T0309246

Analog Superpowers

Analog Superpowers

HOW TWENTIETH-CENTURY TECHNOLOGY
THEFT BUILT THE NATIONAL
SECURITY STATE

Katherine C. Epstein

THE UNIVERSITY OF CHICAGO PRESS
CHICAGO AND LONDON

The University of Chicago Press, Chicago 60637
The University of Chicago Press, Ltd., London
© 2024 by Katherine C. Epstein
Published 2024
Printed in the United States of America

33 32 31 30 29 28 27 26 25 24   1 2 3 4 5

ISBN-13: 978-0-226-83122-0 (cloth)
ISBN-13: 978-0-226-83123-7 (e-book)
DOI: https://doi.org/10.7208/chicago/9780226831237.001.0001

Library of Congress Cataloging-in-Publication Data

Names: Epstein, Katherine C., 1982– author.
Title: Analog superpowers : how twentieth-century technology
theft built the national security state / Katherine C. Epstein.
Other titles: How twentieth-century technology theft
built the national security state
Description: Chicago : The University of Chicago Press, 2024. |
Includes bibliographical references and index.
Identifiers: LCCN 2023058452 | ISBN 9780226831220 (cloth) |
ISBN 9780226831237 (e-book)
Subjects: LCSH: Pollen, Arthur Joseph Hungerford, 1866–1937. |
Isherwood, Harold, 1877–1964. | Fire control (Naval gunnery)—
Technological innovations—Great Britain. | Analog computers—Great
Britain. | Patent infringement—Great Britain—History—20th century. |
Patent infringement—United States—History—20th century. |
Patent laws and legislation—Great Britain—History—20th century. |
National security—United States. | National security—
Great Britain. | Inventors—Great Britain.
Classification: LCC VF520.E67 2024 | DDC 355/.0330730904—
dc23/eng/20240117
LC record available at https://lccn.loc.gov/2023058452

♾ This paper meets the requirements of ANSI/NISO Z39.48-1992
(Permanence of Paper).

To Nick, KK, and Mallee

Contents

Illustrations

Note on British and American Naval Administration

To orient readers who may be unfamiliar with British and American naval administration, here is a brief guide.

The British navy, known as the Royal Navy, was administered by the Board of Admiralty. Its institutional roots went back to the medieval position of Lord Admiral. Over the centuries, instead of having a single individual serve as Lord Admiral, it became more common to put the position "into commission," meaning that it was held by multiple individuals known as the Lords Commissioner of the Admiralty. Collectively, they constituted the Board of Admiralty, for which the term "the Admiralty" is the common shorthand.

The civilian head of the Admiralty was known as the First Lord of the Admiralty, which was a Cabinet position. The uniformed leaders of the Admiralty were known (after 1904) as the Sea Lords, of whom there were four or five in the period covered by this book. We will mainly encounter the Third Sea Lord, also known as the Controller, who was responsible for the procurement of materiel. The Naval Ordnance Department, headed by the Director of Naval Ordnance, reported to the Controller.

On the American side, the US Navy was administered by the Department of the Navy. Prior to the unification of the armed services under a single department in 1947, the Navy Department was freestanding (its army counterpart was the War Department). The Navy Department was run by the Secretary of the Navy. Responsibility for the procurement of ordnance material lay with the Bureau of Ordnance, run by the Chief of the Bureau of Ordnance. The Bureau of Ordnance was divided into sections, of which the most important for present purposes was the fire-control section.

Naval Fire Control
as Beach Reading

Imagine yourself on a beach, standing near the ocean's edge. The sky is blue, the air is clear, and you can see a ship moving slowly against the horizon—about three miles away, as far as the earth's curvature allows the eye to see.

Now imagine that there's a 6-inch naval gun next to you. Your job is to hit the ship with a shell fired from the gun. How do you do so? At a range of three miles, the shell's time of flight would typically be around nine seconds. Because the ship will move during that period, you'll miss if you aim directly at it. Instead, you need to aim the gun where the ship will be when the shell lands on it. In other words, you need to make a prediction about the future location of your target.

What information do you need? At a minimum, you need to know the target's range, course, and speed. With those three pieces of data—assuming the ship is steaming a steady course and doesn't alter speed—you have the makings of a high-school math problem, which you can use basic algebra and trigonometry to solve. To wit: "If a ship moving at 15 knots along a compass bearing of 60° is 5,000 yards at a bearing of 135° from you now, how far and at what bearing from you will the ship be in 30 seconds?" With this data, along with some data about your gun's performance today that you can treat as known constants, you can aim your gun.

Now imagine that instead of trying to hit a ship from a stable platform in a stationary position in good weather, you're on a warship in the North Atlantic. The sky is dark, visibility is poor, and the sea is choppy. Not only is your own ship, like your target, moving along a course at a given speed, but also the waves are making it pitch (from front to back), roll (from side to side), and yaw (corkscrew). If you want to make hits through something other than blind luck, you need to account for your own motion, in three dimensions, as well as your target's. Your targeting problem has become far more difficult.

In essence, this was the problem that two brilliant but nearly forgotten Englishmen named Arthur Pollen and Harold Isherwood set out to solve at the dawn of the twentieth century. The story of their solution illuminates hidden chapters in the history of computing, intellectual property, defense innovation, government secrecy, and great-power competition. Along the way, it also challenges conventional narratives about liberal capitalism in Great Britain and the United States, as well as the transition from the Pax Britannica to the Pax Americana. Cutting-edge in its day, the invention at the center of this book raised issues that remain cutting-edge today, when concerns about computing technology and geopolitical rivalry once again darken the horizon.

DIGITAL ANALOGS AND PATENT SECRECY

In today's world of nuclear weapons and intercontinental missiles, it is difficult but necessary to recall the geopolitical and military importance of battleships. Until aircraft carriers and strategic bombing confirmed their potential in World War II, the big guns of battleships represented the principal overseas strike force and deterrent capability of the great powers (hence, for instance, President Franklin Roosevelt's redeployment of the Pacific Fleet from the West Coast to Pearl Harbor to send a message to Japan in 1940). The ships themselves were enormously expensive technological marvels, representing massive commitments of limited national resources. Accordingly, improving the ability of the big guns to hit their targets was not a minor technical matter but a geopolitical and fiscal imperative.

Hitting the target became much more difficult toward the end of the nineteenth century. As gunnery ranges and ship speeds increased, the problem of hitting acquired a new name: fire control—as in, controlling the fire of the guns. The prevailing response in the British and American navies was to try to tackle the problem piecemeal. Enterprising naval officers invented new instruments to generate rough-and-ready predictions. The mathematics behind their predictions consisted of basic algebra—the multiplication and division of distances over finite time intervals—to derive average, unchanging rates of relative motion that could be used to predict the target's position at some future point in time. But because the rates actually changed from instant to instant under almost all conditions, their predictions relied on what would now be called data smoothing: that is, they "smoothed out" variations in the rates within the given time interval. The extent of the error introduced by this smoothing depended on how far their calculated rates diverged from the actual rates, and human judgment was required to assess the significance of the error. Accordingly, naval officers' solutions to the fire-control problem relied heavily on the human part of a human-machine interface.

Pollen and Isherwood, who were civilians, took a radically different approach. Instead of discrete instruments and approximate data, they insisted that only a systematic solution based on precise, accurate data could enable hitting under likely combat conditions. Their demand for precision and accuracy moved them out of the world of algebra and into the differentials and integration of calculus. Because they understood that the rates of relative motion between two ships changed instantaneously and infinitely under most conditions, they were not content to work from rates calculated as the average for a finite amount of time. Moreover, they believed that human beings could not perform their more demanding mathematical calculations without introducing intolerable degrees of error. Thus, where naval officers looked to preserve an important role for (their own) human judgment amid the mechanization of fire control, Pollen and Isherwood looked to maximum mechanization—that is, to artificial intelligence. From their perspective, human computers might work for the conceptual world of algebra, but only a mechanical computer would do for calculus.

The computer they envisioned and built was analog rather than digital. Whereas digital computers represent quantities in the problems they solve as digits (most commonly ones and zeroes), analog computers represent quantities in direct proportion to their original values. Another way to describe the difference between digital and analog is to say that digital computers work with data discontinuously (one-on, zero-off), while analog computers work with data continuously. Gears, cams, and so forth in mechanical computers, as well as currents in electrical computers, can be manipulated to analogize to the quantities involved in the equations governing a physical problem, such as the relative movement of two ships. Although Pollen and Isherwood did not call their calculating and predicting machine a computer, it has occasionally been recognized as a landmark in computing history.[1] In their day, the term "computer" typically referred to people (think of the book and movie *Hidden Figures*).[2] To indicate the mechanical character of their invention, they, and most of their contemporaries, referred to it as a "clock," an old term for a wide range of calculating instruments.

Pollen's and Isherwood's clock placed them in distinguished company. The challenge of solving calculus problems through electrical, mechanical, and digital means has attracted some of the finest scientific and mathematical minds and generated some of the most famous inventions in modern history. Lord Kelvin's "harmonic analyzer," Charles Vernon Boys's integraph, and Vannevar Bush's "differential analyzer" all belonged to the same technological cluster as the Pollen-Isherwood computer.[3] Their invention both dominated surface-gunnery systems and laid the groundwork for anti-aircraft fire control and bombsights (including the famous Norden bombsight) into the Cold War. In certain respects, it even anticipated nuclear missile guidance systems still in use today.

Pollen and Isherwood also broke new ground in electrical, not just mechanical, engineering. They invented their computer at the same time as rapid advancements were occurring in the world of telecommunications. As radio and cables networked far-flung locations across the globe, so Pollen and Isherwood networked locations across a ship, with their computer at its center. In this respect, they anticipated the type of networked warfare that has been the hallmark of high-tech militaries since the 1980s.

At the same time, however, Pollen's and Isherwood's invention provoked deep discomfort among some naval officers. This was not out of any knee-jerk technological conservatism. Naval officers worked with some of the world's most advanced technologies every day, ranging from turbine engines and explosives to radio and optics. Many of them were excited about what Pollen and Isherwood were offering. But others were not. From painful experience, they knew that machines could fail, and there were plenty of crank inventors offering navies the equivalent of snake oil. Moreover, these officers had the same anxieties that workers often have when "labor-saving" machines, robots, and artificial intelligence threaten to replace them or to downgrade the dignity of their work—as Pollen's and Isherwood's invention threatened to do. In this respect too, the issues raised by naval fire-control technology are more familiar than they might appear.

.·.

Telling the story of Pollen's and Isherwood's invention involves much more than situating it in computer history, however. It also requires situating it in the history of intellectual property (IP). This should come as no surprise given how deeply computer technology and IP issues are intertwined today, not least in the context of Chinese efforts to acquire foreign technology like semiconductors.[4] Like many later inventors in the digital age, Pollen and Isherwood had the misfortune of having their invention pirated—only the pirates were not Chinese but British and American.

Piracy is a strong word, but it is apt, accurately reflecting the beliefs of a wide range of actors in this book. The concept of piracy, of course, assumes the acceptance of a certain set of values about private property. These values are neither self-evident nor universal; they depend on cultural beliefs and powers of enforcement. This is not the place to offer a full-fledged summary of the extensive literature on the history of IP. Suffice it to say here that for centuries, the intangible quality of IP, combined with its origins in early modern royal grants and its monopoly character, has made it a particularly fraught species of property in liberal societies that value free competition.

Nevertheless, by the early twentieth century, IP had clearly, if controversially, overcome its image problem and achieved recognition as a legitimate, modern form of private property.[5] All the actors in this book—not just Pollen and Isherwood, but also the government officials and defense contractors who pirated their invention—accepted that perspective. Even when they opposed the scope of Pollen's and Isherwood's IP claims, they believed that the inventors had done something remarkable that merited compensation. They were also quick to make accusations of piracy when they believed themselves to be the victims. Whether they were right to believe in modern Western notions about private property can certainly be debated. But it cannot be debated whether they believed in these notions or whether, within the terms of their beliefs, they pirated Pollen and Isherwood. They did and they did.

These issues were hardly unprecedented in the history of computing, but they arose in distinctive ways in the context of Pollen's and Isherwood's computer. Although historians have produced outstanding studies of the intersection between computers and the IP system for mechanical computers in the early modern period and for electronic computers in the second half of the twentieth century, they have not mapped the particular intersection between analog computing and the IP systems in both Britain and the United States in the early twentieth century.[6] This is too important an intersection to leave unexplored, for both historical and contemporary reasons.

When Pollen and Isherwood invented their computer, both computing technology and IP regimes were in transition stages. Computer development was moving out of the early modern world of natural philosophy and instruments-making, but it had not yet reached the world of digital, and the computing industry was in its punch-card infancy. The British and American IP systems had experienced a combination of statutory changes and court rulings that made them recognizably more modern than they had been even a half century earlier, yet they were still far from what they became a half century later. From the perspective of the early twenty-first century, when instruments-makers still play a crucial role in the most cutting-edge forms of digital computing, debates a century ago can look eerily familiar, even as subtle differences offer a vantage point for questioning contemporary assumptions.[7]

∴

In mapping the intersection between computing and IP in the early twentieth century, this book does something even more original, which is to map the intersection between IP and national security. This latter intersection remains virtually uncharted.[8] Given that inventors of technology with potential military applications have sought IP protection for hundreds of years, and given that IP issues pervade contemporary defense procurement, this is not so much a gap as a chasm in the existing historical literature on IP. It is probably to be explained by the fact that legal historians do not pay much attention to war and national security, and that military and diplomatic historians do not pay much attention to law.

This book builds a bridge across the chasm by investigating the history of patent secrecy. Patent secrecy is as much a contradiction in terms as it sounds: the Latin root for patent is the verb *patere*, meaning "open." In his famous commentaries on the laws of England, which influenced the American founders and are still cited by courts today, the eighteenth-century English jurist Sir William Blackstone explained that patents, or *litterae patentae* (letters patent) were "so called because they are not sealed up, but exposed to open view."[9] Contra Blackstone, Britain passed a law in 1859 creating a category of patents known as "secret patents": patents that were sealed up and *not* exposed to public view. The United States has a rough but inexact equivalent. US "secret patents" are actually secret patent *applications*, not full-fledged patents. Because of certain distinctive features of the US patent system, discussed at length in chapter 5, the only way that the US government has found to keep "patents" secret is to prevent patent applications from issuing as patents. Significantly, it took the United States almost a century longer than Britain to establish even these ersatz secret patents as a permanent legal category (with the Invention Secrecy Act of 1951).[10] As chapter 9 shows, the absence of British-style secret patents has created serious problems for US defense procurement—though as chapter 6 demonstrates, secret patents have hardly proved a panacea for Britain.

Patent secrecy confounds the conventional understanding of how patents came to be regarded as modern legitimate forms of property. According to legal historians, patents made this move largely by assimilation into liberal contract theory, in which inventors received monopoly grants not as marks of special government favor but in exchange for disclosing their invention to the public.[11] Secret patents are not disclosed to the public, however, and thus they violate the terms of the legitimizing bargain. Or do they? It could be argued, as indeed it was by actors in this book, that patent secrecy was actually *necessary* to keep the terms of the bargain with the public: secrecy best served the public interest by denying knowledge of sensitive inventions to foreign powers. The existing historical understanding of the patent system simply has no concept of "secret public use"; it is based on the belief that public use is necessarily, well, public. With so much concern today about the relationship between the patent system and technological innovation in the context of great-power competition, recovering the history of "secret public use" is a timely undertaking.

LIBERAL CAPITALISM, NATIONAL SECURITY, AND SUPERPOWER ANALOGS

In exploring the connections between computer technology and IP, this book also takes aim (so to speak) at several powerful and intertwined narratives that structure common understandings of the relationship between the public and private sectors in Britain and the United States, of government secrecy, and of the emergence of US global hegemony. These are such huge and frequently studied topics that it requires a certain foolhardiness to try to delineate an original contribution to them. And yet the subject matter of this book so obviously has implications for them—not least from the perspective of the actors it studies—that an attempt must be made.

One of this book's central preoccupations is the relationship between liberal capitalism and national security in Britain and the United States.[12] When historians describe Britain and the United States as "liberal-capitalist," they mean something particular with each term. They do not mean "liberal" in its everyday use as "left of center," nor in its twentieth-century sense as "pro-welfare" or "pro-big government." They also do not mean "liberal" as "nice" or "pleasant"; they are acutely aware of how liberalism can coexist with, and even facilitate, violence and oppression. Rather, they mean "liberal" to indicate a set of values—however much honored in the breach—characterized by respect for individual rights, commitment to legal due process, protection for private property, limitation of government power, and a belief that governments derive legitimacy from the consent of the governed. Some of these values are now typically regarded as conservative, or right-of-center. What made them liberal (and modern), as they emerged in the seventeenth century and gathered strength through the nineteenth century, was their rejection of early modern ideas about the scope of monarchical power, the divine right of kings, and natural hierarchies of rank and station.

Capitalism developed in symbiosis with liberalism. The term "capitalism" is used here to refer to a market system in which goods and services are exchanged for money. Capitalist economies do not require markets to be perfectly "free," in the sense of having no government involvement; indeed, they may depend for their very existence on government involvement, however indirect. But capitalist economies have a greater degree of freedom from government power than command economies. Accordingly, prices in them respond more to the market forces of supply and demand as distinct from government fiat. By delegitimizing government intervention in the economy, liberalism tended to facilitate the emergence and growth of capitalism, while, reciprocally, the spread of capitalism tended to legitimize liberalism. Together, moreover, liberalism and capitalism contributed to a new stigmatization of war, previously regarded as the normal (even desirable) human condition, by tending to delegitimize government involvement in the economy on the grounds of military preparedness—like, say, subsidy grants to build up a defense-industrial base at home, or mercantilist restrictions on trade to attack an enemy abroad.

This book argues that the relationship between Anglo-American liberal capitalism and warfare requires reconceptualization. Historians have done a great deal of work showing that there *was* a relationship, notwithstanding the ostensibly pacific character of liberal capitalism, and that this relationship was substantial enough to speak of "liberal militarism." But the implications of "liberal militarism" for property rights and economic activity in peacetime, as well as the way in which it tends to erode the very boundary between war and peace, demand further study.[13] Liberal militarism depends on technology and money to defeat manpower-rich enemies. Precisely because liberal Britain and the United States embraced the free market and were wary of central government power, they have relied heavily on the private sector to supply the technology central to their liberal militarism, rather than procuring it only from publicly owned government arsenals.[14] Perhaps counterintuitively, that *liberal* reliance on capitalist production has impelled both governments to behave *illiberally* toward the IP rights of contractors.[15] Although this tension has not escaped notice altogether, it lacks historically concrete demonstration.[16] This book documents multiple instances in which defense contractors sought to export their IP abroad and governments responded by classifying the IP as secret on national security grounds. This response was, and was understood as, a form of expropriation. Conceptually, it belongs more to the world of the command economies that Britain and the United States defined themselves against than to their self-images as protectors of free markets and private property.

The fact that this treatment of contractors' IP rights often took place when both Britain and the United States were at least nominally at peace— for instance, before World War I and during the interwar period—also merits emphasis. Many scholars accept what one has described as the "pendulum model" of government power in war versus peace: in liberal societies like Britain and the United States, the pendulum swings toward greater government power and hostility to private property rights in wartime, but then it swings back to its peacetime setting.[17] In fact, however, the British and American governments showed hostility toward the property rights of defense contractors before wars began and after they ended, not just during them. The pendulum model does not capture this complexity.

Finally, the geographical location of government hostility to defense contractors' IP claims is noteworthy. Little attention has been paid to persistent breaches of liberal-capitalist norms by governments at the expense of defense contractors, whose elite status—according to the metrics for eliteness popular among historians—has rendered their vulnerabilities invisible or unsympathetic. This book shows that the British and US governments frequently reached into a well-stocked legal toolbox when dealing with defense contractors. The tools included the doctrines of sovereign immunity (the right of a sovereign government to be immune to suit without its consent) and eminent domain (a government's right to take private property in return for compensation), secrecy laws (like the British Official Secrets Act and the US Espionage Act), and secrecy privileges (crown privilege, later the public-interest immunity, in Britain and the state secrets privilege in the United States). These tools enabled the British and US governments to take defense contractors' IP both with and without paying compensation. Their use of these tools makes the enormous size of many defense contractors appear not only as a means of aggressive predation against the public but also as a defensive response to government predation.[18]

∴

In the course of reconsidering the relationship between liberal capitalism and national security, this book also offers a new history of the secretive national security state. Most histories thereof center thematically on nuclear weapons, chronologically on World War II and the early Cold War, and geographically on the United States. The account offered by this book is different: it centers on naval weapons, the long World War I era, and Britain. In effect, it reimagines the nuclear secrecy regime as the end of an old story as much as the start of a new one.

Of particular note, it shows that what is often regarded as the most novel feature of nuclear secrecy—the "born secret" (or "born classified") provision of the Atomic Energy Act of 1946—had earlier precedents. This provision held that all information pertaining to nuclear energy was secret and classified by nature; accordingly, the US government could only declassify, not classify, it.[19] The provision was relatively uncontroversial when applied to information generated within the government or under a government contract, because the government's right to regulate it mapped onto liberal norms about the right to control one's own property. But it was highly controversial when applied to information generated independently by private actors, as became more and more common the farther the Manhattan Project receded into the past.[20] In such cases, the government had no property or contract claim to the information in question and thus no conventionally liberal basis on which to control it.

This was precisely the situation in which the British and US governments repeatedly found themselves before and after World War I concerning the computerized naval fire-control systems at the center of this book. Then, as during the Cold War, in the absence of liberal property or contract grounds for regulating information, they turned to national security grounds. When they prevented the foreign sale of privately generated IP by converting secrecy laws into improvised export-control legislation, they were treating the information contained in the IP as secret by nature ("born secret"), not by right of government property or contract. Similarly, when they invoked a secrecy privilege to prevent contractors from accessing evidence needed to prove the infringement of privately generated patents, they converted cases from the terrain of property rights to the terrain of national security. Notably, the architect of the US Navy's secrecy strategy in two such cases in this book was Commander Robert Lavender, the Navy's leading patent expert and the future patent advisor to the Manhattan Project and Atomic Energy Commission, in which capacity he helped to craft the atomic secrecy regime. Literally embodying the links between interwar naval secrecy and Cold War nuclear secrecy, Lavender nicely illustrates the problem with seeing the latter as something altogether novel.

∴

In recentering the history of the secretive national security state on naval weapons, the long World War I era, and Britain, this book casts the United States not as the hegemon of the post-1945 world but as a rising power that thumbed its nose at international norms benefiting the existing hegemon—for instance, by pirating the hegemon's technology.[21] Moreover, it took not only the knowledge about weapons from abroad but also the legal knowledge of how to "do" national security secrecy. Britain's Official Secrets of 1889 predated and served as a model for the US National Defense Secrets Act of 1911 (the precursor to the better-known Espionage Act of 1917). During World War I, the British Comptroller General of Patents tutored his American counterpart about setting up a temporary patent-secrecy regime. It might be said that the flow of naval technology from Britain to the United States was accompanied by a parallel flow of legal technology. The directionality of these flows punctures narratives of Yankee ingenuity and American exceptionalism. It also mandates a rethinking of the Anglo-American relationship as "special."

Hence this book proposes that the United States engaged in many of the behaviors vis-à-vis Britain that it accuses China of engaging in today. The more common historical analogy from the World War I era for analyzing the contemporary Sino-American relationship is the Anglo-German relationship, and not without reason. But this analogy has the downside of usually centering on the much-misunderstood Anglo-German naval arms race, and accordingly it has contributed to the impoverishment of much US strategic (especially naval) thinking today.[22] The Anglo-American relationship is at least as good a historical analogy. As China is doing to the United States today, the United States, from the late nineteenth century through World War II, challenged British hegemony across a broad front (sometimes in cooperation with Germany).[23] Although Americans' freewheeling political and business culture foiled early attempts at top-down government direction of technology imports, the importation was no less thorough or intentional for being a grassroots affair.[24] Then, during and after the Civil War, the Republican Party fused so closely with the federal government that one scholar has spoken of a "party-state," and greater top-down direction more along the lines of the modern Chinese party-state became feasible.[25] The US Navy established its Office of Naval Intelligence in 1882 principally to collect information about—and pirate—foreign naval technology.[26]

By following the US Navy's pursuit of British fire-control technology, we can observe one important manifestation of the US challenge to British hegemony. We can watch, in real time, as Americans wrote and rewrote the story of their technological development to emphasize their own innovativeness by airbrushing out Pollen, Isherwood, and other inconveniently non-American figures. We can see how historians, by neglecting to draw the United States into the same model of "catch-up development" that they apply to other nations, have effectively reproduced the stories that Americans have long told themselves.[27] And we can learn from the former hegemon a cautionary tale about the geopolitical dangers of self-deluding historical myths that overestimate one's own capacity for originality—with real-world consequences for today and tomorrow.

FINAL NOTES

To substantiate its broad claims, this book spends a fair amount of time down in the proverbial weeds of naval technology and legal doctrine. (This is especially the case in chapters 1 and 2, which are the longest in the book because they have to lay much of the groundwork for what follows.) That said, the "technical" subject matter in this book does not require advanced scientific, mathematical, or legal education to study, because the process by which it acquired a technical character was fundamentally a historical one. The subject matter does require patience: a willingness to tolerate, even embrace, denseness and complexity. Although there are reasons why gardeners try to pull weeds and poets do not write about them, they matter, and they can be unexpectedly interesting. When viewed from far above, or taken for granted, the weeds appear flat and undifferentiated, but viewing them at eye level reveals bustling ecosystems. Only by neglecting the study of these ecosystems can existing interpretations based on the view from 30,000 feet be sustained; conversely, zooming in on the weeds enables and indeed demands a rethinking of existing understandings of great-power transition and the national security state. This book remains neither in the weeds nor at 30,000 feet; it moves between them, showing how reconsideration of one reacts upon the other. Like a macro-history, it seeks to paint on a big, broad canvas, but like a micro-history, it seeks to do so without sacrificing particular stories.

In taking this approach, the book has much to say about the world wars but not, perhaps, in the way that might be expected. While World War I features prominently in chapters 4–6, it is not in the context of rendering judgment on which technology was (or would have been) "best" in combat. Rather, the goal is to trace how participants in fire-control development understood the lessons of the war, and how the war affected the geopolitical balance of power between the United States and Great Britain. Chapter 10 also discusses World War II in the context of the Anglo-American relationship. It would be satisfying to provide some sort of quantification as to the superiority of one system in the ultimate test of combat, or even under trial conditions—for example, "Pollen's system enabled 30 percent more hits than so-and-so's"—but quantification would be specious. The major competing alternatives all pirated Pollen's, so any quantification would to some degree compare Pollen's system against itself (as the report of a board discussed in chapter 4 did). Moreover, head-to-head trials between Pollen's complete system and that of his chief British pirate, the naval officer Frederic Dreyer, were never conducted, though the unambiguous preference of combat-experienced British and American naval officers for Pollen's system over Dreyer's speaks volumes. In the end, the best testament to the superiority of Pollen's system is that both the British and US governments chose it for the sincerest form of flattery: theft.

This book covers an unusual combination of subjects in an unusual way. It has things to say about fire-control technology, but it packages them with discussions of such topics as eminent domain and sovereign immunity. It probes great-power rivalry alongside national security law, and computer history alongside great-power rivalry. Indeed, its central methodological argument is that full understanding of these subjects, each important in its own right, requires them to be analyzed in the same historical frame. They were deeply, if surprisingly, interconnected.

So: come for the naval gunnery and stay for the political economy, come for the great-power transition and stay for the exercise of eminent domain, or come for the secrecy legislation and stay for the computers. This subject matter may not lend itself to a lighthearted literary romp, but to end where we began, there are stranger things to read at the beach.

CHAPTER 1

Invention as Authorship

"[I]n years to come the fact that the invention is mine may not seem so obvious."

ARTHUR POLLEN, 10 AUGUST 1906

How do you invent a solution to a problem that no one knows exists? First, you have to define the problem. This is what Arthur Pollen and his coinventor Harold Isherwood did between 1900 and 1904. Others had grasped pieces of the emerging fire-control problem, but they were the first to attempt a comprehensive statement of it. Before receiving any official assistance from the Admiralty, the two men worked out a pioneering analysis of the mathematics involved in the relative movement of two ships, and they articulated the parameters of a system of instruments to embody their mathematical insights. In 1904, the Admiralty began working with Pollen and Isherwood to help them to develop their instruments. In 1906, the two parties agreed to an extraordinarily novel—possibly unique—development contract, and in 1908 they formally signed the contract.

This chapter traces the development of Pollen's and Isherwood's invention and of their relationship with the Admiralty during these years. The inventors laid as much stress on their definition of the fire-control problem as on their mechanical solution to it. Their mathematical analysis of the equations governing the relative movement of two ships supplied the algorithms they needed to write the "software" code for their computer "hardware."[1] The Apple cofounder Steve Jobs once defined software, which is notoriously difficult to define, as "something that is changing too rapidly, or you don't exactly know what you want yet, or you didn't have time to get it into hardware."[2] On that definition, there was a great deal of "software" in Pollen's and Isherwood's system. But because the computer at its center was a single-purpose analog computer rather than a general-purpose digital computer, the software was built into the hardware: it was the cams, gears, and so forth that mechanically encoded the algorithms derived from their mathematical analysis. In modern computing terms, it might be said that the algorithms were the "source code," while the "object code," instead of being "machine-readable," was the machine itself.[3]

Ironically, the effect of Pollen's and Isherwood's instrumental invention (the hardware) was to render invisible what they regarded as their more fundamental algorithmic invention (the software). Once the problem was defined and its solution proposed, both seemed obvious all along—a technical problem with a technical solution, existing in the eternal worlds of mathematics and machines, abstracted from any particular historical context.[4] But recovering their historical context is vital. Pollen's and Isherwood's invention, like many in the history of instruments-making and computing, raised difficult questions about the boundaries between nature versus human artifice, discovery versus invention, and unpatentable versus patentable subject matter. None of the answers to these questions was self-evident, and debating them was a historical process.

In studying the development of naval fire control, therefore, it is necessary to go beyond the world of physical instruments. Indeed, the contract that Pollen and the Admiralty negotiated in 1906 and signed in 1908 was not primarily about instruments. Pollen insisted, and persuaded the Admiralty to agree, that his and Isherwood's invention consisted of both ideas and instruments, software and hardware. This understanding of their invention invites a capacious sense of what "technology" can be, one not limited to physical objects. Thus conceptualized, other technologies—especially legal technologies like the new form of contract envisioned by Pollen—must be studied alongside the naval technology Pollen and Isherwood invented.[5]

Enlarging our sense of technology beyond physical objects also helps expose connections between the worlds of artistic and mechanical creation. Pollen and Isherwood understood themselves as authors no less than inventors. Pollen, who had a powerful aesthetic sense, drew an analogy between the mechanical and musical worlds, writing admiringly of a gifted naval officer that "his eye for a [mechanical] drawing is infallible, it is like a great conductor's for a score—he does not have to hear the music—he can read it."[6] This analogy both reflected old ways of thinking about invention and anticipated new ones in digital computing: today, with software understood as "the text in the machine," software developers can take out either patents or copyrights on their inventions.[7] (Not for nothing do coders "write" in programming "languages" or artificial intelligence researchers—whose ranks included Pollen and Isherwood, as we will see—study linguistics.) Thus, in the history of computing and intellectual property, Pollen's and Isherwood's story illuminates a previously hidden aspect of the transition from the computing and IP practices of the early modern period to the computing and IP practices of the modern era.

POLLEN AND ISHERWOOD

Born in 1866 to John Hungerford Pollen and Maria La Primaudaye, Pollen made an unlikely but not unprepared inventor.[8] He came from a socially prominent English family that moved in aristocratic and culturally elite circles. He was born in a house rented from family friends Wilfred Blunt (the well-known poet and essayist) and Lady Anne Blunt (a skilled artist, musician, and horse-breeder), and his father was close to the prominent Catholic reformer Cardinal John Newman. Pollen grew up in financial comfort but, because his father had been disinherited upon converting to Catholicism, knowing that he would have to make his own way in life. After attending Newman's Oratory School in Birmingham, he graduated with honors from Trinity College, Oxford, where he proved himself a skilled debater. Seeking a career in the law, he entered Lincoln's Inn in 1893 but evidently found it dull. He unsuccessfully stood for Parliament as a Liberal in 1895. Three years later, he married Maud Lawrence, the daughter of the Conservative MP Joseph Lawrence (who was knighted in 1902). Evidently not holding Pollen's politics against him, Lawrence made his new son-in-law the managing director of his firm, the Linotype Company, which was the premier supplier of newspaper equipment in England and also a producer of scientific instruments.[9] This work placed Pollen at the cutting edge of a revolution in printing. The linotype machine was a complex technological marvel, reportedly dubbed "the eighth wonder of the world" by Thomas Edison.[10] One of Linotype's chief customers was Pollen's friend Alfred Harmsworth, later Lord Northcliffe, owner of the *Daily Mail* and the *Daily Mirror*, at whose estate in Kent Pollen and his wife spent part of their honeymoon.

Far from the grubby businessman that naval officers and officials sometimes imagined him to be, Pollen (fig. 1.1) was the epitome of the Edwardian English gentleman. Debonair and always fastidiously dressed, he moved with ease in genteel social settings. In his great-grandson's words, he was "at home in clubland and a master of establishment pastimes such as deer-stalking, golf and bridge."[11] A keen sportsman, he owned a superb collection of hunting rifles. He was well connected in politics, the press, the arts, and the military on both sides of the Atlantic. His friend J. A. Spender, the prominent journalist, arranged a job for him writing as an arts and literature critic for the *Westminster Gazette*, the mouthpiece of the Liberal Party.[12] He

Figure 1.1. On the left, a portrait of Arthur Pollen in 1917 taken by the well-known American photographer Pirie MacDonald. A neck injury suffered when a tree fell on him as a young man gave him a "'stiff-necked,' almost haughty appearance" in portraits (Jebb, *Leonardo Da Vinci's Miniature Madonna*, 9) (PLLN.9/7/1). On the right, a portrait of the English actress Violet Vanbrugh, pictured in *The Sketch*, a stage and society magazine of the day. The original caption pays tribute to Pollen as a natty dresser and society figure: "Appearing in 'Trimmed in Scarlet'—and Here Seen in an Arthur Pollen Collar!" (*The Sketch* 107, no. 1380, 9 July 1919, 58).

was friends with Theodore Roosevelt; the American ambassador to Britain (soon-to-be Secretary of State) John Milton Hay attended his wedding and signed the wedding register.[13] His diary from a trip to the United States in 1917 reads like a who's who of American society—he stayed with Mrs. George Vanderbilt at the Biltmore, dined with John Singer Sargent, and met with Edward House, President Woodrow Wilson's close advisor.[14] Pollen also had family members in the Royal Navy, which he described himself as "almost abjectly" admiring, including his brother Francis Pollen and his cousin William Goodenough (who distinguished himself in World War I and rose to the rank of admiral).[15]

Pollen possessed a powerful intellect, deep emotions, and a strong character. He was equally capable of forming intimate friendships and of making vengeful enemies. One of his friends described the "glamour" of his personality, and condolence notes to his widow almost invariably recalled his charm, vitality, and brains.[16] His friend Hilaire Belloc, the celebrated author and philosopher, paid tribute to "the rapidity and exactitude of his judgement," calling him the "most remarkable member of a remarkable family."[17] The art critic Kenneth Clark formed just as intense but less favorable an impression. Recalling a dinner with Pollen in his memoirs, Clark portrayed him as conceited bloviator who was rude when he did not get his way.[18]

While nothing in Pollen's background foretold his success as an inventor, it equipped him in key respects. His legal training gave him some preparation for the myriad contract and intellectual property issues that would arise in attempting to develop new technology. His debating experience stood him in good stead when confronted with the task of winning over skeptics of his work. His directorship of the Linotype Company familiarized him with the design and production of complex, precision-manufactured machine tools and instruments, and it afforded him access to skilled mathematicians and engineers—most importantly Harold Isherwood. The company also gave him extensive day-to-day commercial experience dealing with the patent system in both Britain and the United States, since manufacture of the linotype was closely bound up with patents. At a time when naval officers routinely turned to hunting analogies to describe shooting at a moving target, Pollen's interest in grouse-shooting may have primed him to understand the challenges involved and express himself through analogies that many officers understood.[19] Although he lacked formal scientific or engineering training, his intellectual and rhetorical gifts enabled him to understand quickly the technical points at issue in naval gunnery and to articulate their broader significance for nonspecialists.

Last but not least, his social prominence gave him an entrée to the Admiralty unusual for an ordinary outside inventor, which was both an asset and a liability. When he wished the Admiralty to consider his invention, for instance, he wrote directly to the First Sea Lord, a family friend, while his father-in-law contacted the First Lord on his behalf.[20] Pollen's ability to go straight to the top did not always endear him to the often middle-class naval officers over whose heads he went. Asked by the First Lord for advice, the miffed Director of Naval Ordnance replied, "I know the Pollen family personally they are all pushing and persistent."[21] Naval officers who lacked Pollen's social standing sometimes envied it. Although he formed close friendships with some, his possession of connections and his willingness to use them caused resentment in others. Sociologically, his background did not equip him well to navigate the culture of the naval officer corps. It may help to explain why, in the great feud between the snobbish Lord

Charles Beresford and the bourgeois Sir John "Jacky" Fisher, Pollen backed the wrong (i.e., aristocratic) horse.

Far less is known about Isherwood than about Pollen. Unlike the latter, the former died childless and left no personal papers. The loss of the corporate archive for the firm established to develop Pollen's and Isherwood's invention makes it difficult to get at their relationship, but enough survives to indicate that Pollen's dominance of the extant historical record should be interpreted as absence of evidence about Isherwood, not as evidence of Isherwood's absence. In correspondence with others, Pollen referred to Isherwood as "my partner and co-inventor," and Isherwood returned the respect, writing as an inscription in a book for Pollen that he had "ever retained a fervent admiration for [Pollen's] Genius."[22] They complemented each other well: Pollen brought business acumen, connections, and articulateness; Isherwood, design and engineering genius.[23] While Pollen seems to have initiated the development of their invention, it would almost certainly be a mistake to view him as the ideas man and Isherwood as a "mere" mechanic—or, for that matter, to view Pollen as ignorant of mechanical details. What survives of Isherwood's voice in court testimony from the 1930s shows that he shared Pollen's big-picture sense of what they were trying to achieve; conversely, Pollen's papers reveal close understanding of the mechanical particulars of their invention.

Isherwood was born in 1877 in Lancastershire, about 20 miles northwest of Manchester. While attending Manchester Technical School in the evenings, he began, at the age of 15, a series of apprenticeships, working mainly with machine tools as a fitter, turner, and draftsman, but also doing a short stint at the British General Electric Company (no connection with the American giant) working with electrical machinery. In 1901, he became superintendent at Linotype. Isherwood impressed a number of important people along the way. When he was proposed to join the Institution of Mechanical Engineers in early 1917, his supporters included Sir William A. Tritton, an expert on agricultural machinery and contributor to the development of the tank; Ernest H. Lamb (later Baron Rochester), an electrical engineer specializing in telephony and future minister in the government of Ramsey MacDonald; and Bernard G. Arkwright, manager of the Engineering Department at William Armstrong & Co., the armaments giant, as well as the great-great-grandson of Sir Richard Arkwright (the celebrated inventor of the water frame and party to one of the most famous cases in the history of patent law).[24] In short, although Isherwood did not have Pollen's connections to the most aristocratic, genteel, and culturally elite members of society, he was professionally well connected and well regarded in his chosen field.

Figure 1.2. A photograph of Harold Isherwood in May 1918. (Courtesy of Martha Specht Corsi.)

In addition to their intellectual affinity, Isherwood and Pollen had other things in common. Like Pollen, Isherwood was a patriot and an admirer of the Royal Navy, which he joined as a reservist during World War I. Like Pollen, Isherwood had strong connections with the United States. During the war, the Royal Navy sent Isherwood to Washington, DC, to assist the US Navy with mine development, work for which the US Navy awarded him the Navy Cross. His second marriage was to Charlotte Evans, the formidable daughter of the US naval officer Admiral Robley "Fighting Bob" Evans, best known as the commander of the famous Great White Fleet. Isherwood moved during the interwar period to the United States and after World War II to Italy, where he and his wife rented rooms from an expatriate US army officer. The officer's daughter, who became like a granddaughter to the Isherwoods, remembered "Hal" (fig. 1.2) in terms that must have endeared him to Pollen. Isherwood, she recalled, was "extremely elegant, a tall good looking gentleman always perfectly dressed," "with a special slightly ironic twinkle in his eyes," and fascinated by mechanical problems—"he and my father shared a work room where they both loved to putter." Deeply in love with his wife, Isherwood always rose when she entered a room (once, when he did not, she bellowed, "Aren't there any GENTLEMEN in this room!"). They also dressed for dinner—"she in long and lovely tea-gowns, he in shiny pumps, a dinner jacket and bow tie."[25] He died in Florence in 1964, only months after his wife.

THE TEXT IN THE MACHINE

Pollen embarked on his career as an inventor by chance. While visiting family in Malta in 1900, Pollen accepted an invitation from his cousin William Goodenough to watch a gunnery practice by a cruiser and a battleship, in which the two vessels took turns firing at a target at a range of 1,500 yards. That morning, Pollen happened to have read in the newspaper that naval guns hauled onto land in the Boer War had fired effectively at a range of five miles (8,800 yards). Why, then, he asked his companions, were the same guns being fired at less than five times that range at sea? The answer, he was told, was inadequate rangefinders.[26]

Intrigued, Pollen began to investigate. Rangefinders at this time were a recent development. When Pollen had been born, navies expected to engage at such short distances—under 1,000 yards—that finding the range was unimportant. Ships simply laid their guns parallel to the surface of the oceans and fired at more or less point-blank range. Because the trajectory of the shell was practically flat rather than parabolic across such a short distance, the firing ship did not need to know the target range. In the 1890s, however, through a complex causal interaction between new technologies and tactical ideas, the expected range in battle began to lengthen. As it grew, the trajectory of a shell changed from flat to parabolic, making knowledge of the range necessary so that the firing ship could "drop" the shell onto its target.

At the same time, instrumental assistants to the human eye known as rangefinders became necessary. Rangefinders worked on the trigonometric principles governing right-angled triangles: given one side of a triangle and an angle, they computed the side of the triangle that was the range. Two main kinds of rangefinder were in use by the 1890s. One was a depression rangefinder invented by the British army colonel Henry S. S. Watkin, designed to be used by forts on land to determine the range of target ships.[27] The Royal Navy found it unsuitable for use at sea.[28] The other main type of rangefinder—the one used by the Royal Navy—was a 4.5-foot horizontal-base rangefinder invented by the Scottish optics firm Barr & Stroud. Horizontal-base rangefinders used the width of their base as the known side of a triangle to the target. The width of the base limited the range at which these rangefinders were accurate; the wider the base, the longer the ranges at which they were accurate.

Having had the gunnery problem framed for him as one of rangefinding, Pollen initially directed his attention to widening the base of the triangle but quickly realized that the problem went beyond rangefinding as conventionally understood. Before sitting down to sketch designs of instruments, he first tried to understand the mathematics of relative movement. He tasked engineers at Linotype—including, almost certainly, Isherwood, who dated his own involvement in fire control to 1901—to analyze the most difficult gunnery scenario he could imagine: two high-speed (25-knot) cruisers converging from 10,000 yards and then diverging on parallel courses.[29] The engineers offered two ways to approach the problem by graphically representing, or *plotting*, the range (the distance between own and target ship) and bearing (the angle between the line of own course and the line of sight to the target) data that could theoretically be observed in such a scenario. One, later known as a *true-course plot*, showed the estimated courses of both ships; and the other, later known as a *range-rate plot*, showed estimated ranges against time. These are illustrated in figure 1.3.

Pollen's and Isherwood's analysis of the range-rate plot produced a key insight. Not only did the range change from moment to moment, but also the rate at which the range changed—better known as the rate of change of range, or *range rate* for short—itself changed from moment to moment. Crucially, under most conditions, the range rate changed continuously and instantaneously *even when* one's own ship and the target did *not* change their courses and speeds.[30] The fact that not only the range but also the range rate were changing instantaneously and continuously moved the problem from the world of trigonometry and basic arithmetic (multiplication or addition of ranges divided by a finite period of time to arrive at the average rate for that period) to that of calculus (differential and integral functions dealing with instantaneous and infinite time). If the range rate was known, then the relative movement of the two vessels could essentially be neutralized; in effect, the much easier conditions of firing on land from one fixed point at another fixed point could be reproduced at sea. In order to determine the changing rate—rather than the rate at a particular instant represented by the tangent line to the range curve—knowledge of own and target course and speed were necessary.[31]

Pollen and Isherwood had two other mathematical insights about the relative movement of two ships from the start. The first—which Pollen later described as "the first piece of knowledge I had on the subject"—was that the range rate and the *bearing rate* (the rate at which the bearing changed), on the one hand, and courses and speeds, on the other, were mathematically interconvertible.[32] That is, knowledge of the range and bearing rates and of own course and speed would yield knowledge of target course and

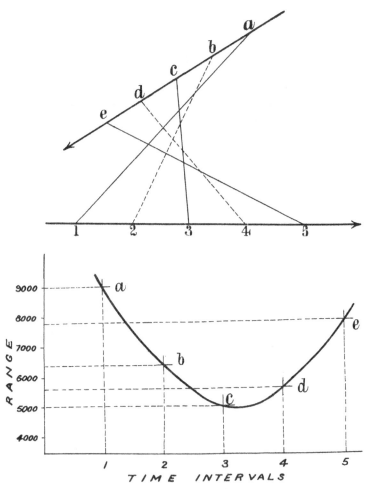

Figure 1.3. These diagrams illustrate the principles of true-course plotting and range-rate plotting.

The diagram on the top shows a true-course plot. When own ship is at position 1, target ship is at position a; when own ship is at position 2, target ship is at position b; and so on. The line 1-5 represents own course, while the line a-e represents target course. The lines 1-a, 2-b, etc. represent both the range and the line of sight from own ship to target. The bearings are the angles between own course and the line of sight to the target (a-1-5, b-2-5, c-3-5, etc.).

The diagram on the bottom shows a range-rate plot. Ranges on the y-axis are plotted against times on the x-axis. At time 1, the range (a) is 5,000 yards; at time 2, the range (b) is roughly 6,400 yards; and so on. If the range was changing at a constant rate, the points on the graph would form a straight line, and the rate of change would be the slope of the line. In this plot, the rate is changing continuously, so the line forms a curve, and the instantaneous rate is the tangent line to the curve at that instant. ("Elements of the Change of Range," figs. 1 and 3, PLLN.8/2.)

speed, while knowledge of own and target course and speed would yield knowledge of the two rates. In mathematical terms, therefore, it made no difference whether one began with rates to get target course and speed or one began with target course and speed to get rates.

The inventors' second mathematical insight was even more fundamental—indeed, it was the basis of their entire approach to the fire-control problem. They realized that ranges and bearings, as well as the rates at which both changed, varied with each other, and thus knowledge of one amounted to knowledge of the other. Pollen subsequently recalled that he had realized the importance of the bearing rate "from the earliest time."[33] Pollen's and Isherwood's emphasis on bearings and bearing rate, though mathematically correct, was by no means obvious: as we shall see, in pirating their invention, both the Royal Navy and the US Navy initially failed to recognize the importance of bearing rate and its interconnection with the range rate.

Pollen and Isherwood drew a critical inference from their insight into the importance of bearings and bearing rate: knowledge of these variables would enable feedback between observed data and calculated data. That is, if the latter diverged from the former, the calculating machine could be "tuned" to bring its predictions in line with observations. Pollen's early writings make clear that he not only understood feedback but was the first to explain it.[34] In a 1904 pamphlet, for instance, he wrote, "As it is unthinkable that the enemy could be at his right bearing but at the wrong range, or at the right range but on the wrong bearing, every observation from the [observing] station, whose observation is taken as his original bearing, will be an automatic check on the range in use."[35] The "check" was feedback. Indeed, the whole thrust of Pollen's and Isherwood's early thinking was to replace the existing method of feedback, which was to "spot" the fall of shot and then re-lay the gun to correct the observed error, with a method that would waste less ammunition by exploiting mechanically graphed and calculated data.[36] That is, where the existing feedback loop was between human beings—the gunlayer and the spotter—Pollen and Isherwood wanted to reduce the scope for error by replacing one human side of the loop with mathematics and machines.

Pollen's and Isherwood's emphasis on bearings led them to become early participants in "gyro culture"—"a whole set of knowledge, skills, ideas and devices based around the gyroscope."[37] To supply the necessary degree of accuracy at the ranges they contemplated, bearings had to be corrected for *yaw*—the rotational motion of a ship around an imaginary vertical axis from its deck through its hull due to wave action.[38] Figure 1.4 illustrates the effect of yaw on bearings.

Figure 1.4. The arrow line represents the true course of the ship, or the course line. Wave action causes the ship to yaw from side to side around its true course. The lines drawn from the fore to the aft of the ship—the keel lines—show the difference between the keel lines and the course line. Bearings taken from the keel lines (or *keel-line bearings*) would differ by several degrees from bearings taken from the course line (or *course-line bearings*, also known as *yaw-free bearings*). ("The Elements of Change of Range," fig. 5, PLLN.8/2.)

Pollen's and Isherwood's first thought was to take bearings from the magnetic compasses then used by the Royal Navy. However, consultation with the renowned physicist Lord Kelvin, who served on the Linotype board of directors, convinced the men that magnetic compasses would not produce sufficiently accurate course-line bearings. They therefore determined that some form of gyroscope, providing a stable course-line reference in *azimuth* (within a horizontal plane), would be necessary to correct bearings for yaw.[39]

In addition to these specific insights, Pollen and Isherwood generally identified maximum rapidity and accuracy of operation as essential elements of a successful naval fire-control system—including the transmission as well as the recording and calculation of data—and automation through mechanization and electrification as the best means of securing them. In early 1901, Pollen was calling for a "rapid, continuous, and accurate" system "rendered possible by a machine."[40] At a time when navies relied on rough visual estimates to acquire data on target course and speed and vocal transmission to communicate gunnery data, Pollen's insistence on the need for accurate, electromechanically acquired and transmitted data was highly original. It derived from his and Isherwood's mathematical analysis, which established that small, seemingly insignificant errors could propagate through a fire-control system and feed each other in unquantifiable and unpredictable ways. In modern systems-engineering parlance, it might be said that he and Isherwood sensed the need for an "error budget"—that is, a total allowable amount of error—and the improbability that visual estimates and manual methods could stay within budget.[41] When small errors in data inputs could make the difference between hits and misses, and when not only ranges but also rates varied instantaneously and continuously, inaccuracy and delay in data acquisition, calculation, and transmission had to be minimized.

Pollen's confidence that only machines could perform with the necessary rapidity, accuracy, and automaticity reflected his background as manager of Linotype's large engineering works. "The experience of those engaged in the management of a factory, where uniformity and punctuality in getting results is the first criterion of success," he once wrote, "will bear me out in saying that it is an industrial axiom to eliminate the unnecessary man, and never to employ labor, whether skilled or unskilled, where an automatic machine can get you the result."[42] The linotype itself was a labor-saving machine that automated work previously carried out by multiple human beings. Unsurprisingly, then, automation for Pollen meant the replacement of human beings, not turning human beings into automata by making their jobs less skilled. In his vocabulary, the antonym of "automatic" was "polyanthropic"—many-humaned. To borrow a concept from economic history, in his and Isherwood's eyes, the nonhuman qualities of their invention made the information it generated more "credible," in much the same way that people's behavior can make them more or less "credible"—more or less worthy of credit and investment—in the eyes of financial institutions.[43] In effect, Pollen and Isherwood equated automaticity with electromechanization and saw it as superior to human calculation. Not everyone would agree with them.

ANALOG ALGORITHMS

Pollen's first approaches to the Admiralty, in early 1901, incorporated the fruits of his analysis to date. Observing that the lack of a rangefinder accurate at long ranges was holding back gunnery at sea, Pollen suggested a novel form of rangefinding based on bearings—an early reflection of his unusual emphasis on bearings. Whereas existing rangefinders measured the range directly, without taking bearings, Pollen proposed to exploit the mathematical interconvertibility of ranges and bearings by using two bearing observations to calculate the range. The indirect approach, so to speak, to ranges via bearings would enable ranges to be calculated accurately at much longer distances than with the direct approach of existing rangefinders, the accuracy of which was limited by the length of their base. With two observers stationed far apart in the ship's superstructure, each taking bearings, the base of the triangle to be solved trigonometrically for range was nearly the whole keel line of the ship, such that ranges could be taken accurately out to the horizon at 20,000 yards (11+ miles).[44]

Pollen went much further than this long-base rangefinding scheme. He saw that to take yaw-free bearings, it was necessary to combine "the telescope for observation with an arrangement of one or more gyrostats."[45] Ranges and bearings would then be used to make a true-course plot. There is no evidence that anyone had suggested using a true-course plot for the purposes that Pollen identified (let alone actually produced a workable true-course plotter). At the same time, Pollen suggested a new machine—a pantographic calculator—to perform the trigonometric calculations. He justified the development of new instruments with a demand for accuracy in the acquisition of data.[46] The whole proposal was sketchy compared with his later ideas, and the two-observer system for taking bearings, as it turned out, involved insuperable technical obstacles. And yet one can see, in this early document—written before he and Isherwood received cooperation from the Admiralty—all the hallmarks of their mature thought: the articulation of a three-part system of instruments (a rangefinder, a plotter, and a computer), the emphasis on bearings alongside ranges, the demand for gyro-corrected bearings, the quest for accuracy, and the preference for machines rather than human beings in fire-control work.

Equally evident in this initial proposal was Pollen's belief in the inseparability of the mental and material aspects of invention.[47] This inseparability was a characteristic feature of instruments-making, the field in which the Linotype Company specialized and from which mechanical computers emerged. For centuries, instruments-making—which involves mental labor as well as manual labor, scientific thought as well as technological practice, basic science as well as applied science, design as well as engineering, art as well as science—has defied the binary categories popular in many ways of thinking about invention and IP.[48] Thus, it has long raised fundamental and persistently relevant questions about the line between discovery and invention, between the naturally occurring and the humanly made, between principles that should be open to all and creations that should be enclosed as property.[49] Alive to the importance of these questions, Pollen wrote that, in advance of submitting any drawings, "we shall have to ask that a binding pledge of secrecy shall be given, and an undertaking in no kind of way to imitate or use the entirely novel mechanical and mathematical principles incorporated in the machine."[50] Conceptualizing the invention in terms of not only material instruments but also mental labor—mathematical insight (or software) as well as mechanical ingenuity (or hardware)—he expected the Admiralty's assurance to cover all of it. Unsurprisingly, the Admiralty declined this first approach. Pollen opted not to try to sell abroad, regarding patents as "no real protection against government user in foreign countries," but instead to try to sell his idea to the British armaments giant Armstrong Whitworth.[51] It also turned him down.[52]

In 1904, he—or rather his father-in-law—reapproached the Admiralty, which proved more receptive this time around. In June of that year, Pollen produced a more elaborate explication of his ideas, criticizing the Royal Navy's existing reliance on visually "spotting" the fall of shot to correct the gun range and explaining how plotting could address the problem of instrument error.[53] Six months later, he came out with a still more rigorous and extensive analysis in a new pamphlet, the immodestly Newtonian subtitle of which conveyed his sense of himself as a scientific author as well as inventor: "An Essay to Define Certain Principia of Gunnery, and to Suggest Means for Their Application." Therein, he explained that mist, smoke, and an inability to distinguish which splash came from which gun could all make "spotting" impractical. It became another hallmark of Pollen's approach to emphasize the need for any fire-control system to work under conditions of temporary target invisibility. Instead of guesswork, he insisted that the Navy needed "a scientific and accurate system" of range-finding based on thorough identification of all relevant variables and their precise instrumental measurement.[54] Given the necessary "principia" of his title and accuracy in the acquisition of data, the rest would be "a mere question of suitable mechanisms" to perform calculations and lay the guns in accordance with the results.[55] Mental labor first, instruments second—a capacious but hierarchical conception of invention was clear here.[56]

Pollen's characterization of his proposal as a "scientific" "system" was also significant. By these terms he meant that his invention proceeded from as thorough an effort as possible to identify all mathematically relevant variables, and then used instruments to achieve accuracy and rapidity of operation.[57] "Science" and "system" were then gaining prestige in the public mind and industrial management, making his use of these words self-interested as well as sincere: a civilian who lacked the credibility conferred by wearing the uniform, he invoked science and system as alternative sources of credibility.[58] He was trying to find arguments that would count with naval officers.[59]

∴

Of the instruments proposed by Pollen in 1904, the most important and challenging was one to predict the range at a future moment in time. The Royal Navy had recently acquired two machines to assist with this process. The first was a slide rule called a Dumaresq (pronounced Doo-MER-ick), named after its inventor, Royal Navy Lieutenant John Dumaresq. The instrument worked from Dumaresq's realization that the vector of relative movement between two ships did not depend on their range. It is shown in figure 1.5, along with a diagram illustrating the underlying mathematical theory.

Deflection—that is, the component of the vector of relative movement perpendicular to the line of sight—was *not* the same as bearing rate;

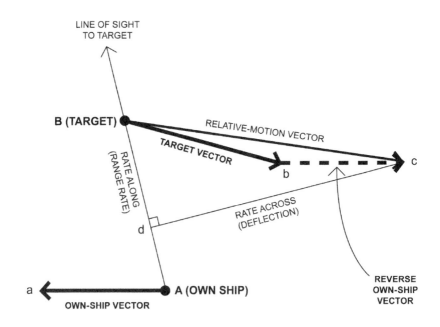

LINE OF SIGHT
TO TARGET

B (TARGET)

RELATIVE-MOTION VECTOR

TARGET VECTOR

RATE ALONG
(RANGE RATE)

RATE ACROSS
(DEFLECTION)

b

c

d

REVERSE
OWN-SHIP
VECTOR

a

A (OWN SHIP)

OWN-SHIP VECTOR

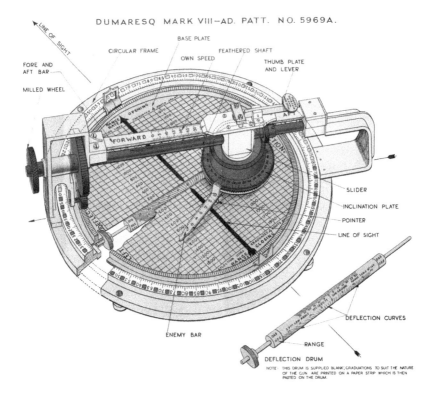

DUMARESQ MARK VIII—AD. PATT. NO. 5969A.

LINE OF SIGHT

BASE PLATE

CIRCULAR FRAME

OWN SPEED

FEATHERED SHAFT

THUMB PLATE
AND LEVER

FORE AND
AFT BAR

MILLED WHEEL

FORWARD

SLIDER

INCLINATION PLATE

POINTER

LINE OF SIGHT

DEFLECTION CURVES

ENEMY BAR

RANGE

DEFLECTION DRUM

NOTE: THIS DRUM IS SUPPLIED BLANK; GRADUATIONS TO SUIT THE NATURE
OF THE GUN ARE PRINTED ON A PAPER STRIP WHICH IS THEN
PASTED ON THE DRUM.

mathematically, it was equal to the bearing rate times the range. Thus deflection and bearing rate could be interconverted, but only with knowledge of the range, which the calculation of deflection using the Dumaresq did not require. The instrument worked best when the range rate and deflection were not changing at all, and next best when they were low and changing only slowly, so that manually unclamping and reclamping the bars to calculate the new rates (or simply treating them as constant) introduced relatively small errors. When the rates were higher and changing more quickly, however, the time required to reclamp the bars and read the data introduced larger errors. Moreover, to cope with even a small change in the rates, the Dumaresq required the target to be visible, so that the enemy bar could be kept trained on it. In other words, the Dumaresq was incapable of producing accurate results if the rates were changing while the target was temporarily invisible.

The second machine recently acquired by the Royal Navy to help to predict ranges was known as the Vickers clock, manufactured by the British armaments giant Vickers. At its heart was a *variable-speed drive*, in which a roller (shaped like a coin) drove a cylindrical output shaft that was held by a spring in contact with a rotating disc. These were well known in the art; James Thomson and his brother William (the future Lord Kelvin) had famously described a disc-and-roller drive (with the roller shaped like a ball)

Figure 1.5. These images illustrate the principle on which the Dumaresq worked (top) and the Dumaresq itself (bottom).

Referring to the top diagram, let A be own ship and B be target ship. The vector A-a represents own ship's course (the direction of the vector) and speed (the magnitude of the vector), and the vector B-b represents the target's course and speed. The line AB represents the range along the line of sight from own ship to the target. To produce the vector of relative motion, subtract own-ship motion from target motion by reversing the vector of own ship, which now appears as the dotted vector b-c, and adding it to the target vector. The new vector B-c is the vector of relative motion. Now draw a line at a right angle to the line of sight from the tip of the vector B-c. The vector component d-B is the *rate along* the line of sight, while the vector component d-c is the *rate across* the line of sight. The rate along is known as the *range rate*, while the rate across is known as *deflection*.

Referring to the bottom image, the plate carrying the grid lines is rotated so that it is pointing in the direction of the line of sight from own ship to the target. The large bar across the top, labeled "forward" and "aft"—known as the "fore and aft bar"—represents the course and speed of own ship as a vector, while the smaller bar, labeled "enemy bar," represents the course and speed of the target ship as a vector. When set with own and enemy course and speed, the Dumaresq calculated the range rate and deflection, which were read off using the grid lines. (*Handbook on Minor Fire Control Instruments*, BR 1534, Plate 1, AL.)

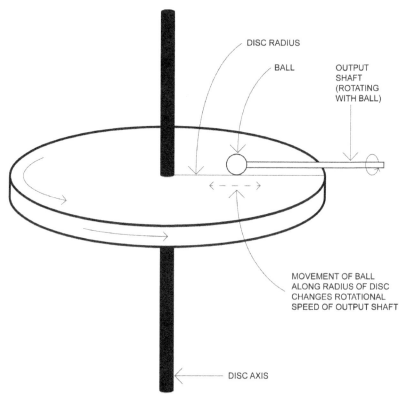

DISC RADIUS

BALL

OUTPUT
SHAFT
(ROTATING
WITH BALL)

MOVEMENT OF BALL
ALONG RADIUS OF DISC
CHANGES ROTATIONAL
SPEED OF OUTPUT SHAFT

DISC AXIS

Figure 1.6. This diagram illustrates the principle on which variable-speed drives worked. The ball (or roller) can be moved in or out along the radius of the rotating disc. The closer to the center of the disc that the ball is placed, the slower it rotates; the farther away from the center of the disc, the faster it rotates. The output shaft controls the speed at which a pointer rotates around the face of the clock, indicating the ranges.

in the 1870s, and William used multiple such drives in his harmonic analyzer for predicting tidal heights.[60] Within the Royal Navy, disc-and-roller drives were colloquially known as "potters' wheels." Because the angular speed of any point on a rotating disc varies with its distance from the center, moving the position of the roller along the disc's radius varied the speed at which it drove the output shaft. This principle is shown in figure 1.6.

Rather like a timekeeping clock, the Vickers clock, when set to an initial range and rate of rotation (such as the range rate calculated by the Dumaresq), would "keep" the range as time passed; thus, for instance, if set to an initial range of 3,000 yards and a rate of +200 yards/minute, the Vickers clock would show a range of 3,200 yards after one minute, 3,400 yards after two minutes, and so on. Unlike a range*finder,* which could take a range only at a given instant of time, the Vickers clock was a range*keeper*, able—*all other things remaining equal*—to predict the range over time. If the range rate changed, however, then the Vickers clock had to be adjusted by hand to a new rate, by moving the roller closer to or farther from the disc's center. The more frequently the rate changed, the greater the error introduced by the time required to reset the clock rate. Furthermore, moving (or rather dragging) the coin-shaped roller across the rotating disc to reset the rate scoured the disc. Wear to the disc in turn generated unpredictable error.

Pollen proposed to make a clock that could cope with high and frequently changing rates. By the time he wrote his pamphlet in December 1904, he was familiar with both the Dumaresq and the Vickers clock.[61] In a sense, he was proposing to build on their capabilities while overcoming their limitations. The trick was to turn them from essentially static instruments, optimized to handle unchanging or slowly changing instantaneous rates, into dynamic instruments, capable of handling rapidly changing rates. "The additions and subtractions made from the original range" by his new clock, he wrote, "will, of course, not be a fixed amount per minute"—that is, the result of a constant rate as on a Vickers clock—"but the actual amount of change" resulting from a changing rate. In order to generate the actual amount of change, Pollen's and Isherwood's clock, unlike the Vickers clock, would generate bearings as well as ranges; hence Pollen's description of it as a "change of range *and bearing* machine" (emphasis added).[62] This plan to use bearing rate, which required knowledge of the range, distinguished his proposed instrument from the Dumaresq, which used deflection. The use of bearing rate was crucial to move from the Dumaresq's mechanical solution of two static rates to Pollen's envisioned mechanical solution of two continuously varying rates. Accordingly, the switch from deflection to bearing rate may be regarded as the fundamental insight on which the whole of Pollen's and Isherwood's system was built.

Testifying in the 1930s, Isherwood made exactly that point, and in so doing expressed the same sense of a continuum between the mental and the mechanical as expressed by Pollen. Isherwood was asked about the nature of his and Pollen's invention by an attorney seeking to show that the discovery of mathematical principles could not be considered an invention, let alone a patentable one. At issue was a diagram in a patent illustrating the mathematical theory underlying Pollen's and Isherwood's "change of range and bearing machine," shown in figure 1.7.

Cross-examining Isherwood, the attorney suggested that the term "Rdβ" in the patent was really no different from what Dumaresq called "deflection," designated "BN" in the patent. Both referred to the component perpendicular to the line of sight of the vector showing the relative

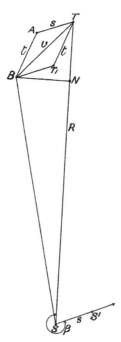

Figure 1.7. This diagram illustrates part of the mathematical theory behind Pollen's and Isherwood's clock. (Arthur Pollen and Harold Isherwood, "Range Clock," fig. 1, US patent 1,162,510.)

To paraphrase the patent, S represents own ship's starting point and T represents target's starting point; the range between them is ST, or R, and the bearing is the exterior angle β. The vector SS¹ represents the movement of own ship at speed s, the vector TT¹ represents the movement of the target at speed t, and the vector TB (consisting of TT¹ minus own vector SS¹, or plus own vector SS¹ reversed in direction) represents the relative motion of own and target ship at speed v.

TN and BN are the components of the vector TB. TN is the component along the line of sight from own ship to target, and BN is the component across (i.e., at right angles to) the line of sight. In the short time period under consideration, the dimensions of the triangle TBN are small compared to the magnitudes of SB and ST—or, put differently, the change in target position is small compared to the range. Thus the change of range in the time period, or range rate, designated dR, is represented by TN, the difference of SN (the projection of the new range SB onto the original range ST) minus ST (the original range). The rate across, or deflection, is BN. Let the change in bearing over the time period, or bearing rate, be called dβ (equivalent to the angle TSB). In circular measure—that is, trigonometrically, on a unit circle—dβ is represented by BN/SB. Again, since the dimensions of the triangle TBN are small compared to the magnitudes of SB and ST, ST (or R) can be substituted for SB, giving the equation BN/R = dβ. On these assumptions, BN/SB equals BN/ST or BN/R. Thus, BN/R = dβ, or, expressed differently, BN = Rdβ. This displacement BN = Rdβ is set up on a variable-speed gear so that the resulting velocity is proportional to Rdβ and drives a second variable-speed gear that reduces the velocity in the ratio 1/R, that is, divides the velocity Rdβ by R, giving a velocity dβ. If a dial is set to bearing β and driven at the velocity dβ, it will indicate the correct instantaneous bearing.

movement of two ships; indeed, the patent gave the equation $Rd\beta = BN$. Isherwood pushed back:

ISHERWOOD: I rather think . . . that I object to your calling the component at right angles to the line of sight as $Rd\beta$, because it was never called $Rd\beta$ by Dumaresq. That length [BN] was called deflection.
ATTORNEY: Is it what you call $Rd\beta$ in your patent . . . ?
ISHERWOOD: Yes, because we took into consideration the rate of change of bearing, but Dumaresq does not take that into consideration.
ATTORNEY: The component of movement across the line of sight was no different then in 1903, or whenever it was that Dumaresq did this, from what it was in 1914, or whenever it was that you did it?
ISHERWOOD: Oh, yes, there was a different consideration of it.
ATTORNEY: So by giving it a different name you got a different quantity?
ISHERWOOD: In a way, yes.[63]

What Isherwood was trying to convey was that although he and Pollen treated deflection (BN) as instantaneously equivalent to the range times bearing rate ($Rd\beta$), they were not conceptually equivalent: Dumaresq dealt with deflection as a static or discontinuously varying quantity, independent of the range, whereas Pollen and Isherwood dealt with deflection as a dynamic and continuously varying quantity by constantly relating it to the range, or, put differently, by working with bearing rate rather than deflection. Hence the algorithms underlying the two machines were different.

The switch from deflection to bearing rate reflected the essential contrast between Dumaresq's approach to the problem and Pollen's and Isherwood's. The Dumaresq was optimized for low rates and target visibility; those conditions minimized the significance of the errors introduced by data smoothing—that is, by discontinuously reading off the continuously varying range rate and deflection. For Pollen and Isherwood, whose goal was to give accurate results when the rates were varying instantaneously and infinitely in relation to each other, and when the target was invisible, deflection did not suffice. They could not stretch out an instant without introducing errors that they regarded as intolerable. They needed to know the deflection at every instant in time—which is to say that they needed to know the bearing rate. Hence, to fulfill their ambition, as distinct from Dumaresq's, Pollen and Isherwood had to discover/invent the mathematical principle called bearing rate and give it mechanical expression in their clock. From one perspective, the principle had always been there, like a planet, waiting to be discovered; but from another, it did not exist until Pollen and Isherwood invented it in their quest for a material instrument that embodied it.

∴

Pollen's and Isherwood's intention to make their clock give accurate predictions even when the rates were changing and the target was invisible was analogous to the quest for "black box" navigational technologies. At the same time as they were envisioning their fire-control system, other participants in "gyro culture" were using gyroscopes to design guidance and navigational systems that could function without reference to the outside world—hence the term "black box." The gyroscopic guidance system for torpedoes was the first such technology, the navigational gyrocompass was the second, and eventually inertial guidance systems for nuclear missiles would emerge from the black-box dream.[64]

Pollen and Isherwood wanted their range-and-bearing clock to be a black box too. But unlike guidance systems, the machinery inside of their black box would be a form of artificial intelligence (a "machine that uses intelligence," in the words of a future student of their system).[65] Their clock's intelligence derived from the fact that it mechanically interconnected the range and bearing rates so as to autogenerate bearings as well as ranges and make accurate predictions about the target's location even when the target could not be observed. The interconnection between the rates was what gave their computer its processing power; it was, so to speak, an integrated and integrating mechanical circuit. As shown in figure 1.8, their clock as ultimately developed was literally inside a black box, which encased the artificial intelligence inside it as a skull does a brain.

Pollen also made clear in his 1904 pamphlet that he and Isherwood intended their system to be *helm-free*—that is, to acquire and calculate accurate data when own ship was turning (i.e., "under helm"), rather than moving on a steady course. On the plotter he described, "changes in own course can be simply allowed for," and the clock would also "be corrected accordingly."[66] To be clear, helm-free operation did *not* mean that his system would produce accurate results during periods when the *target* was changing course (or speed)—that was impossible. But in calling for a system that would work *both* when the target was invisible *and* when own ship was under helm, Pollen was calling for something original. It was ambitious, too, because a prerequisite for fully mechanical helm-free operation during periods of target invisibility was a computer that could mechanically reproduce the interrelationship between instantaneously and continuously changing range and bearing rates—which neither the Dumaresq nor

Figure 1.8. The black box / skull containing the clock / brain. (File R-2-a, Register 3184, RG38/E98/B1254, NARA-I.)

the Vickers clock could do. Hence an American naval officer who viewed Pollen's and Isherwood's finished clock in 1914 remarked that it was "such an improvement over the Vickers clock that it should be called by another name."[67] The radical difference he perceived is starkly visible in figure 1.9, which shows vertical cross sections of the Vickers clock and the finished Pollen-Isherwood clock.

Pollen's and Isherwood's invention was not *de novo*, but it was original. They developed their ideas at a time of great ferment in naval gunnery, when others were coming up with discrete instruments—like the rangefinder, Dumaresq, and Vickers clock—to deal with components of the fire-control problem that Pollen and Isherwood were the first to define comprehensively. In some sense, the system that they envisioned had to incorporate the capabilities of all three of these other inventions, or

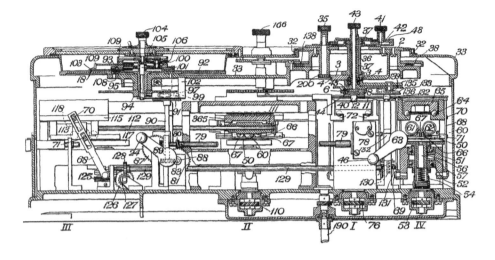

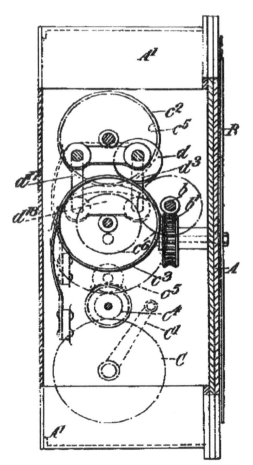

Figure 1.9. The image on the left is a vertical cross-section of one embodiment of the Vickers clock, showing its single variable-speed drive. The image on the top is a vertical cross section of the Pollen-Isherwood clock, showing its four variable-speed drives (one in each of the sections labeled I, II, III, and IV across the bottom of the image) and the intricate interconnections between them. No explanation of the parts in each image is necessary to convey that the Pollen-Isherwood clock was a far more complex piece of hardware, because its software sought to do very different (and much more difficult) things than the Vickers clock. (Trevor Dawson and James Horne, "Improvements in and relating to Apparatus for Indicating Variations of Range or Distance between Moving Objects, more especially for use in Naval Gunnery," fig. 8, GBP 9,461/1904, and Arthur Pollen and Harold Isherwood, "Range Clock," fig. 3, USP 1,162,510.)

functional equivalents thereof. Pollen and Isherwood saw the need for something to find ranges (like the rangefinder), something to solve the vector of relative movement (like the Dumaresq), and something to predict future ranges (like the Vickers clock). In another sense, however, they saw their needs as very different, conceptually and functionally, from these three inventions. They needed something to take bearings as well as ranges, and they needed the bearings to be gyro-corrected for yaw—so not a rangefinder. They needed something to solve the vector of relative movement continuously and instantaneously, while own ship was under helm and the target was invisible, and thus something that worked with bearing rate rather than deflection—so not a Dumaresq. And they needed something to autogenerate not only ranges but also bearings, and to do so according to two rates that were continuously and instantaneously varying—so not a Vickers clock. Moreover, they needed to link these discrete systems together electromechanically into an *über*system, or what would now be called a "system of systems." That way of thinking about fire control was itself an innovation. Pollen's and Isherwood's inventive text had a context, therefore, but it also expressed an original authorial voice.

The electrical and plotting elements of their system similarly rode yet diverged from contemporaneous currents in the Royal Navy. At the same time as they were devising their system, the naval officer Percy Scott was working with Vickers to develop his "director," a sort of master gunsight for centrally firing the individual guns through electrical connections. Like Pollen and Isherwood, he perceived the potential for and desirability of new electrical technologies to network and automate naval gunnery. Simultaneously, Admiral Sir John Fisher, the First Sea Lord, was exploiting wireless and wired telegraphy—the so-called "Victorian internet"—to implement a new, virtually real-time plot at the Admiralty of all merchant and warship movements around the world, as well as to give the Admiralty unprecedented command-and-control of warships.[68] What he wanted to do at the strategic level in London, Pollen and Isherwood wanted to do at the ship level: take decision-making power and responsibility from multiple distributed locations (individual gun turrets) and concentrate it in the plotting room.

Nor was Pollen's and Isherwood's inventive context purely naval. Their desire to combine multiple parts within a single coherent system mirrored the inspiration behind the design of the linotype, the inventor of which, Ottmar Mergenthaler, had sought to build it as a single machine that could perform and automate functions previously requiring multiple machines and operators.[69] Thanks to Isherwood's experience and Pollen's connections, they were in touch with the latest developments in mechanical engineering and able to draw for advice on such luminaries as Lord Kelvin and Charles Vernon Boys, both of whom were inventors of mechanical integrators. Not only would the system envisioned by Pollen and Isherwood contain mechanical marvels; it would also be a shipboard intranet version of the "Victorian internet" powering the development of the field of electrical engineering. Pollen and Isherwood had links with this world too, due to Isherwood's short stint at General Electric and through Kelvin and Boys, who worked on electricity as well as machinery. Unsurprisingly, in view of the porousness of the boundary between mechanical and electrical engineering at the time, the legal issues raised by Pollen's and Isherwood's mechanical inventions closely paralleled those simultaneously arising in the telecommunications industry.

LEGAL TECHNOLOGIES

When Pollen approached the Admiralty for the second time in 1904, he met with a more favorable reception than he had in 1901. After appointing a committee to examine Pollen's ideas at the end of 1904, the Admiralty agreed to pay for a set of experimental instruments to be designed and built by him.[70] These were tested on HMS *Jupiter* in late 1905 and early 1906 with Pollen's and Isherwood's two-observer rangefinder and plotter, though not their clock. The *Jupiter* trials were the first and last trials in which Pollen and Isherwood had the Navy's cooperation, though its financial support was not as generous as they had hoped, and they had to improvise some equipment as a result. The trials revealed such serious flaws with the rangefinder and plotter that Pollen terminated them in early 1906 in order to overhaul the designs. Fortuitously, at just this time Pollen and Isherwood learned that a new 9-foot base Barr & Stroud rangefinder, which could work more accurately at longer ranges than the 4.5-foot base version, would soon enter service.[71] (Barr & Stroud, incidentally, began spying on Pollen and Isherwood to try to figure out what they were up to.)[72] The revised designs were completed and sent to the Admiralty in June 1906. They included a one-observer rangefinder in lieu of the old two-observer system, a continuously running gyroscope to correct bearings for yaw at the plotter (or alternatively at the rangefinder), a fully automatic true-course plotter to chart ranges and bearings transmitted from the rangefinder, and a clock.[73] Still, the redesigned instruments existed only on paper.

Pollen and Isherwood now found themselves in a position familiar to "macro-inventors": those who, unlike "micro-inventors," seek a quantum leap rather than incremental change.[74] They had what they believed to be a revolutionary system—the systemic quality of which was part of what made it revolutionary. "[W]hat I have to sell is not instruments but a system," Pollen told the First Lord of the Admiralty,

> the embodiment of certain laws ["principia"] of gunnery which I have been the first to codify. My instruments as at present designed, will no doubt soon be superseded by others that embody the essential features of my system more completely. The monopoly of instruments is only incidental. It is the knowledge of the system which they make workable, and the exclusive knowledge of it, to which high, possibly supreme, value attaches.[75]

As soon as Pollen and Isherwood could demonstrate that their system was, to borrow a characteristically unpretty German term, *Entwicklungsfähig* ("development-feasible"), micro-inventors were likely to swarm it and seek patent protection at their expense.[76] How could they secure the credit and pecuniary rewards adequate to their role as pioneers?

One option was to seek a pioneer patent (sometimes called a master patent).[77] The classic pioneer patent in their day was Alexander Graham Bell's telephone patent.[78] Pioneer patents were unusually broad grants that butted up against normal limits on the scope of patentable subject matter. The most fundamental such limits excluded the products of nature and purely mental processes from patent protection: some inventive act was required to transform them into patentable subject matter. These limits corresponded to the distinction drawn by the patent system between discovery and invention, and they still inform patent law today, notably in the fields of gene editing and computer code. But this distinction often blurs in practice. At the turn of the century, pioneer patents constituted one such instance of blurring: especially in the nascent telecommunications industry, they straddled the boundary between mental processes and the manipulation of physical substances.

On the face of it, pioneer patents seem as though they would have been a good choice for Pollen and Isherwood. For one thing, the men regarded themselves as pioneers. For another, as noted above, there were striking parallels between their proposed system and telecom technology. By the same token, the encoding of mathematical insight into a physical computer mirrored the encoding of mathematical insight into physical telecom devices: both types of technology had a "text in the machine" (which helps to explain why the telecommunications industry became closely connected with the computing industry).[79]

In fact, however, pioneer patent protection was not a viable option. Pioneer patents required publicity campaigns conducted through the press to establish would-be patentees as "heroic inventors" who merited a relaxation of the rules that applied to everyone else.[80] The pamphlets that Pollen circulated among naval officers constituted a publicity campaign of sorts, but he limited their circulation and did not draw on his many contacts in the press for greater publicity. The reason was that he and Isherwood, as both patriots and men of business, wanted to give the Royal Navy a monopoly on their invention and to be compensated accordingly. That strategy mandated that they keep their invention secret—that is, not give it the sort of extensive publicity campaign required to obtain a pioneer patent. Their strategy also precluded the normal methods of raising private capital to fund the development and exploitation of a pioneer invention, since no one was likely to fund a technology they could not see the patents on.

Another option was to seek secret patents (described in the introduction). Secret patents would give them property protection without revealing their invention to foreign governments. But there being no known case of a secret pioneer patent, secret patents would have to limit the extent of their claims in the ordinary way. Hence, while secret patents were attractive as far as they went, they did not go very far—a limitation with which Pollen's legal training and business experience made him familiar. Certainly Pollen and Isherwood did not want to rely on such limited patents as their primary method for protecting their invention. Writing to a fellow inventor who had published a sketch of an invention "totally unlike" something that Pollen wanted to use but "undoubtedly embod[ying] its principle," Pollen expressed his desire to pay the inventor for the use of his invention, regardless of whether it was covered by patents, "as I am rather sensitive to the rights of inventors, and do not think them adequately protected by the patent laws of any country."[81]

In this respect, Pollen's and Isherwood's timing was unfortunate. In the early modern period, patent law (such as it was) had regarded invention as a dynamic process embedded in the context that produced it. Over the course of the nineteenth century, however, British patent law had come to objectify inventions twice over: first, by requiring them to be materially embodied; and second, by reducing them to their textual representation in patents.[82] Ironically, this emphasis on the text of patents had the effect of hiding the text in the machine—that is, the continuum between mathematical insight and material embodiment. The old habit of referring to a "copyright in inventions" and a "patent for authors," which persisted into the nineteenth century, lent itself to awareness of the continuum. But it too had recently disappeared, as the modern boundary between copyright and patents firmed up, and as professional third-party "ghostwriters" displaced the authors of inventions as the authors of patent texts.[83] In the second half of the twentieth century, the establishment of copyright in addition to patents as a legitimate form of IP protection for computer software restored greater recognition of the continuum between the mathematical text and the material embodiment. But that came a half century too late to help Pollen and Isherwood. They fell between two stools.

A third option for them was to seek what would now be called a development contract with the Admiralty. The novelty of such a contract was bound to make it a risky proposition, but pioneer patents or secret patents carried risks of their own. As a legal technology, a contract had the benefit of greater flexibility than patents; with careful negotiation and drafting, it could potentially define the object of property protection essentially in the broad terms of a pioneer patent, but without the need for a secrecy-destroying publicity campaign.[84] In other words, it could effectively combine pioneer patent protection with secret patent protection, recognizing Pollen and Isherwood as the "heroic inventors" of a developing invention that needed to be kept secret for national security reasons. So they decided to pursue a development contract as their primary means of protection, with secret patents as a backup.

∴

Pollen proposed such an arrangement to the Admiralty. Rather than develop his invention commercially, he asked the Admiralty to monopolize it in order to keep it secret.[85] By linking monopoly and secrecy, he was asking to be made a "captive contractor": one working only for the Navy and not trying to sell abroad.[86] For captivity to work for both parties, monopoly and secrecy had to be mutual and indivisible. In return for his giving the Admiralty a monopoly on demand (i.e., a monopsony), it would give Pollen a monopoly on supply; while in return for his keeping the invention secret from foreign powers (thereby preserving the Admiralty's monopoly on demand), the Admiralty would keep Pollen's invention secret from other competitors (thereby preserving his monopoly on supply). Such an arrangement would meet the Admiralty's national security interest in secrecy and his financial-security interest in charging monopoly prices.

What Pollen initially wanted, he later recalled, was "the Admiralty's co-operation in materializing the system shown by the analysis to be required"—an arrangement he characterized as "joint authorship." The Navy had knowledge of seagoing conditions that he lacked and greater access to scientific and engineering experts than he possessed. He was "quite content with the role of the discoverer of the problem, and the originator of the theoretical solution."[87]

But the Admiralty was not content for him to play that role only. His proposed division of labor—conceptualization by him, instrumentalization by the Admiralty—would have required a sharp departure from the Admiralty's regular contracting procedures. As one official told Pollen, "inventors usually have to perfect their inventions at their own expense, or else grant very favorable terms to others who will find the money for them."[88] That is, the private sector bore all the risk of development and sold finished products to the navy. Even the softer division of labor that Pollen fell back on for the *Jupiter* trials, in which he undertook the work of materialization but with the Admiralty's cooperation, demanded a radical paradigm shift: the Admiralty still would not be contracting for a perfected invention. The term "development contract" did not yet exist because development contracts did not yet exist. A development contract would be practically another invention—a legal-technological invention to accompany his naval-technological invention.

Pollen faced stratospheric institutional hurdles in persuading the Admiralty to give him this new kind of contract. Both its accounting techniques and its procedures for fostering technological change were grounded in the old procurement paradigm. These were not simply bureaucratic routines: they represented deeply embedded habits of thought. For centuries since the Glorious Revolution of 1688, the financial culture of the British government, not just the Admiralty, had emphasized control of expenditures and transparency to Parliament.[89] The purchase of finished products from the private sector fitted this culture: the government knew going in what it had to pay and what it was getting for the payment. There was a material concreteness and temporal finality to the transaction. By contrast, a development contract involved immaterial ideas and temporal open-endedness. Pollen had not actually built the instruments he was proposing, nor could he say when the system as a whole, as distinct from its parts, would be complete—if ever. In a very real sense, the Admiralty would be paying not for a thing but for a brain; not for a static object but for a dynamic process. Financial uncertainty pervaded the transaction.

The magnitude of the sums under discussion made the Admiralty even more uncomfortable. When it asked Pollen to suggest terms for monopoly and secrecy in August 1906, he proposed a royalty arrangement that, officials calculated, would have amounted to £300,000 over fifteen years.[90] Advised that a lump-sum payment would be preferable, Pollen suggested the still eye-watering amount of £120,000—equivalent, to provide some perspective, to the cost of building two submarines. From his point of view, this was necessary to compensate him for the loss of both British and foreign rights and justified by the value of what he was offering, which he attempted to quantify in various ways.⁹¹ From the Admiralty's point of view, he was asking to be paid for an unproven system, which he could not develop without the Admiralty's financial assistance, an amount comparable to what it had paid Robert Whitehead, the inventor of the modern torpedo, for his developed invention.⁹² Facing huge political pressure to reduce expenditures, the Admiralty had haggled with Pollen over paying £4,500 for the *Jupiter* trials and was haggling with him again over paying some £8,000 for another round of trials. An institution acculturated to demanding an explanation of the difference "between the charge of £57.3.9. for the Vertical Rack, etc. for aft instrument, and charge of £26.15.5. for the Vertical Rack for forward instrument" was bound to balk at the imprecise, open-ended, six-figure development contract that Pollen was proposing.⁹³

Like the government's accounting and procurement habits, the Admiralty's existing procedures for encouraging technological change also did not match Pollen's proposal. To be sure, the Royal Navy had a long tradition of technological tinkering and a body for rewarding (or rather incentivizing) it: the Admiralty Awards Council, composed of the naval members of the interdepartmental Ordnance Council. But existing nodes of research, like William Froude's testing tank at Torquay and the torpedo school HMS *Vernon*, formed an institutional archipelago, not a centrally directed institution built on an appreciation of the research-intensive nature of much naval-technological development. That awaited the impact of World War I, which led to the creation of the Admiralty Research Laboratory (1921) and the Admiralty Gunnery Establishment (1931), devoted largely to questions of fire control. It also took World War I for the Admiralty to create the new category of "research worker" alongside the older category of "service inventor": unlike the latter, a uniformed officer who invented in the course of or incidental to his primary duties, the former was a civilian employed specifically to invent.⁹⁴

Both because and as a result of this institutional structure, the Admiralty was ill suited to cope with the sort of long-term, research-intensive project that Pollen envisioned. Some insightful naval officers grasped that civilians like Pollen and Isherwood could actually be better positioned than themselves to tackle certain types of problems. According to the assessment of their work by Edward Harding, the chief advisor on fire control to the Director of Naval Ordnance (DNO) at the time, naval officers had not produced "an equal analysis of the fundamentals of the problem" of naval fire control, "and naturally so, because the N[aval].O[fficer]. is practically always up against the immediate requirements of his profession, which tends to produce an attitude of mind rather foreign to a wide outlook on the whole problem, and hitherto we have not produced the consultative and advisory machinery to undertake this type of research work." As a result, Harding argued, the fact that "Pollen has been ahead of general service thought on the subject" was less shocking than it might seem.[95]

Harding was well positioned to judge. An officer in the Royal Marine Artillery, he had been intensely interested in naval fire control for years and had authored a series of essays on the subject, leading to his appointment as the DNO's chief advisor on fire control in December 1903. He cared little about the technical aspects of fire control per se; what interested him were the tactical benefits, and particularly the tactical freedom, that might flow from technically superior (especially helm-free) fire control. His interests, in short, were the inverse of Pollen's, who worked from the technical out to the tactical. As Harding explained in 1913, "Pollen's ideas upon the requirements of artillery technique agree absolutely with mine, but they are reached from entirely different points of view and by entirely different lines of reasoning."[96] Because his point of view was so different, he did not instantly believe in Pollen's and Isherwood's system. Only after careful study did he become convinced that they had something original and important to offer the Royal Navy—and that the directionality of the offer from civilian to uniform was no accident.

∴

Many other officials struggled to believe that the Navy had anything to learn from civilians. Confident in their own abilities and experienced with crank inventors, they assumed that knowledge would flow in the other direction. Accordingly, their fear of financial exploitation merged with their fear that Pollen would acquire secret knowledge from the Navy in the course of jointly developing his system and then threaten to sell the knowledge abroad unless the Navy paid him higher prices. These fears channeled long-standing prejudices against defense contractors, like mercenaries, as avaricious, disloyal, and ineffective.[97] Pollen "could not fail to acquire further knowledge of range-finding in general, and of British Naval methods in particular," one official worried, and "it might be serious to us if we then decided to let him go abroad with that knowledge; we might in fact be almost obliged to accept his terms so as to keep that knowledge from others."[98] Such officials could conceive only that civilians like Pollen and Isherwood would be intellectually and financially in the Admiralty's debt, not vice versa.

Pollen was well aware of these views and did his best to dispel them. In effect, he had to undertake a dual-track education and advertising campaign, not only to persuade the Admiralty of the technical merits of his system but also to explain why the Admiralty's default assumptions about procurement did not fit the situation. He pointed out that the Whitehead example was inapt, because the Admiralty had not monopolized Whitehead's system, and that the Admiralty could have paid far less for the Whitehead torpedo had it accepted the inventor's offer of monopoly—which it had balked at for the same reasons it was balking at Pollen's monopoly offer.[99] He demonstrated that, contrary to its claims, the Admiralty had not in fact borne the whole cost of development thus far.[100] He explained that he was not financially dependent on the Admiralty to develop his invention; he could seek private financing, although doing so "would rob me of control" and thereby endanger his ability to preserve secrecy.[101] If the Admiralty decided to take the financial risk, it would do so because it believed that the risk was worth the benefit of monopoly—not as a favor to Pollen. If it decided not to take the financial risk, then it could not accuse him of being "an unpatriotic, money grubbing, blackmailer" should he sell to foreign governments.[102]

Nor was the financial risk one-way. A monopoly agreement would oblige Pollen to forgo the prospect of foreign sales and perhaps leave him with less money from the Admiralty than he might have made on the global market. Moreover, just as he might steal knowledge from the Admiralty, so too might the Admiralty steal knowledge from him. As he put it, the Admiralty had admitted him to intercourse with the Navy "not because I was learning, but because I had an analysis and constructive view to put forward that entitled me to a hearing."[103]

Indeed, the process of disclosing ideas to the government had long carried significant risk for inventors. In the seventeenth century, to give a famous example, an inventor seeking a reward or patent had submitted a telescope design to the Venetian Senate, which appointed as examiner a man who promptly gave the design to his close friend Galileo.[104] This risk was well known to, indeed infamous among, British inventors dealing with the Admiralty and the War Office.[105] Britain's laws concerning secret patents went some way toward alleviating the disclosure risk for inventors by stipulating that the act of disclosure would not count as publication invalidating the grant of a patent.[106] In a reflection of his close familiarity with the patent system, Pollen cited the relevant clause of the law in drawing the Admiralty's attention to the fact that his disclosure of ideas did not affect his subsequent right to patent them.[107] But this clause did not guard against government use of his inventions without his consent. While the Patents, Designs, and Trade Marks Act of 1883 required the government to compensate patent owners for the use of their patents (thereby overturning the notorious 1865 ruling in *Feather v. Regina* and arguably bringing government patent infringement into the framework of eminent domain), the law permitted the crown to settle terms with the patentee after use of the patent, or to have the Treasury settle terms if the patentee refused to consent to use.[108] Furthermore, whatever protection the patent laws afforded to the patented elements of the patent owner's invention, they offered no protection to its unpatented parts.

Pollen thus insisted that the patent issue had to be dealt with up front in the contract negotiations. This itself required a change from the Admiralty's normal contracting procedures. It is a measure of the significance attached to Pollen's proposal that the Admiralty was willing to make the change. Normally, Admiralty contracts contained a boilerplate patent clause. It was not open to negotiation, nor did it need to be negotiated when the contractor was selling an ordinary, patented finished article. Such cases did not call for Admiralty officials to reflect deeply on the relationship between the patent system and invention; rather, they encouraged officials to regard patents as straightforward proxies for invention. But Pollen was not selling an ordinary finished article, and he did not believe that patents could adequately cover the article under development. He was asking Admiralty officials to reexamine their usual equation of inventions with patents and to consider that inventiveness might exceed patentability. In effect, Pollen and Isherwood wanted Admiralty officials to see them as the authors of new algorithms, not just as the inventors of new instruments.

Other obstacles stood in Pollen's and Isherwood's way of getting what they wanted. The recent sharp separation of patent from copyright made it even more difficult than it would have been for Admiralty officials to understand Pollen's and Isherwood's sense of themselves as author-inventors or to compensate them as they believed appropriate. Part of the compensation they sought was pecuniary, of course. Pollen liked his gentlemanly lifestyle, and as he reminded one Admiralty official, "I am nearly forty years of age, I have a wife and family to provide for; I am to a great extent dependent upon what I earn."[109] This was not as easy for civil servants and naval officers to understand as might be thought: unlike the inventors, they had guaranteed salaries and pensions. There was a fundamental asymmetry in personal financial security. At this stage, Pollen and Isherwood were inventing on the side of their Linotype jobs and did not even have a start-up firm to market and sell their invention, let alone a large armaments corporation with a diversified product line that could make up for losses in one area with gains in another. But as author-inventors, Pollen and Isherwood did not just want money. To a greater degree than invention, authorship seeks credit for creativity not only in the form of money or property but also in the form of attribution, typically expressed as citations.[110] As

Pollen once put it, he was "keener on credit than on cash."[111] He and Isherwood wanted the Admiralty to recognize them as the authors of a new fire-control text, broadly defined, that interconnected the mental and the material—what they called their "system." This was certainly in their interest; the question was whether naval officials could be persuaded that it was in the service's interest too.

A MEETING OF THE MINDS

A year and a half after his second approach to the Admiralty, Pollen managed to secure an important concession on the patent question. In August 1906, at a conference called to discuss his terms for monopoly, he "explained his claim to be that, whether or not the actual apparatus used was technically an infringement of his patents, if his general principle is employed, the Admiralty should pay the same as if his patents were actually infringed, and that they should not question the validity of such claim."[112] He defined the "general principle" the next day: "the system for obtaining the data for gunnery by the use of ranges and bearings taken simultaneously and used in connection with a chart gyroscopically corrected."[113] With a pioneer patent out of the question for secrecy reasons, he was asking for a contract that would define his invention with the broad scope of a pioneer patent. The Admiralty agreed that "my Lords, as at present advised, have no intention of questioning your claim to be regarded as the sole inventor and originator," quoting Pollen's language, "of the system for obtaining the data for gunnery by the use of ranges and bearings taken simultaneously and used in connection with a chart gyroscopically corrected."[114] Here was a written commitment to recognize Pollen's pioneer status and *not* to define his invention and intellectual property in terms of ordinary patents—a remarkable conceptual innovation for Admiralty officials to accept, and a measure of their interest in what he was offering.

The notably broad and vague definition of Pollen's system reflected the circumstances of its production. At this stage, Pollen and Isherwood had not yet committed to one of the two different methods for gyroscopically correcting bearings for yaw then under development. Whichever method was chosen, it involved the formidable technical challenge of designing a gyroscope that would run continuously, rather than for only several minutes as other gyroscopes then in existence did.[115] The definition of Pollen's and Isherwood's system thus reflected the fundamental importance of their insight into the need for gyroscopic correction and the difficulty of embodying that insight in a suitable new type of gyroscope, but in such a way as to avoid limiting their system to a particular method of embodiment.

The software could be expressed in multiple hardware configurations, so to speak. Here was Steve Jobs's insight in action.

The mention of plotting in the definition struck a similar balance. Having made both a true-course plot and a range-rate plot in his initial 1900 analysis of fire control, Pollen went exhaustively into different plotting methods with Harding in 1905 and 1906. In addition to true-course plotting and range-rate plotting, both men later claimed, they also analyzed bearing-rate plotting (like a range-rate plot, but for bearings instead of ranges) and virtual plotting (a course plot in which the motion of own ship is thrown off onto the target, so that the plot shows a single combined "virtual" course rather than two separate "true" courses).[116] According to Harding, they decided to proceed with true-course plotting because they thought it was the most straightforward solution, and if they could get it to work, it would be easy to get any other kind of plotting to work.[117] Given the variety of plotting methods under discussion in the run-up to Pollen's definition of his system, it made sense to adopt an inclusive rather than exclusive definition—to think in terms of a mathematical spectrum along which various solutions might fall. Although it is unquestionable, as we shall see, that Pollen preferred true-course plotting to rate plotting, it is equally unquestionable, based on the written record, that the system of which the Admiralty recognized him as "the sole originator and inventor" in 1906, and incorporated into the signed contract of 1908, included rate plotting.

The scope of the definition of the system worked together with another clause negotiated in the fall of 1906 to protect both parties. In defining his system, Pollen asked that the Admiralty "undertake not to employ any such system, whether in detail exactly as I have claimed in my patents or not, except subject to agreement with me, as if the method actually used were a method validly protected by my patents"—in other words, to commit to ensuring that "my invention shall not be pirated." He apologized for making this request, which might seem "a mere matter of common honesty and therefore superfluous." But he (presciently) continued, "in years to come the fact that the invention is mine may not seem so obvious—and the protection given by the clause may be advisable."[118]

When the Admiralty refused to give the undertaking in the form requested lest it forswear the crown's right under the patent laws to use inventions without inventors' consent, Pollen found a mutually agreeable alternative.[119] His lawyers advised him that he needed language that would make the Admiralty his partner in development—in effect, creating a fiduciary relationship.[120] He suggested suitable language in a meeting with Admiralty officials in mid-September 1906, which the Admiralty summarized in a letter sent the next day: "The terms herein set forth to include any future improvements that you may make in the system without further cost to the Crown beyond manufacturing cost and any improvements or alterations that the Admiralty themselves may desire to make in the system to be made in the same manner."[121]

Pollen believed, with reason, that the new language, though framed as an obligation on his part, set up a mutual obligation for the Admiralty. In effect, by compelling him to turn over subsequent improvements, the Admiralty recognized that it was not buying a set of discrete instruments as they existed at a particular moment in time but a set of ideas along with the dynamic, integrated system they governed. The implied converse of Pollen's duty to provide improvements was the Admiralty's duty to receive them, which necessarily meant that both parties had to keep the system secret from others. These were the essential terms of a development-captivity contract. In Pollen's later words, the new relationship created by this agreement

> was not merely contractual. It set up definite equities, because it was obligatory henceforth on both parties to act in abounding good faith one to the other. Each was, so to speak, a trustee of the interests of the other and the action of each other towards the other would have to be dictated, and most ultimately be judged, by the principles governing all fiduciary relations.[122]

"Fiduciary" was a legal term of art. From Pollen's perspective, the heart of the Admiralty's fiduciary obligation—or its "trusteeship"—was to refrain from defining his system narrowly in terms of patents. His interpretation accorded with the documentary record of the contract negotiations and was soon to be verified (as shown below) by the Director of Contracts himself; it was later endorsed by an independent royal commission, as we will see in chapter 7; and it was indirectly confirmed by the identical terms of a contract negotiated between the US Navy and its lead fire-control supplier. Indeed, given the nonexistence of development contracts as an established conceptual or legal category, the agreement almost *had* to be fiduciary. Without a clear roadmap, the parties would to some degree have to make it up as they went along, each trusting the other to be governed by the cooperative spirit of their undertaking.

·.·

Harding, the Admiralty fire-control expert, saw clear advantages in a fiduciary relationship. In what he called a "regular snorter" of a memorandum for the DNO,[123] written "in order to have a record of the considerations affecting the Admiralty point of view, and to define clearly and beyond future criticism the basis upon which the Admiralty offer," Harding picked apart the Admiralty's arguments against Pollen's price for monopoly.[124] Harding's analysis made clear that many of Pollen's insights that the Admiralty later tried to argue were obvious—such as the need for accurate data—became so only because Pollen made and communicated them. "The great advance in principle" of Pollen's system, Harding wrote, "is that it recognises the necessity for accurate data and substitutes a system of exact observation for one of merely personal estimation."[125] Because, as Pollen insisted, the development of material instruments depended on having the thoughts that made them seem necessary, the value of his invention "cannot be regarded only from the point of view of ingenious instruments for obtaining even a great advance in Artillery technique but must be looked upon as an essential link in a far reaching chain of development."[126]

This conception of invention as a combined mental-material process had important implications for secrecy. "Undoubtedly the idea of plotting the course can occur and has occurred to many," Harding acknowledged in his report for the DNO, "but ignorance as to its importance and the obvious difficulties in the way of its successful application and its apparent complexity have deterred would-be inventors from following up the idea."[127] In other words, to use the German term introduced above, Pollen's fundamental contribution was to make better fire control "development-feasible" (*Entwicklungsfähig*). Outside the Royal Navy, the importance of knowing the range rate, rather than merely the range, was unknown, and "consequently the means for its determination are <u>unsought for</u>." Similarly, the necessity for some form of gyroscopic correction of bearings "is probably totally unrecognized."[128] So long as potential competitors lacked the necessary ideas, they would never develop the necessary instruments— there could be no "know-how" without the "know-why."[129] The loss of secrecy (and monopoly) through independent discovery "really depends on the state of mind and habits of thought of the possible discoverers," Harding reasoned. Since foreign navies lacked Pollen's state of mind and habits of thought, Harding judged the risk of independent discovery to be "negligible."[130]

Moreover, Harding argued, Admiralty arguments against the high price that Pollen wanted for monopoly rested on a misunderstanding of the nature of the transaction and of its own interests. Not only did the preservation of secrecy require Pollen to forgo British and foreign patents, but it precluded normal methods of commercial financing. "Under these conditions," Harding explained, "the Admiralty for their own ulterior advantage finance the trials," as "an insurance" against foreign acquisition of the invention, not to "reliev[e] the inventor of financial risk."[131] If the Admiralty did not pay the insurance premium now, it might have to pay a far higher price in the open market for the finished invention later (as had occurred with the Whitehead torpedo). Similarly, paying a high lump-sum price protected the Admiralty's interests by precluding Pollen from demanding payment for every new instrument or method he might invent in the course of developing his system.[132] Nor could Harding imagine a way for the Admiralty to solve the important problem that Pollen had defined without disregarding his patent rights. "Obviously if the development of the requisite mechanism is hampered by the necessity of avoiding infringement of the original patents," he presciently warned, "a method of obtaining the same results will be extremely difficult."[133] Even without a pioneer patent, Harding judged, Pollen could acquire enough ordinary patents that there would be no way around them.

Harding occupied a key position at the Naval Ordnance Department, but he was by no means the only gunnery expert or naval officer convinced that the Navy must cooperate with Pollen. Percy Scott, the Inspector of Target Practice and inventor of the director, compared the reliance on visually spotting the fall of shot to a game of chance and saw Pollen's system as necessary to improve the odds. "I do not get the data before I put my money on the table, the data only comes after a miss," he wrote of spotting to Pollen: "here is a field for your predictor."[134] Harding also testified to Scott's support. The command and experimental staff of the gunnery school HMS *Excellent* and the Director of Naval Intelligence—Charles Ottley, a talented inventor in his own right—were all persuaded, along with Harding and Scott, that the Admiralty should secure the monopoly and secrecy of Pollen's system. It was on the strength of their unanimous endorsement, not just Harding's, that the DNO, John Jellicoe (better known as the commander of the Grand Fleet in World War I), urged the Admiralty to enter into the radically new kind of contract that Pollen proposed.[135]

The First Sea Lord, "Jacky" Fisher, had his own reasons to support such a contract. Jellicoe was one of his protégés and put forward arguments that Fisher found "cogent and convincing."[136] Perhaps more importantly, Pollen's system promised to advance his construction agenda. Contrary to popular (and much scholarly) belief, Fisher's ideal capital ship was not the battleship HMS *Dreadnought* but the battlecruiser HMS *Invincible*, which would carry the same armament as a battleship but achieve the speed of a cruiser by sacrificing battleship armor. The reduction in armor would make battlecruisers more vulnerable to enemy gunfire—unless they had a fire-control system that would enable them to hit the enemy under conditions in which the enemy could not hit in return. This ability could compensate, so to speak, for less armor protection—and it was exactly what Pollen's system sought to deliver.[137] Last but not least, Fisher, an early supporter of the Whitehead torpedo, had bad memories of the Royal Navy's decision to decline Whitehead's monopoly offer. Pollen's case "is marvellously [sic] like the introduction of the Whitehead torpedo," he wrote to the First Lord. "We could have had the absolute monopoly of that wonderful weapon (and Mr. Whitehead body and soul into the bargain!), but the Admiralty of that day haggled over £80,000. . . . I hope we shan't make such an idiotic mistake over Pollen!"[138]

∵

In October 1906, the Admiralty and Pollen settled on the terms of a draft contract, which included all the language he thought necessary to establish a fiduciary relationship. The following month, on the strength of this agreement, the Admiralty paid him £6,500 to fund the development of his redesigned instruments for a new round of trials.[139] Just how extraordinary this was needs to be stressed: no less a figure than Alexander Graham Bell had failed to get a similar contract from the British government.[140] Pollen had managed to overcome the skepticism of many uniformed officers toward civilian opinions on naval warfare and to persuade government officials with very good reasons for their normal contracting rules to make an exception and spend public money on an unfinished invention. The Admiralty's willingness to put aside centuries-old habits speaks to its recognition of the importance and the uniqueness of what Pollen and Isherwood were offering.

While the Admiralty's willingness to agree to Pollen's terms was remarkable, it was also fragile, as the year following the agreement on the draft contract showed. In the first place, discomfort with the novel nature of the contract soon manifested among the contract specialists at the Admiralty and the lawyers in the Treasury Solicitor's office—though not among the naval officers who favored the new agreement with Pollen because they perceived the military importance of his invention. Put differently, the executive higher-ups were sold on the need for the new type of contract, but their bureaucratically minded administrative underlings had minds of their own. When the Admiralty sent Pollen the "legal form" of the draft contract agreed to in October 1906—that is, the form written by the Treasury Solicitor's office with input from the Admiralty Contract and Purchase Department—it contained several significant changes from what had been agreed in previous correspondence.[141] One, to take a representative example, was a boilerplate patent clause inserted by the lawyers, who had no reason to appreciate the inapplicability of standard procedures in this particular contract. They can have received little education from the Admiralty's Contract and Purchase Department, since its director, Frederick W. Black, had assumed the position only in May 1906, thereby missing most of the two years of discussions that led up to the draft contract of October 1906.[142]

Knowing more about the history of the negotiations than Black, Pollen immediately objected to the new clause. The Admiralty's justifications of it, he wrote, "seem to me to show a radically different conception of the bargain between the Admiralty and myself to that on which I have acted"— namely, that it was not about patents, but "a system of which I am the inventor."[143] Upon examination of the files, Black was forced to concede the point. The language on the life of patents was "usual and reasonable" in "ordinary cases," he wrote. But "there is force in Mr. Pollen's argument that he is offering a system the value of which does not depend upon patent rights."[144] Due to uninformed misunderstandings like this one by the Contract and Purchase Department and the Treasury Solicitor's office, the process of translating the draft contract of October 1906, negotiated between Pollen and naval officers, into legal form occupied more than a year. The formal contract was finally signed in February 1908.

Pollen would go on to carry out his side of the bargain, dutifully communicating his and Isherwood's ideas and improvements to the Admiralty. But the Admiralty would not keep its side. In the period between the negotiation of the draft contract in 1906 and its formalization in 1908, the naval officers with whom Pollen had negotiated the draft contract all left their positions at the Admiralty as part of routine personnel turnover. With them went the main sources of institutional memory of what Harding had called "the considerations affecting the Admiralty point of view, and . . . the basis upon which the Admiralty offer" this novel form of contract to Pollen. Like the instinctive discomfort with the agreement among contract and legal specialists, this personnel turnover and the loss of corporate memory marked another source of fragility in Pollen's understanding with the Admiralty. As we shall see in the next chapter, it turned out to be fatal.

CHAPTER 2

Infringement as Plagiarism

"I have followed the development of the integrating machine in its various forms for over 30 years, including the ball, disc and cylinder integrator used by Lord Kelvin in his harmonic analyser. I have no hesitation in saying that the integrating mechanism used in the 'Clock' is the most perfect of all that has been done in this direction."
CHARLES VERNON BOYS, 1 NOVEMBER 1912

Although the Admiralty and Pollen experienced a genuine meeting of the minds in agreeing to a novel development contract in 1906, the institutional mind that had met Pollen's was already changing by the time the contract was finally signed in 1908. In the interim, new personnel had begun to replace those in the Naval Ordnance Department who had negotiated the 1906 draft contract. Not only were the new people unaware of the history of the negotiations; they were ignorant of the contract's underlying assumptions. In a reversion to the form that Pollen had tried so hard to shake the Admiralty out of, they thought about invention in terms of patents and material objects. Moreover, while they could readily imagine that the Royal Navy had a great deal to teach civilians, they could not believe that civilians had anything significant to teach the Royal Navy. Pollen's appeals to the "scientific" character of his "system" could not overcome their prejudices, and he found himself back at square one.

What ensued over the next seven years could be regarded as a comedy of errors had its consequences not been so serious. On the one hand, Pollen and Isherwood built a system acclaimed by leading scientists of the day as an extraordinary achievement, at the center of which was an analog computer with artificial intelligence. On the other hand, a naval officer named Frederic Dreyer pirated Pollen's and Isherwood's system, but he pirated it incompetently.[1] Although many—almost certainly a majority—of gunnery experts preferred Pollen's and Isherwood's system to Dreyer's, he was able to exploit his insider position, his connections with institutionally powerful patrons, and naval officers' ideological prejudices against civilian contractors to push through the adoption of his system.

The theft of private-sector inventions by public officials and officers was hardly unusual.[2] What *was* unusual was Dreyer's ability to capture the Admiralty's corporate memory about fire control, and the Admiralty's willingness to let him. His talent as an author of historical fiction exceeded his talent as an author of computer algorithms. With breathtaking audacity, Dreyer inverted the historical record to accuse Pollen and Isherwood of pirating *him*, and he persuaded key Admiralty officials to adopt his false history. This was an exercise in what might be dubbed the "economics" of historical memory, or an attempt at "technology laundering." By scrubbing his "invention" of its actual origins, Dreyer redirected credit and development funds from Pollen to himself and from Pollen's firm to a different one. That firm, which became a major player in British computing, in turn suppressed the memory that it owed its start in computing to Pollen.[3] As we will see in subsequent chapters, the willingness of Admiralty officials to cede institutional control of the historical narrative to Dreyer set British fire-control development back for years after World War I, because their reputations came to depend on dissuading anyone from asking awkward historical questions.

To deconstruct what happened requires precise understanding of the historical record and methodological rigor. In describing his invention and constructing his alternative history, Dreyer relied on the technical ignorance of his peers to get away with gross imprecision. Calling certain things "details" and other things "significant" was an important part of his rhetorical strategy. He and the Admiralty facilitated the success of this strategy by adopting a methodologically naive approach to history. They engaged in what might be called an outcome-based approach: given a technological outcome, they inferred inventors' intentions from it. That is to say, they read history backwards. Good scholarly practice is to take an intent- or process-based approach—that is, to read history forwards.[4] Indeed, such an approach is mandated by the protean quality of computer software, as defined in chapter 1.

DREYER'S FIRST PIRACY

In April 1907, Commander Frederic Dreyer replaced Edward Harding as chief advisor on fire control to the DNO, and four months later, Captain Reginald Bacon replaced Jellicoe as DNO. Their arrival at the Admiralty initiated a reversal in the Admiralty's attitude toward Pollen. Bacon possessed impressive technical proficiency—he served as the first head of the

submarine service and the first captain of HMS *Dreadnought*—but he was
not a gunnery specialist. More importantly, notwithstanding his technical
proficiency, he worried about the tendency of complex technology—which
Pollen's and Isherwood's system certainly qualified as—to fail under the
stress of seagoing conditions. "[H]ow far mechanism should supersede the
human brain involves serious practical considerations," Bacon told Pollen.[5]
Moreover, from his experience working closely with contractors on submarine development, Bacon came to the position wary of Pollen's claims
and deeply suspicious of extraordinary commercial arrangements like the
one agreed to with him.[6]

Unlike Bacon, his deputy Dreyer—who had served under Bacon on
board HMS *Dreadnought*—was a gunnery specialist. But like Bacon, Dreyer
generally evinced skepticism, if not outright suspicion, of the private sector. He provides strong support for the insight of one historian that the War
Office and Admiralty "fortified themselves so effectively against frauds that
they became prejudiced against any 'outside' innovation."[7] As DNO himself during World War I, Dreyer pushed to reduce the Navy's reliance on
defense contractors for the design of gunnery materiel.[8] He also displayed
a certain impatience with the niceties of liberal property norms.[9]

Dreyer was highly competent in certain respects but also perceived to
have significant character defects. Even before qualifying as a gunnery officer, he displayed an interest in improving the fleet's gunnery equipment,
first submitting an invention to the Admiralty (which rejected it) in 1899.
Several years later, with him serving as gunnery lieutenant of HMS *Ex-
mouth*, the ship won multiple fleet gunnery competitions, indicating that
he was good at his job. Moreover, as we will see, Dreyer had a talent for
ingratiating himself with powerful superior officers. The verdict from his
subordinates, however, was mixed. While they invariably remembered
him as highly proficient, they also observed less attractive aspects of his
personality. Admiral Sir William Davis, who had served under Dreyer long
before becoming Vice Chief of the Naval Staff, recalled him as "a very clever
and able man" but also considered him "a complex and uncertain character."[10] In Davis's words, "he was inordinately ambitious and he had a bit
of a chip on his shoulder, and if he thought you thought he was not such
an impressive and powerful chap as he outwardly seemed—WOE BETIDE
YOU."[11] Another former subordinate remembered him as "a caricature of
the Navy's stock notion of a gunnery officer, an idea which does not fit most
gunnery officers whom I have known, who were nice, able, normal people."[12] According to Alfred Duff Cooper (later created Viscount Norwich),
First Lord of the Admiralty in the late 1930s, Dreyer was "[u]niversally dis-
trusted and disliked in the service."[13]

Dreyer had met Pollen in 1905; they were friendly though not close, and Pollen sent Dreyer copies of the confidential pamphlets he printed to circulate his ideas among naval officers.[14] Meanwhile, Dreyer began to dabble in fire-control inventions. In December 1906, he submitted a design for a "rate of change calculator."[15] It was a slide-rule for taking a range rate, not— contrary to his later claims—a range-rate plotter (range-rate plots plotted ranges against time, to refresh readers' memories from chapter 1). In mid-1907, Dreyer proposed a new invention with his brother John, an army officer in the Royal Artillery. This occurred shortly after Dreyer began his stint at the Naval Ordnance Department. As it happens, he had recently visited the Linotype works in the course of his official duties, where he saw Pollen's gyro-stabilized rangefinder mounting and automatic plotter in the course of construction, as well as almost certainly the designs of his clock.[16] Dreyer later claimed that this 1907 invention was also a range-rate plotter; again, it was not. Indeed, when he formally submitted it, Dreyer explicitly claimed that its originality consisted of its rejection of *any* form of plotting. To justify this rejection, Dreyer pointed to problems with range-rate plotting, which he described as an "adapt[ation]" of the course-plotting technique he attributed to the army officer Henry Watkin (encountered in chapter 1).[17] This marked the debut of Dreyer's almost obsessive tendency to narrate the development of naval fire control around Watkin.

It is important to establish the character of these 1906 and 1907 inventions in order to understand the role they played in Dreyer's subsequent retelling of history. When he proposed them, Dreyer had no delusions of inventive grandeur; he did not suggest that he was doing anything other than operating in the Navy's tinkering tradition, which had generated valuable technological advances over the years by seeking to improve existing equipment rather to make a quantum leap from it. But as he came to see Pollen and Isherwood as rivals, and as they came to accuse him and the Admiralty of impropriety, he began to reinvent himself as a pioneer rather than a tinkerer. This self-reinvention required the invention of a new history. Because Pollen and Isherwood preferred to use true-course plots, Dreyer made his own use of range-rate plotting (which was mathematically interconvertible with the courses and speeds shown on true-course plots) the basis of his claim to inventive originality and depicted their true-course plotting as a mere adaptation of Watkin's technique (i.e., how he described range-rate plotting in 1907). It would be tedious to document every instance in which he attempted to portray Watkin, who was at most marginal to the development of naval fire control, as a major figure and the real originator of Pollen's system.[18] Suffice it to say that Dreyer seems to have convinced himself of his own propaganda about Watkin's great historical

importance, which, as we will see in chapter 7, bewildered competent outside experts. Dreyer's dependence on range-rate plotting to establish his
inventive originality drove him to try to push his use of it all the way back to
his 1906 and 1907 inventions, before it was plausible to suggest that he had
gotten the idea from Pollen and Isherwood. Hence his placement of narrative weight unsupported by the historical record on these early inventions.

·.·

While Dreyer labored in a conceptual universe that Pollen and Isherwood
had departed long ago, they pushed ahead with new trials of their equipment aboard HMS *Ariadne* in late 1907. As we saw in chapter 1, although
the Admiralty had not signed a formal contract with Pollen by this point,
it had paid him £6,500 in October 1906, on the strength of its draft contract with him, to develop the gyro-stabilized rangefinder mounting and
the plotter in his system for trial. Pollen and Isherwood had already begun
design work on their clock, but it was not ready in time for the *Ariadne* trials.[19] To superintend the trials, Bacon appointed the recently retired Admiral of the Fleet, Sir Arthur K. Wilson, who was not a gunnery specialist; to
serve as Wilson's technical assistant, he appointed Dreyer, who had served
as Wilson's principal gunnery advisor in the Channel Fleet not long before
joining the Naval Ordnance Department. Before getting down to business
in the official trials, Pollen and Isherwood used the preliminary trials to
experiment with range-rate plotting.[20]

By chance, Pollen and Dreyer rode the train together down to Portsmouth before the *Ariadne* trials. Dreyer took the opportunity to inform
Pollen that he hoped to "crab" (spoil) Pollen's instruments at the trials. Not
seeing him as a threat—Dreyer was, after all, an official of the institution
obliged to protect his interests—Pollen offered to let Dreyer see the series
of plots, including the experimental range-rate plot, made in the preliminary trials.[21] Whether Dreyer accepted the invitation is unclear, but in any
case he still might have seen a range-rate plot that Pollen had included in a
pamphlet privately circulated to naval officers that fall.[22] Wilson certainly
received a copy of that pamphlet and would have seen the range-rate plot
made on *Ariadne* during the preliminary trials.[23]

The *Ariadne* trials generated an outcome adverse to Pollen by ignoring
the obligations that the Admiralty had undertaken to him in 1906. While
Pollen's new gyro-stabilized rangefinder mounting and automatic true-
course plotter were tested aboard the *Ariadne*, another ship, HMS *Vengeance*, was undergoing the same trials in parallel. Unbeknownst to him, this
ship carried Dreyer, working a primitive, strictly manual virtual-course

plotter (a third type, different from both rate and true-course plotters) at Wilson's direction that used bearings uncorrected for yaw. Furthermore, the trials posed conditions of yaw, speed, course, and rates far easier than those Pollen and Isherwood had designed their gyro-stabilized rangefinder mounting and automatic plotter to handle.[24] Wilson refused Pollen's request for more difficult test conditions and then abruptly ended the trials, informing him that a "vastly superior" system had superseded his.[25] Although Pollen and the Admiralty signed the formal contract embodying the 1906 draft agreement (including the key clauses reviewed in chapter 1) in February 1908, a month after the conclusion of the *Ariadne* trials, the Admiralty informed Pollen that it was not exercising its option to purchase the monopoly of his system and that he was free to sell it abroad.[26]

In making this decision, the Admiralty relied on the ostensibly expert technical advice of Wilson—behind whom stood Dreyer, the gunnery specialist he relied on. In truth, the "vastly superior" Wilson-Dreyer system for which the Admiralty threw Pollen's overboard had operated under practically the only set of conditions in which it could hope to achieve a modicum of success. Harding, who compared the plots made by *Ariadne* with those made by *Vengeance*, recalled his reaction when he read Wilson's report: it "was so wholly inconsistent with the plain evidence of the results obtained in the test runs that I was wholly unable to understand how anyone, even rudimentarily familiar with the problem, could have come to such a conclusion."[27] As we will see in chapter 7, Harding was not the only competent observer to be aghast.

Regarding the judgment after the trials as transparently absurd, Pollen resisted the Admiralty's rejection of his system. At the end of 1907, he had established a start-up, the Argo Company, to move his and Isherwood's fire-control work out of Linotype.[28] Determined to develop their system for the Royal Navy only, Pollen launched a campaign to convince the Admiralty to reconsider. What most angered him was the appearance of corruption in the trials. Pollen was convinced that Bacon and Wilson both opposed his system. As for Wilson's assistant,

> It is an odd chance that Dreyer, who, as far as I know, is the only gunnery man who has ever been crossed to my views, should, by an accident, be put into the curious position, of having a former Captain [Bacon], who is not a gunnery man himself, as his superior as D.N.O., and then be able to call as judge between his own system and mine an ex-Admiral [Wilson] whom he had kept at the top of the Fleet in Gunnery for years, and who does not appear to have even the vaguest idea of what the problems of modern gunnery are.[29]

He added that "an unpleasant flavour" would be "thrown over the whole transaction by the fact that the system in favour of which [mine] was rejected is nothing more or less than what will be called a belated and inferior imitation of it."[30] Pollen's imputation of impropriety proved uncomfortably difficult to refute and produced the desired effect: in June 1908, the Admiralty agreed to pay him £11,500 for his services to date and to preserve secrecy for another eighteen months.[31]

∴

In the meantime, Pollen and Isherwood kept at work developing their system. By this point, designs of the clock were sufficiently advanced for them to take out two secret patents.[32] These two patents underscore the dangers of outcome-based rather than intent-based history. They were connected with Pollen's and Isherwood's ongoing investigations into different methods of embodying their system, not all of which they ultimately selected. These included an idea, dating back to 1906 but later abandoned, for meaning the range observations from multiple rangefinders, either mechanically or by plotting, so as to reduce the effect of individual errors—an idea that Dreyer took out of their wastebasket and made a key component of his system.[33] Pollen never believed that the scheme involving this idea could be relied on as the primary means of fire control, but at that time he thought it might provide a useful supplement to true-course plotting under certain conditions.[34]

Having suffered from personnel turnover at the Admiralty, Pollen also worked to protect his interests from any future turnover by recruiting more naval officers to his cause. In a new pamphlet condemning the Wilson-Dreyer system used aboard the *Vengeance*, titled "Reflections on an Error of the Day" (a gunnery pun), Pollen decried the system's reliance on manual methods and made the same criticisms of range-rate plotting that Dreyer had made a year earlier when submitting his second invention to the Admiralty. The pamphlet pointedly emphasized the dangers of range-rate plotting without bearings.[35]

Unsurprisingly, Pollen's pamphlet deeply wounded Dreyer's naval *amour propre*. Unconcerned about civilian *amour propre*, Dreyer castigated the pamphlet to a brother officer as "scurrilous." "It is a great pity," he complained, "that trusting N.O.'s [naval officers] will go and discuss 'Confidential' matters with any private man." Dreyer also criticized Pollen's preference for electromechanical automation of fire control and his demand for bearings to be corrected for yaw. "A lot of rubbish re auto-transmission to the sights is loosely talked of, but the cold fact remains that you must have the man of brains to decide when to throw out and when to include the R[ange].F[inder]. readings as se[n]t down," he wrote. Rejecting automation as unnecessarily complex, he elaborated that Pollen

> made some very complicated machinery at the Linotype works of which he is a Director. The simpler we keep our ships the better. A [magnetic] Chetwynd compass [which produced yaw-corrupted bearings] in the transmitting station and a pointer that is worked by the R.F. training, a deal kitchen table and a range bar that is all we want.[36]

Dreyer expressed his views clearly, and they were simplistic. Although he and the Admiralty would later claim that mechanization and gyro-correcting for yaw had been "obvious" all along, manifestly they were far from obvious to Dreyer in 1908. Moreover, while Dreyer evinced a grudging awareness elsewhere in the letter that some form of bearings, not just the ranges he previously relied on, might be useful, he still had no idea *why* bearings were so important in Pollen's system. Like Bacon, whose reservations about mechanization he shared, his priority was to ensure that the human brain, not any electromechanical brain, remained uppermost in naval fire control.

Notwithstanding Dreyer's commitment to preserve the position of the "man of brains," he did not rate the intellectual capacities of his fellow naval personnel highly—especially of those inferior to him in rank. One future admiral who served under Dreyer as a junior officer recalled that he "seemed to expect nothing but idiocy from his junior staff."[37] But where Pollen believed the solution to the shortcomings of the human brain lay in using an electromechanical brain, Dreyer thought it lay in subdividing manual operations so as to reduce the skill level required of operators. "When organising the system of control," the 1908 Admiralty pamphlet on *Fire Control* describing the Wilson-Dreyer system advised, "it should be borne in mind that the guiding principle should be 'ONE MAN, ONE JOB.'"[38] Necessarily, this approach was, to borrow Pollen's term, "poly-anthropic." It required a much larger number of personnel than did Pollen's—roughly forty to fifty versus five—and thus it introduced a correspondingly larger probability of human error.[39] Put another way, where Pollen wanted mechanical automata, Dreyer wanted human automata; or where Pollen wanted to format an electromechanical computer, Dreyer wanted to format the human.[40]

In any case, the failure of the Wilson-Dreyer system, and particularly of range-rate plotting, in the 1908 battle practice induced Dreyer to produce a manual version of Pollen's automatic true-course plotter. Pollen was not amused. "Information that I cannot distrust has reached me," he notified the First Lord, that Dreyer was developing a plotter "that is a mere slavish copy of mine, and which is based upon some of my patented as well as upon some of my unpatented inventions." If the Admiralty adopted Dreyer's plotter, it would be "falling foul both of my rights in the matter, and of the honourable understanding that has been established between the Board and me."[41] Pollen reminded the DNO that the patented or patentable status of his inventions did not define the Admiralty's obligations to him.[42] Politely but firmly, he was accusing the Admiralty of letting one of its own officers steal his ideas. He was not the only one to reach this conclusion. Rear Admiral Percy Scott, arguably the Royal Navy's most distinguished gunnery expert, who had seen the plans of Dreyer's equipment for himself, pronounced it a "piracy" of Pollen's system.[43]

BUILDING THE MACHINE FOR THE TEXT

The Admiralty dragged its feet in replying to Pollen's embarrassing charges. In the interim, he forged ahead with his efforts to sell his system to the Admiralty. In January 1909, he sent the Admiralty a description of the improvements to his and Isherwood's gear since the *Ariadne* trials. He communicated his intention to make the true-course plotter, which was already automatic, helm-free as well—that is, to make it able to cope with changes when own ship turned. Helm-free operation was a goal that he and Isherwood had been chasing for years and that gunnery experts like Edward Harding wanted because of the tactical freedom it would confer, as we saw in chapter 1. Pollen also advised the Admiralty that Argo was working on a mechanical (not magnetic) compass—that is, a gyrocompass—so that it could be connected to the plotter and correct bearings both for yaw and for changes in course. The gyro-stabilized rangefinder mounting had already been tried on the *Ariadne*, the clock was at last nearing completion, and arrangements had been made for automatic transmission of data throughout. Accordingly, Pollen informed the Admiralty, he was now in position to offer the whole system, rather just parts.[44] After months of bargaining, the Admiralty agreed to order a gyro-stabilized rangefinder mounting, the new plotter, and the clock for trial. It also arranged to make monthly payments to Pollen to give him the funds to carry on his work in return for undertaking to keep his system secret past November 1909.[45]

Here again it is critical to distinguish between the paths that Pollen and Isherwood were considering and the paths that they ended up taking under Admiralty direction. Read with other evidence, Pollen's January 1909 approach to the Admiralty plainly shows that he and Isherwood were working on making the electrical transmission of data from the rangefinder to the plotter and from the clock to the guns "synchronous" (a term of art in electrical engineering, the details of which are unimportant here but are discussed at length in chapter 8).[46] Pollen's and Isherwood's pursuit of synchronous transmission makes clear that they saw its importance a decade before either the Royal Navy or the US Navy did. As events unfolded, for lack of time and money, they were unable to make their synchronous transmission system work then; it was one of the remarkably few "reverse salients," or critical problems in the development of naval fire control, that they anticipated but did not manage to solve themselves.[47] Instead, they ended up licensing nonsynchronous equipment from Vickers, the British armaments firm. Even so, their reliance on Vickers was not one-way: their work on transmission, which they patented, proved to be so significant that Vickers found itself obliged to purchase their patents for use in its own fire-control system, as we will see in chapter 8.

The trials of Pollen's and Isherwood's new gear agreed to by the Admiralty in April 1909 ended up occurring on HMS *Natal* in two stages. In late 1909, the plotter was tried; in mid-1910, the clock was tried. In between, several whiplash-inducing changes in Pollen's fortunes occurred. First, Bacon departed the post of DNO, and his deputy Arthur Craig Waller, who liked Pollen's system, temporarily took over the Naval Ordnance Department. A noticeable warming of relations ensued. Shortly thereafter, Pollen found a powerful new supporter of his system in the captain of the trial ship *Natal*, Frederick Ogilvy. An outstanding gunnery officer, Ogilvy shared Pollen's belief that correctly analyzing the fire-control problem was more difficult and important than the details of particular designs. To Pollen's delight, he also agreed that the system must be developed to cope with the most challenging possible conditions of battle, rather than with the much easier conditions of battle practice, and accordingly that helm-free operation was essential.[48]

Within two months, however, Pollen's fortunes changed. In a devastating turn of events, Ogilvy died from food poisoning. At the same time, Archibald Moore, who would prove even more hostile to Pollen than Bacon, took over as the new DNO. Then, in January 1910, shortly after Moore's appointment as DNO, Pollen's old antagonist and Dreyer's supporter Arthur Wilson replaced "Jacky" Fisher as First Sea Lord. An abrupt change in policy followed. Just a month earlier, in December 1909, it had looked as though Pollen would receive an order for seventy-five of his gyro-stabilized rangefinder mountings as well as a new agreement to preserve the monopoly and secrecy of his system. On the strength of the mountings order, and realizing that the purchase of Linotype by its American parent firm would render it unsuitable to build secret British naval equipment, he bought a controlling share in the optics and instruments-making firm Cooke & Sons as a vehicle to manufacture Argo's system.[49] But in April 1910, the Admiralty abruptly informed him that it wanted to end secrecy and to buy only fifteen of the mountings, which it expected him to supply at lower prices per unit now that he was free to sell abroad (which Pollen did not want to do).[50]

Pollen was beside himself, but, as in 1908, he fought back.[51] If the Admiralty ordered forty-five mountings, he wrote to the First Lord, he would be willing to maintain secrecy without compensation for the loss of foreign markets, so little did he want foreign powers to benefit from his system. But he was tired of what he dubbed the "fraudulent contractor theory" that he was seeking excessive profits or engaging in blackmail,[52] so he also wanted the Admiralty to acknowledge, in writing, that he was "patriotic[ally]" accepting less money than he was commercially entitled to in order to keep his system in British hands.[53] The Admiralty gave him only part of what he asked for. On the one hand, it agreed to order forty-five mountings from him at a price high enough to cover the extension of monopoly and secrecy to the end of 1912. On the other hand, it did so on the condition that he withdraw his accusation of piracy against Dreyer's manual true-course plotter. Pollen decided to accept this proposed compromise.[54]

∴

The second round of trials on *Natal* followed on the heels of the April 1910 agreement. These tested the plotter, hastily modified to enable helm-free plotting and given an extemporized arrangement aboard the ship for range-rate and bearing-rate plotting; the trials also tested, for the first time, the clock, which was not yet modified to be helm-free. Both instruments suffered from numerous electrical and mechanical defects under seagoing conditions—not surprisingly, given the Admiralty's decision to kick Pollen's experienced staff off the ship and replace them with ordinary seamen who had received no special training.[55] Despite this, the instruments performed well enough to demonstrate their soundness in principle, and the teething problems were relatively simple to rectify.[56]

The clock, which became known as the Argo Mark I (or *Natal*) clock and was covered by a secret patent (360/1911), marked a breakthrough. Here it is important to understand that Pollen and Isherwood had chosen to tackle the clock in stages. From the start, as we saw in chapter 1, they knew that they wanted their clock to be capable of operating when the target was invisible and when own ship was turning. For operation when the target was invisible, they knew they needed to mechanically interconnect the range and bearing rates so that the clock autogenerated bearings. Without such an interconnection, a supply of visual bearing observations was necessary to calculate the bearing rate to put on the clock—and visual observation was impossible when the target was invisible. For helm-free operation, they knew they needed two things: a straightforward electromechanical linkage between the clock and the gyrocompass, and a complex mechanical interconnection between the range and bearing rates. The former was necessary because own ship's course changed so rapidly during a turn that only an electromechanical linkage with the gyrocompass could enable the clock to reproduce the variation quickly and accurately enough. The latter was necessary because the rates changed so rapidly during a turn that only mechanically interconnected rates could reproduce the variation quickly and accurately enough.

The January 1909 description of the Argo system made clear that Pollen and Isherwood were working on developing their own gyrocompass with a view to connecting it with the clock, but they decided to prioritize the mechanical interconnection between the rates in the Argo Mark I clock (hereafter dubbed the "Argo I clock"). As an engineering matter, it was far more difficult than the comparatively easy connection with the gyrocompass. In the course of building the Argo I clock, Pollen and Isherwood encountered a "reverse salient" and became aware of the need for a special kind of variable-speed drive to enable both helm-free operation and operation when the target was invisible, which in turn posed a difficult engineering challenge. Accordingly, the construction of the new drive became their second priority after interconnecting the rates, and the connection to the gyrocompass was left till last, as a sort of simple mopping-up matter.

In the Argo I clock, Pollen and Isherwood successfully interconnected the rates, something no one had previously attempted. As we saw in chapter 1, the Vickers clock accounted only for the range rate (not the bearing rate) and had to be manually adjusted if the range rate changed, while the Dumaresq calculated the deflection but not the bearing rate. In mathematical terms, Pollen and Isherwood needed their clock to continuously and instantaneously convert deflection into bearing rate by mechanically dividing the deflection by the range. In terms of existing machines, their requirements could be thought of as the addition of a second Vickers clock (for the bearing rate) plus a series of interconnections between the two Vickers clocks and the Dumaresq—except that no one had thought of the problem this way before, let alone invented the machines to solve it. With the Argo I clock, Pollen and Isherwood sought to show that this new problem could be solved in a new way, by interconnecting the rates so as to autogenerate bearings. To supply proof of concept as quickly as possible,

Pollen and Isherwood did this in such a way as to prevent automatic helm-free operation, knowing that they would overcome the issue in their next iteration. Thus, even though the Argo I clock did not fully achieve Pollen's and Isherwood's vision of helm-free operation, it went a long way toward fulfilling the desiderata for a "change of range and bearing" clock that Pollen had articulated in his 1904 pamphlet on "principia." This clock could be set either by courses and speeds, as derived from true-course plotting, or by rates.

MORE PIRACY

In July 1910, shortly after the conclusion of the second round of trials on the *Natal*, Dreyer reentered the picture. Now also outside of the Naval Ordnance Department and serving on HMS *Vanguard*, he submitted a proposal for what he called a fire-control "table" to the Admiralty.[57] The Admiralty funded its manufacture by the instruments firm Elliott Brothers Ltd. Dreyer's table used data generated by and automatically transmitted from Pollen's gyro-stabilized rangefinder mounting. In its design, moreover, it moved in directions long advocated by Pollen: it was much more of an integrated system than Dreyer's previous lash-up jobs, and it added a bearing-rate plot to the range-rate plot (so it may be said to have used *two-rate plotting*).

Soon after receiving Dreyer's submission, the Admiralty, with his proposed two-rate plotting in mind, asked Pollen to modify the design of his clock so that it could be set by rates as well as by courses and speeds.[58] Taken aback, Pollen pointed out, and the Admiralty was forced to acknowledge, that the Argo I clock *already* could be set by rates—in fact, instructions for doing so were engraved on the relevant dial.[59] The reasons why the Argo I clock possessed this rate-setting feature are important to understand, since they differed from those that the Admiralty later assumed when it read history backwards. The inclusion of the rate-setting capability had *not*, contrary to the Admiralty's subsequent interpretation, grown out of any preference for two-rate plotting as the primary form of plotting; as we have seen, Pollen consistently preferred true-course plotting. Instead, it originated partly in Pollen's and Isherwood's understanding of feedback. As Pollen had explained in 1904, if bearing observations sent down from the rangefinder disagreed with the bearings autogenerated by the clock, it was a sign that the clock was working at the wrong rates, and thus it was desirable to be able to reset the rates, not just courses and speeds.[60] The clock's rate-setting feature also traced back to Argo's experiments with sending rates directly from the rangefinder to the clock and with rate plotting as a secondary form of plotting useful under certain circumstance.[61] It was this cluster of ideas going back years that had caused Pollen and Isherwood to incorporate the rate-setting feature in the Argo I clock.

It was also this cluster of ideas that had prompted Pollen to take up the development of a rate plotter, which he told the Admiralty about in August 1910, just weeks after it had received Dreyer's latest proposal.[62] Blissfully ignorant of this multiplicity of original intentions, and skeptical of civilian expertise, the Admiralty engaged in the worst sort of outcome-based history. It assumed that the rate-setting feature of the Argo clock could have arisen only from an interest in two-rate plotting like Dreyer's, and thus it assumed that Pollen was working along identical lines as Dreyer. Accordingly, the worried Admiralty directed Dreyer at once to take out a patent (which became 22,140/1910) covering two-rate plotting. "This action is considered desirable," the DNO Moore explained, "in order to protect the Admiralty from any developments of Mr Pollen."[63] From the Admiralty's perspective, the principal purpose of secret patents was to establish priority of invention—that is, that one inventor's invention predated another's—and the Naval Ordnance Department, encouraged by Dreyer, assumed that the naval officer must have made the invention prior to the civilian.[64] To Moore's assistant and Dreyer's friend Joseph Henley, it was inconceivable that Pollen himself had invented the idea of rate plotting; he confided to Dreyer, "Personally I expect he has heard of your scheme through somebody and that this has given him the idea."[65] Dreyer and the Admiralty hastened his lodging of his provisional patent specifications in order to beat Pollen to the punch.[66]

Then Moore suddenly noticed a problem: although Pollen did not hold patents on *rate* plotting, he did hold patents on *automatic* plotting, which Dreyer's provisional specifications contemplated. Accordingly, interpreting the Admiralty's obligations to Pollen in the narrow terms of patents that it had forsworn in 1906, officials instructed Dreyer to reframe his complete specification so as "not to claim anything covered by the Pollen patents."[67] As Harding had predicted, the Admiralty was struggling to improve its fire-control system without infringing Pollen's patents—though not for lack of trying.

In September 1910, Dreyer made—or rather passed along—another suggestion for his system: the addition of a "clock pencil" to his range-rate plots.[68] The clock pencil took its name from the fact that it was driven by the range-rate clock rather than by the rangefinder (making it a sort of integraph). While the pencil driven by the rangefinder plotted observed data, the clock pencil would plot calculated data. This pencil, which was later incorporated into the bearing-rate plot as well as the range-rate plot, eventually became the single most useful feature of the Dreyer tables, because it enabled, in visually convenient form, the sort of feedback between observed and calculated data that Pollen and Isherwood had pursued by other means. By comparing a meaning line drawn through range observations from the rangefinder with a meaning line drawn through ranges calculated by the range-rate clock, an operator could "tune" (i.e., adjust) the clock to a new rate that brought it into alignment with observed data. The tuning process had the potential to mitigate the effect of errors introduced by the limitations of the Dreyer table's later clock designs. But all that was in the future. The contemporary evidence shows that the "clock pencil" was not Dreyer's idea and that he had no conception of using it to enable feedback, though the officers who suggested it to him—both of whom were familiar with and admired Pollen's system—probably did. At the time, Dreyer was careful to note that the clock pencil was not his idea—the officers who suggested it were his equal and superior in rank and bound to see his proposal—but in later years he was less scrupulous about crediting them.[69] Thus the "clock pencil" is an instance in which reading Dreyer's intent backwards from a later outcome or from his own later writings would produce an incorrect interpretation.

News of Dreyer's latest ideas did not reach Pollen, though news of Pollen's improvements reached Dreyer. Instead of protecting Pollen's interests, the Admiralty was manipulating information flows to its own (and Dreyer's) advantage and Pollen's detriment. On the one hand, the Admiralty refused to disclose information about Dreyer's rate plotter to Pollen.[70] On the other hand, Henley, the DNO's assistant, exploited his access to the files as an Admiralty official to keep his friend Dreyer updated on Pollen's efforts to design a rate plotter.[71] By imposing a knowledge embargo against Pollen while facilitating the flow of Pollen's knowledge to a rival inventor, the Admiralty was breaking the reciprocal terms of the development/captivity contract negotiated from 1906 to 1908: instead of keeping his invention secret (in return for him keeping his invention secret), the Admiralty was sharing it with a rival in order to erode his monopoly on supply (while maintaining its own monopoly on demand).

Accordingly, Argo had to develop its own rate plotter independently of Dreyer's. It did so simply by adding an attachment to the true-course plotter used on the *Natal*. It informed the Admiralty that its rate plotter was ready in November 1910—six weeks after Dreyer lodged his two-rate plotting application.[72] The following month, Pollen sent Henley drawings and further details of the rate-plotting attachment, as well as the design of a mechanical linkage that, when set with own course and speed, enemy bearing, and the range and bearing rates from the rate plots, would indicate the target course and speed to be put on the clock.[73] In August 1911, the Admiralty decided to order Pollen's rate plotter for trial. In so doing, it told him that rate plotting was covered by an Admiralty secret patent.[74] This was Pollen's first official intimation that Dreyer, who had already copied an aspect of Pollen's plotter once, had again picked up and built upon one of the ideas that he and Isherwood had discarded.

"THE HIGH WATER MARK" OF ANALOG COMPUTING

Throughout 1910, Argo had been hard at work. To continue the work, in early 1911 Pollen raised £25,000 by issuing new shares in the firm. Precluded by his secrecy obligations from showing potential investors detailed technical information about what they would be investing in, he generated credibility in part by drawing on his social circle and in part by arranging for letters from five well-known naval officers attesting to the value of his invention.[75] His reputation and their word had to substitute for patent specifications. The investors included Otto Beit (the financier, philanthropist, and art collector, probably best known for having been Cecil Rhodes's visitor at the time of the Jameson Raid), Julius Wernher (a baronet closely connected with Beit), Ernest Ridley Debenham (of department-store fame), James Buchanan (the distiller), Alexander Kay Muir (another baronet and head of the Scottish cotton merchants James Finlay & Co.), Robert Francis Dunnell (a railroad lawyer and future baronet), James Pender (a baronet and son of the founder of the Eastern Telegraph Company), Henry Fitzalan Howard (the 15th Duke of Norfolk, whom Pollen likely knew through Cardinal Newman's circle), and two brothers of the late Captain Frederick Ogilvy, whom Pollen's gear had so impressed on the *Natal*.[76]

Argo directed most of its energy toward improving the design of the Argo I (*Natal*) clock in order to make it fully helm-free, as the plotter already was. Work on the clock continued to proceed in stages. Having achieved a mechanical interlinkage between the range and bearing rates so as to enable autogenerated bearings in the Argo I clock, the next step was to change from what Pollen and Isherwood called the "simulacrum" principle of the Argo I clock, which precluded helm-free operation, to the "rate" principle of construction, which enabled helm-free operation by changing the breakdown of the vector representing the motion of own ship.[77] By May 1911, Argo had made enough progress to communicate details on the new clock, dubbed the Mark II clock (hereafter the Argo II clock), to the Admiralty. Although the Argo II clock design had the new variable-speed drive and dispensed with the design feature that precluded the *Natal* clock from operating helm-free, it did so by changing the mechanical interconnection between the range and bearing rates in such a way that it could not autogenerate bearings—and the autogeneration of bearings, as we have seen, was critical both to fully helm-free operation and to operation during periods of target invisibility. However, in sending the Argo II clock design to the Admiralty in May 1911, Argo included a description of an additional linkage and variable-speed drive that would restore the capability to autogenerate bearings and so transform it from the Argo II to the Argo III clock design.[78] At Henley's explicit request, Argo then sent drawings of this linkage, in what turned out to be an important detail.[79]

Additional minor improvements to the design over the summer and fall of 1911 transformed the Argo III design into the Argo IV design. Unlike the Argo II and Argo III designs, the firm actually constructed a prototype clock to the Argo IV design. Work on the Argo IV clock had advanced sufficiently for Pollen and Isherwood to submit provisional specifications on a secret patent (19,627/1911) covering it in September 1911, and Argo alerted the Admiralty that the final design was nearing completion in November 1911.[80] Like the Argo I clock, the Argo IV clock could be set either by courses and speeds or by rates. Both the provisional and complete patent specifications for the Argo IV clock made clear that the origin of the rate-setting feature lay not in rate plotting but in other sources.

The crown jewel of the Argo IV clock, incorporated since the Argo II design, was the new variable-speed drive designed by Isherwood. For reasons that will become fully apparent in chapters 4 and 10, it is important to understand in some detail what Isherwood did. As we saw in chapter 1, conventional variable-speed drives, like the one used in the Vickers clock, consisted of a disc-and-roller mechanism similar to the one used by Kelvin in the harmonic analyzer. Pollen and Isherwood had found that this mechanism could not satisfactorily reproduce continuous changes in the range and bearing rates—and thus enable derivations of instantaneous rates, ranges, and bearings—because of slippage: instead of gliding across the surface of the rotating disc, the roller driving the output shaft would slip discontinuously from spot to spot; the heavier the load on the drive, the worse the slippage. Isherwood wrote, "It has been found that the most ordinary form of variable speed drive, the disc and roller, is ineffective during the period of changing speed, and the evident reason for this is that the drag of the roller across the disc nullifies the driving friction."[81]

Although Kelvin had endeavored to design his drive to avoid the slippage encountered with previous disc drives, physical realities reduced theoretical performance. Specifically, in the words of the American computer pioneer Harold Hazen, who worked on the famous differential analyzer at the Massachusetts Institute of Technology in the interwar period and studied Kelvin's design, the "elasticity" of the materials used, the "area of contact [between the ball and disc]," and "the mechanical load imposed upon the driven member" compromised the performance of the Kelvin drive.[82] "The job was to keep the roller from slipping," agreed Hazen's supervisor, the legendary Vannevar Bush—a fellow American computer pioneer best remembered as the director of the Office of Scientific Research and Development, which housed the Manhattan Project, during World War II. If the roller "carried any appreciable load, it would slip, and then the integrator would be highly inaccurate."[83] As the ball slipped, moreover, it scoured the disc; the wear, in turn, led to more slippage; the slippage then led to more wear; and so on. The result was a vicious feedback loop bound to produce the sort of computational error—unpredictable and unquantifiable—that Pollen and Isherwood (and Kelvin, Hazen, and Bush) most detested.[84]

Accordingly, Isherwood overhauled the Kelvin-type design in such a way as to decrease slippage, indeed practically eliminating the problem for his and Pollen's purposes. To reduce the "elasticity of materials," as Hazen termed it, Isherwood made both the disc and rolling ball of hardened steel. To reduce what Hazen called the "area of contact" between the ball and disc, Isherwood replaced the simple arrangement for holding the ball in contact with the disc with a sliding "carriage;" it moved in such a way, in his words, that "the Ball is rolled across the disc instead of being dragged across."[85] Whereas Kelvin's drive in the harmonic analyzer held the ball in place against flat surfaces on either side, Isherwood reduced the "area of contact" here too by replacing the flat surfaces with cylindrical ones. These changes enabled Isherwood's drive—unlike Hazen's and Bush's differential analyzer of the late 1920s—to work without the use of a servomechanism for amplifying the torque generated by the drive. The new drive became known as the "infinitely variable slipless" drive—the sliplessness making it possible for the drive to vary infinitely rather than discontinuously. Its construction, which was far more complex than the original Kelvin drive or the drive of the Vickers clock, is illustrated in figure 2.1. Four of these were inter-connected in the Argo IV clock.[86]

Informed opinion of the day regarded the Pollen-Isherwood clock as a phenomenal scientific and technological achievement. Pollen had consulted leading scientists in the course of its development. One, as we have seen, was Lord Kelvin. Another was Charles Vernon Boys, the eminent applied physicist and gifted instruments designer, who, like Kelvin, had expertise in both mechanical and electrical engineering: he too was the inventor of a mechanical integrator, as noted previously, as well as a frequent expert witness in patent cases, including the extended litigation over

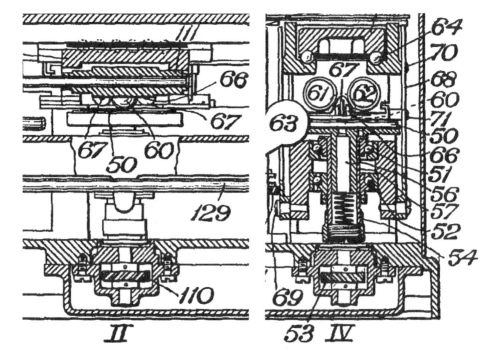

Figure 2.1. Argo's slipless variable-speed drive, introduced in the Argo II clock design. The numbers refer to the same parts in both diagrams, which are close-ups of sections of the diagram of the Argo clock shown in Figure 1.9. (Arthur Pollen and Harold Isherwood, "Range Clock," fig. 1, USP 1,162,510.)

To closely paraphrase the patent, a spring (54) imparted upward force through a cylinder (56) to a disc (50) so that it remained in contact with a ball (60—the outline of the ball is very faint in the middle-right diagram) and the ball remained in contact with two rollers (61 and 62). The ball (60) imparted its speed of rotation around the disc (50) to the rollers (61 and 62). The rollers (61 and 62) were mounted in a frame (63), which could slide as a whole on balls (64); the spring (54) also kept the frame (63) in contact with the balls (64). Movement of the sliding frame (63) moved the ball (60) along the radius of the disc (50), thus changing the ball's speed of rotation imparted to the rollers. To ensure that the ball remained in the correct position, it was embraced by a fork (66) carrying rollers (67) arranged to move parallel to the sliding frame (63) and driven thereby at the proper speed by the lever (68) pivoted around a fixed center (69) and provided with a slot in which a pin (70) carried by the sliding frame (63) and a pin (71) carried by the fork (66) engaged.

the Marconi radio patents.[87] Paralleling Kelvin, Boys was a fellow of the Royal Society; both he and Kelvin served as presidents of the Physical Society. Boys credited Peter Tait, Kelvin's co-author of the *Treatise on Natural Philosophy*, which was described by Vannevar Bush as "something of a classic," with sharpening his understanding of mathematics.[88] Acclaiming

Isherwood's "genius," Boys wrote of the clock, "it is as near perfection as any mechanism which I have ever examined critically."[89] Contra the later statement by Hazen (who knew of Boys' integraph) that "pure rolling contact [between the ball and disc in mechanical integrators] is never achieved" due to "the mechanical load imposed upon the driven member," Boys observed of Isherwood's drive that "the motions in all cases are pure rolling without sliding."[90] He continued:

> I have followed the development of the integrating machine in its various forms for over 30 years, including the ball, disc and cylinder integrator used by Lord Kelvin in his harmonic analyser. I have no hesitation in saying that the integrating mechanism used in the [Argo] "Clock" is the most perfect of all that has been done in this direction. . . . Perfect as the integrators are as elements in the design of the "Clock", the manner in which they are cross connected so as to provide a constant mechanical solution of the ever varying triangle of velocity [i.e. vectors] is equally so, and the conception and execution of the "Clock" as a whole represents in my opinion the high water mark of invention in this field.[91]

In modern parlance, the Argo clock contained extraordinary computing power for an analog device.

Argo made these glittering inventions on a remarkably small resource base. Compared with big defense contractors like Vickers or Armstrong Whitworth, it was a boutique outfit. It benefited not only from Pollen's excellent eye for talent but also from his unusual ability to keep it. In addition to Isherwood, a key participant in the development of the Argo system was Halvor Landstad, who along with Isherwood would help to design a new fire-control system for the Admiralty in the 1920s (discussed in chapter 6). Another was Percy Gray, an employee at Cooke's when Pollen purchased control of it, who would go on to found Vickers's anti-aircraft fire-control program after World War I (discussed in chapter 5). In short, what Argo lacked in quantity of resources it made up for in quality of talent.

STILL MORE PIRACY

In the months following Argo's May 1911 communication to the Admiralty of its Argo II clock design with the linkage for autogenerating bearings, information about the clock flowed freely among the Admiralty, Dreyer, and the firm building the Dreyer table, Elliott Brothers Ltd. Over the summer and fall of 1911, the lead designer at Elliotts, Keith Elphinstone, visited Cooke's works at York in his capacity as an Admiralty contractor, as did Henley, the Naval Ordnance Department official and Dreyer's friend. They saw the Argo IV clock there in the course of construction. Henley, Elphinstone, and Dreyer corresponded frequently with each other during this time discussing possible improvements to the rival Dreyer table.[92] Several proposed by Dreyer moved in the direction of greater mechanization of the table.[93] Another concerned the drive of the range clock, which, in the first experimental Dreyer table, Elphinstone had made electrical rather than mechanical. He told Dreyer that he had preferred a mechanical drive all along, "but it looked so awkward and cumbersome on paper" that he had turned to the electrical drive as an "expedient." However, after seeing the Argo clock in the course of construction, Elphinstone performed a volte-face, now telling Dreyer, "I don't see the least difficulty in making the drive mechanical instead of electrical."[94]

The original Dreyer table, without the improvements being contemplated in the summer of 1911, received trials on HMS *Prince of Wales* in the fall of 1911. Dreyer had been serving on the *Prince of Wales*, the flagship of the Atlantic Fleet, for nearly a year—not as executive officer but as flag commander to the fleet commander, who happened to be John Jellicoe. Fleet commanders chose their flag staff, meaning that Jellicoe had requested Dreyer. Jellicoe had supported Pollen's system as DNO in 1906 but evidently had a change of heart thereafter, perhaps during his tenure as Controller, when Dreyer served in the Naval Ordnance Department, which reported to the Controller. It goes beyond the scope of this book to explore how Jellicoe's change of heart may have related to his ideas about battle tactics. It is difficult to be sure of his thinking in any case, since his personal papers contain no correspondence with Pollen, even as Pollen's personal papers contain correspondence with him; it may not be impertinent to note here that Dreyer was one of Jellicoe's literary executors and thus responsible for arranging his papers before they were turned over to the British Library.

Jellicoe had been impressed by Dreyer's performance as gunnery officer under Wilson.[95] Like Dreyer, he clearly took umbrage at Pollen's criticisms of the Admiralty's decision to select the Wilson-Dreyer system in the wake of the *Ariadne* trials. He echoed Dreyer's wounded naval *amour propre* when he told Pollen, "you have consistently failed to appreciate the fact that you are not and never can be as conversant with service requirements as those whose lives have been spent at sea."[96] When Pollen later solicited Jellicoe's views on the merits of his system versus Dreyer's, Jellicoe piously declined to comment on the grounds that with equipment from both in ships under his command, "My duty is to keep an 'open mind' naturally"—then six months later cheerfully relayed to Dreyer a comment on the superiority of his system over Pollen's.[97]

In the *Prince of Wales* trials, Dreyer got his gear tried on his own ship, served by his own crew—whereas Pollen and his staff had been ordered off the *Natal* during trials of their gear.[98] Moreover, unlike reports on trials with Pollen's gear, which were written by naval officers with whom Pollen had no official connection, the report on Dreyer's table was written by his own captain, Ronald Hopwood, and then passed through Jellicoe, the fleet commander who had hand-picked him. Without systematically describing the tests to which the Dreyer table had been subjected, Hopwood enthusiastically recommended it for general adoption.[99] In forwarding the report to the Admiralty, Jellicoe added that "great credit is due to Commander Frederic C. Dreyer for the zeal and energy he has displayed in devising this invaluable adjunct to Fire Control."[100] The DNO pronounced Hopwood's report "most satisfactory in every way" and, notwithstanding its lack of detail, also recommended the Dreyer table for general adoption.[101]

It fell to the Controller, the Admiralty official responsible for procurement—lobbied by his assistant William Reginald "Blinker" Hall, who knew Pollen's system and would famously serve as Director of Naval Intelligence during World War I—to suggest that perhaps the Dreyer table should undergo competitive trials against the Argo system (which it never did) before the Admiralty wholeheartedly committed itself.[102] The Controller's intervention explains why, in February 1912, the Admiralty ordered only five new Dreyer tables, embodying the improvements that Dreyer had suggested in July 1911, for the ships of the *Lion* (or *Monarch*) class.[103] These improved tables eventually became known as the Mark III Dreyer tables— confusingly and even misleadingly, since Dreyer and the Admiralty did not use Mark designations for his table at this time, and tables later designated Mark III may have incorporated additional suggestions not made until December 1912.[104]

A month after ordering these five new Dreyer tables, a parade of Admiralty officials, including Henley, trooped through Pollen's office in London to see the completed Argo IV clock. Because it had only a manual, not an electromechanical, connection to the gyrocompass, which Pollen and Isherwood had "long contemplated" (recall their January 1909 announcement that they were developing a gyrocompass), it was still not fully "helm-free," but making it so was clearly straightforward.[105] Even though mechanizing the connection to the gyrocompass was simple from an engineering perspective, Pollen and Isherwood did not have any time to waste: their monopoly and secrecy agreement with the Admiralty, extended in 1910, was scheduled to expire at the end of 1912. They judged that the Argo IV clock design contained enough improvements over the Argo II and III designs communicated to the Admiralty in May 1911 to construct it and offer it to the Admiralty for trial. The Admiralty duly borrowed the prototype Argo IV clock for trials on HMS *Orion*, which eventually took place in November 1912, once again without Argo's experienced staff on board. Despite the lack of a mechanical connection to the gyrocompass, the clock managed to cope successfully with a 67° turn by the firing ship during the November trials.[106] Less than a year after the trials, Argo installed the long-contemplated mechanical linkage to the gyrocompass and achieved fully helm-free operation with the Argo V clock.[107]

By then, it was too late. In mid-1912, without awaiting the results of the trials of the Argo IV clock or ordering head-to-head tests against the Dreyer table, the Admiralty informed Pollen that it did not wish to preserve monopoly past the end of the year. One of the two men chiefly responsible for this decision was Jellicoe, to whom Dreyer was still serving as flag commander, now in the Home Fleet. The other was Moore, who had been promoted from DNO in March 1912 to become Controller.[108] To acquire a monopoly on the Argo system would have required Moore as Controller to reverse the policy he had pursued as DNO—that is, to admit that he had been wrong. He preferred infallibility.

A reversal also would have required a fundamentally different attitude toward the private sector than that prevailing at the Admiralty. At the very same time as it was deciding to end its monopoly agreement with Pollen, the Admiralty was also trying to escape an agreement that gave Vickers an effective monopoly over the Royal Navy's submarine procurement.[109] As in Pollen's case, the escape attempt required less-than-perfect solicitousness toward private-sector intellectual property. Together, the two cases indicate that the Admiralty did not like to rely on contractors for its most important and secret technologies, least of all on a monopolistic basis. But whereas Vickers was an established multinational arms manufacturer with a long product line, Argo was a start-up with only one product to sell. As Harding put it, the market for Vickers "is not limited to anything like the same extent," and so " 'what they lose on the swings they make up on the roundabouts.' "[110] Vickers's size gave it protection—evidently necessary protection—in its dealings with the Admiralty, which could draw on the full resources of the British state (as it would against Pollen and Argo).

In the meantime, the Admiralty continued to ignore Pollen's interests. He had loaned the prototype Argo IV clock to the *Orion* for trials on the explicit condition that the Admiralty not let Dreyer see it. "[M]y attention has been drawn to the fact that Commander Dreyer has brought out an automatic clock which is in some sense a competitor to mine," he wrote to Moore in April 1912. "I think it is not unreasonable to stipulate that until the monopoly question is settled no competing inventor should be allowed access to our machine."[111] The Admiralty promptly flouted Pollen's stipulation. Sometime in the summer or fall of 1912, Dreyer produced a specious comparison of the Argo IV clock with his own Mark III table in the *Monarch*.[112]

As before, improvements to the Dreyer table quickly followed Dreyer's exposure to Pollen's system. In December 1912, a month after the *Orion* trials with the Argo IV clock, Dreyer took another step away from the "kitchen table" methods he had once so dogmatically advocated toward the mechanization that he had previously condemned Pollen for preferring. He proposed improvements to the Mark III Dreyer table in order to make it "more automatic"—that is, more mechanized—"than at present."[113] By now, the Mark III table design included a bearing clock in addition to the original table's range clock; Dreyer proposed to mechanize more of the connections between the Dumaresq and the range and bearing clocks. Because the mechanization was only partial, however, his table still did not mechanically interconnect the range and bearing rates, mechanically convert the deflection shown on the Dumaresq into bearing rate, or autogenerate bearings, meaning that it was not fully helm-free and could not keep the range during periods of target invisibility. Dreyer took out another secret patent (21,840/1912) to cover these improvements.[114]

Ignoring Pollen's request that Dreyer not even be allowed to see the Argo IV clock on HMS *Orion*, the Admiralty gave Dreyer the captaincy of the ship in October 1913. The appointment was extraordinary, in more ways than one. *Orion* contained more Argo gear than any other ship in the fleet; in addition to the clock, it also had an Argo gyro-stabilized rangefinder mounting and the Argo rate plotter that had been ordered for trial two years earlier. The Admiralty official responsible for Dreyer's appointment to *Orion* was Jellicoe, back at the Admiralty as Second Sea Lord, the Board member with the personnel portfolio. *Orion* belonged to the Home Fleet's Second Battle Squadron, which contained the four ships of the *Orion* (1909) class and the four ships of the *King George V* (1910) class. These were the Royal Navy's most modern battleships and thus the most prestigious commands in the fleet. At the time of his appointment, Dreyer had all of four *months'* seniority in rank. The captains of the other seven ships in the squadron had all been in rank for more than four *years* (six of them for the more normal eight to nine years).[115] In other words, Jellicoe and the Admiralty went far out of their way to appoint Dreyer to the *one* ship then containing an Argo clock, to which he now acquired unfettered day-to-day access for studying its internal workings.

One of the design changes to his table before the war, embodied in the Mark IV Dreyer table, was to complete the mechanical interconnections between the Dumaresq and the range and bearing clocks in such a way as to mechanically interconnect the range and bearing rates and autogenerate bearings, just as the Argo clocks did. In effect, the interconnections transformed the Dreyer tables' range and bearing clocks from two independent clocks into the interdependent variable-speed drives of a single clock—like the drives of the Argo clocks. While Dreyer's table (unlike the Argo IV clock, but like the Argo V clock) had a mechanical connection to the ship's gyrocompass, it still lacked a key element necessary for helm-free operation in Pollen's and Isherwood's sense: because its clocks did not have Isherwood's infinitely varying slipless drive, they could not reproduce the rapid variations of the rates that occurred during a turn with the same accuracy as Argo's clocks.

(INCOMPETENTLY) PLAGIARIZING
THE TEXT IN THE MACHINE

Notwithstanding this difference and others between Dreyer's system and Pollen's, the surviving evidence overwhelmingly indicates that the former plagiarized the latter. "Plagiarism," of course, is a term associated with literary rather than mechanical theft. But given the textual quality of Pollen's invention, as discussed in chapter 1, plagiarism captures what Dreyer did better than infringement. To be clear, despite his attempts to get around Pollen's patents, Dreyer probably infringed them; an expert legal commission in 1925 explicitly invoked the language of patent infringement to describe what Dreyer had done, as we will see in chapter 7. But the paradigm of patent infringement privileges the mechanical aspects of invention, at the expense of the text in the machine—the algorithms, or software, that Pollen and Isherwood regarded as the more fundamental part of their invention. Plagiarism also captures the highly personal nature of what Dreyer did. Unlike piracy, which preserves an author's name in order to preserve the market value of the product, plagiarism "severs the link between the work and the name of the author and then reestablishes it with a different name."[116]

That is what Dreyer did: he took Pollen's and Isherwood's intellectual labor and credited it to himself. He did not so much invent the Dreyer table as he invented an alternative history for the Dreyer table, which hinged on his so-called original discovery (but later than Pollen's) of so-called range-rate plotting (but not actually a range-rate plot) in 1906. The extraordinary contortions required to narrate the history this way reflected his "anxiety of influence," to borrow a famous term coined by a literary critic: that is, the anxiety that authors feel, knowing that they have been influenced by others, to demonstrate their own originality.[117] Dreyer's first actual use of range-rate plotting was in 1908, immediately following his exposure to Pollen's ideas about it, and he moved thence to incorporate Pollen's ideas into his system after having initially disparaged them. From regarding range-rate plotting as adequate by itself, advocating manual "kitchen table" methods, and defending yaw-corrupted bearings in 1908, he had moved step-by-step to integrate yaw-corrected bearings and mechanization into his system. Those features of the Dreyer table that differed from Pollen's system had either been invented by Pollen and Isherwood (like range-rate plotting) or by someone other than Dreyer (like the "clock pencil"). In effect, Dreyer had pulled his ideas out of Pollen's trash bin—when he did not take the ideas that Pollen had chosen to develop.

But Dreyer's plagiarism was imperfect, because he did not fully understand the algorithmic text in Pollen's and Isherwood's machine. Nowhere was this imperfection clearer than in the drives of his range and bearing clocks, which did not replicate the infinitely variable, slipless capability of the Argo drives, even as his system strove to reproduce the linkages between the range and bearing rates characteristic of Argo's clocks. Dreyer's clock was designed for different algorithms, because he never fully understood the reasoning behind them. He tried to copy Pollen's and Isherwood's text without understanding its context.[118] From Pollen's very first analysis of naval fire control in 1900, when he set two high-speed cruisers on converging courses, he had picked the most tactically and mathematically challenging parameters he could think of, on the logic that if his system could handle those, it could handle anything. Hence his request to Wilson for *more* difficult trial conditions in 1908. By contrast, Dreyer always worked within parameters defined by current Royal Navy practice, which were far easier. Whether he was trying to find a quicker way to get the range rate to set on existing instruments (as with his proposal for a "rate of change" calculator in 1906), or to make Wilson's virtual-plotting system work on the *Vengeance* (as with his proposal for range-rate plotting in 1908), or to overcome the humiliation of the 1908 Battle Practice (as with his 1910 proposal to add a bearing-rate plot), Dreyer never attempted to define the parameters of the fire-control problem for himself from the ground up. If Pollen's and Isherwood's algorithms were a Shakespearean sonnet, then Dreyer turned them into doggerel ("Thou art smoking hot, like a summer's day / My kingdom to horse around in the hay").[119]

Functionally, the underlying limitation of Dreyer's tables was that they were not designed to cope with high or rapidly changing rates or with periods of target invisibility. As he himself had pointed out in 1907 when arguing against range-rate plotting, unless the range rate was steady, a meaning line drawn through range observations would make a curve (the same was true of a bearing-rate plot).[120] Not only was it more difficult to draw an accurate meaning line through a curve than to draw a straight meaning line, but the instantaneous rate indicated by the tangent line to the curve was out of date the instant it was taken. Moreover, while the clock mechanism of the Mark IV Dreyer table had two features necessary for optimal helm-free operation—its mechanical linkage to the gyrocompass and capacity to autogenerate bearings—it lacked the third: an infinitely variable slipless drive like Isherwood's. Despite Dreyer's moves toward artificial intelligence by mechanically interconnecting the range and bearing rates, his system required so much manual intervention and preserved such an important role for human judgment that one US naval officer who observed it in action during World War I summed up, "after all their elaborate system, they show they are afraid of it and fall back on simpler methods."[121] Thus, the Dreyer table came with limitations that Pollen and Isherwood had designed their system to avoid.

As a result, even the most developed forms of the Dreyer table did not offer—did not seek to offer—the accuracy at long ranges or the tactical freedom that Pollen's system promised. Instead, the Royal Navy retained tactics within the limits of Dreyer's system. In so doing, it made self-perpetuating the feedback loop between limited fire-control equipment and limited tactics that Pollen had hoped to break: limited fire-control equipment limited tactics, which in turn made limited equipment seem adequate, which in turn limited tactics, and so on. These tactics envisioned a battle in which two fleets sought to deploy onto parallel lines at medium range (of course, they relied on the enemy obliging). During the period of parallelism, the range and bearing rates would be low and steady enough for Dreyer's system to cope.[122] Officers who preferred simple tactics under centralized command-and-control rather than more complex ones with distributed command-and-control probably viewed Dreyer's proposed system as an improvement on old fire-control equipment rather than as an obstacle.[123] In effect, the mentality of Dreyer and like-minded officers was to make battle more like Battle Practice, rather than to make Battle Practice more like battle.

There was a striking parallel here to the Soviet experience with computers and combat during the Cold War. As Dreyer did to Pollen, the Soviets carried out a sustained campaign to steal information about and copy US digital computing technology, especially semiconductors, which are to modern artificial intelligence what the mechanical interconnection of the range and bearing rates was to naval fire-control clocks. Although the Soviets understood the mathematical and scientific context of US semiconductor technology better than Dreyer understood the context of Pollen's and Isherwood's clock, they were unable to reproduce the industrial context—the machine tools, the spare parts, and so forth—that enabled the Americans to materialize their mathematical and scientific text into semiconductors with precision and at scale. Because US leaders had confidence in their electronics, they developed a new style of warfare around "smart" munitions and networked information.[124] By contrast, because Soviet leaders did not trust their electronics, they "minimized the use of electronics and computers in military systems" and adapted their style of warfare to existing technology—they "fell back on simpler methods," so to speak.[125] That is, the Soviets' continued reliance on human intelligence rather than artificial intelligence for munitions fire control subordinated tactics and operations to technological limits, while the Americans emancipated tactics and operations by overcoming technological limits. Similarly, the Royal Navy's continued reliance on human intelligence rather than artificial intelligence for naval gun-fire control subordinated tactics and operations to technological limits, while Pollen and his supporters like Harding offered emancipation.

·.·

Just as Dreyer admitted no debts to Pollen and Isherwood for influencing his invention, so he belittled the contributions of its chief design engineer, Keith Elphinstone. Dreyer's patent applications bore his name only, unlike Pollen's, who took them out jointly with Isherwood from the start. Dismissing Elphinstone's work as "purely that of a manufacturer executing the ideas put before him," Dreyer argued that "there is therefore no reason for including him as an Inventor of the Table."[126] This formulation denied Elphinstone credit not only for his own important role in pirating Pollen, but also for his understanding of the significance of key points lost on Dreyer—such as the fact that a patent covering the Mark III Dreyer table failed to show a working mechanism for autogenerating bearings, and that the method adopted to fix the issue in the Mark IV Dreyer table infringed one of Pollen's and Isherwood's patents.[127] Calling the faulty mechanism "only a detail," Dreyer either failed to understand or chose to minimize the significance of the fact that mechanically generating the bearing rate was essential for fully mechanical helm-free operation when rates were high and changing.[128] Acknowledging it would have meant that his invention lagged behind Pollen's and that he needed Elphinstone's help to get as far as he did.

Remarkably, Dreyer regarded the credit due to him as the credit due to a martyr. However improbably in view of his inside position, Dreyer saw himself as a lonely hero fighting on behalf of rate plotting against Pollen's siren song of true-course plotting, which had ensnared the Navy until Dreyer came to the rescue. "I often feel sorry for having taken the matter up as it appears my labours have actually done me harm," he sighed to Jellicoe before the war. "My fears are that in order to <u>convince</u> Mr Pollen [that no reward has been made to me] I may never be promoted."[129] He need not have worried. In 1915, George Warrender, the admiral commanding Dreyer's squadron, recommended that the Admiralty make him a retroactive monetary award for the Dreyer tables. A junior officer under Warrender's command at that time later could "not remember [him] taking any interest in the technicalities of our armament."[130] Though Warrender insisted that Dreyer "had nothing whatever to do with this submission, which is entirely my own idea," his recommendation unmistakably bore Dreyer's intellectual influence. Dreyer had performed a great service by inventing his table, Warrender wrote:

> It is well known that Mr. A. H. Pollen would have received the sum of £100,000 for his second set of Fire Control Apparatus had it been accepted, and very large Royalties on further sets, but it is probably not generally appreciated that Captain F. C. Dreyer with sounder views <u>alone</u> stood in the path of Mr. A. H. Pollen.
>
> It is certainly not generally realized that the Argo Clock—the only Pollen instrument of any value—is based <u>entirely</u> on Captain Dreyer's system.[131]

Warrender's submission made its way through the Admiralty just as Dreyer was insisting on Elphinstone's ancillary role in his invention. In May 1916, the Admiralty informed Dreyer that it was awarding him £5,000, roughly equivalent to three-and-a-half years' salary.[132]

While Dreyer exaggerated less than usual in claiming sole credit for blocking the adoption of Pollen's system, he still exaggerated. For his efforts to succeed, others had to protect and enable him. In deciding to adopt Dreyer's system, Admiralty officials accepted his assurances as to its superiority not only because influential, ostensibly disinterested officers who were in fact close to Dreyer (like Wilson and Jellicoe) endorsed it, but also because Dreyer's system, like many knockoffs, seemed to cost less money than the real thing. In recommending the Dreyer table for adoption following the tests on *Prince of Wales* in late 1911, Moore argued that it would cost less than a quarter of the price of the Argo system.[133] Whether it was actually cheaper is another question. The mechanism of Dreyer's system cost less than Pollen's, but the personnel cost more, because it required many more human operators, who were in chronically short supply; Moore did not factor in wage calculations or ripple effects on personnel needs when assessing the two systems.[134] Moreover, the Admiralty's refusal to place large orders with Pollen constrained his ability to reduce his unit prices; what his prices would have looked like had the Admiralty given him the fully cooperative relationship he had always sought must therefore remain in the realm of conjecture.

Although the Admiralty's selection of the Dreyer table might appear the choice of an insider over an outsider, it is better understood as a choice between two factions of insiders. As Pollen put it, the controversy seemed "the case of a layman quarrelling [sic] with the Admiralty," when in reality "there are two conflicting schools of thought in this matter in the Service."[135] Many naval officers did not share the Admiralty's preference for the Dreyer table over the Argo system. Officer after officer, including many gunnery experts who did not have a prior close relationship with Dreyer or Pollen, came to admire the Argo system.[136] Institutionally, support for Pollen was concentrated in, though by no means limited to, HMS *Excellent*, the Royal Navy's premier gunnery school and research center, as well as in the Inspectorate of Target Practice.[137]

Foreign observers picked up on unhappiness with the Dreyer tables throughout the fleet. The US naval attaché wrote in 1913 that the Admiralty had adopted a system that it regarded as superior to Pollen's, but that "many, if not most, of the officers actually engaged in fire control work are heartily in favor of the Pollen system."[138] In 1917, a US observer who visited the Grand Fleet wrote that British officers "complained rather bitterly of the 'penny-wise' and 'pound-foolish' neglect of the Admiralty prior to war in failing to provide all capital ships with director fire system and the necessary fire control equipment which, although not absolutely necessary in target practice, made the difference between success or defeat in war."[139] In effect, a clique, with Dreyer as its champion, had taken over the Royal Navy's fire-control policy and rewritten its history. The effects on the Royal Navy and British power, as the next four chapters will show, were grievous.

[CHAPTER 3]

Official Secrets

"[W]hile we are founding our case on what is purely a matter of fact, namely, whose is the invention? the Admiralty are founding theirs on an administrative necessity, namely, to prevent a device being put upon the market which could endanger the secrecy of the Service System."

ARTHUR POLLEN, 14 JULY 1913

When Pollen and the Admiralty had negotiated their development/captivity contract between 1906 and 1908, both parties had clearly understood the connection between secrecy and monopoly required to meet both parties' interests. Already, however, instead of keeping Pollen's system secret, the Admiralty had facilitated Dreyer's and Elliotts's piracy of it to break his monopoly on supply. Now it would attempt to sever the link between monopoly and secrecy from a different direction: by deploying the Official Secrets Act, passed in 1889 and revised in 1911, as an improvised method of export control. Classifying Pollen's intellectual property as national security information would maintain the Admiralty's monopoly on demand without having to pay for it. It might be said that the Admiralty was using the secrecy law as a legal technology to avoid paying for Pollen's naval technology.

The Admiralty justified its deployment of the Official Secrets Act in two distinct ways. One was to layer it atop Dreyer's secret patents on his system while trying to imbue them with pioneer status. This use of the Official Secrets Act grounded the Admiralty's assertion of secrecy on liberal property norms, which in turn rested upon Dreyer's historically false narrative that he was the original inventor of his fire-control system and Pollen the derivative one. But in the face of pushback from Pollen's lawyers and its own hand-picked patent expert, the Admiralty abandoned these grounds and fell back on straight-up prerogative: Pollen's system was secret regardless of who had invented it and whose property it was. By severing secrecy from the liberal legal technology of property, this use of the Official Secrets Act anticipated the "born secret" provision of the US Atomic Energy Act of 1946. The fact that it occurred in the context of the Admiralty's efforts to avoid paying Pollen for monopoly and secrecy lays bare the political-economic implications of secrecy, which historians of US atomic secrecy have not typically emphasized.

The Admiralty's deployment of Dreyer's patents and the Official Secrets Act also involved shifting claims about the relationship between the mental and material aspects of invention, or between software and hardware. As we saw in chapter 1, Pollen had long insisted that these aspects were inseparably intertwined, against the Admiralty's tendency to reduce invention to its patentable, material aspects. With control of Dreyer's patents and an interest in expanding the scope of secrecy, Admiralty officials found it convenient to reconsider their stance on this point.

Tracking these shifts requires close attention to the precise language used in the correspondence between Pollen and the Admiralty. As their relationship deteriorated, the documents they exchanged were ever more likely to become evidence in court, and words were chosen increasingly carefully. Pollen awoke only gradually to the reality that the Admiralty had no interest whatsoever in negotiations and had already made up its mind to prevent him from selling his system abroad. But although the correspondence charted no change in the Admiralty's intentions, it showed how far beyond legal norms the institution was prepared to go in order to achieve its objective.

LEGAL WEAPONS TECHNOLOGY

For Pollen, the Admiralty's decision in 1912 not to extend its monopoly of his system past the end of that year necessarily implied the end of secrecy: if the Admiralty would no longer pay for monopoly, then he was free to sell abroad. Pollen realized that the prospects for monopoly were bleak in the spring of 1912, when the Director of Naval Ordnance, Archibald Moore, intimated that the Admiralty would order at most five of the Argo IV clocks.[1] He accordingly began to make arrangements for selling his system on the open market in the summer of 1912. With the end of secrecy freeing him to raise private funds or turn over production, he also launched negotiations with Armstrong Whitworth and Vickers, Britain's two largest armaments firms.[2] In July, he met with the retired rear admiral and current managing director of Armstrong's, Charles Ottley, who had seen the promise of Pollen's system while serving as Director of Naval Intelligence from 1905 to 1907. Ottley, Pollen recorded in his diary, "is mad keen to get us. I ought to be a Director of Armstrongs etc—all sorts of real gush. . . . So it looks as if, supposing [Admiralty] chuck us, we shall be in easy street soon—which will be a comfort."[3]

No comfort was forthcoming. The Admiralty officially notified Pollen in August 1912 that it would not extend monopoly past the end of the year. In doing so, it reminded Pollen of his obligation to maintain the secrecy of confidential information "which may have come under your notice in your association with the Navy," while informing him that foreign business should enable him to lower the price of the Argo IV clock.[4] By this point, not only had Admiralty officials seen the clock for themselves and had it installed aboard HMS *Orion*, but they had also, as the Admiralty later acknowledged, seen the complete specifications for the patent covering the clock.[5] Thus the Admiralty knew exactly what it was authorizing Pollen to take abroad—indeed, encouraging him to take abroad in return for lower prices.

Shortly after sending this notification, the Admiralty informed Pollen that his rate plotter, for which he had just submitted the patent specifications, infringed an Admiralty secret patent (Dreyer's 1910 two-rate plotting patent). The Admiralty used this patent to claim rights not only over Dreyer's specific material embodiment of rate plotting but over rate plotting altogether: "The Admiralty hold all patent rights over Time and Range and Time and Bearing Plotting," it informed Pollen.[6] This was not the same set of arguments about patents and patentability that the Admiralty had consistently deployed against Pollen. Having used patentability as a bludgeon to exclude principles and limit the scope of Pollen's system to its specific material embodiments, the Admiralty now treated Dreyer's 1910 patent as covering the principle of rate plotting, and with it any and all reductions of rate plotting to material form. The hardware now covered the software. In effect, the Admiralty was trying to treat Dreyer's patent as a pioneer patent, despite it being secret.

Pollen pushed back, to no avail. He could not lower prices on the clock until he had foreign orders in hand that justified the investment in additional plant, he explained, and he could not get them in hand before the end of secrecy, nor would two firms that he had contacted about manufacturing the clocks do them for any less.[7] As for rate plotting, he indicated his desire to meet the Admiralty's wishes but noted that he had made a range-rate plot during the *Ariadne* trials more than four years earlier—meaning that the Admiralty's patent could cover only a particular instrumental embodiment of rate plotting, not the principle.[8] This was the same logic of patentability that the Admiralty had long deployed against him. The Admiralty was not amused at the tables thus being turned: it insisted that Pollen should be able to lower his prices, and it reminded him, apropos of the news that he had asked two other firms about manufacturing, of his obligation to preserve the secrecy of his system.[9] Thus, the Admiralty was demanding lower prices by virtue of foreign sales on the one hand, while refusing to relax the secrecy that prevented Pollen from securing them on the other.

∴

Although on the previous occasions Pollen had fought back when the Admiralty tried to end monopoly, this time he felt resigned to his fate. The Admiralty's decision, in violation of its promise, to kick his staff off HMS *Orion* during the trials of the Argo IV clock—he presumed because it did not trust Argo to safeguard naval secrets—infuriated him. But what really inclined him to give up the fight for monopoly was that since early 1911, when Argo issued additional shares to be able to carry on its work, he had new responsibilities to investors and employees.[10] Even so, he continued to loathe the prospect of selling abroad a system that he regarded as vital to naval efficiency. "I am in a dilemma between my duty as a citizen, and my interests as a shopkeeper," he agonized to a friend.[11] Preliminary results with the clock on *Orion* temporarily renewed his urge to fight. In October 1912, he offered to let the Admiralty set the price for monopoly so long as it was recommended by an impartial inquiry.[12] In making this offer, Pollen again warned the Admiralty of the danger of letting his system go abroad: "The day my system becomes public property you have no secret of any kind left in your naval gunnery. In so far as you have adopted a restricted and mutilated form of my system, you have obviously no secret of any value."[13] He meant, of course, that Dreyer had plagiarized him. Backchannel signals that his warning had gotten to the Admiralty encouraged him: "They are badly hit by my saying that with my show published they have no gunnery secret left, so after all the situation <u>may</u> be saved."[14]

Pollen may well have been right that his warning shook the Admiralty—but he misunderstood why. Around or shortly before this time, prompted by learning that HMS *Orion* was trying Argo's rate plotter as well as its clock, Dreyer had begun developing a counternarrative arguing that Pollen had plagiarized *him*. His point of departure was, as ever, that Pollen merely replicated the invention of the army officer Henry Watkin by basing his system on true-course plotting, whereas he, Dreyer, had invented the genuinely novel method of rate plotting (originally described by him as an "adaptation" of Watkin's work), which (he claimed) was the basis of his entire fire-control system. Dreyer now moved to charge that Pollen had gotten the idea of rate plotting from him and infringed his 1910 patent.[15]

The inference to be drawn from this counternarrative was that publication of Pollen's system would leave the Royal Navy with no fire-control secrets not because the Navy had stolen its system from Pollen, as Pollen intended, but because Pollen had stolen his entire system from the Navy. Reflexively adopting Dreyer's perspective, the Admiralty reiterated its claim to control all rate plotting through Dreyer's patents, still using the patent system as a legal technology to protect its interests.[16]

It soon found an even more potent legal technology: national security secrecy. When Pollen offered to keep rate plotting secret, despite his own invention of it, the Admiralty took an axe to this olive branch.[17] In bureaucratically ominous terms, it informed him of its "every confidence" that his "legal obligations under the Official Secrets Act will be faithfully observed."[18] Violation of this act was a criminal offense carrying a mandatory prison sentence of three to seven years.[19] Lest Pollen miss the point, the Admiralty followed up with an even sharper letter. Parroting Dreyer's counternarrative that Pollen had gotten the idea of rate plotting from him, the Admiralty argued that it had a right under the Official Secrets Act that it would not otherwise have to contest Argo's efforts to take out a regular (nonsecret) patent on its rate plotter.[20] This formulation linked the power to invoke the Official Secrets Act to the Admiralty's theory that Pollen had acquired the secret in question—rate plotting—from the Royal Navy: the technology of secrecy was still tethered to, not independent of, the technology of property. Moreover, the Admiralty's secrecy and property claims still went no further than its patent claims, however expanded by the assertion of pioneer status, in that it continued to define the secret and property in question as rate plotting, which it believed Dreyer's rate-plotting patent to cover.

Blob-like, the scope of the secret took only days to expand, and with it the reach of the Official Secrets Act. The initiative for this expansion seems to have lain with Moore's successor as DNO, Frederick Tudor, who adopted an even more antagonistic stance toward Pollen than had Moore. In an interview, he informed Pollen that the Argo clock—not just its rate plotter—used a service secret. Tudor struggled to articulate exactly what the secret was but thought it had something to do with a dial on the clock to set it with the bearing rate. Pollen found it "very difficult to understand" how this point could have arisen:

> The only possible explanation is that the fact that there are two rate indications in addition to that of range, may have led someone not familiar with the subject to believe that this conjunction necessarily implied the obtaining of these two rates by plotting. But obviously the Clock

indicators are in themselves merely the expression of mathematical truths and the fact of indicating these two rates of itself affords no suggestion that they can be obtained by automatic rate plotting.[21]

What was obvious to Pollen was by no means obvious to the Admiralty—or it simply did not care. Having experimented with rate plotting and clock-setting by rates in his efforts to map all the parameters of naval fire control, as we saw in chapter 2, Pollen knew that there were multiple roads from multiple origin points leading to the conclusion that it was desirable to be able to set a clock by rates. But the Admiralty's desire to be able to set a clock by rates had flowed, and thus in its limited imagination could only flow, from rate plotting. Accordingly, it reasoned, dials to set the clock with rates necessarily revealed the service secret that the Royal Navy used rate plotting, which ostensibly Dreyer had invented and Pollen had learned from him. Thus, after years of trying to limit Pollen's claims to specific instrumental embodiments of his ideas, the Admiralty had discovered in the context of secrecy—as it had in the case of Dreyer's patent—that the mental and material aspects of invention were inseparable: a dial could reveal the idea of rate plotting.

Only at this juncture did the Admiralty seek professional legal advice about the position it was attempting to argue. The Treasury Solicitor's office poured cold water on the Admiralty's employment of the Official Secrets Act, declaring "that there would probably be much difficulty in holding Mr. Pollen criminally responsible."[22] But the Admiralty pressed on. A couple days after receiving the Treasury Solicitor's opinion, it provided Pollen with a fuller, but no clearer, definition of the scope of the secret. Pollen could safely be allowed to take out foreign patents on the Argo I *Natal* clock, the Admiralty told him, because, it incorrectly claimed, that clock could not be set by rates (this was the clock that Pollen had once reminded the Admiralty contained an engraved plate with instructions for setting it by rates). But he could not be permitted to take out foreign patents corresponding to his secret patent on the Argo IV clock. The dials to set the clock by rates "are in no way germane to the Aim Corrector system," the Admiralty blustered, "but are evidently fitted to admit of the clock being used on the Service system." It continued,

> You have already been informed that the Admiralty has certain secret patents by another inventor [Dreyer] *relating to the utilization* of Rates of Change of Range and Rates of Change of Bearing, *whether obtained by plotting or otherwise*, and that such processes are regarded as Service secrets. [emphasis added]

This imprecise language reflected the ignorance of Admiralty officials over details and served to muddy the waters. Was the secret the dials, or was it the utilization of rates by the clock? The former was a specific instrumental embodiment of an idea, while the latter was the principle on which the clock worked. In the next breath, the Admiralty returned to the dials:

> If therefore you were offering your Clock to a foreign purchaser, and putting your patent [in question] before him, and if he should ask the use of the two dials referred to, you would be debarred from answering his question. He would, however, speedily draw his own conclusions as to the alternative method of using the Clock, and as to your reasons for silence.

Whether the inclusion of the dials infringed Dreyer's patent, the Admiralty wrote, was a matter for an outside patent expert to determine. But regardless of the patent question, publication of the Argo IV patent "would most seriously imperil an important Service secret of which you have obtained knowledge from your connection with the Service, and, if made by you, would constitute infringement of the Official Secrets Act."[23] The Admiralty still linked its power to invoke the act to Pollen's acquisition of the secret from the Navy, but now it was pushing beyond the scope of Dreyer's patent on rate plotting.

In effect, the Admiralty was trying, *against* the crown's best legal advice, to use the Official Secrets Act to convert Pollen's intellectual property into national security information. Alternatively, it could be said that the Admiralty was using the Official Secrets Act as improvised export-control legislation. This maneuver enabled the Admiralty to pursue secrecy without paying for monopoly. The Official Secrets Act functioned as a trump card, even more powerful than Dreyer's rate-plotting patent, over the Admiralty's contract with Pollen, which clearly envisioned secrecy and monopoly as inseparable.

AN AWKWARD EXPERT OPINION

At the same time as it invoked the Official Secrets Act, the Admiralty notified Pollen that it was retaining an expert to assess the whole patent situation.[24] It declined his suggestion to have the expert review the whole record of correspondence between the parties on the ground that the patent record was sufficient—and then supplied the expert with two long additions to the patent record, which Pollen had no input into or knowledge of.[25] The first was produced by the Contract and Purchase Department. It painted Pollen as an unpatriotic ingrate who had received large sums of public money to develop his system, acquired secrets from the Navy, and then repaid this trusting generosity by threatening to sell abroad unless the Admiralty gave him more money.[26] It also insisted, aping Dreyer, that Pollen's system was derivative of Watkin's, and it was "not of first importance to the Navy in view of the alternative Service apparatus available."[27]

These claims tracked closely with the second document, composed by none other than Dreyer, with the assistance of Cecil V. Usborne, Henley's successor in the DNO's office. It was titled *Pollen Aim Correction System. Technical History and Technical Comparison with Commander F. C. Dreyer's Fire Control System.* To paraphrase Voltaire loosely, it was neither technical nor a history. Ostensibly a précis, it was actually a polemic, camouflaged in the language of neutral "technical" expertise. Typical of the document's half-truths and falsehoods was its treatment of yaw-corrected bearings as an obvious technical need, not a point unrecognized by Dreyer as late as 1908 despite Pollen's years of impressing it on the Admiralty.[28] Condescending that Pollen's system "is the embodiment, perhaps the most perfect embodiment, of a system conceived by a civilian," Dreyer and Usborne concluded that the Dreyer table "is in every way a practical instrument designed to meet the real requirements of Naval action, in so far as we can foresee them, and no one but a Naval Officer, working with ample personal experience of fire control behind him, could have produced it."[29] All Pollen's talk of "science" was as nothing compared with the authority of the uniform.

Given a documentary record by the Admiralty designed to prejudge the outcome, the patent expert retained by the Admiralty, James Swinburne, delivered a careful and qualified opinion open to multiple readings. Swinburne was one of the leading patent experts of the day, frequently called upon by the Admiralty.[30] According to his biographer, he had such a high reputation in legal circles for giving "clear unshakable and completely honest evidence" that "any firm knowing its case to be on slippery ground would avoid employing him."[31] Alas for the Admiralty, thanks to Dreyer and its own prejudices, it had no real idea of the true ground on which it was standing—or just how slippery it was.

On its surface, Swinburne's report told the Admiralty what it wanted to hear: technically, the Dreyer system did not infringe Argo patents, and "to allow the Pollen clock to be sold to other Powers would be giving them all the knowledge that is embodied in the Dreyer apparatus."[32] Yet his report was done so artfully in places as to suggest that he smelled a rat. Rather than comply with the Admiralty's request that he comment on the "veracity" of Dreyer's *Technical History*, Swinburne side-stepped: "[t]his document is largely historical, and I have no knowledge of history, except as gathered from the patent specifications." Instead, he reframed his brief, saying that "[t]he simplest way is to discuss the patent question and call attention to any point of difference between" himself and Dreyer.[33] The patent record convinced him of Pollen's and Isherwood's "high inventive ability"—just the opposite of the conclusion that Dreyer's *Technical History* sought to manipulate him into drawing.[34] Moreover, his comparison of the two systems pointed out that Pollen's could do things that Dreyer's could not. Indeed, when read with knowledge of the full documentary record—that is, with the correct dates and chronology not found in Dreyer's doctored narrative—Swinburne's report amounted to an unambiguous endorsement of Pollen's claims as to his own originality, Dreyer's plagiarism, and the limitations of Dreyer's system.

The nature of Swinburne's endorsement comes through most clearly in his analysis of both the Mark III Dreyer table and the Argo IV clock vis-à-vis the Dumaresq. "Both instruments have the Dumaresq," he wrote. The Dreyer table contained an actual Dumaresq along with range and bearing clocks; in the Argo clock, the Dumaresq "does not look like a Dumaresq but it is practically a Dumaresq with the ships below the dial." Swinburne then explained why:

> Instead of merely reading off the distances of the ships' bows from the two centre lines of the Dumaresq, to find the range rate and the bearing rate X R, Pollen provides slots so that the position of the bows actually controls the range rate and the bearing rate X R. There is a second variable speed gear in the bearing rate mechanism whose speed varies inversely as R, and this divides bearing rate X R by R giving the bearing rate (angle), and this is the speed at which the ships are turned relatively to the line of sight, and this turning affects the bearing and range rates.[35]

What Swinburne dubbed "X R" was what Pollen and Isherwood, as we saw in chapter 1, called $BN = Rd\beta$. He was describing the foundational conceptual leap that Pollen and Isherwood had made from Dumaresq's use of deflection, which did not require knowledge of the range, to their own use of bearing rate, which did require knowledge of the range.

Swinburne was also describing how Pollen and Isherwood had embodied their conceptual leap by building a clock that mechanically interconnected the range and bearing rates so as to autogenerate not only ranges but also bearings. The Mark III Dreyer table (which, unlike the original Dreyer table, contained a bearing clock in addition to a range clock) could *not* autogenerate ranges and bearings, because Dreyer had not (yet) mechanized the necessary interconnections as Pollen and Isherwood had. "Dreyer has no mechanical connection corresponding to the two slots under the Dumaresq in Pollen [sic]," Swinburne noted; instead Dreyer relied on human operators to make the connections. Hence Swinburne's statement, on the one hand, that the Argo clock "looks as unlike the Dreyer apparatus as it well could; but it is really on almost the same lines," and on the other hand, that "Pollen's arrangement as a machine is much more complete than Dreyer's, and given accurate data it will do much more."[36] It was precisely the same realization that led Dreyer and Elphinstone subsequently to mechanize in the Mark IV table the connections that they had not mechanized in the Mark III.

Dreyer's failure to mechanize the connections between the Dumaresq and the clocks may have accounted for a nasty surprise for the Admiralty in Swinburne's report: he judged that the Dreyer table infringed *Dumaresq*'s patents.[37] Because the conversion of deflection into bearing rate in the Dreyer table was not mechanical, the conversion did not turn the Dumaresq from a machine that calculated deflection independent of the range into a single part of a larger machine that calculated the instantaneous bearing rate by mechanically dividing the instantaneous deflection by the instantaneous range. Put differently, in the Dreyer table, the Dumaresq remained a Dumaresq.[38]

Swinburne's report displayed a level of skill fully justifying his high reputation. Indeed, he read the patent record so intelligently that he understood better than Dreyer (though not Elphinstone) how central the bearing rate and bearings were to the operation of the Dreyer table. "The broad principle of the Dreyer apparatus is thus range and range rate plus bearing and bearing rate," Swinburne wrote. "But the apparatus involves the combination of these so that each can help the other, *and especially so that the bearing and bearing rate can give the range and range rate*" (emphasis added).[39] Hence Swinburne was correct that the differences between the Mark III Dreyer table and the Argo IV clock did not prevent the latter from "being similar to Dreyer's in the sense of involving secret knowledge."[40] It was just that Swinburne had no way of knowing, given how much information the Admiralty deliberately withheld from him, that the secret knowledge was Pollen's rather than Dreyer's. The fact that the Admiralty's own expert powerfully, if unwittingly, sustained Pollen's judgment that the lack of secrets in the Dreyer table was due not to Pollen's plagiarism of Dreyer but to Dreyer's plagiarism of Pollen likely explains why the Admiralty did not retain Swinburne as an expert when the Pollen-Dreyer controversy erupted into court in the 1920s (when Swinburne was still very much alive).

BORN SECRET

Pollen, meanwhile, shaken by the prospect of criminal prosecution under the Official Secrets Act, had brought in his own legal experts—who, unlike Swinburne, received the full record of his communications with the Admiralty. One was the patent specialist Russell Clarke, whose first order of business was to determine what exactly the secret was, since the Admiralty's references to the dials for setting the clock with rates and to the utilization of rates by the clock pointed in two different directions (pun intended). He concluded that the Admiralty meant the second, broader definition relating to the utilization of rates. The documentary record from Pollen convinced Clarke that Argo had given the idea of using rates to the Admiralty, not vice versa. It also convinced him that Argo had not gotten the means for embodying the idea from the Admiralty—nor did the Admiralty suggest that it had. Instead, the Admiralty

> must go so far as to say that no inventor may invent or disclose any mechanism for determining speed and course from rate. They claim in fact a secret monopoly not to any mechanism or apparatus but to an idea, or mathematical principle.

The utilization of rates, Clarke insisted, "must be clearly distinguished from Rate Plotting." While the Admiralty had claimed rights over rate plotting for years, it had raised no objection to the Argo clock's utilization of rates until more than a month after its secrecy and monopoly arrangement with Argo had expired—and until months after it had encouraged Argo to sell its clock abroad in order to drive down prices. "The threat of a prosecution under the Official Secrets Act may be totally disregarded," Clarke accordingly advised Pollen. "The act was not intended to be used against inventors who have expended large sums of money in developing something wanted in the service, nor was it intended to be used as a lever to cause the inventor to accept a lower price."[41]

For additional legal advice, Pollen also retained the prominent firm of Coward & Hawksley, Sons & Chance (now part of Clifford Chance). At the time, its clients included Cecil Rhodes, Marconi Wireless, and Barings Bank. Pollen's point of contact was Ernest Bourchier Hawksley, a friend from Oxford, who was the son of one of the firm's founding partners and himself made partner in 1910.[42] Characterizing the Admiralty's mention of the Official Secrets Act as a "very serious threat," Coward & Hawksley echoed Clarke's arguments in writing to the Admiralty on Pollen's behalf.

Argo did not wish to go abroad, the firm maintained, "but they cannot be expected to stand by and see their rights disregarded in the manner contemplated nor can they submit to spoliation of those rights by a threat of prosecution under an Act of Parliament which they are advised has no possible application in their case."[43]

After a month, during which period Pollen had to delay foreign patent applications, the Admiralty responded with an indignant broadside. Characterizing its purpose in invoking the Official Secrets Act as "assisting your clients by giving them timely warning in general terms of the existence of certain restrictions"—a sort of friendly reminder from their neighborhood national security state—the Admiralty "repudiate in the strongest possible manner the suggestion" that it had "disregarded" Pollen's and Argo's rights or that "an attempt has been made to despoil them of those rights by a threat of prosecution under the Official Secrets Act." Conceding that the Act could apply only to knowledge that outsiders had acquired from the Navy, and not to knowledge that outsiders generated on their own even if the Navy wanted it kept secret, the Admiralty acknowledged that "there might be reasonable ground" to pay Pollen for the continuance of secrecy "if further secrecy were desired by the Admiralty in respect of patents *which embody the inventor's own unaided ideas alone*" (emphasis added). Referring to the dials to set the Argo clock by rates, however, it insisted "that the fact of the adaptation of the Pollen Clock to utilise the data in question was due entirely to knowledge and experience confidentially gained from the Service." To support this statement, it claimed, again relying on Dreyer's false chronology, that "the system embodying the utilisation of the data above referred to was used in the Navy in 1908, 1909, and 1910." In any case, the Admiralty blithely (and absurdly) assured Pollen, his system would be "in no way impaired" by removing the dials.[44]

With access to Pollen's documentary archive, Coward & Hawksley proceeded to drive a truck through the holes in the Admiralty's arguments.[45] Publicly, the Admiralty refused to budge with Argo.[46] Behind the scenes, however, officials prepared a defensive line, consulting the Treasury Solicitor about the Admiralty's legal position if Pollen sued it for breach of contract.[47] Pollen, for his part, leveraged his journalistic and political connections, now that secrecy was at an end, to stir up discussion of the Admiralty's questionable selection of Dreyer's system over his in the press and in Parliament.[48] He also solicited further legal advice from Sir Robert Finlay, a former Attorney General and future Lord Chancellor.[49] At the same time, without giving ground on the merits of the case, he conveyed Argo's willingness to withhold mention of the rate dials and of the linkages for resolving rates into courses and speeds in its foreign patent applications on the clock. He still hoped, at this point, "not to engage in active hostilities with the Admiralty unless compelled to do so."[50]

The Admiralty compelled him to do so. On June 30, in reply to a question from a Member of Parliament coordinated by Pollen, First Lord of the Admiralty Winston Churchill informed the House that the Royal Navy had chosen a "more satisfactory" system than Pollen's, and that the Official Secrets Act would preclude him "from disclosing Service secrets of which his connection with the Admiralty has given him knowledge." A few days later, the Admiralty responded to Pollen's offer to withhold mention of the rate dials and linkages by demanding still more omissions, one of which was a feature already disclosed in a public patent held by Barr & Stroud. Pollen at last realized that the Admiralty had no intention of shifting its position, only of entrenching more deeply. "This shows their hand so obviously, that I think we should not delay 24 hours from Monday morning before sending in our ultimatum to the Admiralty," he told his lawyers. "[I]t is quite clear that the Admiralty are determined, if they can successfully stop it, to prevent our having a Clock that is of any value at all."[51]

Pollen duly fired off the ultimatum on Tuesday, July 8.[52] "[I]n view of the First Lord's recent allusions in Parliament to the Official Secrets Act, and the injurious comments to which they have given rise," Pollen wrote, "we feel bound to clear ourselves forthwith of all suspicions by having our rights legally determined."[53] Acting on Finlay's advice, he informed the Admiralty that he would apply for complete foreign patents on July 20. Since sovereign immunity—that is, a sovereign government's right to be immune to suit without a waiver of immunity—prevented Argo from initiating "proceedings for clearing our own good name" without the crown's consent, it had to force the Admiralty to initiate proceedings by seeking an injunction that would stop Argo from submitting whatever foreign patent applications it wished.[54] This method, Pollen explained, would give Argo the legal determination it needed while affording the Admiralty an opportunity to make its case before the publication of anything it considered secret.[55] He had no qualms about taking this course, he told a friend, since "[t]he lawyers are unanimous that the Admiralty threat is a brutum fulmen"—an empty threat.[56]

Its bluff called, the Admiralty scrambled. It professed itself "at a loss to understand" Pollen's sudden unwillingness to continue discussions over modifications to his foreign patent applications.[57] Pollen explained that, until the Admiralty requested changes to his foreign applications going beyond the rate dials and linkages, he had understood the question at issue to be one "of ownership only." That is, the Admiralty claimed that it had invented these features and communicated them to Pollen, and this claim supplied the basis of its invocation of the Official Secrets Act. The Admiralty had to take this ground, Pollen's lawyers advised him, for its invocation of the act to be legal:

> We are advised that were [the features in question] truly Service inventions, and communicated to us, the Admiralty would have legal grounds for demanding their suppression; but if they were our own unaided inventions, and not communicated to us by the Service, then the Admiralty could have no legal grounds for such a demand, whatever the consequences of publication.

When the Admiralty demanded the omission of a feature from Argo's foreign patent applications that had already been published in another patent, Pollen realized that the Admiralty was invoking the Official Secrets Act on different grounds: it did not matter who had invented the features in question. That is, Pollen realized that the Admiralty was severing national security secrecy from the liberal norms of property and taking "ground outside the law." This illegal severance ruled out any possibility of agreement between Argo and the Admiralty. "[W]hile we are founding our case on what is purely a matter of fact, namely, whose is the invention? the Admiralty are founding theirs on an administrative necessity, namely, to prevent a device being put upon the market which could endanger the secrecy of the Service System," Pollen summarized. "[I]f the Admiralty's position is based not on ownership but on policy"—that is, not on property grounds but on national security grounds—it followed that further discussion was a waste of time. Argo's only recourse was the courts.[58]

The Admiralty could mount only an inconsistent reply. In order to defend itself against the charge of inconsistency in its grounds for invoking the Official Secrets Act, it fell back on its previous imprecision in defining the scope of the secret and on Dreyer's counternarrative of invention. While averring that it had always maintained that Pollen got key knowledge from the Navy, in practically the next breath it characterized "the main point" of its case as being "that the presence of the device in question on the Argo Clock *whether or not your own invention* gives a key to the service system, which ought not to be disclosed."[59] This claim to have been arguing on the grounds of secrecy rather than on the grounds of property contradicted the Admiralty's previous acknowledgment, exactly in line with what Pollen's lawyers told him, that the legality of invoking the Official Secrets Act turned on the question of ownership—that is, on whether Pollen's patents "embody the inventor's own unaided ideas alone." Here was the logic by which the US Atomic Energy Act of 1946 made nuclear knowledge into "restricted data," secret by its nature: when knowledge was "born secret," its parentage was irrelevant.[60]

Disputing the Admiralty's arguments in their entirety, Pollen informed it that he could see no point to continuing the correspondence and reiterated his invitation to the Admiralty to seek an injunction against his foreign patent applications.[61] Unwilling to give Pollen his day in court, which would have required a defense of its self-admittedly illegal position, the Admiralty resorted to retribution. If it initiated legal proceedings, the DNO Tudor delicately minuted, "it is probable that the Admiralty's reasons for prosecuting the Argo Co. would be misunderstood."[62] The Admiralty had already, at some point in 1913, torpedoed Pollen's chances of reaching "easy street" through a deal with Armstrong Whitworth by informing the company that the Official Secrets Act would prevent it from selling all of the Argo system.[63] Upon learning that Pollen had followed through on his ultimatum and shown the Argo IV clock in its entirety to foreign naval attachés, Admiralty officials judged "that the action of the Argo Company was most reprehensible and rendered it necessary to consider punitive measures." Accordingly, they decided to strike Argo from the list of approved Admiralty contractors and very publicly informed the entire Royal Navy that "no further intercourse was to be held with it." The latter method the Admiralty judged "particularly important as the only means of officially breaking off all existing relations between Mr Pollen and individual naval officers."[64] For a man who counted his "friendship and intimacy with naval officers" as his "greatest pleasure in the last five years," this was perhaps the cruelest cut of all.[65]

The Admiralty's deployment of Dreyer's patents and the Official Secrets Act constituted interventions in both the domestic and international political economy. Domestically, the Admiralty viewed patents and secrecy as tools, or technologies, to redistribute resources between the state and the private sector: it used them to take from the latter and give to the former. Internationally, the Admiralty used patents and secrecy as mechanisms to try to prevent a redistribution of resources between states. In order to maintain British power and naval supremacy, the Admiralty did not want vital fire-control technology going abroad. It was convinced that Pollen's system was significant, albeit on the totally backwards logic that his system's significance derived from its incorporation of Dreyer's system. Because the Admiralty had no legal way to prevent the export of Pollen's system besides paying him for monopoly and secrecy, and it was unwilling to do so, it had to let him go. As we will see in the next chapter, the US Navy was very glad to take him.

CHAPTER 4

Westward the Course of
Piracy Makes Its Way

"I think, however, we may be able to modify the Ford instrument a little bit and embo[d]y the best features of the Pollen clock. The government will have to pay for this, of course after the war."
WILBUR VAN AUKEN, 3 MAY 1918

The end of Pollen's agreement with the Admiralty freed him and Isherwood to sell their system on the global market. This freedom offered both risk and reward. On the one hand, what they lost in exclusive sales to the world's largest Navy, they gained in a larger pool of potential customers. On the other hand, attracting new customers required them to share knowledge about their system in advance of receiving payment. The time lag between exposing the system and signing a contract created a vulnerable period—the same as they had encountered during their early negotiations with the Admiralty—during which a foreign navy or firm might pirate the system and build it themselves. As a US naval officer with intelligence-gathering experience remarked in 1912, "Commercial firms especially naturally do not relish turning loose the results of their efforts for possible use by similar firms at home."[1]

International patent law, US patent law, and the culture of patenting at key US firms exacerbated the threat of piracy. The 1883 Paris Convention for the Protection of Industrial Property, the world's first intellectual property treaty, was built for ordinary commercial patents, not secret patents like the ones that Pollen and Isherwood held in Britain. While secrecy no longer ruled out pioneer-patent protection by preventing them from pursuing the public status of heroic inventors, as it had in Britain, their status as foreigners effectively did so in the United States, given Americans' cultural commitment to their sense of self as the most heroic inventors in the world.[2] The same pressure to reduce inventions to material form that discouraged Pollen from making nonpioneer patents his primary means of legal protection in Britain existed even more strongly in the United States, which required inventors to break down their claims to an greater degree. For pioneering foreign inventors like Pollen and Isherwood, this feature of US patent law posed a threat. With inventive claims so subdivided, it was easier for Americans to claim specific instrumental expressions of foreigners' fundamental inventions, thereby appropriating foreign inventiveness for themselves. The business culture of the US firms that entered the fire-control industry was to take full advantage of this aspect of the US patent system.

These firms, along with the US Navy, had no interest in Dreyer's system, which they quickly judged inferior to Pollen's. It was thus to the latter and not to the former that these Americans paid the sincerest form of flattery: imitation, or rather piracy. Initially repeating Dreyer's failure to grasp the importance of bearings and bearing rate in Pollen's solution, the Americans needed three rounds of knowledge transfer to understand just how much farther ahead of them Pollen was. The US Navy's interest in Pollen's system predated the outbreak of World War I in August 1914, and prior to US entry in April 1917, naval officers believed that the first two rounds of knowledge transfer had enabled a US defense contractor to build a clock as good as Pollen's. But once admitted to regular contact with their British counterparts, US naval officers learned that the Dreyer tables' inadequate arrangements for bearing, which the existing US clock mirrored, were now regarded by gunnery experts as a major liability under combat conditions. Thus alerted that they had not plagiarized Pollen as thoroughly as they had thought, they acted to complete the process. The result was a more competently plagiarized version of Pollen's and Isherwood's system than Dreyer himself had managed to achieve.

ROUND ONE

Prior to learning about Pollen's and Isherwood's system, the US Navy remained far behind the Royal Navy in the realm of fire control.[3] The most important American firm in the field was the Sperry Gyroscope Company. The well-known inventor Elmer Sperry had founded the company in 1910 to carry on his work for the US Navy.[4] This had begun with his invention of an enormous gyrostabilizer for ships, intended to dampen the ship's roll and provide a more stable gunnery platform, followed shortly by his construction of a gyrocompass.[5] He built on his gyrocompass work by designing an electrical system for transmitting target bearings between observation positions aloft, the plotting room below, and the turrets.[6] This work evolved into an attempt to build a full-blown director system—technology pioneered in Britain by Percy Scott and Vickers to facilitate centralized fire control, discussed at greater length in chapters 1, 5, and 8. In 1911, Sperry became interested in developing a gyro-stabilized rangefinder.[7] Around the same time, he also initiated work on a plotter, which his company called the "battle tracer."[8] Thus, by the time World War I broke out, Sperry had in hand the development of two of the three major components of Pollen's and Isherwood's system, of which he was clearly aware: a gyro-stabilized rangefinder and a plotter, but no clock—which was the heart of the Argo system.[9]

During the life of Pollen's agreement with the Admiralty, very little information had trickled out about the nature and design of his system, or, for that matter, about Dreyer's. A US naval attaché report on the trial of their inventions on HMS *Ariadne* and HMS *Vengeance* in early 1908, for instance, incorrectly stated that the goal was "to find out whether suitable fire control systems can be installed behind armor."[10] Accurate information about Pollen's system began to appear only toward the end of 1912, when prospects for agreement with the Admiralty faded and he started to approach foreign naval attachés about selling his system on the global market. His earliest correspondence with the US naval attaché dates from this period.[11] Several months went by without leaving any trace of negotiations in the extant documentary record, but in August 1913, Pollen confided to his diary that he had received an order from the US Navy.[12]

In fact he had not received an order so much as premonitions of one. The well-connected US naval attaché, Powers Symington (uncle of future Secretary of the Air Force and US Senator Stuart Symington), thought highly of Pollen's system. "I am very much impressed by the value of the scheme," he informed the Navy Department, "and consider its immediate purchase as most desirable and important."[13] The American attaché had been in touch with numerous British naval officers who regarded Pollen's system as much superior to Dreyer's. "The Admiralty have abandoned their undoubted monopoly and state that they have a system of their own [i.e., Dreyer's] that is superior," Symington wrote. "Many, if not most, of the officers actually engaged in fire control work are heartily in favor of the Pollen system."[14] After viewing the system for himself, Symington agreed with their assessment. In another note to a fellow officer, Symington described Pollen's system as "far and away superior to anything that we have or that I have ever heard of."[15]

At first, Symington's superiors were skeptical that a foreign inventor could be so far ahead. The US Navy Bureau of Ordnance, which was responsible for fire-control technology, requested further information about Pollen's system but refused to buy a set at his asking price, and it ignored Symington's suggestion to send a board of officers to view Pollen's system.[16] Reginald Gillmor, the Sperry Gyroscope Company's representative in

London, advised that Pollen's system was too complex and too expensive to buy at the price he was asking.[17] Most dubious of all was William Sims, perhaps the navy's leading gunnery expert—thanks to his mimicry of Percy Scott's gunnery reforms in the Royal Navy.[18] Observing that "[a]ll of Mr. Pollen's conclusions in reference to fire-control seem to be based upon the remarkable assumption that extreme precision is required of all elements, and that this is attainable in practice," Sims disagreed on both counts.[19] He insisted that Pollen offered no improvement on the US Navy's existing fire-control methods.

This opinion in the US Navy soon changed. In May 1914, Pollen crossed the Atlantic to bring modern fire control from the old world to the new. Symington urged him to make the trip and did his best to prepare the ground for Pollen, emphasizing to the chief of the Bureau of Ordnance, Joseph Strauss, that Pollen could teach the US Navy not only about his own system but also about European gunnery more broadly.[20] Symington's colleague Frank R. McCrary, a torpedo specialist and future aviation pioneer, joined the chorus. After inspecting Argo's works in England, McCrary admitted that he had first thought Pollen's instruments to be "unnecessarily complicated," but "after seeing the instruments I was forced to modify that idea." He reserved special praise for the Argo clock—"it is one of the most perfect and complete machines I have ever seen"—singling out Isherwood's slipless variable-speed drive. McCrary advised that the US Navy should order at least the clock for trial.[21] Strauss replied that the Bureau was uninterested in Pollen's plotter, because it had high hopes for the domestic Sperry "battle tracer," but it was interested in his clock and rangefinder.[22] Already, it was clear, the US Navy would not buy his system as a system, but at most select components piecemeal.

Upon arriving in DC, Pollen went immediately to the Navy Department, where he met with several officers, including Strauss and Frank C. Martin, who headed the Bureau of Ordnance's fire-control section. Pollen was optimistic about his chances: "I fully expect to get an order—or at least to arrange finally for one—before I go."[23] The following week, he wrote to Secretary of the Navy Josephus Daniels making the case for his system.[24] Strauss advised Daniels that Pollen's plotter and rangefinder offered no major advantages over expected or existing US versions. By contrast, "The superiority of Pollen's clock is undoubted," and Strauss recommended purchasing one for trial.[25] Yet the Secretary hesitated. He informed Pollen that although US officers held his system in high regard, the navy did not want to buy his system until it had tested "some new instruments" of its own development that "worked along the same lines" and were "designed to accomplish similar results."[26] Thus no purchase would be forthcoming.

By the time of his visit to the United States, Pollen had been working on his system for thirteen years. Before his visit, the US Navy had the Vickers clock, but there is no evidence that the Navy or any of its contractors was working on any clock of their own, while there is strong evidence—including Gillmor's and Sims's dismissals of his clock as overly complex and unnecessary—that they were not. Yet within less than a year of his visit, two US defense contractors—Sperry and his former employee Hannibal Ford—had proposed clocks of their own, which the US Navy referred to as "rangekeepers." While Ford (who, like Pollen, also came from a printing background) and Sperry were unquestionably talented inventors in their own rights, exploitation of foreign developments was part of the corporate culture at Sperry Gyroscope.[27] In the careful judgment of Sperry's biographer, his interest in gyroscopes likely went back to his boyhood, but the design of his first marine gyrostabilizer owed much to the work of the German naval engineer Otto Schlick.[28] Ford recalled a similar process concerning the German Anschütz gyrocompass. He and Sperry "had an Anschutz book and we were studying it trying to get every significant fact out it," he told an interviewer. "Neither one of us knew anything about gyro-compasses."[29] US naval officers familiar with the Anschütz provided additional help.[30] According to Sperry's biographer, he himself acknowledged that his "inventive technique" was that "he looked for the weak points in earlier devices invented by others . . . and concentrated on surmounting those."[31]

In other words, Sperry Gyroscope's business model was to scan foreign patents on fundamental inventions with an eye to stealing a march—and the spoils. Sperry and Ford were not pioneering inventors themselves. Certainly Sperry's success owed much to "drive, resourcefulness, persistence, and courage," as his biographer claims—but the secret sauce, so to speak, was the prior work of pioneering inventors.[32] This secret sauce was bound to bring Sperry and Ford into conflict with the intellectual property claims of foreign inventors, as it did with Pollen (as well as Anschütz).[33]

It is scarcely plausible that Sperry and Ford managed, through sheer Yankee ingenuity, independently to conceptualize in less than a year and invent in less than two years what had taken Pollen and his ingenious British team a dozen years to conceptualize and invent. The alternative explanation is that they "virtually stole" Pollen's technology.[34] In addition to the chronology, other evidence strongly points to this conclusion, even though it is difficult to pin down the nature and method of the theft with precision. At a minimum, it would have involved a verbal description of Pollen's clock by a Bureau of Ordnance officer, most likely Martin, the head of the Bureau's fire-control section. At a maximum, it would have involved passing

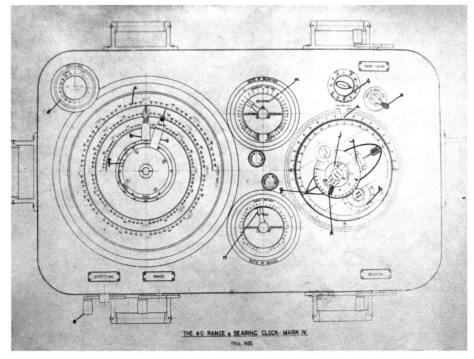

Figure 4.1. This is a copy of a drawing of the Argo clock viewed from above sent by the US naval attaché in late 1913. It shows the various dials seen and manipulated by operators. Though no internal machinery is visible, the dials provide some sense of the information that Pollen and Isherwood regarded as necessary to the solution of the fire-control problem. One clue of potential significance—not understood by the US Navy in 1914, despite the Admiralty's fears covered in chapter 3—was the inclusion of not only a range-rate dial but also a bearing-rate dial (the two medium-sized circles in the middle—the bearing-rate is the one on top). (File U-1-i, Register #S6925, RG38/E98/B1294, NARA-I.)

Pollen's written description, drawings, and photographs of his system—which Symington had sent to the Office of Naval Intelligence for circulation to the Bureau of Ordnance in August 1913—to Sperry and Ford. These were not full engineering drawings showing tolerances and other information necessary to build the instruments, but they nevertheless contained much in the way of potential clues, as shown in figure 4.1.

While Sperry and Ford began working on their clocks, the Bureau of Ordnance maintained its interest in Pollen's. In early September 1914, Strauss lobbied Daniels to reverse his decision on Pollen's clock, asking him to approve the purchase of one from an American firm. Although very little documentation about this initiative survives, presumably the firm would have built under license from Pollen. Strauss advised the secretary that Pollen's clock, "the most important" part of Pollen's system, was "a vast improvement over the clock in use in the U.S. Navy."[35] This was a reference to the British Vickers clock.[36] Daniels remained unmoved, however, vetoing the initiative.[37] There relations between the US Navy and Pollen rested for almost two years.

During this period, Sperry and Ford made substantial progress on their new clock designs. By this point, they were rivals—Ford left Sperry Gyroscope to form the Ford Marine Appliance Corporation (soon to become the Ford Instrument Company) in January 1915. Sperry and Ford proposed their clocks to the Bureau of Ordnance within a day of each other in May 1915. Significantly, while both designs called for a range-rate dial, neither called for a bearing-rate dial; like Dreyer initially, both Sperry and Ford focused on range.[38] Also significantly, Pollen's and Isherwood's US patents on their clock had not yet been published, meaning that Sperry and Ford were relying on other information—that forwarded by the US Navy—about the Argo clock.[39] Ford's proposal, unlike Sperry's, shows that he recognized that knowledge of the bearing rate as well as the range rate was mathematically necessary for accurate predictions of the range, but unlike Pollen and Isherwood, he did not provide means for the clock to autogenerate bearings, nor did he mechanically interconnect the range and bearing rates. Instead, he called for bearings to be introduced into the clock from a target bearing transmitter, which required the target to remain visible.[40] A prototype of Ford's clock was tested in May 1916.[41] The Navy chose it over Sperry's clock.[42]

ROUND TWO

In early 1916, US interest in Pollen's system reawakened. In January of that year, the new US naval attaché to Britain, John Towers, visited Argo's works. Coming off a recent stint as fire-control officer on the battleship USS *Michigan* (with his career as a pioneering naval aviator yet to come), Towers reported favorably. "I was greatly impressed by the Argo system as a whole, and think that it solves more of the problems of fire control than any other system I have seen or heard of in either the British of American Navy," he told the Office of Naval Intelligence. Like McCrary, he gave special praise to the Argo clock, "which seems to be a splendid instrument."[43] Towers took it upon himself to interest Reginald Gillmor, Sperry Gyroscope's London representative, in Pollen's system, "in the hopes that Mr. Gillmor might find it to the interests of the Sperry Gyroscope Company to make a thorough investigation of the subject, with the idea of making some arrangement for the developing of the Pollen system in America."[44] Symington, the previous naval attaché who had so admired Pollen's system in 1913 and remained in London, also approached Gillmor.[45]

Despite his earlier skepticism toward the Pollen system, Gillmor was the perfect man for the job. A Naval Academy graduate, he had come to Sperry's attention while serving on the USS *Delaware* during trials of Sperry's gyrocompass.[46] Sperry poached him from the Navy and put him in charge of the firm's European sales office in London. When the United States entered the war in 1917, the Bureau of Ordnance arranged for the Navy to commission Gillmor as a lieutenant in the Naval Reserve. He volunteered to work on the staff of Admiral William Sims, who headed the US naval mission to Britain and made Gillmor Assistant Naval Attaché.[47] Once Gillmor was in the Naval Reserve, the Navy permitted Sperry to correspond with him through the diplomatic mails in order to evade British censorship.[48] Thus, Gillmor wore two hats—one as past and present naval officer, one as Sperry employee.[49]

Gillmor's investigation of Pollen's system led him to undergo a conversion experience and become a true believer. He visited Pollen's works in early spring 1916, after which Pollen sent a long description of his system, along with an analysis of how it might have helped British ships to handle the fire-control conditions they had encountered in various actions during the war.[50] The Battle of Jutland, on 31 May 1916, which Pollen seized upon as evidence of the inadequacies of the Dreyer tables and as vindication for his own ideas, likely further stimulated Gillmor's interest.[51] In late July, Towers sent one copy of Gillmor's ninety-page report to the Office of Naval Intelligence with a request that it send a second copy to Sperry, in order to avoid interception and censorship by British intelligence (which was extremely thorough in such matters).[52]

Gillmor's report was an impassioned attempt to spread the gospel. Having been stunned by his own realization of how far ahead Pollen was, he understood why others struggled to believe. The heart of his report consisted of his analysis of the basic fire-control problem as he had come to understand it. Having intensively studied the fire-control systems used in European navies, including the Dreyer tables, Gillmor concluded

> that the Pollen system is vastly in advance of any other system in the world. This [is] because (a) Pollen is the only man, who as a result of many years of study and analysis, has a clear and complete understanding of the many factors involved and the relation which each has to the others, and (b) Pollen and his Company are the only people who have

carried on a continuous process of development, experiment, trial and improvement in means for completely fulfilling the functions of fire control.[53]

Gillmor wholeheartedly endorsed Pollen's critique of (Dreyer's) rate-plotting technique, which he agreed could not produce sufficiently timely data to be accurate when rates were changing. Moreover, with a better understanding of the Pollen clock, which three years earlier he had dismissed as unnecessarily complex, Gillmor now acclaimed it as "by far the most important unit of the Pollen system."[54] "I did not believe in Pollen's system when Capt. Symington first described it to me," he penitently admitted, "and as I look back at it now, I know that my attitude was due to the fact that I did not have a thorough analytical knowledge of the whole subject."[55] Pollen was so far advanced that without an agreement with him, Gillmor judged, "we would have to surmount a tremendous number of difficulties, and—in my opinion—it would take us a very long time and a great deal of money to equal the result Pollen has attained."[56] This was essentially the same argument that Edward Harding had made to the Admiralty in 1906.

Rather than start from scratch, Gillmor recommended that Sperry Gyroscope purchase the US rights to Pollen's system. Wearing his Sperry hat, Gillmor saw contracts with the US Navy as the most promising growth area for the firm, and he regarded fire control as the most promising basis for such contracts. Switching to his Navy hat, Gillmor envisioned Sperry Gyroscope performing a key function for the Navy. "In the American Navy, the constantly changing personnel has limited this development and they really need some organization such as ours [i.e., Sperry Gyroscope] to take hold of these things and carry them out," Gillmor told Sperry.[57] Gillmor detected in the Navy Department the same weaknesses that he believed had doomed the Admiralty in fire-control development, and he imagined Sperry playing for the Navy Department the role in which the Admiralty had failed to cast the Argo Company. "You will no doubt think it strange that the Admiralty should refuse to adopt the Pollen gear if it is in fact as efficient as I have described it in this letter," Gillmor acknowledged to Sperry, but he insightfully explained:

To me this is not at all strange—fire control systems admit of many compromises, and the officers responsible for making a decision on this subject in the Admiralty happen to be those who believe in rough and ready and simple methods. Because the subject is complicated and full of detail it could not be decided by the higher officers, and therefore had to be referred to subordinates. These subordinates were capable naval officers, and capable gunnery specialists, but did not have sufficient training to be able to carefully, thoroughly, and correctly weigh all the phases of the subject of fire control. This is often the case in other lines, and is to be expected where the officers in control are constantly shifting.[58]

By contrast, at Sperry Gyroscope, as at Argo, expert personnel remained in the same jobs and could develop fire control along the most promising lines over the long term. Gillmor was echoing Harding's arguments here too.

In another way, Sperry Gyroscope was in a better position than the Navy to stay abreast of foreign developments. "We are in a position to not only carry on this work in a progressive and efficient manner," Gillmor observed, "but we are also able to get the best ideas from abroad and to obtain the American rights to foreign developments which will be useful to our Navy."[59] As a private firm, Sperry Gyroscope could acquire information through channels closed to the Navy. One naval officer seeking to collect intelligence abroad remarked, "[Our attaché] could not get any thing because he is attaché and if one attaché gets any thing all others from the different countries expect the same," adding, "You can see how this handicaps the attaché."[60] Naval officers working as inspectors at foreign works stood a better chance of getting valuable material. Upon receiving a report full of sensitive information about foreign ordnance development from such an inspector, the Director of Target Practice sighed, "You cannot get stuff of this kind in our Office of Naval Intelligence."[61] But private actors dealing with private actors were better situated still. It was more difficult for a government to control information transfers between private parties than when itself or another government was involved.[62]

PATENT TROUBLES

Gillmor's report spurred Sperry into a flurry of action, largely focused on investigating Pollen's US patent rights. In his report, Gillmor had both raised doubts and sought to reassure Sperry on this score. "Pollen says himself that his patent protection in America is not all that it might be," Gillmor wrote. "You will appreciate, however, that in the case of such developments as his, protection is derived not from patents but from an extensive knowledge of all the factors of theory, design, manufacture and construction which can only be obtained by many years of work and development."[63] For revolutionary inventions like Pollen's, Gillmor was saying, "tacit knowledge"—unwritten knowledge about theory, design, manufacture, and construction—was acutely necessary.[64] Sperry was not reassured.

From the start of his career, he had taken a keen interest in the workings of the US patent system; by 1916, he held more than two hundred US patents.[65] He used patents as competitive weapons: they enabled him to secure market share, served as assets against which to raise capital, and so on. He always kept one eye focused on the patent implications of his inventive work.[66] Accordingly, patents meant something very different to him from what they meant to Pollen. For the latter, they captured only small parts of an invention, and they offered too little protection to be relied upon as sources of profit or security, for which Pollen instead looked to a development contract with the Admiralty. For Sperry, patents were functionally equivalents to invention, and they were leading sources of profit and security.

When Sperry looked into Pollen's US patent situation, he saw vulnerabilities. By this point, Pollen's and Isherwood's main US patent on their clock had been published, along with several others. Pollen was asking 15 percent royalties but would not commit to maintaining his US patents, since he had no US organization for that purpose.[67] Moreover, in Sperry's judgment, the patents themselves were poorly drawn:

> The patents have been ground through purely mechanically without any adequate understanding on the part of the attorneys as to the points that should be safeguarded. Not one single generic claim exists in any of the patents, they being all confined to some foolish statement, which so limits them as to make them almost valueless. For instance, by changing from a dial marked in yards to a dial marked in meters a great many of the claims could be overcome. In other words, P's patent attorneys have fallen down completely and have failed to protect his invention as it should be.

Given the weakness of Pollen's patents, Sperry was loath to take on the expense and risks of manufacturing Pollen's system under license.[68] As he put it to Gillmor, "American manufacturers are so keen regarding patent matters"—he knew whereof he spoke—"that the moment a matter is called to their attention they look into it, and we would simply be working on the name [i.e. Pollen's] without any real patent protection whatsoever."[69]

One reason to accept Sperry's assessment of Pollen's US patents is that he seems to have been telling the truth when he said he wished they were otherwise—albeit for his own sake, not Pollen's. He saw Pollen's US patent rights as a weapon against his rival Ford and as bait for the Bureau of Ordnance. Sperry complained that Ford's clock design constituted "a direct attempt on his part to short circuit our further sales of the battle tracer."[70] He thus asked Gillmor to provide "all information you have respecting F[ord]," and he solicited information from the Bureau of Ordnance with an eye to evading any patents Ford might take out.[71] (Ford, for his part, snarked to a Bureau of Ordnance official that he had "no doubt that Mr. S. was all eyes" when examining Ford's clock as a member of the Naval Consulting Board.)[72] Sperry hoped that he might find a way to use a connection with Pollen to stem his loss of business to Ford, his former employee turned competitor. If Sperry's company could adequately protect itself against the weaknesses of Pollen's US patents, he explained to Gillmor, "there would be certain extraneous considerations connected with this P. situation, in that it would put us in a very desirable and confidential relation with our Government that might possibly give us a leverage in other directions."[73] Not only a carrot for the Bureau, Pollen's US patents might also make a stick against Ford. Sperry saw that Ford's clock "infringes one of those patents and may have some value to us on this basis."[74] In view of "the vital weakness of P[ollen]'s patent situation," however, Sperry lamented that he did not "see very much hope of being able to stop the other fellow [i.e., Ford]."[75]

There are other grounds to accept Sperry's evaluation of Pollen's patents as weak. For reasons discussed in chapter 1, the legal issues raised by Pollen's invention within Britain or the United States required specialized knowledge even within the specialized world of patent attorneys; for reasons discussed below, the task of translating his British patents into American ones required still more. In Britain, Pollen bought the highest-powered legal talent money could buy—former attorneys general, Barings's lawyers, and so on. In the United States, he did not. His lead patent attorney was Robert Fletcher Rogers, who had graduated from Harvard, done a stint as a patent examiner, and was a name partner in the New York firm of Rogers, Kennedy, and Campbell.[76] Pollen selected him not after an exhaustive national search but because he was already acquainted with Rogers as Linotype's US patent attorney and regarded him as a close personal friend.[77] As such, Rogers may have reduced his prices for Pollen or worked for free. But he was nowhere near as distinguished as Pollen's English lawyers.

∴

The vagaries of international, US, and British law complicated Pollen's US patent situation. As we saw in previous chapters, Pollen and Isherwood took out more than a dozen British patents in the course of their association with the Admiralty—but these were secret patents. Their secret character effectively precluded recourse to otherwise available means for translating intellectual property protection across national borders. Under the terms of the 1883 Paris Convention for the Protection of Industrial Property, inventors could apply for foreign patents identical to their domestic patents within a certain period of filing for the latter.[78] The United States became a party to the Paris Convention in 1887 (though enabling legislation was not passed until 1897).[79] Both the Paris Convention and the US enabling legislation made the date of filing for domestic patents, not the date of publication, the moment when the clock started counting down toward the deadline for filing for foreign patents; the US legislation set the window at two years. This standard debarred Pollen from filing for US patents identical to most of his British secret patents once the Admiralty waived secrecy and his British patents were published because he had filed for most of his British secret patents more than two years before the end of his secrecy agreement with the Admiralty permitted him to apply for foreign patents.[80] As Sperry wrote to Gillmor, "most of [Pollen's US] patent applications have been finally rejected, the prior issue of P's patents in England being an absolute bar to their issue here."[81]

Even when a patent could clear this bar, translating a British one into a US one was not straightforward. While patents in both countries contained a specifications section (to explain the invention) and a claims section (to define the scope of the property protection), the grammar of the two patent systems differed.[82] "The British practice permits an inventor to use alternative and functional expressions in the claims, or, in other words, to set forth the real inventive idea," according to Paul Blair, a patent lawyer employed by the Bureau of Ordnance, "instead of the numerous specific claims required by the United States Patent Office." In US practice, claims had to be "drawn to the structure shown."[83] Pollen's (or rather Rogers's) attempt to translate the basic British patent on the Argo IV clock into an American patent ran into precisely this problem. Rogers originally, and rather lazily, submitted merely a verbatim copy of the British patent, containing the same eight claims, for the US patent on the Argo IV clock.[84] The patent examiner summarily rejected them for the reason identified by Blair: "As drawn, the claims recite movement of a part in a manner proportional to a trigonometric formula. The claims should be drawn to structure and not to such indefinite matter as the above named formula."[85] To meet this requirement, Rogers had to multiply while simultaneously narrowing Pollen's claims.[86] This feature of US patent law made it even more difficult for Pollen to protect what he regarded as the most important part of his invention, namely, the algorithmic articulation of the mathematics of the problem, to which he built the structure that the US Patent Office required him to claim on.[87] The requirement to subdivide claims likely reflected the

United States' commitment to "democratizing invention"—that is, making it easy for ordinary inventors to take out patents—but it also conveniently opened the field for Americans to patent particular instrumental expressions of fundamental inventions made by foreigners.[88] In that respect, the US patent system was engineered to facilitate piracy.

By equating inventiveness with (or rather reducing it to) patentability, as the Admiralty had done for its own reasons, Americans could deny the inventiveness of foreigners and rationalize their own plagiarism. Sperry's correspondence with Gillmor offers an excellent example of this process. Being "obsessed" by the Ford clock, in Sperry's words, the US Navy had told Sperry "to take the data from the battle tracer exactly the same as P[ollen]. takes his data from the battle tracer."[89] In other words, the Navy and Sperry were taking their design inspiration from Pollen's linkage of the plotter and the clock, adopting his breakthrough idea of an integrated system as preferable to disintegrated components—without paying Pollen any money for his idea. Rather than acknowledge his debt to Pollen's intellectual labor, Sperry instead speculated that "P's belief in his own system borders either on bigotry or fanaticism, and I do not think he is enough of an engineer himself to realize that there are many ways in which these matters may be worked out."[90]

Pollen had managed to fall into the interstices of international law, the British secret patent system, and the US patent laws. The upshot of the fact that neither the Paris Convention nor the US patent laws had been written with British secret patents in mind was that, regardless of how well or poorly his US patents were drawn, the strength of Pollen's US patent position was bound to vary inversely with that part of his British patent position predating the two-year Paris Convention window. Even where the Paris Convention did not preclude Pollen from filing US applications equivalent to his British patents, US patent law did, and in such a way as to play perfectly into the hands of Sperry, Ford, and the Bureau of Ordnance.

ROUND THREE

Despite Sperry's concerns about Pollen's US patents, he and other Americans remained interested in Pollen's system. "There is no question but that there is some value in [Pollen's] name," Sperry acknowledged to Gillmor, who for his part kept up the pressure.[91] Pollen also acquired a new and important supporter in Eugene C. Tobey, a US naval officer in the paymaster corps recently stationed to the London embassy. Despite his title, Tobey did much more than handle routine office expenses. Tobey's actual job was industrial espionage.[92] His reports went straight to the chiefs of the technical bureaus, with whom he also maintained direct semiofficial correspondence.[93] "Spying doesn't pay, and the other extreme of an Attache [sic] with an established social and official position is apparently even less fruitful of what we want," another practitioner of industrial espionage explained. "Strangely however, there is a mid-position in which a tactful chap with a game of frankness, if armed with the right kind of credentials and power of attorney, can walk off with material seldom secured and most needed."[94] Tobey was a tactful chap. He headed to London with a letter of introduction to Gillmor from Sperry, who told his lieutenant that Tobey was "on a very important special mission—in fact, as special Naval Attache."[95] Admiral William Sims, whose staff in London Tobey joined in 1917, wrote that the paymaster "has a capacity as a mixer that enables him to inspire confidence in the people who have the information that we want, and his business head is such that he can dope out from this just what the matter is." "[Q]uite outside of this," Sims added, "he is one of the best collectors of information even on technical subjects which are supposed to be of no interest to his corps."[96] Tobey quickly established warm personal relations with Pollen, whom he described as "a most delightful companion and friend."[97] Whether he captured Pollen or Pollen captured him is unclear. In any case, he swiftly joined Gillmor in agitating for Pollen's system.[98]

The Bureau of Ordnance was intrigued but cagey. Its officers rated Pollen highly and were eager to pump him for information—but they did not want information, especially about Ford's clock, to flow to Pollen in reverse. Like the Admiralty, they pursued a knowledge embargo. Martin, the head of the Bureau's fire-control section, wrote to Sperry, "I think Mr. Pollen gives us credit for being a little more dense than we really are, and I don't know but what this is a good thing, because the more he preaches the better I like it. He is a very clever man, and well worth listening to."[99] Martin advised the new chief of the Bureau of Ordnance, Ralph Earle, that "the secret of the Ford Rangekeeper should not be divulged by any form of argument or controversy with Mr. Pollen." He continued:

I believe that we should try a Pollen Rangekeeper, find out its price, time of delivery, and not let Mr. Pollen know that we have a mechanical rangekeeper of any description. It will be better to throw him off the track and let him feel that we are still using ordinary plotting methods which have been developed to a great degree of accuracy by constant training of the personnel. He now has heard somewhere that we have some form of rangekeeper—that it is being made by Mr. Sperry, etc. (He probably heard this from Gillmor, in London, who gets a great deal of his information on the English Navy from Mr. Pollen). In connection with the buying of the Pollen system *even though it is no better than the Ford Rangekeeper*, we can certainly use one set on a ship to advantage and in this way get lots of dope from Mr. Pollen and keep him on our side. [emphasis added][100]

Notably, at this stage, after two rounds of knowledge transfer from Pollen but prior to US entry into the war, Martin erroneously thought that Ford's clock—which did not yet autogenerate bearings—already equaled Pollen's. But he still wanted to pump Pollen for other information. Earle promptly asked the Navy Department to authorize the Bureau to bring Pollen over for consultation.[101]

No money was forthcoming from the Department, but fortunately for the Bureau, funding materialized from another source. Pollen had published a series of widely read articles in *Land and Water*, a British magazine, on the course of the war at sea. After the United States entered the war in April 1917, the US Navy League conveniently organized a paid public lecture tour for him in the United States.[102] His trip also received quiet support from the Department of Information at the Foreign Office—the British government's war propaganda office and the rough equivalent to the US Committee on Public Information.[103] With Tobey having urged Pollen to make the trip and done his best to prepare the way on the fire-control front, Pollen headed across in June 1917.[104]

A further source of expert knowledge about Pollen's system followed him to the United States several months later and stayed for a few months after he left: Harold Isherwood. In January 1916, Isherwood was made a temporary lieutenant commander in the Royal Naval Reserve and attached to HMS *Vernon*, the Royal Navy's center for torpedo and mining research.[105] After the United States entered the war, he was one of several British naval officers sent by the Admiralty to the Bureau of Ordnance to help it with mine development.[106] Pollen was pleased to have Isherwood stationed in the Bureau. "Now that Isherwood is here," Pollen wrote to his wife, "I am much easier" about developments with the Navy Department.[107] He duly suggested that Bureau of Ordnance officials turn to Isherwood for help in understanding their fire-control system.[108]

Despite the knowledge embargo pursued by the Bureau of Ordnance, Pollen developed suspicions that Ford's rangekeeper plagiarized the Argo clock. According to Sperry, Martin told him that Pollen believed that Ford "stole it bodily from him."[109] Nor was Pollen the only one to suspect. A British officer visiting the United States, Commander Richard Down, who examined Ford's clock and spoke at length with US officers, pointedly remarked that Ford's clock was "very similar to Pollen's Clock."[110]

Without regarding themselves as plagiarists, US naval officers also believed at this stage that they had learned all they could from the Argo clock. To be on the safe side, Earle decided to order a set of Pollen's instruments in June 1917.[111] But he and his officers "were not enthusiastic in any way, nor can any of us see that his arrangement is as good as the Ford range keeper now being issued to the battleship fleet," Earle told Sims.[112] Gillmor also came to think that the Ford clock was better than Pollen's. Once he returned to the United States and had a chance to examine it, according to Earle, Gillmor "pronounced it at least 20 per cent ahead of anything of which he had knowledge."[113] By this time Gillmor had adopted the self-serving tendency of his boss, Sperry, to minimize Pollen's inventiveness. "If the Pollen fire control gear had been designed by Pollen I don't think it would have amounted to anything—it was the results [sic] of the efforts of many other more scientific people," Gillmor now told Sperry in October 1917."[114] Gillmor's reference to "more scientific people" revealed more about Sperry Gyroscope's corporate self-perception than about reality; a US naval officer described Sperry's own designers as "trial and error men."[115]

Believing that the Ford clock replicated the functionality of the Argo clock, Pollen put the accusation of plagiarism in writing at the end of October 1917. In a letter to Earle, he asked, "Should not an equitable arrangement be made with my company in the matter of our patent rights in this country?"[116] With the request for equity turning on his only leverage, his inadequate patent rights, Pollen's implicit charge was easy for Earle to parry: he fought on the narrow and favorable ground of patent infringement rather than on the broad and unfavorable ground of plagiarism.[117]

Pollen responded by formally withdrawing his accusation of plagiarism— not because he accepted Earle's assurances, but because he now realized that Ford had plagiarized him much less competently than he had thought. "[A] rather extraordinary situation has arisen at Washington, the details of which I will explain to you when I get home," Pollen reported to his wife.

> Briefly, the point is this. Ever since I came here, in June, I have been dealing with the Bureau of Ordnance on the understanding that the Ford range clock, which the American Navy has adopted, was an exact reproduction of my clock. This turns out to be a complete misunderstanding, with two results. First, there is no case for the Department buying out my system before the trials take place. Secondly, if the Ford clock is not a competitor after all in what I believe to be the most important aspect of fire control, the disappointment of not selling the system is completely counter-balanced by finding that the system is still unique![118]

Having realized how imperfectly Ford had plagiarized him, Pollen retracted his accusation. "[M]y letter of October 31st would not have been written," he told Earle, "but for my having gathered, from information previously given to me, that the functions of the Ford clock and the Pollen clock were, for all practical purposes, identical, and consequently that the patents granted on the Pollen clock might, in the ordinary course, be supposed to be of such validity as to constitute the Ford mechanism an infringement."[119]

What Pollen had come to understand, sometime during the month between the two letters to Earle, was that Ford had plagiarized him just as incompetently as Dreyer, and in just the same way: focused on ranges rather than bearings, Ford had not mechanically interconnected the range and bearing rates in his clock so as to automatically generate bearings under helm and when the target was invisible, the feature that Pollen and Isherwood had made the basis of their solution to the fire-control problem. One day after withdrawing his accusation of patent infringement, Pollen wrote Earle a long letter on this point. The Ford rangekeeper, Pollen told Earle, had reached only the stage of the Argo I clock. This clock, it will be recalled from chapter 2, autogenerated bearings through the mechanical interconnection of the range and bearing rates and thus could keep the range during periods of target invisibility, but it was not helm-free. A clock that could not autogenerate bearings *both* during periods of target invisibility *and* when own ship was under helm, Pollen explained to Earle in his long analysis, was useless for probable tactical conditions.[120]

∵

In fact, the Ford clock at this stage may have been even less further along than Pollen thought. Without question, the Ford clock had already moved some distance toward automatic bearing generation. A letter by Martin, the head of the fire-control section, in May 1917 indicates that the Bureau of Ordnance had ordered a new version of the Ford rangekeeper that "generates its own bearing."[121] But read in conjunction with other evidence, it seems certain that what Martin meant by "generates its own bearing" was not the *auto*generation of bearings through *mechanical* interconnection of the range and bearing rates but rather some means for *manual* interconnection of the rates. Probably this means consisted of using a newly added bearing "pointer"—i.e., a bearing dial to match the range dial—to determine the deflection through the operation of a bearing-rate / deflection conversion drum, like the arrangement in the Mark III Dreyer table. A report by the commander of the Atlantic Fleet, Henry T. Mayo, in February

1918 noted the new dial "simplifies somewhat the work of the operator and should result in greatly increased accuracy." He continued,

> It is not known whether or not the addition of the pointer was due to the original tests [of the Ford rangekeeper] conducted in the Fleet. A conference, held in the Bureau of Ordnance, during which Mr. Pollen explained his system of fire control, brought out very forcibly the necessity for the additional pointer.[122]

An analysis written in April 1918 by the electrical officer of the USS *Wyoming*, Frederick Van Auken, makes clear that the Ford clock was still unable to keep the bearing during periods of invisibility. A British officer, Van Auken reported,

> was particularly anxious to find whether a Ford Range Keeper provided the means for establishing this point of aim in azimuth automatically from the previously established rate of change of bearing after the target had been lost through the [smoke]screen. The writer thinks this officer was rather disappointed in that the Ford could not do this in view of the fact that it can do practically everything else.[123]

As we saw in previous chapters, accurate bearings could be generated during periods of target invisibility only if they were autogenerated through mechanical interconnection of the rates. The fact that the Ford rangekeeper could do "practically everything else" reflected Ford's plagiarism of Pollen; the fact that it could not do this particular thing reflected the limits of his plagiarism thus far.

Other reports by other US naval officers show how Dreyer's failure to understand the crucial role of bearings and bearing rate in Pollen's system had the effect of convincing the US Navy not to make the same mistake in the Ford rangekeeper. Eugene Tobey, who did not think much of the Dreyer table he inspected ("as a simple matter of design, the whole system is not well worked out"), noted that "[t]he bearing plot instrument is not generally taken seriously. One imagines that it was added so that the system could not be criticised as deficient in this respect by Mr. Pollen, or others, rather than for the reason of its actual necessity itself."[124] The Second Battle of Heligoland Bight underscored the inadequacy of Dreyer's provision for bearings and bearing rate. In this action, which occurred on 17 November 1917—eleven days before Pollen sent his long explanation of the importance of bearings and bearing rate to Earle—the Germans employed smokescreens, and the British proved unable to hit them while their ships were invisible. Following the battle, as we will see in chapter 6, the Royal Navy established a committee to investigate the problem of firing at an invisible enemy, and the committee seized on an invention then under development known as Gyro Director Training, which was intended to remedy the defects of the Dreyer tables with regard to bearings and bearing rate. Husband Kimmel, the senior gunnery officer of the US squadron serving with the British Grand Fleet (better known as the commander of the US fleet at Pearl Harbor in 1941), caught wind of these developments and reported on them in early December 1917:

> The rate of change of bearing instruments [i.e., Gyro Director Training] used in connection with the Dreyer Plotting Table is [sic] still in the undeveloped stage, but it is considered by many officers with whom I talked as the coming method, that is, that this method will in time supercede all others. The great thing advanced in its favor is that it is much easier to obtain bearings than range-finder readings.[125]

Although Kimmel himself did not understand the significance of bearings, he accurately reported the recognition by British officers of a fundamental limitation of the Dreyer system: Dreyer's failure to understand the importance of bearing-taking and bearing rate in Pollen's solution of the fire-control problem meant that his table could not keep the bearing and range during frequent periods of target invisibility.

Van Auken picked up on the same British unhappiness with the Dreyer tables. British officers, according to Van Auken, had been trying to fix this weakness in the Dreyer tables "for a long time" and regarded a fix "as of the utmost importance." The Ford rangekeeper, he continued,

> actually *now* [emphasis added] does give—say to twenty minutes of arc— the rate of change of bearing by means of the automatic bearing pointer. Hence, it is unquestionable that the Ford Range Keeper can be made to give this point of aim in azimuth <u>automatically</u>.[126]

By using the automatically generated bearing rate to drive a pointer indicating the instantaneous bearing, Van Auken concluded, the Ford rangekeeper could accomplish what Dreyer had failed to do.

ADMISSIONS AND INDEMNIFICATIONS

Having been made aware by Pollen in November 1917 that Ford's rangekeeper could not do everything that his own did, and alerted by reports

from abroad of the importance which combat-experienced British gunnery officers attached to the autogeneration of bearings, the Bureau of
Ordnance acted to complete the process of plagiarizing Pollen. Wilbur Van
Auken (not to be confused with Frederick), who had recently taken over
the fire-control section from Martin, promptly instructed Ford to "to take
full advantage of the generated bearing feature," adding "I forsaw [sic] this
point last November [1917] after Pollen's visit here."[127] Citing Frederick Van
Auken's letter, Van Auken continued,

> At the present time, the British are trying to get in a predicted bearing
> scheme with the Dreyer system. *Mr. Pollen is quite right that they have
> already and are now adopting some of his principles to their scheme.* We
> will in the United States have learned a great deal from Mr. Pollen in
> fire control. *I do not believe that any one quite fully appreciated the great
> value of rate of change of bearing.* My previous conception of it, which I
> have had for the past five years [was] as the use of the bearing element
> [i.e., deflection], but not as a rate of change of bearing. We virtually did
> that in the use of the rate of change projectors [the US equivalent of the
> Dumaresq],—but we had nothing which could or might be used when
> firing at a target obscured from the firing ship. The integrated rate of
> change of bearing is in my estimation one of the most potent factors in
> the whole fire control problem. [emphasis added][128]

Indeed it was—but the US Navy had not understood it until Pollen and
Royal Navy officers unhappy with the Dreyer system had explained it to
them. This failure of understanding, which paralleled Dreyer's, helps explain why Pollen and Isherwood may be said, in some sense, to have invented bearing rate.[129]

Van Auken explicitly linked the Navy's intellectual indebtedness to Pollen and Isherwood to financial remuneration. Conceding that Ford's clock
did not offer "as good a scheme of predicted bearing" as Pollen's, he wrote,
"I think, however, we may be able to modify the Ford instrument a little bit
and embo[d]y the best features of the Pollen clock. The government will
have to pay for this, of course after the war."[130] Here was the responsible official acknowledging, in writing, his intention for Ford to incorporate part
of Pollen's design and thus the need to compensate Pollen. This acknowledgment amounted to a reversal of Earle's announcement to Pollen that
the Bureau did not believe it owed him any money. But no one notified
Pollen of the change—and he was never paid.

No surprise. In the next breath after admitting that the Navy morally
owed the Englishmen money, Van Auken wrote, "I shall take good pains

however that neither Isherwood nor Pollen ever get to feel that they are in any way responsible for the invention of the Ford clock."[131] He kept up the effort when he wrote a history of US naval ordnance development in the late 1930s, remarking that "[t]he noted inventors, Elmer A. Sperry and Hannibal C. Ford, aided the Bureau's officers in the [sic] fire control development," and omitting any mention of Pollen and Isherwood.[132] The US Navy also obscured its dependence on Pollen and Isherwood through continuity in the Mark numbers assigned to the Ford rangekeeper. Instead of introducing a new Mark (or even Modification) number when it incorporated Pollen's automatic-bearing feature—a major change by any standard—the Ford rangekeeper remained the Mark I.[133]

∴

The degree to which Isherwood and Pollen were in fact responsible for ostensibly all-American inventions comes through in an analysis of the theory underlying the Ford rangekeeper produced in 1918. It expressed in mathematical terms the same indebtedness to Pollen's and Isherwood's use of bearing rate that Van Auken had expressed. The analysis was written by Lieutenant (junior grade) H. M. Terrill, whose low rank does not convey the qualifications he brought to the task. He was a Columbia University mathematician and physicist whom the Navy commissioned during World War I. Terrill explained how the relative movement of two ships could be represented as a vector and its components solved for range rate and deflection—that is, the theory underlying the Dumaresq. Then, in terms almost exactly matching the disclosure in Pollen's and Isherwood's basic US patent on the Argo IV clock (as well as Swinburne's analysis discussed in chapter 3), Terrill wrote:

It may be remarked that

Rate = distance changed in 1 unit of time = dR[ange] / dT[ime]
Arbitrary Deflection = bearing changed in 1 unit of time = dB[earing] / dT

Ordinary deflection as given in knots may be written RdB / dT.
Loosely, we may speak of [Range] Rate and Deflection as dR and RdB, it being understood that the differentiation is performed with respect to the [t]ime.[134]

Recall Isherwood's insistence, quoted in chapter 1, that he and Pollen had "invented" the term RdB. The mathematics of bearing rate was theoretically available to everyone, in much the same way that the science of the atom was theoretically available to everyone—but not everyone discovered the former, just as not everyone discovered the latter. In Ford's case, knowledge from Pollen and Isherwood made possible his discovery of bearing rate and its importance.

Ford also plagiarized the crown jewel of the Argo clock: the slipless variable-speed drive designed by Isherwood. The absence of evidence, particularly of the Ford Instrument and Argo corporate archives, makes it impossible to explain precisely how the plagiarism occurred. But given how many other aspects of the Argo clock Ford plagiarized, and given the speed with which he overcame the problem of slippage that had taken Isherwood years to overcome, plagiarism must have played a role. This is not to deny Ford's engineering skill, nor that the drives contained numerous differences in mechanical detail. For instance, Ford superimposed a second ball on top of the first and interposed a carriage between the two. But both drives contained a ball (or balls) held by a spring in contact with a spinning disc and with an output shaft mounted on a frame. From there, Ford essentially inverted Isherwood's design: whereas Isherwood's frame moved with the ball, Ford held his frame stationary and had the carriage interposed between the balls move with them. The second ball functioned as a large ball bearing—or at least that was the initial judgment of the patent examiner who evaluated his application.[135] Moreover, Ford adopted and adapted Isherwood's solution to a defect in Kelvin's original design, discussed in chapter 2 above, which was to convert the flat surfaces in contact with the ball(s) into cylindrical ones.[136] Like Isherwood's, Ford's drive did not resort to a servomechanism. Ford's drive was thus an example of a hybrid technology, one that combined elements of Isherwood's original with his own contributions. It was not that Ford's design involved no creativity or innovation; it was that his creativity and innovation rested squarely on the foundation of Isherwood's. In 1919, a board of US naval officers on USS *Louisiana* conducting competitive trials between Ford's system and the trial set of Pollen instruments ordered two years earlier observed, "[t]he principle of mechanical integration and operation of the Pollen range keeper is very similar to that of the Ford"—indeed, but vice versa.[137]

∵

Along with Pollen's clock, the US Navy also plagiarized his rangefinder mounting.[138] But it was the theft of the predicted-bearing feature for the clock that led the Ford Instrument Company to issue the first of two requests for the Navy Department to indemnify it against infringement of Pollen's patents. Knowing what he had done, Ford was afraid that he was liable and wanted to protect himself by shifting responsibility for the plagiarism onto the Bureau. Arguing that his company had added the predicted-bearing feature only at the Bureau's demand, Ford asked the Bureau to assure him that the government would be "entirely responsible" for the payment of any royalties or litigation costs arising from his incorporation of this feature.[139]

Ford's request for indemnification waded into churning legal waters concerning liability for patent infringement on government contracts. At least since the Supreme Court's ruling in the 1878 *McKeever's Case*, patents had been more or less recognized as a form of private property requiring the government to compensate patent-owners for unauthorized use in accordance with the Takings Clause of the Fifth Amendment.[140] In 1910, Congress effectively endorsed this recognition by passing a law, subsequently known as the Act of 1910, that extended the jurisdiction of the Court of Claims—a court established a half century earlier with a waiver of sovereign immunity to hear certain types of claims against the US government—to include claims for patent infringement (in all but name).[141] In the 1912 ruling *Crozier v. Krupp Aktiengesellschaft*, the Supreme Court held that the Act of 1910 brought government takings of intellectual property within the framework of eminent domain.[142] This ruling was widely interpreted to mean that eminent domain covered contractors doing government work, such that aggrieved patent-owners should sue the government in the Court of Claims, not contractors in district court, for alleged infringement.[143] However, in the 1918 ruling *Cramp & Sons Ship & Engine Building Co. v. International Curtis Marine Turbine Co.*, the Supreme Court rejected that interpretation.[144] Its decision opened up contractors to ruinous infringement suits and unsurprisingly led them to feel "a sudden reluctance" to undertake vital wartime work for the government. Importuned by the Navy, Congress hastily passed a new law, known as the Act of 1918, intended to clarify that patent infringement by government contractors amounted to a government taking—with government liability—under eminent domain.[145]

Notably, Ford's initial request for indemnification predated the *Cramp* decision. Earle attempted to punt until after the war. But the *Cramp* decision led Ford to make his second and broader request—filed with similar requests from other contractors in the Secretary of the Navy's office—for the government to indemnify him against infringement of Pollen's patents.[146] It was in response to this second appeal that Assistant Secretary of the Navy Franklin Roosevelt, who had dined with Pollen during his visit to the United States, issued the requested indemnification to Ford.[147]

The addition of the predicted-bearing feature, on top of the slipless infinitely variable drive, completed the Bureau's and Ford Instrument's plagiarism of the Argo clock. Because, in the end, they had plagiarized Pollen so much more completely and competently than Dreyer had, the US Navy, unlike the Royal Navy, could afford to conduct honest trials between the Argo clock and its plagiarized rival, and the plagiarized rival could hold its own. The US Navy's board appointed to test Pollen's clock on USS *Louisiana* judged it superior to Ford's in some respects and inferior in others, making no recommendation either way regarding further purchases.[148] Earle was being truthful when he told Pollen, "[t]he many fine points of the Argo Clock have been admired by a number of officers of our service, but it is not felt that it has, on the whole, advantages over our Ford range keeper."[149] This was because the Americans had successfully milked Pollen and Isherwood dry without paying them anything. As Van Auken put it, "[a]fter a few months use, neither Pollen nor Isherwood can tell us anything about the Pollen system that has not already been found out." He reported ingenuously telling Isherwood "that we wanted to get all the good points of all fire control systems."[150] Indeed.

For all that the US Navy matched the Admiralty's ruthless disregard of Pollen's and Isherwood's interests, the former's determination to get the best compares favorably with the latter's record. The Admiralty's massive conflict of interest where Dreyer was concerned—his superiors' reliance on him as an ostensibly disinterested source of judgment about competing fire-control systems—necessarily meant that it had an agenda other than getting the best fire-control system. Comparatively speaking, the Navy Department had no other competing agenda. It would be a mistake to think of the Admiralty's record on the Dreyer table as evidence of British decline, since, after all, Pollen's system was every bit as much a British achievement as Dreyer's. But the contrast between the Admiralty's procedural corruption and the Navy Department's single-minded determination to get the best possible system does point to British decadence—a certain complacency about remaining at the apex of the global power rankings, while the Americans climbed over anyone to get to the top. In the face of such a challenger, institutional corruption came with a heavy geopolitical price tag. As the next chapter will show, the US Navy was no less ruthless toward British interests when it came to other technology.

CHAPTER 5

Secret Patents and the Pax Britannica

"I am strongly inclined to believe that the highest result can be reached by starting with the British system and following it as closely as possible until the first system has been made and tried. . . . Why shouldn't we start with the principles of design and construction which have been proved by five years of experience in target practice and battle?"
REGINALD GILLMOR, 17 JANUARY 1917

When Europe went to war in 1914, the US Navy felt confident in its gunnery technology. In 1916, President Woodrow Wilson proclaimed his ambition to build "a navy second to none"—meaning equal to the Royal Navy, the backbone of British hegemony, which Wilson intended to challenge.[1] By the end of that year, the US Navy had learned, rather awkwardly, that it was not only behind the Royal Navy but at least a generation behind. To fulfill Wilson's ambition, it had to close a large gap. The plagiarism of Pollen's and Isherwood's clock was an important step in that direction, but hardly sufficient. The US Navy needed to acquire further British naval technology and know-how, and it needed to foster a domestic industry capable not only of reproducing British technology but of going beyond it.

The British Admiralty was not keen to play along, perceiving that American acquisition of British naval technology undermined British power relative to the United States. Fortunately for the US Navy, the Admiralty, under Dreyer's influence, which was magnified when he became DNO in 1917, did not appreciate what it had in Pollen's system. But its head was not buried so deep in the sand that it was blind to the glint from other jewels in the Royal Navy's technological crown. These included Percy Scott's director system, to which the British armaments giant Vickers owned the rights, and various inventions made by James Henderson, the Royal Navy's leading gyroscope expert. These the Admiralty guarded closely, permitting the inventors to take out only secret patents, not regular ones, and minimizing the leakage of information as far as possible.

While the Admiralty potentially blocked the US Navy's goals from abroad, there were other complicating factors at home. Having cooperated to pirate Pollen's system, the Bureau of Ordnance, Sperry Gyroscope, and Ford Instrument began to squabble over the division of the booty, and the tensions between them only grew as the prospect of additional booty came into view. Moreover, although the US patent system had facilitated attempts to pirate the Pollen clock, it now complicated the import of additional technology. Unlike Britain, the United States did not have secret patents. Wartime moves in the direction of greater patent secrecy under British tutelage satisfied neither the Admiralty as to secrecy nor Vickers as to property protection. In effect, the United States' inability to import British legal technology blocked its import of British naval technology.

Amazingly, what removed the blockage to this new round of naval-technology transfer were the fruits of an earlier round—namely, Ford Instrument's development of the pirated Argo clock. The Royal Navy's interest in the Ford rangekeeper, which most British naval officers did not recognize as the Argo clock in disguise, gave the Bureau critically needed leverage in its negotiations with the Admiralty over the Vickers director system. In other words, the only "American" naval technology sufficiently ahead of British naval technology to entice the Admiralty was in fact pirated British technology. There could be no better demonstration of both the depth of the US Navy's dependence on foreign technology and the damage to British interests wrought by the Admiralty's selection of the Dreyer tables over the Argo system.

CAPTURING FORD INSTRUMENT AND
PURSUING THE DIRECTOR

In its quest to foster a domestic fire-control industry, the Bureau of Ordnance formed exactly the type of relationship with Ford Instrument that Pollen had sought with the Admiralty. The Bureau paid Ford Instrument for monopoly and secrecy and helped the firm to develop its fire-control system; in return, the firm was forbidden from exercising the normal right of inventors to authorize the Patent Office to issue patents for which they had applied. Recognizing the continuum between mental and material knowledge (or between software and hardware) that Pollen had pushed the Admiralty to acknowledge, the Navy paid Ford Instrument for providing not only knowledge reduced to material form ("apparatus," "plans," "specifications"), but also knowledge ("data and information") not reduced to material form. Moreover, because the Navy understood that multiple types of knowledge could be commercially valuable, it saw that

Ford might use the supply of different kinds of knowledge as grounds for claiming additional compensation, and it protected itself against corporate covetousness by defining the valuable knowledge covered by the contract as comprehensively as possible.[2] In effect, it did with Ford exactly what Edward Harding had advised the Admiralty to do with Pollen in 1906: it made him a "captive contractor."[3] The terms of captivity—monopoly and secrecy, linked together—were precisely those that the Admiralty had tried to break with Pollen in 1913.

Moreover, unlike the Naval Ordnance Department in Britain, which had cast aside Pollen's system in favor of Dreyer's despite substantial support in the fleet for Pollen's, the Bureau of Ordnance was proud of itself for developing a clock plagiarized from Pollen, and it supported Ford despite substantial opposition in the fleet to the Ford rangekeeper. The lead skeptic was Donald C. Bingham, the chief gunnery officer of the Atlantic Fleet.[4] Contrary to the Bureau's efforts to cast itself as a heroic knight of technological progressivism battling the evil dragon of technological conservatism in the fleet, Bingham and other officers in the fleet did not oppose the mechanization of fire control per se.[5] Rather, they worried about whether the poor workmanship of the American-made rangekeeper—an issue not coincidentally within the knight's cognizance rather than the dragon's— would enable it to survive sea service. Multiple observers compared Ford Instrument's workmanship unfavorably with Argo's, including the US naval officers who, having tried the Pollen clock on the USS *Louisiana*, reported that "at the present time they have considerably more confidence in the Pollen than in the Ford."[6] At this stage, moreover, the Ford rangekeeper lacked any plotting element and had not yet fully incorporated Pollen's automatic bearing-generation feature, meaning that it could not operate helm-free in the conditions of target invisibility that officers expected to encounter in combat. Even the Dreyer tables, which Bingham detested, had plots.[7]

While the Bureau worked to improve the Ford rangekeeper, it also sought to acquire additional fire-control technology from the Royal Navy. Top of its wish list was Percy Scott's director system, developed before the war and owned by Vickers, as mentioned in chapter 1. The basic idea behind it was that instead of each gun of a ship directing its own fire, a single "director," located high in the ship to facilitate observation, would operate as a sort of master rangefinder, gun sight, and firing key, serving as a central source of target range and bearing readings and controlling the fire of the individual guns. Whereas the Pollen system sought both to calculate and to transmit data and involved roughly corresponding mechanical- and electrical-engineering challenges, the director system sought mainly to transmit data and thus posed mostly electrical-engineering challenges. Scott, who liked Pollen's system and shared his belief in the need for greater electromechanization, hypothesized that centralized control would improve firing accuracy. Unlike Pollen, he sold the rights to his invention to a large firm, Vickers, rather than trying to sell directly to the Admiralty.[8]

The US Navy saw value in the idea of director firing but hoped to do without paying for the Scott-Vickers system. Prior to the war, it had passed on an offer from Vickers and instead contracted with Sperry Gyroscope to build its own director system, which was tried on the USS *Delaware* in 1913.[9] In March 1914, the chief of the Bureau of Ordnance, Joseph Strauss, announced his intention to install Sperry's director system on all battleships.[10] Reflection on the British experience in the Battles of the Falkland Islands (December 1914) and Jutland (May 1916) further convinced the US Navy of the importance of director firing and likely spurred Sperry Gyroscope to undertake a significant redesign of its version so that it would more closely resemble the Scott-Vickers system.[11]

Hitherto, unlike the British system, Sperry's director generated corrections only for gun-laying in elevation (i.e., for range), not for training in azimuth (i.e., for deflection), and it did not operate on the "follow-the-pointer" principle. "Follow-the-pointer" was a way of displaying data that gunners found intuitive. In follow-the-pointer displays, one pointer on a dial showed the actual elevation and/or training of a gun, while another pointer showed what the elevation and/or training should be according to predicted data. The gunner's job was simply to "follow the pointer"—that is, to keep the pointer showing the actual setting of his gun married to the pointer showing what the setting should be.[12] An analysis produced by the Bureau of Ordnance in 1918 found that gunners processed information more quickly and reliably from follow-the-pointer displays than from other kinds, such as reading numbers from dials.[13]

Prior to US entry into the war, US naval officers overestimated the state of US director technology compared with Britain's, just as they initially had overrated Ford's not-yet-fully-plagiarized system relative to Pollen's. According to Reginald Gillmor, the Sperry Gyroscope employee and US naval officer whom we encountered in chapter 4, "the officers in the American Navy have no idea of the tremendous amount of fire control development work that has been done in other Navies."[14] Gillmor did not think much of even his own firm's product line. "Taking a broad aspect of this matter without consideration to any particular technical details, I am strongly inclined to believe that the highest result can be reached by starting with the British system and following it as closely as possible until the first system has been made and tried," Gillmor wrote. "Why shouldn't we start with the principles of design and construction which have been proved by five years of experience in target practice and battle?"[15] This was not what Sperry wanted to hear.[16] Seriously underestimating Vickers's achievement (and overestimating his own), he judged his system to be at most one generation behind the Vickers system, when in fact it was more like two generations behind. He wrote "omit" next to Gillmor's recommendation, which was duly excluded from the version of Gillmor's letter that Sperry forwarded to the Bureau of Ordnance.[17]

So long as the United States remained out of the war, British secrecy helped Sperry to evade any reckoning over the limitations of his system. The Royal Navy kept director development so secret that, in Gillmor's words, "in five years no word of it has leaked out."[18] His own description of it to Sperry was based on crumbs of information and "necessarily lacking in detail."[19] The US naval attaché submitted a couple of reports on the Vickers system, but British secrecy made reliable data hard to come by.[20] Thus the US Navy was not in a strong position to resist Sperry's manipulation of the truth.

US entry into the war in April 1917 changed this. As the Royal Navy dropped the veil of secrecy, the US Navy was suddenly able to witness British technology close-up. It immediately saw that Sperry's system was much inferior and sprang into action. In May 1917, Ralph Earle, the chief of the Bureau of Ordnance, asked the Secretary of the Navy to open negotiations with Vickers about purchasing its director system for the control of auxiliary guns.[21] Two months later, the Bureau asked Ford Instrument to develop its own director system in competition with Vickers and Sperry Gyroscope.[22] The month after that, in August 1917, the Bureau of Ordnance initiated negotiations with Vickers to purchase its director system for controlling the main battery.[23]

By this point, it had become clear to British as well as American observers that the US Navy-Sperry Gyroscope director system lagged far behind Britain's. "The Director has not been developed to anything like the same extent as with us and until quite recently its importance had not really been fully realized," Richard Down, a British naval officer, reported to the Admiralty after an inspection tour of the US Navy."[24] A report by a US naval officer, G. W. S. Castle, who inspected the British Grand Fleet, emphasized in all-caps, "THE VICKERS' 'FOLLOW-THE-POINTER' SYSTEM FOR RANGE ELEVATION AND TRAIN IS THE ESSENTIAL THAT MAKES THEIR FIRE CONTROL SYSTEM BETTER THAN OURS."[25] Earle himself admitted that "we are certainly behind the English in many respects as to fire control."[26] The quickest way to make up the gap was to acquire British technology.

SUPERPOWER STATUS AND PATENT SECRECY

The British were not so keen to help. From their perspective, the United States was looking to profit from British blood, labor, and expenditures. "They know us to be fools and suspect us of being crooks," Powers Symington, the US naval attaché in London, reported.

> They have hoped against hope all this time that we would come in with them, but they have been disappointed too often and too long. They do not believe anything that our Government says. They suspect that even if we went to war, we would very shortly change our minds and make peace, and if we did not make peace, we do not know what war means, and would not know how to conduct it.[27]

British suspicions were not unfounded. Within the international political economy, the United States was looking to grow its power at Britain's expense. At an interdepartmental conference dealing with the possibility of reciprocal exchange of information with Britain's allies, officials dryly noted, "We have been 3 years at war, and numerous inventions of all kinds had naturally been brought to us (not necessarily made by Englishmen) which the latecomers such as USA would obtain gratis."[28] The US authorities want "officers sent over occasionally who are conversant with technical details and Grand Fleet procedure, with a view to keeping them in touch with our methods," Admiral John Jellicoe, the First Sea Lord, cynically agreed, "but their idea is not so much that we should learn from them as that they should learn from us."[29]

Of course, the British had *some* incentive to share *some* scientific and technological knowledge with the Americans: the fastest possible improvement of US naval materiel might help bring the war to an end more quickly. But they, like every other combatant, kept one eye firmly fixed on the postwar world. The two time horizons were in conflict: the optimal strategy for maximizing British chances in wartime was not the optimal strategy for maximizing Britain's relative power in the postwar world. An overwhelmingly one-way flow of scientific and technological knowledge from Britain to an ally—which the United States technically was not, since it insisted on fighting as an "Associated Power" to preserve its independence from suspect Europeans—amounted to helping the recipient compete more effectively against Britain once the war ended without any comparable help in return.[30]

∴

In addition to their concern about the postwar implications of a one-way knowledge flow, the British also worried about the United States' ability to keep sensitive knowledge secret while protecting the intellectual property of British nationals. The United States had no equivalent to British secret patents, which were full-fledged patents withheld from publication. In the United States, patent applications remained effectively secret while they were pending, but this form of patent secrecy did not belong to a national security secrecy regime: rather, it existed to protect inventors' interests. Once patents were granted, US patent law required that they be published. Inventors could prolong the period of pending status, and thus of effective secrecy, up to a point, but if they did not prosecute a patent application by responding to communications from the Patent Office within a statutory time frame, US patent law held their application abandoned.[31] As chapters 8 and 10 will show, inventors could, and did, game the system to keep their applications in pending status for years by delaying their replies to Patent Office communications until the end of the allowable time frame and by repeatedly amending their applications. But these techniques were at best a stopgap measure. Not only did they require inventors willingly to delay full patent protection, but the Patent Office tried to stop them as antithetical to the spirit of the patent laws.[32]

The absence of British-style secret patents in the United States resulted from two somewhat intricate features of the US patent laws.[33] First, US patent law required that patents granted must "be printed and published on their issuance."[34] No exceptions were possible, even on national security grounds. Second, the US patent laws included a system of so-called interferences, which had no analog in the British system. Interferences were conflicts between a new patent application and an existing application or patent, the resolution of which required a determination as to priority of invention. Like the British Patent Office, the US Patent Office was obliged, when it received a new patent application, to search prior applications and patents for evidence of prior invention—but here their obligations diverged. The US system required the Patent Office to notify prior applicants and patentees when it discovered that a new application interfered with theirs, at which point they had the right to see the new interfering application.[35] The British Patent Office had no such obligation. Instead, the British system made prior applicants or patentees responsible for protecting themselves by searching published specifications for repetitions of their claims—but since secret patents were not published, there was no way to discover whether they repeated prior claims.[36] Thus, while British secret patents could remain secret even if a subsequent application interfered with them, the US Patent Office had no way to preserve the secrecy of an application it found to be in interference. Accordingly, unlike Britain, the United States had not found a way to adapt the liberal property norms of the patent system to the pressures of national security—or vice versa—on a permanent peacetime basis.

The prospect and then reality of entry into World War I brought changes, but only on a temporary wartime basis. In July 1916, as an impulse to prepare for war swept the country, Congress amended the US patent laws to move them in the direction of patent secrecy, but not all the way to British-style secret patents.[37] For one thing, the amendment obtained secrecy only by preventing patent applications from issuing as patents, whereas British secret patents were issued patents. For another thing, the provision required the US government to make the application its property.[38] The US Department of Justice interpreted the property requirement to exclude a mere license and instead to mandate assignment of the full title to the invention.[39]

US entry into the war brought still more significant changes to the patent system but no commitment to preserve them on a permanent peacetime basis. These changes were part of a broader expansion of the government's ability to regulate knowledge.[40] The month after the US declaration of war, the Commissioner of Patents formed a committee of his examiners to ascertain which inventions in Patent Office records "should be called to the attention of the War or Navy Departments."[41] No longer would the fighting departments have to do their own digging: the Patent Office would undertake to act in the national interest, thereby becoming an agent of the national security state rather than of inventors. In effect, a regime of national security patent secrecy, intended to protect the interests of the state, was replacing the normal regime of patent secrecy, which was intended to protect the interests of inventors while their applications were pending. In June 1917—four days after passage of the Espionage Act, which enlarged the government's power to control information in the name of national security, but four months before receiving formal statutory authority to do so— the Patent Office amended its *Rules of Practice* to permit the Commissioner to suspend action on a patent application when he believed that granting a patent might "be detrimental to the public safety or defense or might assist the enemy or endanger the successful prosecution of the war."[42]

The changes continued. In October 1917, Congress passed two major knowledge-regulating laws on the same day: first, "An Act to prevent the publication of inventions," and second, the better-known Trading with the Enemy Act (Section 10 of which related to intellectual property).[43] A week later, President Wilson, exercising authority conferred on him by the latter act, issued an executive order vesting in the Federal Trade Commission the power to order that any invention it adjudged potentially dangerous to national security "be kept secret and the grant of letters patent withheld until the end of the war."[44] Unlike the July 1916 law, this executive order provided a means for the government to keep patent applications pending and thus secret without acquiring ownership—but still only until the end of the war. In February 1918, the Patent Office amended its *Rules of Practice* to permit army and navy officers, not just patent examiners and parties to interferences, to see pending applications.[45] The amendment marked a further penetration of the normal patent secrecy regime by national security secrecy. Compared with the state of play before the war, these were large and significant changes.

But they did not much impress the British, who had been doing secret patents for over half a century. As the Americans played catch-up, the British worried that they were amateurs when it came to plugging gaps through which knowledge might leak from them to their enemies. What was the procedure in the United States, the British asked in July 1917, for keeping patents secret?[46] The British Embassy politely renewed its inquiry a few months later, passing along evidence that a US firm—in wartime—was attempting to take out patents on its military invention in enemy Germany and Austria as well as the ostensibly neutral Netherlands, through which considerable property originating in Allied countries passed to enemy belligerents.[47] (The behavior of the US firm too might have been an instance of trans-Atlantic knowledge flow, since many British firms did a scandalously large trade with Britain's enemies, often via neutral countries.)[48] The State Department and the Patent Office promptly lost track of this second inquiry for a year.[49] Wisely, the British had not put all their eggs in one basket. Their Comptroller-General developed a direct correspondence with his American counterpart, who managed to keep track of his letters and played the role of eager pupil, absorbing the legal techniques being shared.[50]

A SIX-WAY TANGO

The idiosyncrasies of the US patent system, from the British perspective, and the temporary character of the wartime provision for secret patents complicated the US Navy's acquisition of the Vickers director system. Like most of Pollen's patents on his fire-control system, Vickers's British patents on its director system were secret patents. This meant that communication of its system to the US Navy required Admiralty approval. It also involved commercial risk, because the firm held only a few relevant US patents and had no contract with the US Navy.[51] Earle, the chief of the Bureau of Ordnance, promised that the US Navy "does not intend in any way to jeopardize the interests of the Vickers Company because of their prompt action in supplying" drawings of the director system—a statement of intent soon forgotten by the Bureau, as chapter 8 shows.[52] He asked the Admiralty to permit Vickers to take out US patents and to assist the firm in preparing the applications. If the Admiralty granted Vickers permission to apply for US patents, Earle promised, the Bureau would take "every precaution to maintain the secrecy of these inventions."[53] What these precautions would or could be, Earle did not specify.

While the Bureau worked to acquire the Vickers system, Ford Instrument stole a march on the Bureau. Rather than start from scratch in building a new director system to compete with Sperry Gyroscope's, Ford Instrument, operating on the same logic as the Bureau, decided to start with British technology. Gillmor had urged this logic on Sperry, of course, but Sperry's complacency and Ford's superior technical understanding of Vickers's accomplishment gave him the quicker draw. In late 1917, Ford Instrument negotiated a license deal with Vickers giving it the exclusive US rights to Vickers's follow-the-pointer gear. More far-reachingly, the two firms also signed a joint development agreement.[54] This was a coup for Ford Instrument. In effect, Vickers was identifying it, rather than Sperry Gyroscope, as the leading US fire-control firm. What Pollen had supplied to Ford Instrument in the way of rangekeeper technology, Vickers would now supply in the way of director technology. The key difference, of course, was that Ford Instrument paid Vickers rather than stealing from it.

In a twist, the deal with Vickers also gave Ford Instrument sight of Pollen's work through a back door. Vickers had a long-standing relationship with Thomas Cooke & Sons, the optical firm acquired by Pollen in 1910 to manufacture Argo's system. In 1915, Vickers bought Pollen's controlling shares in Cooke's.[55] In the field of *anti-aircraft*—as distinct from *surface*— fire control, the connection with Vickers enabled Ford Instrument to benefit indirectly from Pollen's work. This was because Vickers's head of anti-aircraft fire control was none other than Isherwood's assistant at Argo before the war, Percy Gray.[56] In due course, Vickers would follow the lead of so many others, both American and British, and airbrush the inconvenient Pollen out of its history of anti-aircraft fire control.[57]

In the field of *surface* naval fire control, access to Pollen's work via the Vickers connection probably did not make much difference to Ford Instrument's plagiarism of the Argo clock, but it did help the plagiarists with their own task of airbrushing. By robbing Pollen of further development funds, Ford's plagiarism in the United States and Dreyer's plagiarism in Britain prevented Pollen from adapting his system to wartime experience while enabling them to do so. Even with this advantage, as we will see in chapter 6, Dreyer never managed to leapfrog Pollen. But Ford did, and his success had the effect of camouflaging Pollen's contribution. By the early 1920s, Ford's system had developed sufficiently that a US naval officer, comparing it with an Argo system recently sold by Vickers to the Spanish navy, judged that the Ford rangekeeper was "much superior" to the Argo clock and that "[t]here are not enough points of similarity to warrant any belief that there has been any interchange of ideas."[58] These comments reveal how the US Navy was rewriting the past in real time. By making a straight technical comparison between the two systems without any inquiry into their development, Americans could transform a story about American plagiarism of British technology into a story about American ingenuity.

Ford Instrument followed up the deal with Vickers by making a small but important advance over Sperry Gyroscope's director system, thereby bringing itself into deeper cooperation and conflict with the Bureau of Ordnance. The technical details are unimportant; suffice it to say that the improvement was known as the directorscope-converter, used a follow-the-pointer display, and was jointly developed by Ford Instrument and the Bureau.[59] Taking credit, the Bureau demanded that it hold all patent rights and have exclusive use of the directorscope-converter and follow-the-pointer system "as designed and as may be developed by the Ford Instrument Company." Ignorant of Ford Instrument's agreement with Vickers, the Bureau further asserted, based on its own discussions with Vickers's American agent, that it held "all patent rights to Vickers' director firing follow-the-pointer system in the United States."[60]

While the Bureau and Ford Instrument drifted toward a collision over the rights to Vickers's US follow-the-pointer patents and the directorscope-converter—if the narrative here seems convoluted, imagine what fun it was to piece together from the original documents—a related piece of British director technology entered the picture. The Scott-Vickers system, for all its strengths, had certain limitations in action: it required that the target be visible, and its sights were not gyro-stabilized, with the result that its operators struggled to keep the target in their telescopes' field of vision as their own ship rolled, pitched, and yawed. James Henderson, the Royal Navy's leading gyroscope expert and a prolific inventor, was attacking these limitations on multiple fronts. Like Pollen and Isherwood, Henderson thought systematically, not piecemeal. His interest was what he called the "internal" side of fire control, whereas theirs was mainly the "external" side of fire control. That is, much as they sought to render firing at sea equivalent to firing on land by canceling the effects of relative motion between two ships, so Henderson sought to cancel the effects of the motion of one's own ship (a process they had started by using gyroscopes to counteract yaw).[61] His first major invention, known as the Henderson Firing Gear, used gyroscopes to provide a stable datum line in azimuth and elevation and to help the operator of the director's training telescope keep the target in his field of vision; this entered service in 1916 and was soon followed by other inventions.[62] The Royal Navy kept the Henderson Firing Gear very secret. Again, Gillmor caught wind of it but obtained few details.[63]

As with the Vickers director, US entry into the war in 1917 suddenly enabled the US Navy to acquire far greater knowledge of the Henderson Firing Gear, along with closely associated developments. In February 1918, Garrett Schuyler, now the US naval attaché in London, submitted a detailed report. He wrote:

> I have included in the last part of the report some remarks on the subject of the Henderson firing gear and ultimate development which they are striving for in the way of gyro elevating and gyro training, so that future naval engagement[s] may be fought by forces entirely enveloped in smoke screens [i.e., with targets invisible] but with only kite balloons observing. Henderson's sight was designed as the first half of the system which will permit this. The director train by gyro angle is being worked out by Elliott Brothers [manufacturers of the Dreyer Table]. There are very few people, even in the Admiralty, who realise just what it is all leading to and appreciate that the Henderson gear in itself would scarcely be interesting whereas in this connection it is very interesting. I believe that the Sperry Company has been kept in the dark on this. At any rate Gillmor never mentioned it to me, as I believe he would have if the Admiralty had let his Company in on it. . . . I do not hesitate to say that I believe that this development will be the next big thing in naval gunnery and that it is very important for the Bureau to realise it and push it along.[64]

Schuyler was describing British attempts to gyro-stabilize their director system in all possible ways, including not only the Henderson Firing Gear but also a related invention known as Gyro Director Training (mentioned in chapter 4 and on which more in chapter 6). Earle promptly submitted a grab-bag request for all British technology related to the director. The Bureau wanted not only "detailed drawings [of the] Henderson gear" but also "any other drawings of Elliott and Company and the Admiralty on director firing for battleships[,] cruisers and destroyers." With a certain whiff of entitlement, he added that it was "important to have full information here to assist in solution [of] director firing problems"—which the Americans could not solve themselves.[65] To Henderson's great future annoyance, the Admiralty authorized the US Navy to see his invention.[66]

∴

Direct US Navy access to the Henderson Firing Gear and other British director technology boded ill for Sperry Gyroscope, and it was not the firm's only problem. Once the US leader in fire-control technology, with exceptional access to British developments via Gillmor, Sperry had twice lost out to Ford on exploiting key British inventions—first the piracy of Pollen's rangekeeper, and then the purchase of the Vickers director. Now the already proven Henderson Firing Gear posed a threat to Sperry Gyroscope's only initiative to gyro-stabilize the director, its "stable zenith" project, which had yet to produce a successful design.[67] To make matters worse, officers in the fleet complained ever more loudly about the quality of Sperry instruments.[68] At the Bureau of Ordnance, Wilbur Van Auken replaced the friendly Frank Martin as head of the fire-control section.[69] By late 1917, the firm's relationship with the US Navy was in trouble. Van Auken pressed Sperry to solve the firm's problems.[70] Wanting to have things both ways, the Bureau hoped that the firm would simultaneously provide competition to and cooperate with Ford Instrument. Gillmor, whom Sperry had recalled from London to fix the firm's management troubles, was consumed by the task and not keen to hurry along development work or collaborate with a rival.[71] But he relented as the firm's financial distress grew, even offering, in June 1918, to put Sperry Gyroscope at the Bureau's behest.[72] This was essentially the role that Gillmor had urged Sperry to play back in 1916, but in the two long years since, Ford Instrument had taken over the part. Now Sperry Gyroscope was left trying to win back the role from its former understudy.

Yet Ford Instrument's relationship with the Bureau had its own tensions. The Bureau was unhappy to learn of Ford Instrument's deal with Vickers. Earle fired off a letter to Vickers accusing it of violating its promise to grant the Bureau the exclusive US rights to its director system.[73] Shortly thereafter, he received a stiff reply from Ford Instrument to his earlier letter asserting the Bureau's rights to the jointly developed directorscope-converter and to Vickers's follow-the-pointer gear. While Ford acknowledged the Bureau's assistance in initiating and advising on the directorscope-converter, he contended that all patent rights belonged to his firm. "The entire system, after preliminery [sic] conferences upon the same, was designed and developed by Mr. Ford," Ford wrote of himself in the third person. He also rejected the Bureau's claim to hold the exclusive US rights to Vickers's follow-the-pointer system, instead insisting that *his* firm held the US exclusive rights and had been planning to make arrangements with Vickers to sell its improvements thereto abroad.[74] A week later, as if to underscore this message, the Bureau's inspector at Ford Instrument reported that Argentine naval officers were visiting the firm and requesting authority to make a "comprehensive study of fire control instruments in production."[75]

In other words, the Bureau's most important fire-control contractor was refusing to play nicely. Like his digital-computing descendants in Silicon Valley, Ford relied heavily on public assistance to get off the ground and then bristled at government regulation. The Bureau had helped facilitate the original transfer of knowledge from Britain (i.e., from Pollen) that enabled Ford Instrument to take off so rapidly with its first major product, the Ford clock. Now Ford could get the knowledge he needed directly from Britain (i.e., from Vickers) to make a second rapid improvement to the director, and he wanted to be able to transfer knowledge back across national borders in the other direction for profit. As the public, security-oriented foundation of his firm receded into the background, and with it his debt to the government, Ford wanted the freedom to behave like a private, profit-oriented actor.

The Bureau resisted any loosening of the leash. By containing Ford's strategically significant technology within the domestic political economy, so to speak, the Bureau sought to maintain the US position within the international political economy. Much as the British Admiralty had seen its (purported) contributions to Pollen's system as grounds for preventing him from exporting his system, so the Bureau saw its (purported) contributions to the development of the directorscope-converter as a method of exerting control. Disputing Ford's account, the Bureau wrote:

> The Bureau having submitted the broad ideas and problem to be solved, together with many suggestions helpful to the solving of the problem, believes that the system *could have been* developed entirely within the Department, had the Bureau a man available for this type of work at the time. Unfortunately, however, the Bureau did not have an available man, and, in order to save time, collaborated with Mr. Ford to construct and design the device in question, as Mr. Ford is considered one of the best fire control and designing engineers. This is no attempt to disparage the fine work done by Mr. Ford in this connection, but it is merely intended to state the Bureau's position in view of the work done by the Bureau and the fact that Mr. Ford was permitted to take part in various Gunnery Conferences where representatives of the fleet met in Commander Van Auken's office. Under these circumstances, it is believed that the Ford

Instrument Company is not entitled to full and unrestricted patent rights in this system, in fact, there is a serious question whether the matter was not one of joint inventorship. [emphasis added]

Accordingly, the Bureau asserted "moral and legal rights in and to the inventions," demanded "the unrestricted rights of use and manufacture of this system," and commanded that Ford Instrument not disclose the system "to outside parties, or representatives of foreign governments, without the express and written consent of this Bureau." Note the similarities here with Dreyer's and the Admiralty's elevated sense of naval officers' expertise: the Bureau *could have* done the work *if only* it had the time, because its knowledge was hierarchically superior to civilian knowledge, and any old engineer could have done the comparatively simple job of implementing the Bureau's brilliant ideas. In this case, to be fair, it is possible that Bureau officers had made more significant contributions than had Dreyer. As for Ford's claim to the exclusive US rights to Vickers's follow-the-pointer system, the Bureau simply added that "[t]here is some difference of opinion as to the correctness of this statement."[76]

While tensions over the rights to the director-converter and the Vickers director system strained the relationship between the Bureau and Ford Instrument, action by the British Admiralty confounded the Bureau's ongoing negotiations with Vickers. In August 1918, the Admiralty denied the Bureau's request that it help Vickers file for US patents on the firm's director system, and it also denied permission for Vickers to file a US patent application corresponding to the firm's secret British master patent on the director. From the Admiralty's perspective, Vickers was trying to involve it in the firm's private business relations, while the Bureau was trying to use it in the Bureau's interests. The Admiralty had no desire to be caught in the middle. While it did not object to the United States making confidential use of the director during the war, it insisted that the US Navy and Vickers work out terms between themselves.[77]

As the Admiralty moved to extract itself from negotiations between the Bureau and Vickers, Ford and Bureau officials met in an attempt to iron out their differences over the rights to the director-converter and to the Vickers director, especially the follow-the-pointer system. The meeting produced a Solomonic agreement to split the US rights to the Vickers system.[78] The Bureau and Ford Instrument also agreed that the Bureau would have the right to contract with other firms for the director-converter, including follow-the-pointer transmission, in return for equitable compensation to Ford Instrument. In addition, the firm undertook not to disclose the system to outsiders or foreigners without the Bureau's consent (so, no more unauthorized visits from Argentine naval officers). In recognition of both parties' contributions to the director-converter, it was to be known as either the "Van Auken-Ford" or "Bureau of Ordnance-Ford" Director Firing System.[79]

Now it was Vickers's turn to assert its interests. The Bureau, having been stymied in its efforts to cut a deal with the Admiralty over the Vickers director, retreated to its fallback position: a bilateral license agreement with Vickers. A license agreement would acknowledge the firm's right to its intellectual property and to compensation for the use thereof, while enabling the US Navy to acquire the director system—but it would not afford Vickers the protection of US patents. Nevertheless, to protect itself, the Bureau asked the firm to indemnify it against patent infringement suits by third parties (such as Ford Instrument and Sperry Gyroscope, which were working on director technology at the Bureau's own instigation).[80] Unsurprisingly, Vickers balked at the suggestion without adequate patent protection in the United States.[81]

As the negotiations between the Bureau and Vickers continued—and as if matters were not already complicated enough—a further complication arrived on the scene in the form of James Henderson. In the midst of a bitter and protracted fight with the Admiralty over control of and compensation for his inventions, the inventor was not at all pleased to learn that the Admiralty had unilaterally offered the Henderson Firing Gear to the US Navy without his consent, thereby lowering the value of its permission to let him apply for foreign patents on the gear.[82] "The Admiralty gave me to understand that I had to make my own commercial agreement with you, and to submit it to them," Henderson informed William Sims, commander of US naval forces in Europe, "but, by supplying you with one of my instruments directly, they have unwittingly deprived me of the power of coming to terms with you before the trials, by making you independent of me in so far as your trials are concerned." A canny operator, he took a firm Scottish line. "My invention is not untried," he reminded Sims. "It has been subjected to the most crucial tests that the Admiralty could devise, and passed through them all and was finally adopted." He insisted on being present at any US trials—and "I submit that you ought to pay my expenses."[83] When the Navy declined to do so, Henderson broke off communication while he considered his options.[84]

Despite these road-bumps, Vickers, Ford Instrument, and the Bureau managed to settle among themselves the vexing matter of the US rights to the Vickers system. They agreed that the Bureau had the right, without any payment of royalty to Ford Instrument, to manufacture or have manufactured the Vickers system during the war and for thirty days after the conclusion of peace between the United States and Germany (which did not occur until March 1921, the ceasefire of November 1918 being only an armistice); Ford Instrument had the right to use Vickers's follow-the-pointer gear during the war, and the Bureau was obliged to place any orders for the Vickers system with Ford Instrument after the war. The parties further agreed to settle the question of compensation to Vickers via bilateral contracts.[85] The Bureau and the firms chose to accept the trilateral agreement, signed in February 1919, "as the best possible solution of the entire situation for all concerned."[86] Neither the Bureau nor Ford Instrument got everything it wanted, but each got enough to make any divorce between them look painful.

At this juncture, early in 1919, the absence of British-style secret patents in the United States became a sticking point. Beseeched by the Bureau, the Admiralty was now willing to agree to let Vickers apply for US patents on its director system—but only on the condition that the United States could guarantee to keep the patents secret for three years or longer.[87] Explaining to the British Comptroller-General of Patents how the laws governing patent interferences rendered British-style secret patents impossible, the US Commissioner of Patents confided that "[w]e have therefore been considerably perplexed as to the best method of keeping secret such inventions as should not be disclosed to the enemy, and while we have solved it in a way, it is quite awkward."[88] That awkwardness revealed itself when Claude C. Bloch, a Bureau of Ordnance officer (and future Bureau chief), interviewed the Commissioner over how to keep secret Vickers's US director patent applications. "The Commissioner stated that he had no provision of law whereby he could grant the request of the Bureau for a definite statement to the withholding of this application from publication," Bloch reported to Vickers's US patent attorney, "but added that he believed it was a matter easily within the control of the attorney."[89] He meant that Vickers's attorneys could deliberately keep the application pending—and thus effectively secret—so long they did not contest any interference declared by the Patent Office or initiate any infringement lawsuits. In other words, Bloch was proposing that a large corporation act against its commercial interests. "As the Vickers Company undoubtedly want to protect the Admiralty in the secrecy of these patents," Bloch reasoned rather hopefully, "the Admiralty can feel assured that the patents will be kept secret for at least five years."[90]

The Admiralty did not feel assured. Bloch had omitted key details, which emerged when the British Embassy took the matter up with the State Department. "[I]t would be only under the condition of ownership by the Government that the invention could be kept secret," Acting Secretary of the Navy Franklin Roosevelt explained, "and even then only under most favorable circumstances"—namely, that no interference was declared. If one was, the Commissioner of Patents could not legally refuse to reveal Vickers's application to the contending applicant, "and there would be no restriction as to secrecy on the part of either applicant." Roosevelt added somewhat desperately, "The foregoing takes no cognizance of what might be accomplished by means of compensation or other means for quieting a later applicant."[91] Thus, the best the US government could offer was the hope of bribing third parties to maintain secrecy.[92]

BOOMERANG AND BREAKTHROUGH

The solution to this impasse came in the most ironic way possible. In late 1917, the US Navy had furnished full information about the Ford range-keeper to the Royal Navy, and in the spring of 1918, a US squadron in European waters loaned a Ford rangekeeper to HMS *Cardiff*.[93] This was not an act of generosity but a Trojan horse. For the US Navy, this rare reversal of the overwhelmingly one-way flow of technology from Britain—a reversal that was really the return leg of a boomerang, since the Ford rangekeeper was plagiarized from Pollen in an earlier transfer of technology from Britain—presented an opportunity to acquire still more knowledge from the Royal Navy. Garrett Schuyler, the naval attaché in London, asked the Admiralty to share its criticisms of the Ford rangekeeper, because it was "a matter of interest to know their views, and it would have been unwise to have neglected this opportunity of learning them."[94]

Schuyler's bait hooked a big fish. He did not identify the author of the British criticisms he quoted in his report, but they bear the unmistakable imprint of Frederick Dreyer, who was then serving as the Director of Naval Ordnance. The British critic wrote of the Ford rangekeeper:

> The instruments are very ingenious and compact and if supplied with the correct data will, if mechanically efficient[,] perform all that is claimed for them. It is, however, considered that too many functions are combined in one instrument. This results in either a large number of operators crowding round the instrument and mutually confusing one another or in putting too much strain on one operator. Experience has shown the desirability of giving each individual in a fire control system as little as possible to do, especially as unskilled men have frequently to be trained to perform important functions in the operation of fire control instruments.[95]

Multiplying the number of operators in order to reduce skill requirements, as we saw in chapter 2, was Dreyer's modus operandi. For similar reasons,

Dreyer also took aim at a distinctive feature of the Ford rangekeeper—one possible only in a derivative of the Argo clock: the use of a cross-wire display to indicate inconsistencies between the predicted ranges and bearings generated by the clock and observed data on ranges and bearings, so that the settings on enemy course and speed could be adjusted until the predicted and observed data converged.[96] "The vertical and horizontal wires to indicate errors in range and bearing rates are not considered of very great practical value," Dreyer sniffed, "as our experience has shown that it is essential to have the range finder range and gyro bearings of the target plotted on two diagrams *to enable the operator to use his judgment* [emphasis added] successfully in correcting the enemy's course and speed."[97] This was a defense of Dreyer's trademark range and bearing plots, and of his system's reliance on human intervention. Schuyler's gloss on Dreyer's comments was perceptive (if ungrammatical): "Summing up, we may say that the British criticism of the Mark I Ford range keeper is that the operations which need to be done are done by many individuals in the British system the very ingenuity of the Ford range keeper in combining everything into a single instrument has a disadvantage."[98]

Other British naval officers disagreed with Dreyer's assessment of the Ford rangekeeper, however. According to a US naval officer serving with the British Grand Fleet, "British Gunnery Control officers have invariably thought the Ford Range Keeper to be a very excellent feature of our fire control system and it certainly is the one feature which creates the greatest interest among them."[99] Indeed, when Ford traveled to London in early 1919, Admiralty officials were keen to speak with him. Schuyler, the US naval attaché, attended the first meeting at the Admiralty, but afterward, Ford telephoned Henry Brownrigg, the gunnery man on the British Naval Staff, and asked for a private chat, remarking that "there were too many people present at the first meeting for free and open conversation to take place." In other words, Ford wanted Schuyler out of the way. After preliminaries, "the meeting got down to the real purpose of Mr. Ford's invitation to Captain Brownrigg": Ford wanted to know if the Royal Navy would be "purchasing his clocks, with a view to his opening a branch in England." Ford then showed the British officials a letter from the US Navy suggesting an amendment to a proposed agreement between Vickers and Ford Instrument—an agreement that Vickers had not seen fit to tell the Admiralty about—to the effect that if the Admiralty ordered Ford rangekeepers, Vickers would build them in England "for the use of the Royal Navy only."[100]

Brownrigg liked the idea of obtaining the services of so talented an engineer as Ford, but he balked at the notion that the Royal Navy's suggestions to Ford would be passed to the US Navy: "Manufacture under such conditions would be very detrimental to our interests." Since the Admiralty's decision, under Dreyer's influence, to let Pollen go had resulted in the US Navy acquiring the Ford rangekeeper in the first place, Brownrigg was unknowingly attesting to the damage which that decision had done to the Royal Navy's interests. To compound the irony, instead of purchasing clocks of Ford's design, Brownrigg favored paying him royalties on any features that the Admiralty incorporated into its own clock design—which is to say that Brownrigg was effectively proposing to pay royalties on features that the Admiralty had funded the development of. Brownrigg added, "[W]e were much impressed not only with [Ford's] inventive capabilities but also with the great rapidity with which ideas are put into effect."[101] That rapidity, of course, had British origins, but they were obscured thanks to Dreyer's capture of the Admiralty's corporate knowledge about Pollen. Dreyer was truly the gift that kept on giving.

Brownrigg's and other British officers' admiration for Ford and his rangekeeper gave the Bureau of Ordnance leverage, but the leverage came with a complication. Like Vickers, but in reverse, Ford wanted to protect his technology in a foreign country by taking out British patents. Like the Admiralty, but in reverse, the Bureau worried that allowing an American firm to license a British firm to produce "American" (originally British) technology would compromise its secrecy. Hence the Bureau's insertion of the amendment in the letter that Ford showed Brownrigg—that Ford rangekeepers built by Vickers be "for the use of the Royal Navy only." This amendment was inserted not to assure the *Admiralty* that Vickers would refrain from selling on the global market, but to protect the *US Navy* against that prospect.[102]

The Royal Navy's interest in the Ford rangekeeper, coupled with Ford's desire for commercial protection in Britain, created symmetry with the US Navy's interest in the Vickers director and Vickers's desire for commercial protection in the United States. The stage was set for a trade—or rather a prisoner swap. Ford filed for British patents on his rangekeeper in June and July 1919.[103] The Bureau then aped for the Ford rangekeeper the Admiralty's demands for the Vickers director. In October 1919, Earle wrote to Sims, "The Bureau of Ordnance guarantees that the [Vickers] instruments in connection with director firing shall not be available for stripping and copying by persons not connected with the United States Navy." In return, "[t]he Bureau desires that you obtain a guarantee from the Admiralty that the Ford Range Keeper shall not be demonstrated or made available for stripping and copying by persons not connected with the British Navy."[104] Two weeks later, Vickers at last began to file for US patents on its director.[105] Although the Bureau and Vickers waited another eighteen months, until Vickers had finished installing its system on US vessels, to sign their contract, the logjam had broken.[106] Ford's rangekeeper served as collateral for the US Navy's promise to preserve the secrecy of the Vickers director after the firm filed for US patents. The ramshackle nature of US patent secrecy laws gave the Admiralty no grounds for confidence—but hostage-taking did. The irony was that their American hostage was a clone of British technology.

Ford took care of one other piece of business on his trip to London in 1919. The Bureau's refusal to pay James Henderson's expenses to attend the US Navy's trials of his gear created an opportunity for Ford to steal another march on the Bureau, just as he had with Vickers. "We are pleased to inform you that we have acquired the exclusive manufacturing rights to all the inventions of Professor James B. Henderson," Ford Instrument trumpeted to the Bureau in June 1919. "Professor Henderson is coming here at our solicitation *and expense*, solely for the purpose of installing and to be present at the trials of his Director Gear" (emphasis added). The firm added, with a touch of smugness, "We trust that our efforts to secure the benefits of the inventions of Prof. Henderson for the United States Navy will meet with your approval."[107]

Whether or not the US Navy approved, it certainly benefited from access to the Henderson Firing Gear. After seeing the gear tested at Ford Instrument's factory in July 1919, the Bureau's inspector there reported, "I think the Ford Company are exceedingly fortunate and also the Bureau is fortunate in having the Ford Company secure the service of Prof. Henderson."[108] Weather conditions during the initial tests of the gear on the USS *North Dakota* a few days later prevented it from showing its full potential, the captain wrote, but the ships' officers believed "that it would be of great value if firing when the ship was rolling heavily."[109] According to Henderson, US naval officials were so impressed that they offered him a job while he was visiting (an offer he promptly used as leverage in his protracted dispute with the British Admiralty).[110] He declined, but the US Navy still had acquired access to his inventions.

∴

World War I was the best thing that ever happened to the US Navy. US entry into the war opened a treasure trove of British naval technology well in advance of what the US manufacturers could produce or even conceive on their own. Highly secret technology, such as the Vickers director and the Henderson Firing Gear, on which the United States had struggled to get reliable information before the war, suddenly became available—along with the "tacit knowledge" derived from daily shoulder-to-shoulder service alongside the Royal Navy. Geopolitically, these transfers undermined the Pax Britannica and helped lay the groundwork for the Pax Americana.

The US Navy's acquisition of British naval technology puts the Wilson administration's wartime pursuit of "a navy second to none," as well as the postwar Washington naval conference, in a different light. Possession of naval technology was critical to becoming a first-class naval power, and becoming a first-class naval power had a decidedly anti-British purpose: the Wilson administration, along with key interest groups among its supporters, felt the political-economic consequences of British naval supremacy keenly.[111] Once the United States, with invaluable British assistance, got far enough along in its pursuit of a navy to rival Britain's, it locked in parity at the Washington naval conference.

Hungry for British knowledge during the war, US naval officers turned very quickly after the war to the task of forgetting who had cooked their feast. Garrett Schuyler—who, as US naval attaché to Britain, served as head waiter—proved a master of selective memory. Writing about a British inventor's broad patent on "flexible shafting" (not as obscene as it sounds) that covered practically any mechanical interconnection of fire-control instruments, Schuyler employed the "rhetoric of obviousness" to minimize British technological achievement: "I cannot conceive how in foreign countries, the idea of doing the obvious can be in any way controlled by existing patents."[112] "I have no doubt that not only in our own service but in other navies people have played with the idea of inter-connecting fire control instruments," he continued, "and that any of them, if they had simply heard that it was absolutely necessary to push the idea through to success by keeping at it, had sufficient skill in design to develop satisfactory gears of this type." This was the same rationalization that the Bureau used against Ford Instrument over the development of the director-converter—we *could* have done it, *if only* we'd had the time—scaled up from the domestic context to the international. "Perhaps in England" the inventor of flexible shafting deserved his patent, Schuyler patronizingly allowed, but not in clever foreign countries like the United States where such a thing was obvious—except that no American had actually invented it.[113]

While the Americans successfully imported much British naval technology, they proved unable to import the British legal technology of secret patents. Even with British tutelage, US law on patent interferences prevented translation. Stuck in remedial school on that subject, the Americans fell back on their expertise in pirating naval technology. The Ford rangekeeper, plagiarized from Pollen, piqued the Admiralty's interest enough that it permitted Vickers to file US patent applications despite the absence of secret patents in the United States. Instead of leading the Admiralty to repair its relationship with Pollen, exposure to the Ford rangekeeper led it to engage in a new round of plagiarizing Pollen, as we will see in the next chapter. Perhaps, then, the Admiralty learned exactly the lesson that the Ford rangekeeper had to teach: if at first you don't succeed in fully plagiarizing Pollen, try, try again.

CHAPTER 6

Breaking Up Is Hard to Do

"[P]articularly in modern times, the use of personal names by service people is the very devil, and leads to untold difficulties. The very fact that Admiral, then Commander Dreyer, called his alternative to the late Mr. Pollen's Argo fire control the Dreyer Table, put back the development of gunnery material many years."

HUGH CLAUSEN, MAY 1947

For the US Navy, reports from British officers about the shortcomings of the Dreyer tables under combat conditions confirmed the wisdom of its decision to pirate Pollen. For the Royal Navy, any decision to repudiate the Dreyer tables was bound to be more difficult. Although liberal scruples about intellectual property rights inhibited the Admiralty as little as they did the US Navy Department, professional considerations inhibited it far more. The reputations of important people—not least Dreyer himself—and of the institution as a whole were implicated in the decision to throw Pollen overboard in favor of Dreyer. Burdened by fear of adverse consequences to their careers, British officers were much more circumspect than their US counterparts when making unfavorable remarks about the Dreyer tables or mentioning Pollen at all.

The atmosphere at the Admiralty in the immediate postwar years also made any attempt to revisit past decisions a perilous undertaking. The Royal Navy had a bad war, failing to perform up to expectations. In the public eye, Horatio Nelson's service seemed to have done very little: Jutland may not have been a defeat, but it certainly was no Trafalgar. For many years after, the feud between John Jellicoe and David Beatty over Jutland consumed the Royal Navy. The daughter of one naval officer recalled that "after Jutland my mother had to keep the factions apart—had two tea parties going, upstairs and downstairs, as the Beattyites could not be civil to the others."[1] Riven by factionalism and personality clashes, the Admiralty resembled the court of Louis XIV more than the Weberian ideal of an impersonal bureaucracy. In official correspondence, authors were trying to tip-toe their way around the institutional equivalents of viperous courtiers.

Despite—or perhaps because of—those constraints, service dissatisfaction with the Dreyer tables came to be expressed through seemingly tangential avenues. They gathered sufficient force to compel the Admiralty to initiate the design of a new system that repudiated not only the Dreyer tables themselves but also the procurement process used to build them; conversely, the new table embraced the principles underlying the Pollen system and the procurement model he had proposed to the Admiralty.[2] But even as the Admiralty acted to plagiarize Pollen's system more competently than Dreyer had done, it refused to relax its official hostility to Pollen personally or to Argo corporately. Turning once again to secrecy—now in the form of a secrecy privilege in legal proceedings rather than the Official Secrets Act—to foil Pollen's pursuit of compensation, the Admiralty managed to pervert the course of justice, at least for the time being.

THE FLEET STRIKES BACK

As the war neared its end, any chance that the Admiralty would reconsider its prewar decision-making on fire control appeared remote. The chief obstacle was John Jellicoe, who not only regarded Dreyer highly, trusted him enough to make him flag captain, and saw him as a personal friend, but also had played an important role in the prewar abandonment of Pollen's system. Jellicoe had no incentive to welcome questions about the effectiveness of the Dreyer tables, and much reason not to. Accordingly, during Jellicoe's tenure as commander of the Grand Fleet and then First Sea Lord, Dreyer had powerful protection; even after Jellicoe's dismissal as First Sea Lord in December 1917, he remained on the active list and nearby. Meanwhile, Dreyer himself was ensconced at the Admiralty as Director of Naval Ordnance until April 1918 and then as the gunnery advisor to the Naval Staff until January 1919. From the former perch, he personally squashed an Admiralty move to reestablish relations with Pollen in March 1918, after Pollen had managed to convince the new civilian First Lord to send a committee to inspect his system. While the committee reported unfavorably on the whole, it acknowledged the ingenuity of the Argo clock, expressed regret that "the ingenuity and mechanical designing ability displayed in producing these instruments have been lost to the Service," and ventured to suggest that "the services of the Inventor and his Staff could be utilized in connection with the design of future fire control instruments."[3] Dreyer would have none of this. Of Pollen, Dreyer wrote, "it would be a grave error to once more put him in touch with the Service at great risk of disturbing the present standardized Fire Control Methods and Machines, in which everyone has complete confidence"—except that the fleet did *not* have complete confidence in the Dreyer tables.[4]

Much of the fleet's dissatisfaction with the Dreyer tables stemmed, as was alluded to from the US perspective in chapter 4, from the inadequacy of its provisions for bearings and bearing rate. These were critical to firing at an invisible target, sometimes known as "indirect fire." Although the various marks of the Dreyer table contained bearing plots, the fleet habitually disregarded them in action because of their inaccuracy.[5] In 1916, a Royal Navy lieutenant named John Dove, with no special training in gunnery and on his own initiative, began working on the problem of indirect fire and swiftly realized the importance of bearings and bearing rate.[6] In early 1917, he communicated his ideas privately to Dreyer, by then the DNO, who took no action.[7] Undeterred, Dove continued his work and steadily gained the support of key officers within the fleet, now under the command of David Beatty—who, unlike Dreyer and Jellicoe, was not implicated in pre-war decision-making about fire control. In the middle of 1917, these officers put Dove in touch with Hugh Clausen, a lieutenant in the Royal Naval Volunteer Reserve who had worked as an electrical engineer in the private sector before the war and possessed the ability to develop Dove's ideas into a workable design. The Royal Navy's inability to hit the Germans behind a smokescreen at the Second Battle of Heligoland Bight in November 1917 heightened the urgency of improving the fleet's capacity for indirect fire. The committee formed within the Grand Fleet to study the problem quickly latched onto Dove's and Clausen's scheme, which would become known as Gyro Director Training, or GDT. It was completed by mid-1918.[8]

Basically, in conceptualizing GDT, Dove and Clausen independently reinvented Pollen's and Isherwood's prewar ideas about the importance of gyro-correction for yaw and of bearings and bearing rate for indirect fire. The "Gyro" in GDT referred to the gyrocompass, which corrected for yaw and provided a stable reference line against which target bearings could be taken. GDT extracted data on bearing rate from the rotation of the clock mechanism underneath the Dreyer table and used it to plot the predicted bearing of the target, while also plotting the observed bearing of the target during periods of visibility. Instead of plotting these data on the principle used by Dreyer (or Pollen), Dove invented a new type of plotting known as "straight-line plotting," in which a pencil made a straight line along a plot so long as the predicted and observed bearings agreed with each other; if they diverged, the line curved one way or the other.[9] During periods of target visibility, GDT enabled the clock mechanism of the Dreyer table to be adjusted so that its predicted bearings matched observed bearings, meaning that it was set to the correct bearing rate; then, if the target became invisible, the predicted bearings generated by the Dreyer table would be accurate so long as the bearing rate remained constant.[10] Of course, as we have seen, the bearing rate typically did not remain constant, and its instantaneous variation could be accurately reproduced only by mechanically interconnecting it with the range rate and by using Isherwood's slipless variable-speed drive. Even so, GDT represented an advance within the limitations of the Dreyer tables.

While GDT indirectly expressed, in instrumental form, the fleet's awareness of deficiencies in the Dreyer table, this awareness found direct expression as well. In September 1918, the Admiralty innocuously asked the Grand Fleet to recommend what type of pencil to use in a modified Dreyer table being built for HMS *Hood*, which was then under construction.[11] Beatty, the commander-in-chief, seized upon this trivial query to form a committee of fleet officers to consider how to standardize the many alterations that individual ships had made to their Dreyer tables, and to make recommendations on the future development of fire-control tables.[12] This committee, known as the Grand Fleet Dreyer Table (GFDT) Committee, was high-powered and exceptionally experienced.[13] Its five members were the fleet's leading gunnery officers, who enjoyed the confidence of its most senior admirals.[14] Before the war, the committee members had not only graduated from the central gunnery school at HMS *Excellent*, but they had all taught on the faculty there too.[15] As noted in chapter 2, the staff at HMS *Excellent* had generally supported the development of the Pollen system before the war. At least one member of the committee, Julian Patterson, was intimately familiar with Argo equipment, having served nearly four years as gunnery officer of HMS *Orion*, one of the six ships in the fleet fitted with an Argo IV clock.[16] The members of the GFDT Committee came from modern ships with the latest equipment in the fleet, including the Marks IV and IV* Dreyer tables. When they judged the Dreyer tables, in other words, they were not judging Dreyer's earliest and feeblest attempts: rather, they were judging the best that he could do with the Admiralty's full development support.

The GFDT Committee delivered a scathing indictment of the Dreyer tables. To a striking degree, its litany of criticisms and its suggestions for future development echoed notes sounded by Pollen before the war. These included the following:

- The Dreyer tables' reliance on range-rate plotting was fatal, especially when conditions of maneuver with high and rapidly varying range and bearing rates replaced the simple tactics that Dreyer had counted on. "*Experience has shown, and it must now be accepted,*" the committee wrote in italics, "*that it will very seldom, if ever, be possible to obtain the rate of change of range from rangefinders.*" It continued, "The frequent alterations of course at high speed which are now the accepted conditions in action will preclude the rate of change of range being obtained with sufficient rapidity from a time and range plot."[17]

- The unreliability of range observations rendered bearings and bearing rate vital. "The measurement of rate of change of bearing is considered of great importance owing to the accuracy with which bearings can be observed, even when the visibility is poor, provided a portion of the enemy or even gun flashes can be seen," the committee remarked.[18] Thus, "all future developments of our fire control system must be designed to deal with the probability of the enemy being for the greater part of the action hidden by a smoke screen . . . or outside the range of visibility."[19]

- Greater automation was necessary. Unlike machines, human beings made mistakes under the stress of combat. "[E]rrors in gun range occurring after alterations of course by own ship or enemy are frequently attributed to an error in rate when in reality they are caused by the neglect or incorrect application of these required corrections to gun range," the committee observed.[20] More broadly, it complained, "our present system necessitates too many operations being carried out by hand"; the future system "should aim at making as many operations as possible automatic."[21]

- The non-slipless drive of the Dreyer tables' clock mechanism was inadequate and consequently generated random errors. "Many complaints have been received that this disc [in the drive] is not sufficiently strong for the work now imposed upon it," the committee reported.[22] It "is not the best available type of variable speed gear," the committee judged in a clear allusion to Argo's slipless drive.[23]

In short, the Dreyer tables did not work under combat conditions. In view of their deficiencies, the committee concluded, "the time has now arrived to reconsider the general design."[24]

Reviewing the GFDT Committee's recommendations, Beatty concurred in withering terms. "The latest pattern of fire control table now existing is in many respects *obsolete*, based as it is on principles *which modern experience has discarded*," he wrote, "and the time has arrived when *a complete re-design* is essential" (emphasis added). While acknowledging the difficulties of putting the committee's recommendations into effect "both from the technical and commercial points of view"—the latter a delicate reference to the Admiralty's fraught relationship with Argo—Beatty urged that "the highest engineering skill available, together with a clear understanding of the practical requirements, must be brought to bear on the problem." He suggested the appointment of a committee including Keith Elphinstone, the managing director of Elliotts, which produced the Dumaresq, the Dreyer tables, and the GDT gear, but he also named Harold Isherwood, "formerly of Argo Company."[25] In addition, he named Dove and Clausen, the inventors of GDT. In effect, Beatty was arguing that the Admiralty could do without Dreyer, but not without Argo's expertise, and especially Isherwood's expertise as the designer of the slipless Argo clock drive.

Beatty's argument received a boost from an entirely different direction as the GFDT Committee was completing its work. In March 1919, Hannibal Ford visited London to explore business opportunities in Britain (a trip covered from the US perspective in chapter 5). In addition to meeting with Pollen to discuss licensing his US rights, Ford also met with Admiralty officials to try to sell his rangekeeper to the Royal Navy.[26] Reporting on two meetings with Ford, the gunnery man on the Naval Staff, Captain Henry Brownrigg, expressed admiration for the relationship that the US Navy had established with Ford—the same "captive contractor" relationship that the Admiralty had established and then abandoned with Argo. "It is patent that Mr. Ford is paid by the U.S.N. to keep the designs secret—an example the Admiralty might well follow," Brownrigg wrote. If the Admiralty did not pay to keep designs secret, he explained, it struggled to prevent domestic firms from using their patents as they wished and selling on the open market.[27]

Brownrigg had conjured the ghosts of Pollen and Argo. Admiralty officials who recognized the apparitions moved quickly to banish them.[28] But Brownrigg persisted. "[T]he Ford Company are the secret Fire Control Design Section of the U.S.N., a policy which it is considered we ought to follow," he insisted—except with a twist. Instead of locating the Royal Navy's new "secret Fire Control Design Section" in a commercial firm, he suggested locating it inside the Admiralty.[29] At the same time, echoing Beatty, he maintained that "the services of Messrs. Isherwood or Clausen, or both, should be obtained permanently."[30] By pushing for Clausen and Isherwood, both RNVR officers with private-sector careers before the war, he was saying that the Admiralty could not do without expertise developed in the civilian world, even if the expertise was brought in-house, and he was saying that one of the experts needed to be from Argo. Brownrigg was treading carefully, but the direction of his steps was clear: away from Dreyer.

THE ADMIRALTY FIRE CONTROL TABLE

Under pressure, the Admiralty appointed a Fire Control Tables (FCT) Committee, under the presidency of Captain Sidney Drury-Lowe. He had been closely connected to the prewar Inspectorate of Target Practice during the inspectorship of Richard Peirse, a stout supporter of Pollen's system.[31] Established in August 1919 and dissolved in December 1920, Drury-Lowe's FCT Committee was essentially transitional, intended to serve as a conduit from the GFDT Committee in the fleet to the Admiralty.[32] As Drury-Lowe himself acknowledged, "the requirements for the future Fire Control Table"—with particular emphasis on the need to operate when the target was invisible—were "based on the report of the Grand Fleet Committee."[33] The five members of the FCT Committee were bureaucratic box-checkers and technical experts, not high-profile gunnery officers or tacticians. The technical experts were John Dove (one of the two junior officers suggested by Beatty) and James Henderson, the Royal Navy's leading gyroscope expert, whom we met in chapter 5. Isherwood, his Argo colleague Halvor Landstad, Clausen, and Elphinstone served as consultants.[34] The composition of the committee, as well as its short duration, suggests that its purpose was to lay down the general desiderata for the new fire-control table, not to carry out the detailed design work.

In early 1921, the Naval Ordnance Department took over responsibility for the design of the new table. By now, the DNO was Roger Backhouse, a long-time admirer of Pollen's system.[35] Bringing Dove into the Naval Ordnance Department, Backhouse was also able to draw for expertise on the "secret Fire Control Design Section" proposed by Brownrigg, which was constituted, in a further addition to the alphabet soup, as the LP & FC (Low Power and Fire Control) Section of the Director of Torpedoes and Mining. Its offices at 80 Pall Mall soon housed Clausen and Isherwood. The LP & FC Section provided the organizational umbrella for the experts hand-picked to carry out the detailed design of the new table, which would become known as the Admiralty Fire Control Table (AFCT).[36]

Behind the miasma of acronyms, the new AFCT was clearly proceeding along the lines indicated by the GFDT Committee and the FCT Committee, meaning that it was *not* an evolution of the Dreyer tables but rather a new departure. This helps explain the recollection of Admiral Sir Frank Twiss, a young gunnery officer in the interwar period who held high positions after World War II, that Dreyer "was cross about the [AFCT]; bad-tempered about the AFCT; clearly anti-AFCT."[37] Echoing the GFDT Committee's appeal to reconsider "the general design" and Beatty's call for "a complete re-design," a pamphlet prepared under Backhouse's oversight and distributed to fleet gunnery officers observed in 1921 that the Dreyer table had reached finality and described the AFCT as "a fresh design."[38] In a minute for Admiralty officials, Backhouse wrote in 1922 that the new table "is entirely different to the existing tables, and includes in its design a number of new features."[39] Tracing the lineage of the AFCT back through the FCT Committee to the GFDT Committee, the official handbook of the new table confirmed that it was "a complete redesign," necessary because the Dreyer table required "too many operations being carried out by hand."[40] From the start through to the end, therefore, the direction of the new table's development led very clearly away from the Dreyer tables. So much for Dreyer's claim in his memoirs that the AFCT was "only a rearrangement of my 'Dreyer Table.'"[41]

In fact, the AFCT was closer to a rearrangement of the Argo system. As conceptualized, designed, and built, it represented the full instrumental realization of Pollen's and Isherwood's conception, plus some new features. Pollen and Isherwood had sought to maximize electromechanical automation, minimize human intervention, and achieve extreme precision and accuracy throughout their system, toward the overall goal of being able to cope with the most challenging conditions of visibility, maneuver, and range and bearing rates. Accordingly, they envisioned a system operating on a synchronous electrical transmission system and employing infinitely varying slipless drives in the clock. They also envisioned using gyro-stabilization as much as possible—so much so that James Henderson himself regarded them as fellow pioneers.[42] They had gotten a long way toward the instrumental achievement of their overarching ambition before the war, most notably with their gyro-stabilized rangefinder mounting and slipless clock drive. But they had been forced to settle, for lack of time and money, for nonsynchronous transmission, as we saw in chapter 2, and they had not accomplished all the forms of vertical and horizontal gyro-stabilization that later developed.

The AFCT picked up where Pollen and Isherwood had left off when the Admiralty yanked development support from them, while also incorporating parts of the Ford clock and British wartime innovations that owed nothing to Dreyer. The Pollenite genealogy of the AFCT was most obvious in the table's incorporation of the Argo slipless clock drive; indeed, the official handbook for the AFCT emphasized the fact that the ball in the variable-speed drives moved across the disc "without slipping."[43] But the Pollenite genealogy went well beyond the clock drive. The AFCT operated on synchronous electrical transmission and sought every possible form of gyro-stabilization with its "master gyro unit."[44] Notably, the AFCT design team experienced no significant delays with the clock—the part of the table that Pollen and Isherwood had already completed—but it did with the synchronous transmission and the master gyro unit.[45] The AFCT clock also used "cross wires," akin to the distinctive cross-wires of the Ford rangekeeper (which Dreyer had criticized), to indicate discrepancies between calculations and observations of the range rate and deflection.[46] The AFCT's plotting elements, which operated on the straight-line principle, emerged directly from wartime modifications to the Dreyer tables suggested by fleet officers and owed nothing to Dreyer himself.

The AFCT also marked a repudiation of Dreyer's and the Admiralty's prewar preference for a fire-control system that was cheaper and mechanically simpler than Pollen's. The cost of the AFCT for a capital ship was £45,000.[47] To put this number in some perspective, Pollen had offered his complete system, which the Admiralty regarded as too expensive, to the US Navy in 1914 for £7,500.[48] The Director of Naval Ordnance (Charles Forbes) acknowledged that the new AFCT was "very expensive," but he advised that "any questions which may arise in future as to whether certain parts of the design are sufficiently important to justify their repetition in new ships should be approached with the recollection that this Table represents the machine produced to cope with the requirements laid down by expert review of the situation after 4 ½ years of war experience."[49] Excellence was expensive, in other words, but the war had shown that excellence was worth the price. Similarly, much as Pollen had defended the mechanical complexity of his system as no more than necessary to solve the fire-control problem within tolerable limits of error, so the DNO wrote of the AFCT that it "may be thought, at first sight, to be complicated and difficult to operate," but in fact "further acquaintance with it removes this impression."[50] He added that "the mechanical problem with which we were faced has been solved," while the Third Sea Lord (Ernle Chatfield) acclaimed the AFCT as "mechanically a great improvement on existing designs"—i.e., the Dreyer tables.[51] In sum, therefore, the AFCT evolved from the war's lessons as understood by the Royal Navy, and the Royal Navy understood the lessons to consist largely of points that Pollen had hammered before the war against opposition from Dreyer.

INTELLECTUAL PROPERTY AND THE NEW PROCUREMENT PARADIGM

The development of the AFCT represented a rejection not only of the Dreyer tables but also of the procurement relationships that produced them. This time around, the Admiralty was determined to get the best design talent available, regardless of the intellectual property issues involved.

One reason why the Admiralty had chosen Dreyer's system over Pollen's was that managing the IP claims of serving naval officers, like Dreyer, was much simpler than managing the IP claims of civilians. Under pressure from the fleet to do better, however, the Admiralty did not want naval officers *qua* naval officers involved in designing the replacement for the Dreyer tables. The sole officer to serve as a lead designer was Dove, who was there in his capacity as the coinventor of GDT. The other lead designers were Clausen, Isherwood, Landstad (his Argo colleague), James Henderson, and Keith Elphinstone—all civilians, but of distinctive statuses. Legally, the tools available to the Admiralty for navigating the IP claims of the different statuses differed.[52]

The Admiralty had the strongest legal tools for controlling the IP of serving naval officers like Dove. Naval officers—be they regular officers like Dove or temporary RNVR officers like Clausen and Isherwood—were bound by Section 415 of the *King's Regulations and Admiralty Instructions for the Government of His Majesty's Naval Service*, which required serving officers to seek the Admiralty's permission before applying for patents and to assign any patents to the Admiralty if desired. In effect, by subjecting themselves to these regulations upon accepting their commissions (akin to signing employment contracts), serving officers forfeited many of the IP rights to which they otherwise would have been entitled. However, because serving officers were not hired to invent, they did not forfeit all of their rights. If they, as quasi-employees who had signed a quasi-employment contract, could make a plausible case that they carried on their inventive work outside the confines of their quasi-employment contract, British courts (like US courts, as we will see in chapter 8) generally held during this period that they, not their employers, owned the rights to inventions.[53] The Admiralty also recognized that making special financial awards to inventive officers stimulated innovation and sometimes made such awards through its Awards Council. Still, the *King's Regulations* meant that serving officers did not negotiate for their IP rights or monetary awards from a position of strength. But once Clausen and Isherwood were no longer serving as RNVR officers, this tool of coercion was no longer applicable.

At the opposite end of the spectrum, civilians outside the Admiralty's orbit, like Landstad and Elphinstone, had the greatest freedom to set their terms according to liberal property and contract norms. While the Admiralty refused any relaxation of its official attitude toward Argo, which remained off its list of approved contractors, it recruited Isherwood (now a civilian) and Landstad to become consultants first to Drury-Lowe's FCT Committee and then to the team designing the AFCT. They signed contracts obliging them to keep their work secret and to assign secret patents to the Admiralty at its request, just as serving officers were obliged to do.[54] Elphinstone must have signed the same agreements as Isherwood and Landstad, as must have his firm, Elliotts. These agreements were intended to deny to contractors the grounds on which Pollen had fought to be paid for maintaining the secrecy of his IP.[55] The flip side of captivity, as Brownrigg had pointed out, was that contractors had to be paid liberally—as Isherwood, Landstad, Elphinstone, and Elliotts were.[56]

While the need to include outside civilians complicated the work of designing the new table from one direction, the need to include James Henderson complicated it from another. By the time Drury-Lowe's FCT Committee started its work, Henderson had been engaged in acrimony with the Admiralty over the IP rights to his inventions for years.[57] A civilian professor at the Royal Naval College, Henderson had worked for Barr & Stroud and as a professor at the University of Glasgow before entering Admiralty employment. Though an insider from one perspective, his employment contract with the Admiralty explicitly permitted him to perform outside work as a consultant, and he maintained a partnership contract with Barr & Stroud after joining the Royal Naval College. In short, Henderson demonstrably carried on his inventive work outside his duties as a professor, and thus he had unassailable grounds on which to claim that he, not the Admiralty, owned the products of his inventive mind. Accordingly, after spending years trying and failing to get Henderson to sign away his IP rights as though he were a serving officer, the Admiralty was finally forced to guarantee him an income of £3,000 a year for five years—more than the annual pay of a full admiral, and on top of any royalties he might earn—before he would agree to work on the new fire control table under the same terms governing Isherwood and Landstad.[58]

Clausen, though a civilian, was in a different category from Isherwood, Landstad, and Henderson. Although he left the RNVR when the war ended, he remained, from an IP perspective, closer to Dove's status as a serving officer than to his fellow civilians on the design team due to his status as a government-employed "research worker." This was a new type of civilian expert in the service of the armed forces: not a civilian like Henderson, who invented outside the course of his regular employment duties, but rather a civilian hired specifically to invent.[59] The nature of research workers' employment contracts gave their employers control over their IP.

While the Admiralty had to deal with the different statuses of the AFCT's designers with respect to IP, the designers had to deal with each other. Their work cannot have proceeded without internal friction over IP rights, especially between Dove, Clausen, and Henderson. These three men were, in effect, rival claimants to have invented various components of the Royal

Navy's wartime and postwar fire-control system (and indeed they all submitted claims to the Royal Commission on Awards to Inventors, discussed
below with reference to Pollen). Decades later, Clausen recalled Henderson's brilliance but made rather cutting remarks about both his inventiveness and his willingness to share credit.[60] Not to be outdone, Henderson
described the Admiralty's decision to adopt Dove's and Clausen's GDT in
lieu of an alternative system of his own design as being "based upon considerations other than those of scientific accuracy."[61] Dove, for his part, was
appointed to the Admiralty for six months in 1930 "to assist [the] Royal
Commission in investigating invention claims of Sir James Henderson."[62]

∴

Further remarks made decades later by Clausen attest to the political sen-
sitivity of designing the new fire-control table in the context of the Pollen-
Dreyer controversy. After the war, Clausen enjoyed a very distinguished
career within the Admiralty's technical establishment, rising to become
the Chief Technical Officer of the Scientific Research and Experiment Department during the interwar period. But he never forgot his early fire-
control work. When Pollen's son Anthony approached Clausen in 1969 in
the course of researching his own book about the Admiralty's treatment
of his father, Clausen replied, "I would be very glad to meet you to gather
more information about the deplorable 'Pollen Dreyer controversy.' I don't
think that your father really had a fair deal, but it is an old story now, probably best left buried."[63] His subsequent letters to Anthony Pollen offered
glimpses as to why he thought the story was "probably best left buried."
"As regards post war events, on which I might be able to help you, we must
be wary," Clausen told Anthony. "I am still subject to the agreement that
I signed on joining the Admiralty staff about the Official Secrets Act; and
injudicious comment might lead to trouble even after all these years."[64]
Several months later, he forwarded Anthony some notes sent to him by
Dreyer—which were almost certainly a précis of Dreyer's and Usborne's
Technical History, discussed in chapter 3. "They were sent to me as a con-
tribution to a historical section I was then writing for an official booklet,"
Clausen explained to Anthony.

> This was never completed. The more I studied past history, the murkier
> and more obscure became the background.
>   It seemed such a dangerous thing to write about that I gave it up. And
> so, although I am about the only surviving man who knew the old pio-
> neers, the booklet will never be written.[65]

The "danger" derived both from the secrecy of the AFCT designers' work and from the threat their work posed to the reputations of powerful people, indeed to the Admiralty as a whole.

The danger notwithstanding, Clausen could not quite hide his dissent from the official story ("I don't think your father really had a fair deal"), his admiration for what Pollen and Isherwood had accomplished, or his contempt for the Dreyer tables. Clausen observed that Pollen "recruited a very powerful design team, including Isherwood and Landstad,"[66] whose work "was quite an inspiration to me as a young man."[67] Conversely, Clausen delivered a blistering verdict on Dreyer and the Dreyer tables. "In a previous paper on gunnery matters I urged that the pernicious practice of attachment of personal names to inventions should never be allowed to raise its ugly head again," Clausen recalled in 1947. "The very fact that Admiral, then Commander Dreyer, called his alternative to the late Mr. Pollen's Argo fire control the Dreyer Table, put back the development of gunnery material many years."[68] Dreyer's hypersensitive ego would not admit that a civilian could ever know more than he did; increasingly, over time, this tendency extended to fellow naval officers as well. They might be able to make detailed improvements to his system, in Dreyer's mind, but the fundamental breakthroughs were his alone and immutable. Hence his desperate characterization in his memoirs of the AFCT as "only a rearrangement of my 'Dreyer Table.'" Dreyer's personification of naval fire control, with the Admiralty's support and encouragement, delayed the development of an improved system.

TO THE RCAI

While the complaints from the fleet about the failure of the Dreyer tables in combat during World War I forced the Admiralty to reckon, however imperfectly, with its prewar decisions about fire control, the institution did its best to foil Pollen's persistent attempts to rehabilitate his firm and to be compensated for the plagiarism of his system. The Admiralty's threat of prosecution under the Official Secrets Act and decision to strike Argo from its list of approved contractors—the latter explicitly intended as retribution, as we saw in chapter 3—cut particularly deeply since they implied that Pollen was unpatriotic and untrustworthy. He refused to go away quietly.

Twice he appealed to new civilian heads of the Admiralty for an out-of-court settlement. In a 1916 letter to Arthur Balfour, who had replaced Winston Churchill as First Lord of the Admiralty after the Dardanelles fiasco, Pollen voiced his anger. "[M]y Company has been struck off the list of Admiralty contractors, officers in the fleet have been warned not to

communicate with us, and we have been spoken of and treated as traitors,"
he wrote—despite the fact that all of his Argo colleagues were serving hon-
orably in the war, and that he himself worked to support the war effort
in a variety of ways.[69] In 1918, Pollen tried again with the new First Lord,
Sir Eric Geddes, pleading that even if the Admiralty refused to compensate him for plagiarizing his inventions, "at least the slur of our conduct as
good subjects should be withdrawn, and our contribution to the science of
naval fire control generously acknowledged."[70] But the Admiralty colossus
refused to budge.[71]

So Pollen started to consider legal remedies. In March 1920, he received
an opinion from John Simon, the former Attorney General and future Foreign Secretary, as well as from W. Eric Bousfield, a patent specialist, advising him on his options.[72] One option was to file a "petition of right"—the
legal term for a suit against the crown. This medieval legal instrument had
evolved to provide subjects with the same redress against the crown as they
would enjoy against their fellow subjects for charges of breach of contract,
but not for alleged torts; the old notion that "the king can do no wrong"
died hard.[73] Since patent infringement was a tort, any petition of right
by Pollen would have to rest on an alleged breach of the 1908 contract.
Simon and Bousfield judged it "very improbable" that such a petition
would succeed.[74]

The other option was for Pollen to apply to the Royal Commission on
Awards to Inventors (RCAI). This was a quasi-judicial body established in
1919 to handle a host of claims arising from the government's use of privately owned IP without compensation during the war. In effect, it constituted a waiver of sovereign immunity—the crown's right not to be sued
without its consent—for a certain type of claim against the crown. The
crown made this waiver not out of grace but out of cold calculation. While
Britain, in both the government and the private sector, had already developed an impressive scientific and technological base for the Royal Navy
before the war—indeed one far in advance of any other country, notwithstanding Britain's supposed "decline"—the war had made clearer than ever
before the vital role of science and technology to the maintenance of British power. The interdepartmental committee that recommended the establishment of the RCAI in a November 1918 report stressed that "it is more
than ever to the public interest to encourage invention by giving inventors
security for an adequate award."[75]

Because ordinary procedures did not give inventors that security, the
government decided that an extraordinary procedure was needed. Since
the passage of the 1883 Patents and Designs Act, the crown had been
obliged to compensate inventors when it used their inventions. Inventors

dissatisfied with the terms offered had the right to appeal to the Treasury for reconsideration—but because the Treasury was responsible for paying any compensation, it had an evident conflict of interest in performing this appellate function. In consequence, many inventors were left dissatisfied. By appointing a royal commission (the RCAI) as the arbiter of awards, the government hoped to instill confidence in the awards process and thereby incentivize innovation.[76] Simon and Bousfield judged that Pollen stood a "very considerably greater" chance of success before the extraordinary RCAI than with an ordinary petition of right. With the RCAI, Pollen would not have to base his case on breach of contract. He would merely have to show that the Admiralty had used his system and that it had done so as a result of his communicating it to the Admiralty.[77]

Notwithstanding this encouraging legal advice, Pollen refrained from immediate action. A letter to Admiral Sir A. Berkeley Milne illuminates his state of mind at the time. When Milne, who had commanded the Mediterranean Fleet in 1914 during the notorious escape of the *Goeben* and *Breslau*, asked Pollen for advice on clearing his name and complained that the Admiralty was withholding information, Pollen counseled against pressuring the Admiralty: "I have been through the thing myself and know what I am talking about and honestly my advice is to leave the thing alone; not because you have not a right to justice, but because if you try to enforce that right a worse injustice may befall you.[78] Pollen tried one more time to negotiate a remedy from the Admiralty. This time, he approached the new First Sea Lord, Admiral of the Fleet Earl Beatty, with whom he had always enjoyed a friendly relationship.[79] While Beatty apparently wished Pollen well, he was unwilling to risk his institution's reputation in the postwar hothouse of public recriminations by obliging Pollen's quest to reopen, in effect, a can of worms.[80]

.·.

In August 1920, accordingly, Pollen began the process of submitting a claim to the RCAI.[81] His first substantive formulation came in December and focused on two issues: gyro-corrected plotting and helm-free integration by the clock. Because the latter lent itself more readily to conventional notions of invention as reduction to material form, it was easier to argue than the former. Pollen claimed that sometime during the war, the Admiralty had modified the clock mechanism of the Dreyer table to make it helm-free and thereby made it "mechanically equivalent" to the Argo clock. Here, Pollen was drawing on an idea from patent law known as the "doctrine of equivalents": even when two inventions differ in certain ways, the differences may be insignificant compared to the similarities, which can be so profound as to render the inventions practically equivalent. Although Pollen possessed few details, he had learned that after becoming captain of HMS *Orion*, then the only ship with an Argo IV clock, Dreyer had fundamentally modified his table so that the Mark IV version, unlike the Mark III, mechanically interconnected the range and bearing rates in such a way as to autogenerate bearings, albeit not as effectively as the Argo clock.[82] The autogeneration of bearings, of course, was a defining characteristic of the Argo system, crucial to fully helm-free operation and to operation when the target was invisible.

Pollen's plotting claim was more complicated. For one thing, rate plotting, though capable of mechanical expression, was a method rather than a machine, making it more remote from archetypal ways of thinking about invention and patents. For another thing, Pollen had consistently preferred to use true-course plotting rather than rate plotting in his system. This did not mean his rate-plotting claim lacked a basis, only that its basis would be more difficult to prove. Pollen (correctly) claimed to have invented and communicated to the Admiralty the rate-plotting method used by Dreyer. Thus, even though Pollen ultimately discarded this approach to the problem, he argued that rate plotting fell within the definition of the system defined in the course of his 1906 negotiations and embodied in his 1908 contract with the Admiralty.[83] Overall, then, he was claiming on the clock specifically and on the system generally. The former fit relatively neatly into the framework of patent law, while the latter would have to be contested within the framework of contract law.

The Admiralty staked out its counterposition in April 1921. On top of disputing many of Pollen's arguments on the merits, the Admiralty also signaled that it would build its case upon the principle of secrecy: "it will be a matter of the utmost importance that the hearing of the case should be conducted in camera [i.e., in secret]." The Admiralty continued, "In particular it will be essential that a large proportion of the matter contained in the Admiralty case, which will necessarily reveal features of the Naval system of Fire Control should not be communicated *either to the applicants* or to the general public in such a way as to afford information as to the Naval System and reasons for its adoption" (emphasis added).[84] In short, the Admiralty would oppose any disclosure of its system to Pollen on secrecy grounds.

With the battle lines thus drawn, the RCAI determined that the case merited a full hearing, enabling a triumphant Pollen to submit his official claim form in November 1921.[85] The Royal Warrant establishing the RCAI had created three categories, or "heads," under which applicants could put in claims. Since Heads 1 and 2 covered patented inventions, Pollen put in under Head 3 of the Royal Warrant, which covered "any inventions, designs, drawings or processes which, though not conferring any monopoly against the Crown or any statutory right to payment or compensation [i.e., not patented], may nevertheless appear from their exceptional utility or otherwise to entitle the inventor, author or owner thereof to some remuneration for such user."[86] Pollen's claim was for "the principle and details of his system of Naval Fire Control," as defined in the 1908 contract (per the 1906 negotiations) and covering the material communicated to the Admiralty from 1901 to 1912.[87] Because he could fight the case on contract rather than patent grounds, he believed he would win.[88] "I cannot for the life of me see what game the Admiralty have left to play except to get the damages reduced as low as possible," Pollen exulted to a friend.[89]

Even so, he still had powerful enemies at the Admiralty, as he well knew. In April 1922, he alerted the RCAI to the possibility that the Admiralty was relying for advice on Dreyer, who had every reason to misrepresent matters.[90] Now gunnery advisor to the Naval Staff, Dreyer was in an excellent position to influence the Admiralty's case. Pollen was quite right to be suspicious. It subsequently emerged that Dreyer supplied a written report on the history of the case for the Admiralty's use in meeting Pollen's claim. Continuing to ignore his obvious conflict of interest, the Admiralty made Dreyer's report the basis of its case.[91]

SECRETS, SECRETS ARE NO FUN

The Admiralty also prepared to rely on secrecy, in the form of an evidentiary privilege anticipating Britain's modern public-interest immunity. Normally, when cases involved private litigants, the parties had a right to "discovery"—that is, a right to obtain evidence from each other, or, conversely an obligation to disclose evidence to each other—overseen by the court. The crown enjoyed certain exceptions to the rules governing private litigants, sometimes on national security grounds, sometimes on sovereign-immunity grounds (which are mixed together in the public-interest immunity).[92] If the Admiralty's attempt to fight the case on its merits along lines laid down by Dreyer failed, its fallback position was that the merits—including the 1908 contract on which Pollen planned to base his case—would be irrelevant and inadmissible. It had used the Official Secrets Act in 1913 in exactly the same way: when it could not win on the merits of its claim to have invented and thus to own the use of rates, it fell back on secrecy.

Pollen had foreseen that the Admiralty might assert an evidentiary privilege way back when the parties were negotiating their agreement in 1906, and he had done his best to protect himself from this possibility. Discovery had then arisen in the context of providing terms for arbitration if the Admiralty opted not to acquire a monopoly of his system. Noting that "I shall be dependent upon the Admiralty for evidence to support my case in the event of it going to arbitration,"[93] Pollen secured the following clause in the 1908 contract:

> Both parties to the Agreement shall be at liberty to be represented by Counsel and to call as witnesses any Officers of His Majesty's Navy who may have been present at the trials or any other Officer or person and to cross-examine the witnesses of the other side. The Arbitrators shall be authorised to take into consideration any circumstances which either party may consider material. No evidence shall be withheld by Naval Officers or by the [Admiralty] on the ground that it is confidential but the whole proceedings of the Arbitration shall be treated as confidential by all parties concerned.[94]

That is, the Admiralty had previously agreed in a contract to refrain from using secrecy as way to shield evidence from Pollen.

Nevertheless, in this regard, as in so many others, the Admiralty disregarded the 1908 agreement in the proceedings before the RCAI. Indeed, its approach was simply to render all history and contracts irrelevant. "Considerations of public policy render it impossible for the Department to disclose present methods of fire control at this stage," the Admiralty flatly asserted, "but if the Royal Commission so direct, the Admiralty are prepared under proper safeguards to explain to the Tribunal and such other persons as they may direct so much thereof as may be necessary for the proper trial of the claim."[95]

The task of representing the Admiralty's case to the RCAI fell to the office of the Treasury Solicitor, the government's lawyers. From their perspective, which was much less personal than the Admiralty's, Pollen's case posed a threat because of the principle at stake: could liberal norms about property, contract, and legal due process trump the crown's prerogative to defend the realm? To protect crown prerogative, the Treasury Solicitor embraced the Admiralty's strategy of secrecy. When Pollen's patent agents in December 1922 petitioned the Treasury Solicitor to disclose as soon as possible the documents on which the Admiralty intended to rely, the office flatly refused, citing the "settled rule of practice that no discovery is given by the Crown."[96]

Pollen of course appealed the crown's deployment of secrecy to the RCAI.[97] At a hearing, the chairman of the RCAI, Charles Sargant, rejected out of hand Pollen's suggestion, which was grounded in the 1908 contract, "that he was entitled to be shewn the confidential reports made by Officers to the Admiralty." For his part, the Treasury Solicitor "on behalf of the Admiralty stated that he had definite instructions to refuse to disclose to Mr. Pollen the system of Fire Control which is now in use in the Navy."[98]

This language implied that the crown's objections to disclosure had something to do with Pollen personally. Aside from seeming to endorse, from Pollen's perspective, the Admiralty's highly personal attack on his character, the crown's refusal to make disclosure to him inflicted a financial wound, since it meant that he would have to hire counsel. For representation, he selected Carrol Romer, a patent specialist with a fascinating life of his own.[99] As an officer in the Royal Engineers on the Western Front during the war, Romer had invented the "Romer," a special ruler for reading the grid lines of a map more accurately; later in the 1920s, he became the editor of the *Nineteenth Century and After*, the well-known British literary magazine.[100] Pollen's legal costs, not just for Romer, would ultimately exceed £8,500—enough to buy a large country home for the Pollen family.[101]

Even with Romer on board, the crown threw up further obstacles to discovery. When Pollen applied for disclosure to be made to Romer, the Treasury Solicitor, on behalf of the Admiralty, agreed to let Romer see the Navy's current fire control system both at Elliotts (where the AFCT was being manufactured) and on a ship, but he refused any disclosure of documents to Romer.[102] The refusal to disclose documents meant that Romer would enter the hearing blind and not on level footing: the crown would know his case, but he would not know the crown's. Significantly, the crown refused any additional disclosure of its system to one of the engineering experts at Pollen's patent agency.[103] This meant that he would not be able to hire expert witnesses, who often played critical roles in IP litigation.[104]

These limitations on discovery placed Romer in an impossible situation. As a patent attorney with some technical proficiency, he was an expert of sorts. However, his expertise was not that of, say, James Swinburne, encountered in chapter 3, who possessed some of the same competencies as Romer but also some that Romer did not possess. More importantly, as Pollen's *lawyer*, Romer could have no credibility with the court as an expert *witness*. Romer understood from the start that his situation was exceedingly challenging; precisely when he recognized that it was unwinnable is unclear.[105] In any event, at some point, he shrewdly decided to fight a rearguard action, seeking to salvage what he could in order to enable a subsequent counterattack.

.·.

The pretrial jockeying finally at an end, the full RCAI hearings began in October 1923. The crown's limits on discovery virtually ensured that the hearing would be a farce, but the chairman, Justice Sargant, injected a further element of absurdity by allotting only three days for the hearings, and he remained obstinately determined to stick to his schedule.[106] As a result, he repeatedly prevented Romer from developing his case. For instance, when Romer tried to explain what had led up to the 1908 contract in order to establish its proper interpretation, Justice Sargant interjected, "When once you have the agreement, the agreement supersedes the preliminary context."[107] Similar instances abounded.[108] Although the outcome was foreordained, certain developments during the hearings proved significant for the future.

The first was a new set of irregularities, endorsed by the RCAI, concerning the handling of evidence. Not having been permitted discovery, Romer learned the Admiralty's evidence for the first time when the Treasury Solicitor's representative, Sir Duncan Kerly, began reading from Dreyer's letters to the Admiralty in order to show the development of the Admiralty's system. Sargant not only allowed the evidence in over Romer's objection, but accepted copies in lieu of the original documents, leading a flustered and struggling Romer to declare, "I have never been met by this situation. It seems to me I must take a formal objection."[109] Then, instead of calling Dreyer to authenticate the documents and testify about the Admiralty system, Kerly put Joseph Henley, Dreyer's old friend (mentioned in chapter 2), on the stand. Henley promptly declined to authenticate the documents or to testify. Romer threw up his hands: "[I]t is no use asking the witness any question with regard to them." Unperturbed by the crown's failure to supply the original documents, call their author as a witness, and make him available for cross-examination, Sargant assured Romer that "[t]he general gist of the documents seems to be pretty intelligible."[110] He went farther, stating that the documents had "a great bearing upon the origin, the history, the evolution of the present naval system."[111] As we will see in chapter 7, treating the documents as unproblematic sources, requiring neither authentication nor investigation into the circumstances of their production, violated normal legal procedure, which involved practices of source criticism akin to those of historical scholarship.

The second important development during the hearings was yet another procedural irregularity involving Dreyer. Unbeknownst to Romer, Dreyer was present at the hearing, even though the crown refused to put him on the stand to authenticate the documents. The reason why the crown wanted Dreyer there does not appear in the transcript but is clear from other documents. At some point in the hearing, the RCAI members and counsel went from the main courtroom into a side room, where Dreyer and a Dreyer table were waiting for them. His notes for his presentation survive in his papers and give a flavor of what he told the court: "Dreyer saved Service huge sums and provided it with the real solution to the Fire Control Problem, the Service Set [i.e., Dreyer Table]. Watkin and Pollen only alternatives and of little use."[112] When Romer started to question Dreyer, Sargant stopped him.[113] The Treasury Solicitor refused to call Dreyer as a witness, ingenuously explaining that "for reasons which the Commission will understand I do not propose to call a gentleman who may be treated as a rival inventor."[114] Remarkably, despite the crown's explicit acknowledgment that Dreyer wore the hat of a rival inventor—in effect a rival plaintiff—the RCAI did not even hold him to the standard of an expert witness called by the crown, which would have meant treating his explanation of his system as evidence subject to cross-examination by the opposing party and inclusion in the transcript of the hearings (where it does not appear). It was treating him like an independent, disinterested expert advisor to the court. This was to regular procedure what Genghis Khan was to peace in Eurasia.

The third important development during the hearings was an extraordinary ruling on the scope of Pollen's claim, one that flew in the face not only of his understanding but also of the Admiralty's.[115] On the third day, as Romer began to question Pollen about the development of the Argo clock, Justice Sargant immediately interrupted: "[T]he case which has been set up has not been with reference to clocks at all; it has been with reference to the general question, quite apart from the clocks altogether, and what we propose to do is to reserve entirely any question of any claim hereafter by Mr. Pollen in respect of the appropriation of any invention of his with regard to the clocks."[116] The RCAI could not rule on the clock, Sargant insisted, because "[w]e really do not know, we have not the least idea, what the exact principles of the Admiralty clock are as compared with the exact principles of the Argo clock. It is impossible to deal with it today," the final day of the allotted three days.[117] When Romer tried to point out that the Admiralty's limits on discovery and Sargant's own time pressures explained why the RCAI had not heard about the clock, Sargant again cut him off: the RCAI could rule on the general system, which he reduced to plotting, but not on "that special question of the subsequent invention of the Argo clock."[118] The best Romer could do—which turned out to be quite a lot—was to get explicit confirmation from Sargant that the absence of a ruling on the clock would not prejudice Pollen's ability to put in a new claim on the clock.[119] The clock was out, on the patently absurd grounds that it formed no essential part of the system for which Pollen was claiming.

The outcome was predetermined. Toward the end of the hearing on the third day, Sargant announced, "[I]t is unanimously our view that the Admiralty system is a different system from Mr Pollen's system."[120] The next day, Pollen wrote to Richard Peirse, the former Inspector of Target Practice and a supporter of his system, who had testified at the hearing, as follows:

> The case ended last night. You can guess from the way Counsel cut down your evidence that the Commission never had one fifth of our story put before them, and our main case, therefore, we have lost, because only the story could have won it.
>
> The Commission are considering whether we deserve an award for having stirred the Admiralty up to adopting some kind of scientific system. I doubt, myself, if they will give one—and, if they do, the amount can only be trivial.
>
> Some day, when we meet, I will tell you briefly about it; it is too difficult to write about it now.[121]

The RCAI's official recommendation, issued days later, merely confirmed what Pollen already suspected. The RCAI did not recommend any award. But—and this was a big "but"—it did reserve Pollen's right to put in a new claim.[122] He would lose little time in seizing this life preserver.

CHAPTER 7

Clocking the Crown

"[I]t is a rather remarkable thing that you have an inventor who makes a very beautiful invention, the Admiralty commandeers it, and without more, deprives him of the benefit of it, apparently for all time, without compensation."

LORD TOMLIN, 7 AUGUST 1925

The failure of Pollen's initial attempt before the Royal Commission on Awards to Inventors (RCAI) in 1923 left him "very depressed," his wife recalled, over the "colossal disappointment when this one chance of putting right an injustice was lost apparently for ever."[1] But Pollen was nothing if not resilient. His lawyer had already laid the groundwork for a renewed assault on the RCAI by extracting from the chairman an assurance that he would have the right to put in a new claim on his clock. Then, in an extraordinary turn of events, none other than Frederic Dreyer gave Pollen grounds for claiming a mistrial. Having helped to prepare the crown's case against Pollen, and simultaneously having been treated as a neutral expert by the RCAI, Dreyer had played a major role in the defeat of Pollen's original claim. As soon as his victim was out of the way, he decided to put in his own claim to the RCAI, not content with the £5,000 award the Admiralty had already made to him for his plagiarized system.

Dreyer's action transformed the legal terrain facing Pollen. Most obviously, it meant that Dreyer could no longer get away with playing the role of disinterested neutral expert on naval fire control. No less importantly, Dreyer's claim drove a wedge between himself and the Admiralty. The result was that instead of there being two "rival genealogies" of invention in play—an Admiralty-Dreyer genealogy, and a Pollen genealogy—there were now three: an Admiralty one, a Dreyer one, and a Pollen one.[2]

Other changes redounded to Pollen's advantage. While the crown continued to assert the privilege that would evolve into the public-interest immunity, the RCAI's new chairman, a distinguished senior judge, proved doggedly independent. Not only was he far less deferential to the crown than Justice Sargant had been; he was also much less deferential than the American judges discussed in chapter 10. Conducted on a less tilted playing field, the new hearings went far differently than the original round. The commissioners became convinced that Pollen and Isherwood had invented a form of artificial intelligence—what they called an "intelligent machine." What made the machine intelligent, in their view, was the autogeneration of bearings through mechanical interconnection of the range and bearing rates, the very feature that distinguished Pollen's and Isherwood's clock from early versions of the Dreyer tables (and of the Ford rangekeeper). Furthermore, the commissioners found, what turned Dreyer's dumb machine into an intelligent one was plagiarizing Pollen, a breach of the Admiralty's fiduciary obligations. When subjected to competent outside scrutiny, which the Admiralty and Dreyer had so long tried to avoid, their claims and doctored evidence collapsed.

GETTING A REHEARING

After the RCAI rejected Pollen's claim in October 1923, it did not take long for the next battle in the campaign to begin. The following month, with Pollen seemingly out of the way, Dreyer wrote to the Admiralty about putting in his own claim.[3] The month after that, Pollen put in a new claim form under Head 3 of the Royal Warrant for "A Fire Control System and apparatus which embodied the features[,] elements and general methods of working of the mechanism of the Admiralty Clock."[4] He was not going to have the RCAI exclude the clock from his system again. Four months later, Dreyer put in a claim of his own for an award for the Dreyer tables.[5] There was also a new claim in the mix from the estate of Rear Admiral John Dumaresq, whose patents James Swinburne had found that the Dreyer tables infringed. Dumaresq had died suddenly in July 1922, leaving behind a family. On their behalf, his brother Reginald put in a claim to the RCAI for an additional award over and above the £1,500 the Admiralty had made to John, seeking money to care for John's widow, who had been institutionalized, and for his five children.[6]

For Pollen, Dreyer's claim was a godsend. It meant that if he managed to secure a new hearing, he would square off directly against Dreyer as a competitor; the Admiralty would not be able to repeat its sleight-of-hand of refusing to call Dreyer as a witness. Indeed, when Dreyer attempted to get a quick hearing of his own claim, the RCAI insisted that Dreyer's and Pollen's petitions be heard together.[7] Dreyer's claim also mattered for Pollen because it fundamentally restructured the three-way relationship between the two men and the Admiralty. Now, instead of being Dreyer's ally, the Admiralty became his opponent—just as it had long been Pollen's. The effect, though certainly not the intent, of this change was to make the enemy of Pollen's enemy his friend.

Hemmed in between two rival inventors, to neither of whom it wished to pay more money, the Admiralty tried to play them off against each other. In its remarkable counterstatement to Dreyer's claim, the Admiralty now admitted that

> During the period 1906–1918 covering the suggestions of the Applicant [Dreyer] was in full touch with the whole of the work being done on fire control for the Navy in an official capacity. *In particular he was thoroughly familiar with the various suggestions and trials of the apparatus of the Argo Company Ltd. and took part to some extent in some of the sea trials of the same.* [emphasis added][8]

That is, the Admiralty was arguing that Dreyer deserved no further award because his official duties gave him access to the knowledge he needed to make his invention—specifically Pollen's knowledge. This was the central fact that the Admiralty had worked for decades to suppress. Equally remarkably, the Admiralty counterstatement acknowledged that Dreyer had acted "in an advisory capacity" for the Admiralty's handling of Pollen's 1923 RCAI claim.[9] In other words, the Admiralty was confessing that it had in fact taken advice about Pollen from a rival inventor with an obvious and substantial conflict of interest. This too amounted to officially admitting the justice of what was probably Pollen's greatest grievance: not that the Admiralty had plagiarized his invention (though that was bad enough), but that it had betrayed its obligations to him in order to do so, even as he had faithfully honored his obligations to the Admiralty.

Pollen immediately appreciated the significance of Dreyer's misstep, and he had other reasons for optimism. "[T]hough you will hardly believe it, Dreyer is, himself, bringing a claim for his system, so that it is inevitable that the whole question that the Admiralty lawyers assumed to be closed so far as I am concerned at the last hearing, will have to be re-opened," Pollen wrote to his friend and supporter Rear Admiral Richard Peirse in July 1924. "In other words, the real inventor of the Dreyer system will have to be found by the Commission."[10] "The colossal cheek of Dreyer is amazing," Peirse replied, "but it seems that when a man becomes a Lord of the Admiralty his sense of morality gets perverted."[11] Moreover, Pollen had again appealed to David Beatty for the Admiralty to relax its position on discovery, with apparent success.[12]

As usual in Pollen's experience, however, the Admiralty followed its momentary attack of conscience with a swift alteration in course. In October 1924, the Treasury Solicitor asked that the RCAI order Pollen to amend his new claim in such a way as to limit it to the clock and preclude it from covering the whole system, on the grounds that the RCAI had already rejected the system claim in 1923.[13] In addition, the Admiralty backtracked on the question of discovery, agreeing to allow full disclosure to Pollen's legal team but refusing to extend it to Pollen himself.[14]

Three days later, Pollen's patent agency filed a formal appeal. No longer content with putting it a new claim for just the clock, Pollen now sought a rehearing of his original claim—in effect, a declaration of a mistrial. This was a major change. In requesting a rehearing, rather than a new hearing, Pollen was petitioning the RCAI to repudiate the 1923 judgment in its entirety, not merely to decide on a new case without implications for the old. He criticized the 1923 RCAI for excluding the clock and thus for ruling on his system without understanding what the system was. More importantly, he charged, the RCAI had accepted evidence about the Admiralty system "without affording the Claimants [sic] Counsel any proper opportunity of cross examination"—that is, without affording Romer an opportunity to cross-examine Dreyer about his presentation of the Admiralty's system— and had "wrongly admitted evidence" in the form of Dreyer's submissions to the Admiralty, without the Admiralty having given notice that it would rely on those documents, permitting Pollen to see them, or affording Romer sufficient time to study them.[15] These were not mere technical complaints: as Pollen put it privately, "a fundamental principle of British justice was ignored" by the RCAI in 1923, "in that the parties were not on equality either in presenting their own case or in answering that of their opponents."[16] Pollen's appeal raised a constitutional question about the RCAI, namely, whether it had jurisdiction to grant a full rehearing. After consulting with the Treasury about jurisdiction, the RCAI agreed to consider the possibility of a rehearing in early 1925.[17]

By this time, two important characters in the cast had changed. One was the chairman, with Lord Tomlin replacing Sargant. Best known for his 1936 ruling in *Inland Revenue Commissioners v. Duke of Westminster*, a famous tax-avoidance case, Tomlin was also the father of Stephen Tomlin, the artist and member of the Bloomsbury Set. The transcripts of the 1925 hearings as compared with those from 1923 reveal a night-and-day difference between the attitudes of the two chairmen. Where Sargant gave the Admiralty a long lead and asked few questions, Tomlin kept the Admiralty on a short leash and peppered everyone—counsel on both sides and witnesses—with queries to make sure that he understood the technical matters under discussion as well as the legal arguments being advanced. The transcripts show a man with a commitment to fairness, a powerful intellect, and a keen engineering mind, able quickly to grasp difficult technical matter.[18]

The second new character was Pollen's new lead counsel, Wilfrid Greene (Romer stayed on as junior counsel). Having "got rather a windfall, and having money in hand now for proper fight," Pollen explained to Peirse, "I retained Mr Wilfred [sic] Greene, who is said to be most brilliant advocate now at Bar."[19] Well on his way to a highly distinguished legal career—he would eventually be raised to the peerage in recognition of his immense contributions to administrative law—Greene proved himself to be worth every shilling. Like Romer, Greene had joined the army during World War I, managing to survive four years in the infantry and earning a Military Cross and the Croix de Guerre plus an OBE. His service included a stint as an instructor of rangefinders, giving him intimate familiarity with some of the technology involved in naval fire control.[20] Bracingly intelligent, rhetorically gifted, and marvelously quick on his feet, Greene provided a crystal-clear exposition of Pollen's extremely complex case, aided by a knack for explaining the arcane matter of fire control in plain, even homespun, English.[21] In the voluminous hearing transcripts, he leaps off the page across the span of a century. Greene developed deep respect and affection for his client, a fellow Catholic and Oxford graduate who shared his interest in art.[22] In Greene, Pollen for the first time had found someone whom he could trust to represent his interests as ably as he himself could.

During the preliminary hearing in March 1925, Greene persuaded the RCAI to grant Pollen a full rehearing of his original claim. Tomlin presided, joined by two members who had participated in the 1923 hearing, plus a new member, the barrister A. M. Langdon. Greene argued that Pollen had intended to include the clock as part of the claim and that the Admiralty had understood his claim to include a clock.[23] "I do not quite understand what it was in the language of the claim which led the Commission at that time to limit the claim to the [plotting element]," Tomlin declared.[24] It seemed to him that Sargant had not understood "what was the real function of the clock at all."[25]

Convinced that the 1923 RCAI had misinterpreted Pollen's claim, Tomlin and his colleagues became suspicious and even troubled by Dreyer's role in the 1923 hearing. Tomlin and Langdon regarded it as a gross irregularity that the Admiralty had entered Dreyer's letters and explanation of the Dreyer table into evidence without calling Dreyer as a witness to testify on them. "Dealing with an old Common Law experience," the barrister Langdon remarked, "I should have great difficulty in deciding a case of documents on which a man was not cross-examined."[26] When the Treasury Solicitor protested that the Admiralty had made Dreyer available for Romer to call as a witness, both Langdon and Tomlin rebuked him. "Surely, speaking technically," Langdon insisted, "the party which puts forward the documents has to put forward the witness."[27] Tomlin agreed.[28] The fact that Dreyer subsequently put in his own claim compounded the Admiralty's violation of basic legal principle. "Prima facie for proof of the documents it was necessary to call him," Tomlin stated, "and it was not apparent at that time that Captain Dryer [sic] himself was a claimant."[29] He added, "I personally attach considerable weight" to the fact "that at the time when the Commission were dealing with this case they had no idea that any claim was going to be put in" by Dreyer.[30] "I take the same view very strongly," Langdon chorused.[31]

Pollen was delighted. As he recounted to Peirse, the Admiralty's unwillingness to call Dreyer as a witness, along with Dreyer's own RCAI claim, swung the case his way:

> To the Commission, therefore, it appeared that having without subjecting [sic] himself to cross examination or being called to prove his invention, assisted the Admiralty both in getting up their case and in putting it before the Commission, he had, as soon as I was safely out of the way and could not contrast his statements with my evidence, come out to ask for the very award which the Commission had refused to me. This revelation caused quite a sensation in the Court, and the Judge and Commissioners seemed to be unanimous in regarding it as a new fact of the utmost importance.... [W]e left the Court convinced that the Commission had 'smelt a rat' and was hotfooted on our side.[32]

The RCAI quickly decided that a full rehearing was necessary.[33] Its decision constituted a full repudiation and remarkable rebuke of the original hearings.

This set the stage for a final round of fighting over discovery. Pollen informed the RCAI that he wanted full discovery, including of all documents that Dreyer and the Admiralty would rely on to make their case, along with full disclosure of the Admiralty's case not only to his legal counsel but also to his technical experts as well as Isherwood and himself.[34] The Admiralty reflexively objected.[35] Yet anxious that Pollen be given a fair trial this time around, the commissioners confined the scope of crown privilege to much narrower limits than the Admiralty wanted.[36] At a hearing in May 1925, in which the Attorney General himself, Douglas Hogg (soon to be the first Lord Hailsham), represented the crown, Tomlin not only ordered Dreyer to disclose to Pollen any private documents in his possession on which he intended to rely, but also ordered the Admiralty to disclose to Pollen's legal team its communications with Dreyer.[37] Despite Greene's strong representations that disclosure to Pollen was vital if he was to instruct Greene properly, however, Tomlin felt unable to overrule the crown and compel it to extend disclosure to Pollen himself.[38] Still, his rulings on Dreyer's documents and the Admiralty's communications with Dreyer made the playing field more level than it had been in the first hearing.

The extension of disclosure to technical experts proved particularly important. As we saw in chapter 6, and as Greene emphasized to the commissioners, the refusal to extend disclosure to technical experts in 1923 had placed Romer in an impossible position and left Dreyer's highly self-interested but ostensibly expert testimony to go unchallenged.[39] Now the shoe was firmly on the other foot: not only had Dreyer's claim revealed his self-interest, but the only technical expert to testify in the case was hired by Pollen. As in his selection of Greene for counsel, Pollen went for top-class talent, hiring William Henry Ballantyne, a distinguished patent agent, consulting engineer, and frequent expert witness in patent cases (including the protracted Sperry-Anschütz gyrocompass litigation), who eventually rose to become the president of the Chartered Institute of Patent Agents. Ballantyne possessed other relevant experience, having been a research assistant to Lord Kelvin, worked for Barr & Stroud, and, like Greene, done a stint as instructor of rangefinders in the army.[40] Curiously, perhaps overconfidently, neither the Admiralty nor Dreyer brought in an expert witness of their own. One might have expected them to call James Swinburne, the Admiralty's go-to patent expert, but his 1913 opinion on the Dreyer tables, discussed in chapter 3, hardly provided grounds for confidence that he would endorse the Admiralty's and Dreyer's arguments—not least because Swinburne had found that Dreyer had infringed the patents of John Dumaresq, who was also now a claimant. The result was that the Admiralty and Dreyer had no one to rebut Ballantyne, whose testimony took up almost two full days and deeply impressed the commissioners.[41]

Even without disclosure to himself, Pollen sensed that he would fare better in the rehearing. "We are already a 'cause celebre,' the Attorney General has been put in to run the case against us, and although Isherwood and I are still excluded from the disclosure of the instruments, we know from our past failure how to present our case this time," he wrote to Peirse. "[W]e have an inestimable advantage in being able to put Dreyer into the Box and to cross-examine him." "The real point," he concluded, "is that we have what we did not have last time, which is a Commission strongly suspicious that there has been crooked work, and absolutely determined to do all in its power to see things are run squarely this time."[42] Except for Tom-lin's unwillingness to compel disclosure to Pollen personally, he was right.

DISCOVERING INVENTION

The rehearing began in late June 1925. Justice Tomlin presided. Greene and Romer represented Pollen. Sir Duncan Kerly, who had represented the crown in the 1923 hearings, reprised his role, now joined by the Attorney General (Douglas Hogg). K. E. Shelley—who had appeared for the crown in the 1923 hearing—now represented Dreyer. Tomlin made clear on the first day that unlike Sargant, he was not going to impose an arbitrary time limit on the hearing.[43] Whereas the first one ran for three days, this one ran for no less than fourteen, including several Saturday meetings. As Tomlin put it, "[T]his a very important case, and I am not going to allow time to prevent the Commission giving to all the parties the fullest opportunity of putting their case before the Commission."[44]

Both Pollen and Dreyer submitted bundles of documentary evidence to support their claims, the former's much larger than the latter's.[45] Pollen included the bulk—though not all—of his official correspondence with the Admiralty from 1900 to 1913, but only a tiny fraction of his extensive unof-ficial correspondence with various naval officials preserved in his private papers.[46] The evidence in their bundles took on different significance in the legal context of the RCAI than it had possessed in its original historical context. Before the war, working within what he believed to be a fiduciary partnership with the Admiralty, Pollen had focused on communicating his inventions to the Admiralty as he made them in accordance with the 1908 contract, not on dating their communication for the purposes of a future legal dispute. One of the more important pieces of evidence from his docu-mentary bundle, for instance, turned out to be a routine note to Isherwood that Pollen had dashed off to apprise him of a conversation with Joseph Henley in May 1911, which demonstrated that Argo had communicated the design of the Argo IV clock to the Admiralty at that time.[47] Clearly Pollen had not written the note with the slightest idea that it would prove legally serendipitous; he was just trying to keep a colleague in the loop. Conversely, naval officials did not always create a documentary record of their dealings with Pollen. When asked whether he minuted all suggestions of importance by Pollen, Arthur Craig Waller, who had served as Assistant Director of Na-val Ordnance in 1909–11, replied, "No, I do not think I did; no."[48] In fact, until the battle over the prospect of Pollen selling abroad in 1912 and 1913, neither party was developing a documentary record with an eye toward future litigation.

In reviewing this evidence, Tomlin, unlike Sargant, resisted procedural irregularities that privileged one party over another. Accordingly, he permitted Admiralty representatives to give their views on technological and historical matters only as witnesses offering evidence; he did not treat them as impartial experts. "[T]his body is a judicial body," Tomlin explained.

> They will decline to be affected by anything that does not come before them strictly in accordance with judicial methods of dealing with it. Therefore if statements are made to them on one side by an expert those statements must be treated as part of the evidence in the case and as such must be subject to cross-examination in the ordinary way.[49]

On multiple occasions, he chided the Admiralty and Dreyer for surprising the court with last-minute additional documents. "I think it is very unsatisfactory cross-examining a witness about something he has never seen," he admonished Shelley.[50] When another document turned up so late that its coauthor had finished his testimony and could not be recalled, Tomlin erupted at the Admiralty.[51]

More broadly, Tomlin treated secrecy as an undesirable exception to legal norms of due process. He displayed markedly less deference to the crown's assertion of a secrecy privilege than the standard later set in the landmark public-interest immunity case *Duncan v. Cammell Laird*.[52] Although he felt unable to reject the Admiralty's demand for secrecy altogether, he used his judgment to determine whether the demand really was necessary on national security grounds in particular instances. He took every opportunity to decrease the scope of secrecy and to increase the scope of disclosure. The insistence on secrecy "is a very great embarrassment to all of us, and it is most unfortunate that it has to be dealt with in this way," he stated. "That is why I am anxious to reduce it as far as possible to a minimum."[53] By setting the default to openness, he effectively put the burden of proof on the crown to show that its assertion of privilege was not arbitrary. The crown struggled to do so.

Tomlin's commitment to judicial independence and the principle of transparency came through in ways large and small. He ruled, for instance, that the Admiralty's refusal to permit Greene to discuss a certain document with Pollen was "perfectly ridiculous" and released Greene from the obligation to keep it secret from Pollen.[54] When Kerly, the Treasury Solicitor's representative, indicated that the Admiralty would object to Pollen attending demonstrations of his own system on the grounds that it had forbidden his presence on any ships in 1913, Tomlin retorted, "Yes, but Sir Duncan, there are limits even to Admiralty Orders. To my mind it is perfectly absurd to suggest that he cannot be allowed to go to a particular place to watch this particular thing which is something in which he himself took part. Of course they can surround him with detectives if they like."[55] In another context, he remarked, "All these instruments for the protection of the State necessarily to a certain extent put a limit on the liberties and rights of the Subject; but they can be administered reasonably or unreasonably."[56] He left little doubt as to his views on the reasonableness of the crown's administration in Pollen's case.

Tomlin's most significant reduction in the scope of secrecy concerned Isherwood, whom the Admiralty sought to exclude from disclosure along with Pollen. Greene, wishing to avail himself of Isherwood's unparalleled expertise in designing both Pollen's and the Admiralty's systems, informed the RCAI that the Admiralty's attitude toward Isherwood was "very extraordinary" given that it had included him in the design of the Admiralty Fire Control Table (AFCT).[57] When Kerly objected that Isherwood did not learn everything about the Dreyer tables while working on the AFCT, Tomlin insisted that the Admiralty distinguish precisely between what Isherwood did and did not know rather than deal in generalities. Kerly responded by insinuating that Isherwood was untrustworthy: "The court wont [sic] forget that these people, the Argo people—I am not saying it at all in disrespect—their business is to get systems of rangefinding and sell them to foreign powers."[58] Tomlin swatted this away and ordered that Isherwood be put on the stand to say what exactly he knew. After listening to his testimony, Tomlin ruled that Greene was free to discuss the mechanical construction of the Dreyer tables with Isherwood.[59]

Despite Tomlin's best efforts to chip away at crown privilege, secrecy still hurt Pollen and his team. The limits on disclosure to him meant not only that could Pollen not see much of the Admiralty's evidence, but also that he could not see parts of *his own* evidence.[60] Moreover, he could not instruct Greene on key points.[61] This handicap had concrete results. For instance, not until the penultimate day of hearings did Greene perceive the potential significance of a letter from Keith Elphinstone to Dreyer in July 1911, submitted as part of Dreyer's bundle of documents for the hearing but forbidden for Pollen to see, which proved that Elphinstone had been in close touch with Joseph Henley as well as with Dreyer.[62] The letter suggested a new possible avenue by which Pollen's ideas might have found their way into the Dreyer table—via Elphinstone rather than Dreyer. Because Pollen did not see the letter and was focused on dating Dreyer's knowledge of his ideas, he had not thought to tell Greene that Elphinstone had frequently accompanied Henley to his works prior to the date when he could prove that Dreyer knew all of his ideas. By the time that Greene realized Elphinstone's potential significance, it was too late to call him as a witness.[63] Thus, the Admiralty's limits on disclosure to Pollen precluded him from putting forward the strongest possible case in support of his claim—despite which it still proved much stronger than his opponents'.

..

Pollen's claim, as finally amended in May 1925, consisted of two parts. The first, identical to the original claim heard in 1923, quoted language from the 1908 contract and covered his system as a whole. The second, not in the original claim, was an alternative wording of the first in order to prevent any confusion over the scope of the claim such as had marred the first hearing. It covered "the principle and details of a Clock, Integrating, or Range keeping Device or Change of range machine."[64] In short, the first formulation of the claim focused on the system as a whole, while the second formulation focused on the clock.

Of the two, the system claim was trickier. It raised the same difficult questions about the nature of invention that had complicated the original contract negotiations. Was invention mental or material? Could one invent a conceptual system apart from the specific instruments for giving material effect to it? During the hearings, Greene argued that, while Pollen had successfully reduced his system to instrumental form, his invention included the system too. Before Pollen could design the hardware, so to speak, he had to identify the algorithms that the system would need to solve. Greene referred to "the governing idea" or "the platonic idea" behind "the concrete embodiment."[65] When Tomlin questioned whether obtaining data on target range and bearing and predicting future target location based on those data constituted part of an invented system or merely a statement of a problem to be solved through invention, Ballantyne insisted that defining the problem was a crucial part of invention.[66] "It seems to be extraordinary," Tomlin interjected: surely, it was "one of the obvious things" that prediction of future target location would have to account for the variation of range and bearing during time of flight.[67] Au contraire, Ballantyne replied:

> Suppose there are twenty-five or thirty factors in the Pollen system, it would not be difficult to say that in itself is obvious to a high class mathematician if he has set out to work it and I should have to agree in every case and I can well foresee the cross-examination of Mr. Pollen and Commander Isherwood and myself being proceeded with on those lines would have that result. Each element of the whole system one could say that in itself is obvious if you know you want to do it, but I may say that

this statement which was drafted by Mr. Pollen, which as Your Lordship has pointed out merely sets out the desiderata of the problem, that in itself gives a rather clear indication of what you have to do and as such it is an important communication to the Admiralty and furthermore that having it in their minds from 1901 to 1904 they were immediately led along lines of the solution which has subsequently been adopted.[68]

So then, Tomlin reasoned, "The importance of it as a communication to the Admiralty depends entirely upon the mental conditions of the Admiralty at the time of the communication?"[69] Ballantyne answered in the affirmative. Edward Harding, who was the only witness called by Pollen, Dreyer, or the Admiralty with independent first-hand knowledge of "the mental conditions of the Admiralty" at the time of the early negotiations with Pollen, confirmed Ballantyne's argument.[70]

As it had during the original 1906 contract negotiations, this definition of invention had legal implications. If the RCAI tried to separate the mental from the material, Greene argued, it would fail to understand how deep the Admiralty's plagiarism of Pollen ran. "The Admiralty are trying to do without Pollen and at the same time to adopt him bit by bit," he told the commission.[71] "[T]hey were driven to it, because Mr. Pollen had shown them the only road that could be taken."[72] On this logic, apparent differences between the Admiralty's system and Pollen's faded into insignificance, because everything the Admiralty did took place within the conceptual framework that Pollen had invented. Without understanding the dual mental-material character of invention, the Admiralty's and Dreyer's debt to Pollen looked smaller than it was.

By contrast, the Admiralty adopted the conventional line that invention was only materialistic—except when it suited its purposes to argue the opposite. Everything that Pollen had done in the conceptual realm, according to the Admiralty, was "obvious." Solving the problem of the relative motion of two bodies, for instance, went back centuries in astronomy, at least to Kepler. "Real" invention, therefore, consisted of "the devising of special mechanical means."[73] Pollen deserved no credit for pushing mechanization. "Isn't that what is done, in a mechanical age such as we live in, in every direction?" Kerly asked.[74] Following lines laid down by Dreyer, the crown also pointed to the work of Henry Watkin as an anticipation of Pollen, as well as to various integrating clocks.[75]

These arguments about Watkin and other ostensible anticipators of Pollen's proved unpersuasive, even risible, before the RCAI. Greene had great fun with Dreyer's fixation on Watkin, asking him, when he saw one of Pollen's inventions, "Did you say 'Hullo! here's old Watkin again', or something like that?"[76] Harding, who, as a Royal Marine officer, of course was familiar with Watkin's inventions from his service in the coastal artillery, could not see their relevance.[77] Ballantyne, under cross-examination by Shelley, bluntly pointed out that the Watkin system could not work at sea.[78] Tongue in cheek, Tomlin pronounced the attempt to use Watkin as an anticipation of Pollen's clock "one of the mysteries of the case."[79] When Kerly moved away from Watkin and tried to suggest that Lord Kelvin's famed harmonic analyzer anticipated Pollen's clock, the stratagem boomeranged on him. Ballantyne shot back, "I was a Research Fellow with [Kelvin] and did a lot of work with it, but I cannot see what that has to do with this."[80] Indeed, Ballantyne maintained, "I think I may say in regard to the Argo clock as a whole that speaking as an engineer I have never seen a more beautiful piece of engineering work although I have seen most of the engineering work that has been done during the last 26 [sic] or 30 years."[81] Greene reported that as Ballantyne was saying this, "There came over him the smile of a really enthusiastic engineer, who knew what he was talking about, and he was not talking as an expert witness, but as an engineer."[82] Ballantyne's testimony carried great weight with the commissioners. All in all, Tomlin summarized on the final day of hearings, "I think at present the Commission are not much impressed by there being nothing new in Mr. Pollen's ideas."[83] So much for obviousness and anticipation.

∴

While the RCAI did not buy the Admiralty's and Dreyer's extreme argument that Pollen had done nothing new, his system claim nevertheless troubled the commissioners, particularly as it related to plotting. Consistent with the view he had always taken (and which Harding shared), Pollen argued that his system embraced multiple methodological and instrumental variants, so long as they fell within the parameters defined in the 1908 contract, and that both rate plotting and course plotting fell within these parameters, even though Pollen had always preferred course plotting. His reasoning was not simply that rate plotting and course plotting were mathematically convertible, though they were—course plotting worked from target course and speed to get the range and bearing rates, while rate plotting worked from the rates to get target course and speed.[84] Pollen also insisted that his system included rate plotting as well as course plotting because he and the Admiralty, represented by Harding, believed it did when they negotiated the 1908 contract, and because he had suggested rate plotting before Dreyer did.[85] Harding corroborated Pollen's claim to have discussed two-rate plotting even before the 1906 negotiations and again to have suggested the idea of bearing-rate plotting in 1906 or 1907.[86] Tomlin accepted that Pollen had experimented with two-rate plotting.[87] He and Langdon further accepted that the Admiralty knew that Pollen had already been working on two-rate plotting for some time before late 1910, when it claimed to have given him the idea.[88]

By contrast, Dreyer could produce no evidence in support of his claim to have invented the idea of two-rate plotting before anyone else.[89] He tried to push his idea of range-rate plotting back to the instruments he had invented in 1906 and 1907, but Tomlin—aided by Greene's pinpoint cross-examination—concluded that the earlier instruments did not in fact make range-rate plots.[90] Nor could Dreyer produce any "contemporary evidence," in Tomlin's words, that substantiated his claim to have done range-rate plotting in 1907.[91] The earliest that Dreyer successfully dated his idea of range-rate (but not bearing-rate) plotting was January 1908, in the trials carried out on HMS *Vengeance* shortly after those on HMS *Ariadne*.[92] Dreyer also attempted to push his idea of bearing-rate plotting back to 1908, but Greene picked apart the only two documents he produced to support this timetable, leaving him with 1910 as the earliest date when he could show that he had suggested bearing-rate plotting in addition to range-rate plotting.[93] This chronology put Dreyer at least one year behind Pollen for the idea of range-rate plotting and at least three years behind Pollen for bearing-rate plotting. The collapse of Dreyer's claim to have invented two-rate plotting in 1908 nevertheless did not deter him from repeating it in his memoirs.[94]

Despite all this, the RCAI was not fully persuaded that rate plotting was part of Pollen's system. The commissioners struggled to escape the view that invention must involve a material component—an idea had to be accompanied by a gadget, so to speak. The instinct to think in terms of material instruments came out of a patent-infringement paradigm familiar to both Langdon and Tomlin, given their legal backgrounds. They seem also to have been reluctant to stray beyond settled law; serving in some sense more as arbitrators than as regular judges, the commissioners felt obliged to apply existing law rather than to create precedent.[95] "[D]oesn't it come to this," Langdon asked Greene, "that your claim must be for the instrument which bridged over, or conquered the difficulty which had been bothering everybody up to that time?"[96] Similarly, Tomlin reasoned, Pollen's claim must be "for the system visualised in the particular form of those mechanical instruments." [97] Pollen's clear preference for course plotting posed a further obstacle to his rate-plotting claim.[98]

At the same time, Tomlin could not bring himself to reduce Pollen's invention to hardware and course plotting alone. He appreciated that Pollen had contributed more to the Admiralty than instruments. "May it not be this," Tomlin summarized, "that a conception of a great mind is gradually penetrating bit by bit into another mind, but it does not follow that you can treat that conception as something entitling you to a reward?"[99] He added that Pollen's evidence "suggests a very strong case for your having influenced what the Admiralty actually did in several respects."[100] From Tomlin's perspective, it was possible that Pollen had invented rate plotting before Dreyer and communicated it to the Admiralty—but that he had no claim to an award for rate plotting, because he had always preferred course plotting. Furthermore, even if Pollen did have a claim to a system apart from specific instruments, the commissioners thought, the Admiralty had already paid him more or less what he thought it was worth.[101]

DISHONOR AMONG THIEVES

While the commissioners' materialistic bias injured Pollen on his system claim, it helped him on his clock claim, which fit a patent-infringement paradigm much more comfortably. The core of Dreyer's and the Admiralty's response to Pollen's clock claim was to try to show that they had developed theirs independently of Pollen, by pushing the invention of their clock as far back in time as possible and by trying to depict it as fundamentally different from Pollen's. The Admiralty thus argued that Dreyer's clock was nothing more than an improved Vickers clock bolted to a Dumaresq—the latter for generating the rates, and the former for integrating them—and that Dreyer had invented the idea of this connection in 1908. For the Admiralty, this date was significant because Dreyer was then employed in the Naval Ordnance Department, meaning that the invention had fallen within the scope of his duties and thus merited no further award.[102] Dreyer attempted to argue that the essential features of his clock mechanism were embodied in all Dreyer tables from the Mark III on, which might plausibly be dated after he left the Naval Ordnance Department but before he heard about the Argo IV clock.[103] Both he and the Admiralty were steering the evidence toward narrow chronological windows that served their respective purposes.

Greene tore their cases apart. In the first place, he argued, and Harding corroborated, that Pollen, not Dreyer, was the first to suggest mechanically connecting the Dumaresq to the Vickers clock and actually did so during the *Ariadne* trials.[104] What is more, in his devastating cross-examination of Dreyer, Greene persuaded the RCAI that Dreyer had gotten the idea for the connection during the *Vengeance* trials from the superintending Admiral Arthur Wilson, who had gotten the idea from watching Pollen do it during the *Ariadne* trials shortly before.[105]

Greene further convinced the RCAI that the Mark IV and V Dreyer Tables, which all parties agreed were very similar to each other, differed fundamentally from a Dumaresq-Vickers clock linkage. Dreyer himself argued, contra the Admiralty, that the clocks in his table did not resemble Vickers clocks: "I do not know why they should be labelled as Vickers clocks . . . they do it entirely differently, as a matter of fact, to the Vickers clock."[106] He further agreed with Greene that in his system, the Dumaresq functioned not as a separate instrument but as part of the clock.[107] Tomlin took the point. "The truth of the matter is, you may put independent things together in such a way as to create a new independent whole," he told Kerly.[108]

Greene further persuaded the RCAI that the Mark *IV* Dreyer table differed fundamentally and significantly from the Mark *III*. Indeed, the difference between them was precisely the difference that Swinburne had identified between the Mark III Dreyer table and the Argo IV clock, as well as the difference between the initial versions and the later versions of the Mark I Ford rangekeeper discussed in chapter 4: the difference was that one could autogenerate bearings, and the other could not. The reason for the difference, Greene and Ballantyne explained, was that the Mark *IV* Dreyer table, like the later versions of the Mark I Ford rangekeeper, replaced the *human* intervention required to connect the Dumaresq, the range clock, and the bearing clock in the Mark *III* Dreyer table with *mechanical* connections.[109] Put simply, the Mark IV Dreyer table attempted to solve the mathematical equations relating own to target movement mechanically, whereas the Mark III attempted to solve them manually. As we have seen, Pollen had always argued that this difference mattered because only mechanical connections could reproduce the continuous variation of the rates under challenging tactical conditions; manual adjustment of the clock was discontinuous. Against his preference for mechanization, the Admiralty had unquestionably preferred human intervention. As Kerly put it, "The essence of our system is that judgment, the man's judgment, intervenes at an early stage and he can always tell how things are going,"[110] whereas "[t]he whole essence of [Pollen's] system is that it is perfect throughout with no room for individual judgment or errors."[111]

Tomlin agreed that the difference between human and machine—or between human and mechanical automata—was fundamental. Listening to Greene explain the significance of this difference in his opening, Tomlin remarked, "You have really in one sense got to have a machine which, so to speak, uses intelligence in the way it works out the data with which it has been supplied."[112] Another term for "intelligent machine" is artificial intelligence. An unintelligent clock—one requiring manual adjustment like the

Vickers clock or the Mark III Dreyer table—"worked at the rate at which you set it but it was not a self-regulating clock to vary its own rate."[113] Even if a human being functioned as an "automaton," merely following a pointer rather than performing a calculation or using independent judgment, Tomlin doubted that human beings were automatic in the way machines were: "I should have thought at the moment you introduced the human element it ceased to be automatic."[114] The lack of mechanical automaticity introduced error into the clock's calculations: the longer the period of delay between manual human adjustments to the clock's rate, the larger the error.[115] Hence, when Kerly claimed that the Mark III Dreyer table could perform through a human link the same operations that the Mark IV could perform mechanically, Tomlin shot back, "I do not care a rap about the human link. The human link has nothing to do with it; so long as the human link is in it, it is not a mechanical thing."[116] All in all, as Tomlin put it on the penultimate day, mechanically generating the correct rates in relation to each other was "the Rubicon," "the frontier line."[117] The Mark III Dreyer table fell on one side of this line, and the Mark IV on the other.

What had enabled Dreyer and the Admiralty to cross the line, Greene showed, was the Argo clock. Greene presented evidence that Dreyer had incorporated various features in his clock only following their disclosure to him by Pollen. The process of plagiarism had occurred at multiple points over many years.[118] But the real key was Dreyer's switch from the "unintelligent" Mark III Dreyer clock to the "intelligent" Mark IV Dreyer clock following the disclosure of the milestone Argo IV clock. Pollen could prove that he had disclosed the Argo IV design to the Admiralty (in the person of Henley) in May 1911—a date the RCAI took pains to nail down—and to Dreyer in July 1911, before exhibiting the finished clock to various officers in early 1912.[119] Dreyer could do no better than prove that he had proposed at least the beginning of the Mark *III* Dreyer table design on 19 July 1911.[120] But neither he nor the Admiralty dared suggest that the design of the Mark *IV* Dreyer table, which they avoided dating altogether, went back that far. Hence their desperation to show that the Mark *III* Dreyer table, which might plausibly have predated disclosure of the Argo IV clock, anticipated the Mark *IV* Dreyer table in all essentials.

Tomlin would have none of it. When Shelley protested that the Mark IV Dreyer table developed immediately from the Mark III, Tomlin remarked, "sometimes it is the last step which takes you there."[121] In the Mark III Dreyer table, Tomlin insisted, "you have not got to the governing principle" of mechanically inter-connecting the rates.[122] Sensing which way the wind was blowing, the crown, which had previously been sailing more

or less in tandem with Dreyer, deftly changed tack and reset on a collision course with Dreyer. "There is no doubt that the Admiralty have taken
the view, and do take the view, that they got the suggestions for the Dreyer
table from Admiral Dreyer," Kerly told the RCAI. "If Admiral Dreyer
got them directly or indirectly from Mr. Pollen, that is another matter."[123]
In other words, if there had been any wrongdoing, Dreyer was solely
to blame.

In any case, the RCAI realized that the capabilities of the Argo IV clock
could have found their way into even the Mark *III* Dreyer table through
sources other than Dreyer, namely, Henley and Elphinstone. Although
the Admiralty's limits on disclosure to Pollen had prevented him, as mentioned, from alerting Greene to the potential significance of the Henley-
Elphinstone connection, the eagle-eyed Langdon spotted evidence of
it in Dreyer's bundle of documents. "[W]hat I want to know," he told
Kerly, "as from the material date of the communications by Mr. Pollen to
the Admiralty, when I find they are communicated on May 27th [1911] to
Captain Henley, what inference am I to draw from the fact that Captain
Henley is in consultation with Sir Keith Elphinstone, who is designing the
particular [Dreyer] Table which is in question here?"[124] Kerly now proceeded to throw Elphinstone overboard as well. Speaking of the idea for
a key innovation in the Mark III Dreyer table, Kerly allowed that "there
might be room for doubt—I say room for doubt—as to whether the actual designer, Sir Keith Elphinstone, did not get it from elsewhere"—i.e.,
from Pollen.[125]

As its case collapsed, the crown struggled even harder to convince the
RCAI that the Admiralty had not adopted the Argo clock's infinitely variable slipless drive. This feature unquestionably did not appear in any of the
Dreyer tables. Whereas Dreyer tried to minimize its importance altogether,
Kerly admitted that "We do know the ball drive [i.e., the slipless drive] instead of the roller drive is an improvement."[126] Indeed they did—hence the
incorporation of the slipless drive into the AFCT. Kerly did his best to disguise this embarrassing truth, but the contradictions in his presentation
did not escape the commissioners.[127]

The RCAI had no doubt that what the Admiralty and Dreyer had done
with the Argo clock was tantamount to patent infringement. Tomlin made
clear just how deep he believed the Admiralty's and Dreyer's unacknowledged debts to Pollen ran. "I am asking you to assume for the moment
that the Argo clock was communicated to the Admiralty," Tomlin directed
Dreyer's lawyer. "Notwithstanding that[,] you devised a clock mechanism
of your own and that turns out to be something which might be described
in a patent action as an infringement."[128] Tomlin addressed Kerly along

similar lines. "I want you to appreciate what is really in my mind, and I will tell you frankly what it is," the chair told him:

> It occurs to me that the Argo clock and the designs of the Argo clock communicated to the Admiralty may have been one of the elements which went to produce in the Admiralty *a frame of mind which realised that a machine generating its own rates was a desirable thing*, and that, having that impression produced in their minds, partly, it may be, by what Admiral Dreyer had already done and partly by their knowledge of what the Argo clock was then, they say: Oh well, if Admiral Dreyer's Mark III is converted into Mark [IV] . . . we get the thing and we will have that. Supposing that is so, it may very well be that the Argo clock is one of the elements which has really led to the Dreyer clock, although you may say that the Dreyer clock in some mechanical respects differs from the Argo clock. [emphasis added][129]

Tomlin added "as a possible view of this case" that Dreyer and the Admiralty "have adapted [sic] more or less entirely the thing that [Argo] were using, so that *it really produced in substance the idea* which had been put into their heads by the other machine; *it became part of their knowledge*" [emphasis added].[130]

This was strong language. In view of the fact that Pollen was not claiming under the patent heads of the Royal Warrant, and that the clock mechanism of the Dreyer tables differed in numerous respects from the Argo clock, Tomlin's explicit invocation of the patent-infringement paradigm shows just how thoroughly he believed Dreyer and the Admiralty had plagiarized Pollen. The plagiarism was so complete, in effect, that it had leapt from the realm of conceptual copying (the realm of plagiarism) and crossed into the realm of material copying (the realm of infringement) despite the mechanical differences. At the same time, as the italicized passages above show, Tomlin restored some of the continuity between the conceptual and the material that he had severed for Pollen's system claim; put differently, he recovered the text in the machine. Even where Dreyer and the Admiralty might not have taken Pollen's exact mechanical construction, Tomlin acknowledged, they took what Greene had called "the Platonic idea": the conceptual breakthrough, or the knowledge, that a clock mechanically generating both rates was desirable.

This finding had significant implications for the Admiralty's lingering threat to prosecute Pollen under the Official Secrets Act. Kerly confirmed that it remained under consideration, telling the RCAI that if Pollen tried to work the still-secret patent—one that the Admiralty had not reassigned to him in 1913—covering a clock with dials for setting it by the two rates, it was "extremely likely" that the crown would prosecute him under the Official Secrets Act.[131] "It seems to me a very remarkable position," Tomlin replied. "[I]t is a rather remarkable thing that you have an inventor who makes a very beautiful invention, the Admiralty commandeers it, and without more, deprives him of the benefit of it, apparently for all time, without compensation."[132] Kerly, who knew only what the Admiralty had told him, allowed that Pollen's claim to have invented the two-rate process before Dreyer had come as a "great surprise," and acknowledged that "[i]f he is right, there seems to be no claim for shutting this thing up under the Official Secrets Act."[133] Here, albeit only in passing, the crown admitted the justice of Pollen's complaint about its deployment of the Official Secrets Act.

∴

Even the forceful comments about the clock and secrecy quoted above do not fully convey just how relentless a shellacking the Admiralty and Dreyer received before the RCAI. This was the first time they had to justify their prewar decision-making on fire control to conscientious, expert, independent scrutiny—the scrutiny that the Admiralty might have applied itself, but for the fact that it incorporated Dreyer into its decision-making despite his conflict of interest. The commissioners remained polite but not deferential, and they could scarcely believe some of what they heard. Admiral Wilson's supervision of the crucial *Ariadne* trials of early 1908 and the Admiralty's subsequent decision to abandon Pollen's automatic plotting system in favor of Wilson's primitive manual methods came in for particularly withering criticism.[134] As Greene walked the RCAI through the correspondence after the *Ariadne* trials, he observed that the Admiralty's manner of rejection was "a little bit hard." "A little bit hard on whom?" asked Tomlin. "On Mr. Pollen," Greene clarified. "I thought perhaps you meant the country," Tomlin retorted. Langdon expressed astonishment that the Admiralty had withheld the results of the trials from Pollen: "That is hardly fair."[135] The commissioners were equally astonished to learn that Wilson understood plotting so little that he had picked trial conditions under which *his own* virtual-course plotting (Pollen's was true-course) would fail. Tomlin voiced his bewilderment: "I cannot understand what the frame of mind was of those who ordered the test."[136]

Dreyer fared even worse than Wilson and the Admiralty. During cross-examination, Greene eviscerated him, systematically tearing down each pillar of Dreyer's case—his claims to have invented range-rate plotting in

1906, bearing-rate plotting in 1908, and the Dumaresq-Vickers link-up in 1908—and showing that Pollen had invented each first. Dreyer was left to splutter that the chronology in his claim form was "very nearly right."[137] In other ways, Dreyer took incoherent positions that flew in the face of the conclusions drawn from the war by the Grand Fleet Dreyer Table (GFDT) Committee. Reading the transcripts, it is difficult to tell whether he was panicking under fire from Greene or whether he simply did not understand basic points. One minute, Dreyer stressed the need for hyperaccuracy in bearing observations, claiming that his system provided this and Pollen's did not.[138] The next minute, he insisted that errors from magnetic compass readings were "easy to exaggerate in general conversation."[139] Similarly, on the one hand, he dismissed the importance of knowing the bearing rate so as to be able to keep the range during periods of target invisibility, which the GFDT Committee had found to be vital (as we saw in chapter 6), as "one of those cases which have been so attractive to some people," because it assumed that "the other gentleman obliges one by going on [i.e., maintaining his course] all the time he is out of sight."[140] On the other hand, he contended that there were many combat situations in which the enemy would obligingly maintain a steady parallel course so as to keep the bearing rate negligible, contra the GFDT Committee's finding that the enemy would frequently alter course. Even the landlubber commissioners scoffed at Dreyer's arguments.[141] Once again, civilians proved to understand more about naval warfare than Dreyer thought possible.

·.·

The commissioners' comments throughout the hearings indicated the lines along which they would rule, but internal documents supply additional evidence about their thinking. One of the commissioners, who had been fairly quiet during the hearings, was William E. Dalby. A long-time professor at Imperial College London, Dalby was a distinguished mechanical engineer who had served on the Admiralty Board of Invention and Research during the war.[142] As the only engineer on the RCAI, Dalby produced a twenty-three-page report explaining the mathematics of fire control and the construction of the various instruments to his fellow commissioners.

His analysis amounted to an endorsement of Pollen's main arguments and a refutation of the cases put forward by Dreyer and the Admiralty. Even on Pollen's plotting claim, which Dalby, like Tomlin, could not quite bring himself to accept, Dalby acknowledged that "the [Admiralty's] conception of plotting and its uses owes much to Pollen."[143] As for the clock claim, Dalby's views were unequivocal. Despite the Admiralty's attempts at obfuscation, Dalby perceived the importance of the Argo slipless drive and the Admiralty's own preference for it. "Admiral Dreyer said that they were satisfied with the results" from the Dreyer tables' clock drive, but Dalby inferred from the Admiralty's admission that it planned to adopt the slipless drive "that experience with the many disc and roller mechanisms fitted with the old roller in comparison with the few fitted with the slipless drive (there are 5 Argo Clocks in the Navy and from the evidence nearly 100 Dreyer Tables) establishes the superiority of the slipless drive."[144] In terms strikingly similar to those employed by James Swinburne, Dalby explained how Argo had used linkages to convert the Dumaresq from an essentially static instrument requiring manual adjustment into a "[s]elf acting instrument"—an "intelligent machine"—and how the Dreyer tables' recreation of Argo's linkages made it "indistinguishable in principle from the corresponding parts in the Argo Clock."[145] "Comparing the instruments used, it is remarkable that the Admiralty with each improvement approach the Argo Clock," Dalby concluded:

> The principle of its action and the details of its construction were regularly communicated to the Admiralty and became known to those at work improving the Dreyer Tables. Considering how vital the Argo clock or any mechanism like it is to the Admiralty system of Fire Control, and how the Dreyer Table Clock has gradually approached the Argo Clock in principle I think Pollen has given substantial aid and guidance to the Admiralty in their evolution of the Mark V Table and their present system of Fire Control.

In his judgment, "Pollen is entitled to substantial reward under [Head] 3."[146]

The RCAI's formal recommendation, signed by Tomlin and issued on 30 October 1925, advised against any award for Dreyer. The RCAI also rejected Pollen's system claim, notwithstanding their sympathy for his arguments. Confirming the materialistic bias that they had expressed during the hearing, Tomlin wrote that "this so called method or system claimed (as it is claimed) apart from any special mechanism for operating it cannot be regarded as an invention, design or process within the meaning of Head 3 of the Royal Warrant." [147] The clock claim was another matter. The RCAI concluded that the clock mechanism of the Mark IV and V Dreyer tables "works substantially on the same principles" as the Argo clock. The recommendation continued:

> Further we are satisfied upon the facts that the principle and details of the Argo Clock were communicated to the Admiralty and to those who

were at work on the Dreyer Tables and directly contributed to the evolution of the clock mechanism of the Dreyer Tables Marks IV and V. The knowledge so acquired made plain the feasibility [*Entwicklungsfähig*] of converting the clock mechanism of the earlier types of Dreyer Table into a form which served the same function and was based upon the same principle as the Argo Clock and while we acquit all concerned of any intention or desire to copy or take unacknowledged the benefit of the claimants' work (and any suggestion of the kind was disclaimed at the hearing) *we think it impossible to question the influence of that work upon the ultimate result.* [emphasis added][148]

"There are also other elements in the Dreyer Tables," the recommendation added, "which in our judgment owe their origin to communications by Mr. Pollen to the Admiralty." Accordingly, the RCAI recommended the unusually large award of £30,000 to Pollen and Argo. Of the nearly 450 claimants heard by the RCAI, only twelve received larger awards.[149] Almost all of these larger awards went to big firms in armaments, automobiles, and aviation, making the award to Pollen and the tiny Argo all the more impressive.

Pollen's victory was even greater than he ever realized. While the RCAI's recommendation made clear that it rejected the Admiralty's and Dreyer's core argument—that they had developed their system independent of Pollen—its internal records, which Pollen did not see, show that it found the Admiralty to have acted in bad faith, just as Pollen had long maintained. In a memorandum for Tomlin prepared ten days before the RCAI published its recommendation, its secretary, Percy Tindal Robertson, crunched the numbers behind the award. Just as in a patent-infringement case, the RCAI used royalties as a basis of calculation. The secretary took the price at which Pollen had sold six clocks to the Admiralty before the war—£2,133 each—to set a royalty of £200 per clock, or roughly 10 percent. To determine the number of ships fitted with Dreyer's infringing clock mechanism, Tindal Robertson consulted Brassey's *Naval Annual* and counted eighty-three. These eighty-three ships generated royalties of £16,600 (£200 × 83), from which Tindal Robertson subtracted £1,200 (£200 × 6) to cover the royalties already paid on six clocks before the war, leaving a total of £15,400. Despite the crown's best efforts to fudge the question of whether the Admiralty had incorporated the Argo clock's slipless drive into the AFCT, Tindal Robertson also calculated royalties for ships not yet built. Assuming that the original 1912 patent covering the Argo clock had a term of eighteen years, making it good for another five years, and guessing that the Royal Navy would build roughly seven new ships per year, Tindal Robertson calculated royalties on future construction of £7,000

(£200 × 5 × 7), bringing the running total to £22,400. He gave the sum of £5,000, with a question mark, for Tomlin to consider for ships that had been scrapped and Dreyer tables used for torpedo rather than gun control; if awarded, this would have brought the running total to £27,400. Finally, and most significantly of all, he asked whether there should be any award "for moral and intellectual damages?"[150] The breakdown of the award shows that the RCAI did include damages.[151]

The inclusion of damages was extraordinary—possibly without parallel in any other RCAI case. In British patent-infringement cases between private parties, plaintiffs could not recover damages if the infringement was innocent.[152] Evidently the RCAI did not regard Dreyer's and the Admiralty's plagiarism of Pollen as innocent. The award of damages constituted a rebuke of the crown and, in effect, a vindication of Pollen's belief in the fiduciary character of his contract with the Admiralty. In the RCAI's view, this was not a case of inventors taking a calculated business risk that simply did not pay off; this was a case of the crown betraying a trust that it had undertaken to uphold. Pollen's friend Francis Russell, Baron of Killowen, who knew Tomlin, confirmed as much a year later. "T[omlin]. told me this morning," Killowen wrote, "that his recollection was that so far from your conduct being in any way open to question, it was rather that the Admiralty's behavior had not been beyond reproach."[153] No less than the finding of infringement and the money, the damages show just how far the RCAI sided with Pollen. Dreyer and the Admiralty had indeed betrayed his trust.

[CHAPTER 8]

Inside the Military-Industrial Complex

"[A]ll the decisions clarifying the employer-employee relationship may be applied to differences between the Government and contractor where development work is concerned and the Government clearly financed the experimentation."

ALFRED G. ZIMERMANN, 3 MAY 1929

World War I had come as both a rude shock and a golden opportunity for the US Navy. On the one hand, increased exposure to the Royal Navy had demonstrated that the US Navy was technologically backward. On the other hand, the war enabled it to close the gap much more rapidly than it might have done in peacetime. But even with the acquisition of British technology—most importantly, Pollen's clock and Vickers's director system—US naval fire control in 1919 reflected the frantic and improvisational nature of wartime improvements. Ships did not have individual fire-control systems so much as a hodgepodge of individual components jury-rigged together. Looking to the future, it was evident to the US Navy, just as it was to the Royal Navy's Grand Fleet Dreyer Table Committee, that a systematic overhaul of existing fire-control technology was necessary.

This chapter traces the overhaul. In so doing, it shows that the tensions over intellectual property rights between the Admiralty and Pollen were neither isolated nor unique to Britain: similar tensions pervaded the relationship between the US Navy and its principal fire-control contractors. In this respect as in others, the military-industrial complex that evolved around naval analog computing during the interwar period anticipated the military-industrial complex that evolved around digital computing during the Cold War. Like their Silicon Valley descendants, the builders of naval analog computers depended heavily on defense funding and were constantly fighting over IP.

The patent system structured how relationships among contractors and between contractors and the government played out. For contractors, patents offered vital security, not only against each other but also against the government.[1] For naval officers, patents were both the cost of doing business with the private sector and obstacles on the path to technological innovation and lower prices. As mutually beneficial as the military-industrial complex could be for both its military and industrial sides, it simultaneously seethed with mutual antagonism. Pressures to cooperate coexisted with pressures to compete.

The broader legal and political context also shaped the development of the military-industrial complex in the fire-control field. The period from the late nineteenth century to 1937 is sometimes referred to as the *Lochner* era, after the 1905 Supreme Court decision that virtually sacralized private-sector contracts and thereby handed organized capital a powerful weapon for resisting government regulation and labor demands. But because defense contractors dealt with the public sector, the sacralization could cut both ways. Bureau of Ordnance officials saw that by analogizing the defense contract to a labor contract, they could turn it into a powerful weapon against organized capital. At the same time, however, lesser-known legal developments during the *Lochner* era benefited contractors. A string of confusing Supreme Court rulings about the application of eminent domain to patents enabled contractors to sue for infringement of their patent rights in multiple jurisdictions, not just one. With the various parties all legally well armed, the stage was set for pitched battles.

GENERAL ELECTRIC ENTERS THE FIELD

Since the US Navy had already done such a thorough job of plagiarizing Pollen during the war, it could focus its postwar attention on other elements of its fire-control technology—most importantly, the director system. Here, what it had was not so much a coherent whole as "a patched up system of a half-dozen types of instruments."[2] Not only did the system need to be streamlined, but the electrical transmission needed to be converted from step-by-step to synchronous.[3] "Synchronicity" meant that the transmitters and receivers displayed the same data. In "step-by-step" systems, the process of synchronizing the transmitters and receivers was manual; in "self-synchronous" (or simply "synchronous") systems, transmitters and receivers automatically synchronized themselves without manual intervention. The need for periodic resetting in step-by-step systems meant that they had serious practical drawbacks in action, and complaints about the time-consuming nature of resynchronization poured into the Bureau of Ordnance from the fleet.[4]

To overcome the limitations of the existing system, the Bureau of Ord-nance turned to the nation's leading electrical company, General Electric. Its interest in GE stemmed partly from a desire to stimulate competition in the fire-control field. In the words of the chief of the Bureau, Sperry Gyroscope and Ford Instrument, despite (or because of) their position as the leading suppliers of fire-control equipment to the Navy, "took no action on improving their equipment until it became known to them that General Electric Company was working on the problem."[5] GE had other qualifica-tions. Far larger than Ford Instrument or Sperry Gyroscope, GE was one of the premier US corporations, a world leader in the development of electri-cal transmission systems and a pioneer of large-scale industrial research. It had already done work for the Navy, supplying, for instance, the gear for controlling searchlights on ships, a function with obvious parallels to the control of guns.

Most importantly, GE had a synchronous motor, developed in 1901 and used to control the locks of the Panama Canal. In the spring of 1918, the incoming head of the fire-control section in the Bureau of Ordnance, Wil-liam Furlong, saw a sample synchronous motor that the firm had sent to the Bureau. Furlong, who held a master's degree in radio and electrical en-gineering from Columbia University, immediately perceived GE's poten-tial to solve the Navy's problem. Over the next two years, he spent several days a month with the GE engineers Edward Hewlett and Waldo Willard educating them about the Bureau's needs. They worked on designing a self-synchronizing director system that would meet Furlong's specifications.[6]

Although the engineers were enthusiastic about the project, GE execu-tives were nervous about entering the fire-control field. The preliminary work alone amounted to well over $100,000; establishing the organization and plant necessary to actually build fire-control systems would require hundreds of thousands more.[7] The chief of the Bureau of Ordnance appre-ciated that the firm was "not especially anxious" for the work—that is, the Bureau needed the firm for its synchronous motor and design talent more than the firm needed the Bureau.[8] To convince GE to take the plunge, the Bureau promised the firm contracts to equip four battleships (which ended up being three), and it intimated that contracts for well over one hundred warships of varying types might follow.[9] GE took the bait.[10]

GE's entry into the field immediately raised considerations about patent rights. It was impossible to evade existing patents altogether, though the Bureau certainly intended to try. "It is scarcely possible to build a com-plete fire control system without infringing in some degree patents taken out by Vickers who built the first complete system," the chief of the Bureau acknowledged, though the designs for the GE system "have been gotten up after months of study of Vickers patents with the idea of getting around them." Similarly, the Bureau felt "certain of infringing Sperry Company to a very slight degree" and "will have to pay him a royalty." It opened negotiations with Sperry Gyroscope, but not with Vickers, over settling potential infringement claims. GE, for its part, flatly refused the Bureau's request to indemnify the Navy against third-party infringement suits when the Navy was ordering it "to produce an apparatus which will solve a particular problem."[11]

In late 1920, the Bureau and GE signed a contract covering installation of GE's self-synchronizing director system on the battleships USS *Maryland* and *Colorado*.[12] To supply the rangekeepers, Ford Instrument served as GE's subcontractor on the deal, in a reflection of the increasingly systemic nature of fire control in the US Navy. With the Navy Department's special approval, the Bureau placed the order on a cost-plus basis, the only one that GE would accept.[13] The firm "state that the work is so entirely new to them and so exacting is the accuracy required that they can not make an estimate of cost," the chief of the Bureau informed the Department, and "they can not take the risk of doing the work" except on a cost-plus basis.[14]

∴

The Bureau also sought to entice other firms into competing against Sperry Gyroscope and Ford Instrument. Along with GE, it courted GE's rival Westinghouse (which declined), as well as Siemens-Halske, the heavyweight German electrical firm that had built the German navy's director system and had already developed a synchronous motor.[15] The Germans posed a serious risk to GE. During the war, the US government had seized enemy IP held in the United States. The Trading with the Enemy Act of October 1917, which, as we saw in chapter 5, helped create a temporary wartime patent-secrecy regime, also established the office of the Alien Property Custodian (APC). In addition to being an enormous boon for the US chemical industry, the seizure of US patents held by German and Austrian nationals was a windfall for the US armed forces.[16] The Navy and the Army purchased a license from the APC to manufacture under these patents for the paltry sum of $100,000, giving it access to the US patents of the armaments giant Krupp, the optical powerhouse Carl Zeiss, the radio behemoth Telefunken, and Siemens-Halske, among many, many others.[17] In 1918, Furlong saw German fire-control equipment built by Siemens-Halske, and it is highly likely that he passed along information about what he saw to GE.[18]

The happy hunting season for the US armed forces and corporations eventually came to an end, however. In March 1921, on the same day that Congress adopted a joint resolution formally ending the war between the United States and Germany, it passed a law creating a six-month grace period during which foreigners could file US patent applications if they had enjoyed the right to do so on 1 August 1914.[19] In effect, the law created an exception to the Paris Convention limits (discussed in chapter 4), enabling foreigners—including former enemy nationals—to file US patent applications corresponding to prewar foreign patents with the same effect as if they had filed before the war. This was bad news for US firms like GE that were accustomed to using German IP for a pittance. Compounding GE's concerns, in the spring and early summer of 1921, the Bureau of Ordnance sent representatives to witness tests of the Siemens-Halske synchronous motor in Berlin.[20]

Fears of German competition and patent liability informed GE's position in negotiations over the patent clause in the contracts for the next two battleships, the USS *West Virginia* and *Washington* (only the former of which ended up being built under Washington Naval Treaty limits). At a conference in July 1921, the chief of the Bureau, Charles McVay, traded rhetorical blows with GE's representatives. Grumbling that "the General Electric Company isn't willing to do what every other Company has done," he refused to waive the requirement for GE to indemnify the government against patent infringement.[21] GE had its reasons to insist otherwise. Thomas Edison and GE, like Elmer Sperry and Sperry Gyroscope, had made patenting foundational to corporate strategy and knew the patent system inside and out.[22] GE was not about to play patsy for the Bureau. "We did not come into this thing because we wanted to come into it," Albert Davis, the head of the GE's Patent Department, reminded McVay. "You knocked at our door." GE would back anything in its normal product line with a patent guarantee, because it knew the patent situation. But the Navy was not asking for a regular GE product. "You come to us and say, 'we have a very peculiar problem, no one else in the world knows this problem, the Navy wants us to do a thing that nobody else wants to do,'" Davis explained. What if defending against a patent-infringement lawsuit cost more than GE's profits—when the infringing principle "was something you gentlemen in the Navy Department asked for"? Davis further pointed to the recent law creating an exception to the Paris Convention limits, which meant that GE's work on the system "might be taken away by any foreigner."[23] GE refused to assume the risk and insisted on another cost-plus contract. Its size and remunerative civilian business, combined with the Navy's desperation and the inability of any

other firm to supply the system, gave it leverage. The Bureau again surren-
dered in the contracts for the *West Virginia* and *Washington*.[24]

GE's insistence on a cost-plus contract proved wise, not only because
patent difficulties did indeed arise, but also because the job turned out to be
more challenging (and expensive) than it anticipated.[25] One of the most difficult technical challenges related to the distant control of massive objects
by relatively low-power sources. This challenge cropped up in the context
of correcting for certain errors through gyro-stabilization. By providing
stable horizontal and vertical reference planes—the combination of which
became known as the "stable element" in US fire control—gyroscopes
could detect the deviation of the guns from their "true" positions in multiple dimensions. The difficulty was getting the faint signals emitted by
the gyroscopes to control guns that could weigh over a hundred tons, a
problem known as torque amplification (which also bedeviled the British).
GE had some familiarity with this problem due to its research on power
electronics. Spearheaded by Ernst Alexanderson, the inventor of the Alexanderson alternator and a pioneer in radio and television technology, GE's
work in this area included development of the "pliatron," a high-vacuum
tube used to amplify sound.[26] However, GE's use of pliatrons to amplify the
signals from the gyroscope in order to control the guns led to a stuttering
oscillation, known as "hunting," as the guns attempted to find an equilibrium point. In gunnery terms, the control of the guns was not sufficiently
"delicate."[27] In the early 1920s, even with Alexanderson assisting Hewlett
and Willard, the task of amplifying faint signals to control battleship guns
with precision was simply beyond GE's capacity to solve, at least within the
time frame of its contracts with the Bureau of Ordnance.[28]

Despite occasional flare-ups, the Bureau proved philosophical and imagi-
native about the difficulties and delays.[29] The officer in charge of the Bureau's
fire-control section deemed GE's equipment "very much superior to any
other fire control equipment we have," worth the time and high development costs.[30] The Bureau got what it paid for—and because it needed GE
more than GE needed it, it actually paid for what it got. It also decided to
waive its usual demand for secrecy in fire-control development so that GE
could sell its self-synchronizing (or "selsyn") systems for commercial use
and thereby, it was hoped, overcome the problem of torque amplification.[31]
"[A]s more uses to which selsyns can be applied are developed," the naval
inspector at GE reasoned, "more rapid will be the development and improvement of all selsyns, which improvements should, of course, show in the
selsyns made for the Navy."[32] This was the logic of "spin-around"—a combination of "spin-off" (when technology flows from the military to the civilian
sector) and "spin-on" (when technology flows from the civilian sector to the

military).[33] The Bureau's willingness to let GE commercialize elements of its fire-control work paid dividends. In the late 1920s and 1930s, Alexanderson and other engineers at GE invented the "thyraton," a vacuum tube filled with inert gases subject to grid or electrostatic control, and the "amplidyne," a power amplifier, both of which had significant industrial uses. The Navy promptly exploited these inventions to improve the control of guns.[34]

∴

Over the course of the 1920s, the Bureau sought to reduce its reliance on GE by directing some contracts toward Ford Instrument and a newcomer to the business, the Arma Engineering Company. Like Ford Instrument, Arma had been founded by two former Sperry employees, Arthur Davis and David Mahood (Arma = ARthur MAhood). Like Sperry Gyroscope, Arma got its start by patterning a gyrocompass on the Anschütz and moving from there into fire control; like Ford Instrument, it used its gyrocompass to try to cut into Sperry's business.[35] Ford Instrument and Arma developed their own self-synchronizing systems, differing in certain respects from GE's. The Bureau awarded them the main director contracts for the battle cruisers (later aircraft carriers) USS *Lexington* and USS *Saratoga*.[36]

To avoid squabbling over patent rights that would hinder development, the Bureau found ways to make cooperation among its contractors worthwhile. Ford Instrument agreed to waive any patent claims against Arma or the US government arising from Arma's contract on the transmission system for the *Lexington* and *Saratoga* in return for the Bureau ordering certain major components of the system from Ford Instrument.[37] Similarly, GE and Ford Instrument engineers working together on the *Maryland* and *Colorado* contract "exchanged [advice] freely," and "neither company felt any part of the system to be exclusively its problem."[38] The two firms almost certainly made agreements to divide up patent applications arising from their work and to cross-license each other. Thus, by the mid-1920s, the Bureau had three fire-control contractors it regarded as reliable. There was some competition among them, but the competition was managed rather than free. The Bureau shepherded licensing agreements to avoid explosive patent disputes and ensured that each firm had a satisfactory slice of the contractual pie.

THE FLY IN THE PUDDING

As the 1920s dawned, Sperry Gyroscope found itself on the outside looking in. While GE, Ford Instrument, and Arma climbed in the Bureau's

estimation, Sperry Gyroscope sank. Although Sperry blamed David Mahood, his former employee who cofounded Arma, for the Bureau's evident
disenchantment, Sperry had brought most of his troubles on himself.[39]
Two of the bets his firm placed during World War I—a ship gyro-stabilizer
and a stable zenith, discussed in chapters 4 and 5—did not pan out.[40] To
make matters worse, Sperry Gyroscope also alienated the Bureau by repeatedly flouting its demand for secrecy in the quest for profits.[41] The firm's
resistance to developing a self-synchronizing director system further exasperated Bureau officers. When Furlong, the head of the fire-control section, who had used (and disliked) Sperry equipment as a gunnery officer
in the fleet, took up with Sperry Gyroscope "the question of their seriously
considering the improvement of their material," the firm "took no action
to improve their system." That failure sent Furlong to GE, at which point
"Mr. Sperry commenced to see that the Bureau was in earnest concerning
the desire for improvement."[42] Sperry began sending Furlong monthly bulletins touting the firm's progress toward a synchronous system.[43] Delusion-
ally (and prematurely), Sperry described the system as "epoch-making."[44]
Reginald Gillmor, the former naval officer who had pushed so hard for
Sperry to stay abreast of British developments during World War I and led
a reorganization of the flailing company in 1918, resigned at the end of 1919
in frustration with Sperry's stubbornness.[45]

As the firm's investments in new developments failed and its relationship with the Bureau soured, Sperry increasingly, to borrow Furlong's
words, "busied himself with patents."[46] Like a patent troll, the firm looked
to collect rents from patents, often on rapidly obsolescent wartime innovations. Of course, as we saw in chapter 4, the corporate culture at Sperry
Gyroscope had long regarded patenting as a crucial component of business
strategy. But that culture had arisen when the firm was on the upswing;
now it was on the downswing. In this context, playing the part of patent
rentier was as much a way to offset the loss of revenue on Navy contracts as
a collateral benefit of applying for patents. It was also a good way to extort
money from firms to which Sperry Gyroscope lost Navy business.

Sperry's first opportunity arose in February 1919, when the Patent Office
declared an interference between an application filed by one of his current employees and another filed by his former employee Ford.[47] Both applications related to rangekeepers, where Sperry had failed and Ford had
triumphed. Nevertheless, the old patent application on the unsuccessful
rangekeeper gave Sperry leverage. He wanted to get out of the contract
that he had signed when Ford left his firm allowing him to continue drawing on Ford's expertise in return for paying Ford royalties on sales of the
battle tracer (for which Ford had served as lead designer) to the US Navy.[48]

So Sperry made a deal. In return for conceding priority in the interference and assigning his rangekeeper patents to Ford, Ford agreed to release him from the battle tracer contract.[49] Sperry had managed to spin straw into gold.

∴

Having used his legacy patents to cause trouble for Ford, Sperry now turned to the task of tying everyone else in knots—a task that required him to minimize foreign achievements so as to maximize his own status as a pioneering heroic inventor. Over the course of 1920, he became increasingly angry at the Bureau's reluctance to fund the development of his own synchronous system.[50] In June, he sent a stiffly worded defense of his company's record and attack on those he regarded as johnny-come-latelies.[51] In October, the firm lodged a formal accusation of patent infringement. Sending Furlong a list of patents, the firm offered a make-believe history of Sperry Gyroscope's role in fire-control development, which Furlong underlined and annotated angrily. Claiming that the Navy's fire-control system "centers about the Sperry gyro compass and it is the Sperry Company which has extended the use of this vital element to the fire control field and which was the originator of the idea [Furlong: 'No'']," the firm lied that the Navy had turned to GE only "after we had agitated the matter with your Department [Furlong: 'Absolutely false statement']." Sperry Gyroscope allowed that GE's system included "certain differences and improvements in detail" over its own, but it submitted that "the basic principles [were] unquestionably covered" by its patents.[52] In other words, the firm was complaining that GE was plagiarizing its ideas while trying to get around its patents—exactly how Sperry had built his company.

Sperry Gyroscope's account was a work of historical fiction to rival Dreyer's. In the case of every single significant naval invention for which the firm claimed credit, it was not inventing from scratch, but making improvements on pioneering foreign inventions: the Schlick and Brennan gyrostabilizers, the Anschütz gyrocompass, the Pollen clock, the Pollen plotter (which Sperry rebranded the "battle tracer"), and the Scott-Vickers director. Indeed, at the very same time that Sperry Gyroscope was accusing GE and the Bureau of violating its patents, Sperry was also attempting to uncover as much as he could about James Henderson's gyroscopic inventions.[53] He was a pirate of a particular—and particularly American—kind. His genius was not that of an inventor or engineer. It was that of a manufacturer and self-promoter. Yet Sperry, who suffered from the same "anxiety of influence" about his own originality as did Dreyer, was desperate to believe otherwise. He did not claim pioneer status merely as a negotiating tactic; he drank his own Kool-Aid. Remarkably, as his private correspondence shows, he managed to convince himself that his step-by-step transmission system had always been synchronous and that the US Navy had been satisfied with it.[54] To be sure, he and the Navy deserved each other, since the Bureau of Ordnance had, by its own admission in internal correspondence (cited above), knowingly infringed his patents.[55]

Over the next several years, Sperry began to test the framework of eminent domain that structured attempts to recover for the infringement of third-party patents by the government and its contractors. The Act of 1918, discussed in chapter 4, seemed to extend the shield of eminent domain to cover contractors and thus to make the government the defendant and the Court of Claims the jurisdiction for third parties seeking compensation for patent infringement. Accordingly, Sperry fired his first warning shots by filing two lawsuits in the Court of Claims in the early 1920s, before withdrawing them and pivoting instead to sue Arma in district court.[56] This lawsuit would rise to the Supreme Court as a test case over the meaning of the Act of 1918. In the meantime, the Bureau strung Sperry Gyroscope along with regard to its infringement claims against the government.[57]

∴

The US Patent Office soon gave Sperry another opportunity to interfere—literally—with the Navy's procurement of fire-control equipment. In March 1925, it declared a series of four interferences on director systems. These interferences, which soon multiplied to include two more, involved not only the major American players in the fire-control industry—Sperry Gyroscope, Ford Instrument, and GE—but also Krupp and Vickers. The applications involved are shown in table 8.1.

Without going into the gory details of the interferences, which could fill a separate (and extremely boring) chapter, there are a couple of points to bring out for present purposes. One was the pioneering character of Pollen's and Isherwood's work on fire-control transmission systems, not just on plotters, gyroscopes, and computers. As noted in chapter 2, they had originally hoped to make their system self-synchronizing but ended up licensing, and improving, a step-by-step system from Vickers. In Interference A, Vickers and GE emphasized the scope of Pollen's and Isherwood's US patents (now controlled by Vickers) on transmission, which they argued invalidated the right of all the parties to the interference to make the counts—that is, claims—in question.[58] Per usual, Sperry Gyroscope attempted to downplay Pollen's and Isherwood's significance in the history of fire control in order

Table 8.1. Applications involved in director interferences

Applicants	Assignee	Ser. #	USP #	Int. A 52,138	Int. B 52,139	Int. C 52,140	Int. D 52,141	Int. E 54,815	Int. F 56,847
Hewlett and Willard	GE	655,358	1,894,822	X	X	X	X	X	X
Akemann	Krupp	424,522	n/a	X	X				
Dawson, Watt, and Perham	Vickers	403,432	1,695,483	X	X	X	X		
Perham	Vickers	413,191	n/a	X					
Sperry and Meitner	Sperry	160,877	1,755,340	X			X	X	
Kortepeter	Sperry	653,445	n/a						X
Ford	Ford	250,226	1,840,497				X	X	
Original no. counts				5 counts	1 count	1 count	4 counts	1 count	2 counts

Note: Count 4 in Interference 52,141 was Count 2 in Interference 52,138.

to inflate its own. In its brief, the firm sniffed that the Pollen patent "may be said to disclose one of the prior intermediate stages of development of the fire control art."[59] Vickers—which, unlike Sperry Gyroscope, actually defined the state of the art in the development of director systems before World War I—forcefully rejected the American firm's narrative. In its review of the history, Vickers identified the system covered by the Pollen and Isherwood patent as the "next important step" after Vickers's own invention of follow-the-pointer indicators.[60] "[I]n our view," Vickers's lawyers wrote (echoed by GE's), "the apparatus disclosed in the application of Sperry & Meitner is the same in all essential respects as that shown in the Pollen & Isherwood patent."[61] The Patent Office agreed, dissolving the interference on the grounds that the counts were unpatentable over prior art.[62]

Despite Sperry Gyroscope's defeat in Interference A, Interferences D and E illustrated its power to paralyze the entire fire-control industry and to threaten further development. In Interference D, GE and Ford Instrument, which had collaborated in the development of a synchronous system, allied against Sperry Gyroscope and Vickers, arguing that the latter firms lacked the right to make the counts at issue because their systems were step-by-step.[63] Vickers conceded the point.[64] By contrast, Sperry Gyroscope dug in its heels and tried to stretch the meaning of the counts to cover its own step-by-step system.[65] To the incredulity of GE and Ford

Instrument, the Patent Office law examiner chose to construe the meaning of one of the counts at issue in such a way as to blur the difference between step-by-step and synchronous transmission; with Vickers out, he declared a new three-way interference (E) between the synchronous pioneers and Sperry Gyroscope.[66] Again, the latter declined to go quietly. After the Patent Office Board of Appeals overturned the law examiner's earlier ruling and held that Sperry Gyroscope lacked the right to make the count because its system was not synchronous, the firm appealed to the US Court of Customs and Patent Appeals.[67]

∴

With its attacks showing promise in two jurisdictions—the Eastern District of New York, where it had sued Arma, and the patent courts—Sperry Gyroscope decided to open a third jurisdictional front. In May 1926, the Supreme Court gave Sperry a win when it affirmed the district court's jurisdiction over the Arma suit and remanded the case back to the lower court.[68] (The Supreme Court's ruling also confused everyone over the meaning of the Act of 1918; in the technical jargon of Sperry Gyroscope's patent counsel, it had " 'wiggled out of' the task of interpreting the law.")[69] Then, in November 1926, Sperry Gyroscope notched additional victories when the Patent Office issued the first round of decisions in the four original interferences. Four months later, Sperry Gyroscope once again filed suit against the US government in the Court of Claims.[70]

In notifying the Navy of the suit, Sperry Gyroscope framed the case in terms of liberal property norms. "[W]e are asking only for compensation for the taking of our property by the Navy Department," Charles Doran, the firm's general manager, wrote.[71] Doran's perception of the asymmetry in financial security between the firm's employees and government officials shaped his approach. "I fully understand that individually none of them cares whether the Government is put to a large expense to defend such a suit or whether we are put to a large expense and outlay of time in prosecuting it," Doran told Sperry. Getting "the thing on a basis of justice being done our Company after an invasion of its rights by the Government" was "about the only argument that can be used in order to get a sympathetic viewpoint from them, as even Navy officers want to appear just rather than unjust."[72] What the firm was really after in its lawsuit was leverage for a settlement. It asked for $2 million in its lawsuit, but Doran was willing to settle for $175,000. "In our claims—just between you and me," he confidentially acknowledged to Sperry, "there are many items which would hardly stand up," though he maintained that others were solid.[73]

At virtually the same time as Sperry Gyroscope filed its lawsuit in the Court of Claims, a new threat appeared on the government's flank. GE alerted the Bureau that it had received a request from Ford Instrument, acting on behalf of Vickers, for royalties on the *Maryland* and *Colorado*. Ford asked for $15,000 per ship as compensation for GE's infringement of Vickers's director patents and patent applications (including the one at issue in the Patent Office interferences).[74] GE declined to admit any infringement, "but it cannot be said," in the legalistic litotes of its patent counsel, that Vickers's claim of infringement "is without some basis."[75]

UN-*LOCHNER*-ING THE FIRE-CONTROL INDUSTRY

The twin infringement claims from Sperry Gyroscope and Ford Instrument prompted Bureau of Ordnance officials to produce a far-reaching and novel legal analysis of the fire-control patent situation. With regard to the Ford-Vickers claim, Bureau officer Lieutenant Commander Don P. Moon (who later commanded a naval task force at Normandy) determined to break Vickers's master patent application on the director system. In his judgment, the application's claims were "so broad and so general" that its issuance would give Ford Instrument, through its deal with Vickers, "a strangle hold on all business."[76] To attack the validity of the application, Moon suggested exploiting the "public use" or "prior use" requirement in US patent law. This held that an inventor could not obtain a patent on an invention that had been "known or used by others in this country . . . [or] in public use or on sale in this country for more than two years prior to his application."[77] Vickers had filed the application in August 1920, so if the Bureau could prove that the invention had been known or used in the United States before August 1918, Moon reasoned, then the patent would be invalid under US patent law. In fact, as Vickers itself had already maintained to the Patent Office in an effort to push its priority as far back in time as possible, the US Navy had acquired knowledge of the invention by 1917 at the latest, on the strength of the Bureau's promise (quoted in chapter 5) that it "does not intend in any way to jeopardize the interests of the Vickers Company because of their prompt action in supplying" drawings of the director system."[78] According to Moon, officers in the Judge Advocate General's office—including Robert Lavender, whom we will meet again in the next two chapters—believed that prior knowledge would bar Vickers from receiving the patent.[79] Thus, in order to avoid giving Ford Instrument a monopoly, Moon proposed to punish Vickers for the communication of its system to the US Navy *at the latter's request* during the war.

The Bureau went even further in its argument against Sperry Gyro-scope. On the one hand, it counseled the Department of Justice to seek as-sistance from GE, Ford Instrument, and Arma, whose interest in breaking the Sperry patents pointed toward a corporatist alliance with the government, and it took a hard line against any settlement of the Court of Claims suit.[80] On the other hand, building on its long-standing argument that Sperry Gyroscope had gotten as far as it had only with government funding and advice—an argument that the Bureau had also made in the context of torpedo procurement—the Bureau audaciously claimed that Sperry Gyro-scope was "in the status of employees of the government carrying out the directions and suggestions of its officers."[81] This status "gives the government not only a shop right in the devices developed but also an implied license to manufacture and use others, even in the case where some suggestions originated with Mr. Sperry."[82]

The notion of a "shop right" and "implied license" to employees' inventions came from the private sector, as the Bureau's citations of case law demonstrated. Over the course of the nineteenth and early twentieth centuries, the courts had resurrected the preindustrial concept of the "master-servant" relationship, injected a dose of modern contract theory, and reinterpreted employee inventions as being contractually owned by their employers, rather than as the property of skilled artisans.[83] The Bureau of Ordnance kept abreast of developments in this area of law in order to guide policy toward naval officers who invented in the ordnance field, so much so that its chief patent expert, Commander Albert L. Norton, developed greater expertise than the Judge Advocate General.[84] The ascent of the labor contract in legal interpretation in the *Lochner*-era United States enabled the Bureau to analogize an independent contractor like Sperry Gyroscope to an employee-contractor like a naval officer—only now, instead of the labor contract protecting employers from government regulation, the Bureau sought to use it as a means for the government to regulate private-sector contractor-employ*ers* as government employ*ees*.

The Bureau's argument soon received judicial support. In February 1929, the Court of Claims handed down its decision in *Ordnance Engineering Corporation v. United States*, making precisely the same analogy as the Bureau had.[85] According to Lieutenant Commander Alfred G. Zimermann, the head of the Bureau's patent section, it was "the first case of which this Section has any record where the parallelism of the relationship existing between Government and contractor and the relationship existing between employer and employee is clearly shown." The implications were far-reaching: "On this basis all the decisions clarifying the employer-employee relationship may be applied to differences between the Government and contractor where development work is concerned and the Government clearly financed the experimentation." Although the court's decision made it likely that the government would win the case against Sperry Gyroscope, Zimermann advised the Bureau's fire-control section that it could open negotiations with the firm about employing isolated units of the Sperry system without jeopardizing the government's case.[86]

Acting on the logic of Zimermann's analysis, the Bureau moved to lay the groundwork for a similar claim to a shop right in GE's synchronous director system. In reply to an inquiry from the chief of the Bureau, Wilbur Van Auken, the head of the fire-control section from 1917 to 1919, asserted:

> [T]he idea and tentative outline of a new system was initiated by the Bureau to meet the demands of the fleet. No citizen or private manufacturer at that time had *sufficient knowledge* of director firing, or the complete needs of fire control, as to initiate a new system. While much credit in the design and production can and should be given to such engineers as Mr. Hannibal Ford and those who represented the General Electric Company, . . . the credit of initiating the design and following it up to a successful conclusion belongs primarily to the Bureau of Ordnance and to the gunnery officers of the fleet who aided the Bureau at that time. [emphasis added][87]

Van Auken's invocation of "sufficient knowledge" implied a rationale for a government shop right that complemented but was distinct from the contractual metaphor at the heart of Zimermann's analysis. It was not merely that the government had employed GE; it was also that the employer had hierarchically superior knowledge to the employee's (just as many British naval officers thought about themselves in comparison with civilians like Pollen and Isherwood). The employer could have done the employee's job, but the employee could not have done the employer's job. This was not necessarily inaccurate in all cases, but it was highly contestable.

Much to Zimermann's chagrin, the Navy's lawyers then threw away the government's advantage. Without checking with the Bureau of Ordnance, the Judge Advocate General agreed to meet with Sperry Gyroscope about a possible settlement, which had always been the firm's goal. In conference, a JAG representative informed the firm that if it revised the sum asked for in its lawsuit, the Navy Department might be willing to settle.[88] Zimermann was beside himself. A settlement "will encourage contractors in their present belief that they own all rights," Zimermann told the chief of the Bureau, and to charge prices "with no regard to the Government's acquired right" in their patents. Conversely, a court decision favorable to the government would force contractors to scale down their prices. The Sperry lawsuit was a crucial test case: "[A] compromise in the present suit is bound to have a noticeable and continuing effect on all future contracts for fire control and other ordnance material similarly developed."[89]

Zimermann did not get his way. Over the summer of 1930, and against the wishes of the Bureau, the Judge Advocate General reached a settlement with Sperry Gyroscope, likely because the Department of Justice did not share Zimermann's confidence in the outcome of the suit.[90] The settlement consisted of two license agreements.[91] The first made a lump-sum payment of $150,000 covering the use of patented Sperry equipment on vessels already completed; the second specified royalty payments for vessels not yet completed.[92] It is difficult to be sure how much money was actually paid under the second agreement, due to a subsequent revision, but it certainly exceeded $300,000 and likely ran around $500,000.[93] Coupled with the lump sum, the payments were considerably in excess of the $175,000 that Doran, the Sperry general manager, had originally been willing to settle for.

The Bureau of Ordnance evidently enjoyed greater success in disposing of the Ford-Vickers claim for royalties of $15,000 per ship on the *Maryland* and the *Colorado*. While acknowledging that some pieces of equipment on the ships "embody claims" of Vickers's US patents, the Bureau maintained that its 1921 bilateral agreement with Vickers, which capped royalties at $4,000 per ship, trumped the 1920 contract with GE for the two ships, which capped royalties much higher.[94] This argument seems to have carried the day without forcing a confrontation over the prior-knowledge question raised by Moon, doubtless aided by the fact that Ford Instrument, unlike Sperry Gyroscope, continued to get business from the Bureau.

THE FORD LICENSE

Moon's concerns about Ford Instrument's monopolistic intentions, especially with regard to Vickers's master patent application on its director system, proved prescient. In late 1929, North American Aviation, a large holding company for aviation-related businesses, purchased Sperry Gyroscope, which had shifted, with support from the US Army, into bombsights and other gyro-related technology for aircraft as it lost business on naval fire control.[95] A year later, North American Aviation also swallowed Ford Instrument.[96] Now operating under the same corporate umbrella, Ford Instrument sent its engineers to help Sperry Gyroscope with anti-aircraft work. The latter's decision to hire Percy Gray, Isherwood's former assistant and Vickers's lead designer of anti-aircraft fire-control equipment, to head its British branch closed the loop between the three firms: Sperry

Gyroscope and Ford Instrument were now connected with each other, and each had a connection with Vickers's anti-aircraft fire-control work.[97]

These incestuous relationships worried Oscar Badger II, the head of the fire-control section in the Bureau of Ordnance (and future admiral). In his view, the purpose of the combination under North American Aviation was clearly "to set up an international control of the fire-control field." Although Ford Instrument had a generally good track record of maintaining secrecy, Sperry Gyroscope did not. Worse, Badger suspected that the US Army was actively encouraging Sperry Gyroscope *not* to maintain secrecy. He noted that the army had ordered Sperry to include "all the features contemplated for the newest type Army A.A. [anti-aircraft] gun director" in purchases by the Soviet Union.[98] He acidly surmised that the Navy's sister service was attempting to shift development costs from its own empty coffers to the Russian government: because budgets were now so tight for the armed forces during the Depression, the US Army could not afford to subsidize technological innovation, so it hoped that the export market would supply the funds—at the cost of secrecy. Badger feared that expertise acquired at the US Navy's expense might go abroad through the newly connected companies, with the corporate monopoly serving to erode the Navy's knowledge monopoly.

His solution, which veered into the realm of fantasy, reflected the mindset of many naval officers. "Fortunately the Navy is in no way dependent upon any of these concerns," he wrote, echoing Van Auken's assumption (and the Admiralty's vis-à-vis Pollen) that the Navy's knowledge was hierarchically superior to that of civilian contractors. "Other fire-control experts are available and others can be developed," on a sort of plug-and-play basis. He suggested that "funds be made available for the establishment of a Naval Fire-Control Factory at the Washington Navy Yard."[99] The notion of government-run facilities was a common dream of naval officers chafing at corporate independence—the US Navy tried it with torpedoes, and the Royal Navy tried it with submarines. Each time, naval officers overrated their own competence, underrated the competence of civilian firms, and ignored patent rights. The very absurdity of Badger's proposal is revealing. Of course the Navy *was* dependent on a handful of contractors, which were also, in complex ways, dependent on the Navy. The service had spent decades funding these contractors, and they had developed their own deep reservoirs of expertise—much of it patented. As one JAG officer put it, "It is definitely not the ordinary situation."[100] The Bureau of Ordnance could not conjure up a factory staffed with knowledgeable personnel by a snap of its fingers, nor, as the litigiousness of US firms in the fire-control business indicated, could it abrogate patent rights without consequence.

Ford Instrument, of course, was singing from a different hymnbook. Unlike Badger, it appreciated the fundamental reality that ownership and control of patents dominated every aspect of US fire-control development and procurement, including next-generation anti-aircraft fire-control systems. Thus it moved to enlarge the monopoly Badger identified by exploiting the master patent application on Vickers's director system, which finally matured into a patent in the late 1920s. Just as Moon had feared, it was so fundamental that it had the potential to dominate all fire-control systems, including anti-aircraft ones.[101] In early 1932, as an anti-aircraft fire-control contract for six warships was about to open to bidding, a Ford executive visited Lieutenant Commander C. H. Jones, the new head of the Bureau's fire-control section, to deliver a copy of the patent and of the 1919 trilateral agreement between Ford, Vickers, and the Bureau (covered in chapter 5). Although the executive did not request any specific action, Jones "assumed that the Ford Instrument Company will proceed formally in this matter"—that is, take legal action—if the new contract was not awarded to them. The claims of the patent "appear to be far reaching," Jones reported, echoing Moon's earlier analysis, "so much so that practically any set of specifications which may be prepared for a fire control system based on the principles we now use will require the use of some of the claims set forth in this patent."[102] Indeed, when the Judge Advocate General's office studied the matter, it concluded that Ford Instrument controlled roughly 90 percent of the patent rights involved in the anti-aircraft system, and GE only 10 percent.[103]

Ford Instrument's assertion of near-monopolistic rights over fire-control technology immediately created friction with GE. Like Sperry Gyroscope before it, GE did not want to be driven out of the fire-control field, and it too could use its patents as leverage to get more business. The firm threatened to sue the US government for damages on fire-control equipment supplied by Ford Instrument unless the Navy arranged a cross-license between it and Ford Instrument. GE also bristled at the asymmetry of commercial risk between it and Ford Instrument: the latter, having achieved a total monopoly of patent rights in the rangekeeper field, received rangekeeper contracts on a proprietary (i.e., noncompetitive) basis, while GE had to compete with Ford Instrument on director contracts. For the Bureau, GE's unhappiness raised the old problem of finding enough business to keep everyone happy. From its perspective, the ideal was to keep GE in the director business in order to preserve an element of competition and prevent Ford Instrument from acquiring a monopoly, while letting Ford keep its monopoly on rangekeepers. From GE's perspective, the Bureau wanted to have its cake and eat it too. As in the early 1920s, the firm was threatening to walk away if the Bureau did not sweeten the deal.[104] As a stopgap, GE and Ford Instrument evidently worked out the cross-licensing deal that GE wanted.[105] The Bureau also rewarded GE with the contract for modernizing the main-battery director of three battleships.[106]

∵

Naturally, the Bureau's attempt to keep GE happy made Ford Instrument unhappy; the available pie was only so big. In July 1933, the firm addressed the Bureau of Ordnance about patent rights. "Individual questions have arisen from time to time and have been disposed of individually without any effort to establish a patent policy controlling other present and future cases," Ford Instrument wrote. "This has in many instances proven so unsatisfactory that we are moved to address you on the subject and suggest a broad discussion of the matter." As an example of its patent rights being violated, the firm cited the Bureau's recent award of the main-battery director contract for the modernization of three battleships to GE.[107]

Although Ford Instrument was proposing precisely the sort of long-term arrangement that the Bureau of Ordnance wished to avoid, it was not without advantages, which the Navy's lawyers were quick to spot. In contrast to Bureau officers like Badger, the Judge Advocate General's office understood that the Navy could not wave a magic wand and make patent rights or dependence on the private sector disappear. Rather than the prevailing method of dealing with disputes on an ad hoc basis, a permanent solution seemed desirable. "[T]here has been much contraversy [sic] over the questions of inventions, patents, and applications for letters patent in the fire control art," the Judge Advocate General noted. "These contraversies have hindered the procurement by the Government of the material desired; they have been prejudicial to the industry in that they have held the contractors aloof from one another, engendering an attitude of suspicion and non-cooperation; they have been the source of litigation and threat of litigation." The situation with Ford Instrument bore "a marked similarity" to that existing with Sperry Gyroscope prior to the negotiation of the two license agreements, and "[i]t is felt that the present situation is susceptible to similar treatment." If the Navy Department could obtain "workable agreements," the Judge Advocate General expected that it "would enjoy a freedom of action not heretofore experienced." He welcomed Ford Instrument's proposal as a "first step" on the path to this nirvana of negotiated patent rights.[108]

While the Bureau of Ordnance was willing to go along with the JAG's wishes, the new head of its fire-control section, Frank H. Dean, contemplated a different approach.[109] From conversations with Ford Instrument officials, he came to believe that the firm did not want a licensing deal so much as an assurance of a steady stream of business. "It is believed that the item of greatest concern to the Ford Company is the matter of competitive bidding on material which that company considers they have spent many years of time and money in developing," Dean wrote. "The question of cost is undoubtedly absorbed in prices bid for material bought (or to be bought) from the Ford Company."[110] That is, Ford Instrument had to charge higher prices to cover its development costs, while larger firms without development costs to cover could bid lower on contracts specifying features developed by Ford Instrument. This was the same problem that Pollen had experienced with the Admiralty, which, like the US Navy Department, wanted innovation without paying high prices.

Dean argued that there was a structural impediment to doing what Ford Instrument wanted. If the Navy could award proprietary contracts to Ford Instrument, then the firm could lower its prices by spreading out its costs. But the Navy could not award it proprietary contracts, and the reason came back, as it often did, to the absence of British-style secret patents in the United States. After the expiration of the temporary World War I–era legislation, the only way to keep patents secret in the United States was to keep them in pending status—that is, to keep applications from issuing as patents. According to Dean, the Navy could issue proprietary contracts only for patented material, not for applied-for-but-not-yet-patented material.[111] So the real solution, in Dean's view, was not to negotiate a license agreement with Ford Instrument paralleling the one with Sperry Gyroscope, but rather to pass patent-secrecy legislation, which "would produce a better feeling of security for some firms now supplying fire control material."[112]

The Bureau of Ordnance had been trying and failing for more than a decade to get patent-secrecy legislation passed, and Dean's attempt continued its dismal record.[113] The most recent proposal had been formulated by Zimermann, the head of the Bureau's patent section, in 1929. Zimermann's proposal does not survive, but something of its flavor—a quasi-royalist impatience with private property—may be gleaned from the criticisms of it made by the Interdepartmental Patents Board. "Among the main reasons for the board's disapproval of the proposed measure," the government's chief patent coordinator wrote to the Secretary of the Navy, "the following are mentioned in its report to this office:

1) Sequestration of patented property of inventors.
2) Difficulty of determining just compensation to inventors whose inventions would be commandeered under the bill.

3) Conflict with the Patent Office regulations of long standing usage now having the force of law.

4) General objection to holding patents secret after issue.

5) Question as to constitutionality of several provisions; for instance,

   (a) Right of Patent Office to withhold a patent from an inventor;

   (b) denying an inventor judicial determination of his rights; and,

   (c) granting patents to other than original inventors.[114]

"Sequestration," "commandeering," "question as to constitutionality": such was the dream United States of the Bureau of Ordnance—one in which other government officials wanted no part.[115] So Dean did not get his patent-secrecy legislation, leaving the Bureau without a way to award Ford Instrument proprietary contracts on equipment covered by patent applications in pending status.

Accordingly, the Bureau and Ford Instrument reverted to a license agreement along the lines of the one with Sperry Gyroscope. It was signed in June 1934. The Navy agreed to pay Ford Instrument $30,000 per year in return for a license to use the firm's patents in material not manufactured by Ford.[116] In return for Ford Instrument extending the license to cover material not yet contracted for, the Navy also agreed to award Ford contracts for rangekeepers, anti-aircraft directors, and certain other directors on a proprietary basis.[117] With this agreement, the Navy had managed to stabilize the patent situation with all its major fire-control contractors.

From one perspective, it is a wonder that any order emerged from the chaos. From another perspective, however, stabilization came with hidden costs. The historian David Mindell has argued that the Bureau of Ordnance entered World War II with serious deficiencies in machine-gun directors, anti-aircraft directors for small ships, and fire-control radar. In his informed judgment, "[b]oth cause and symptom of these problems was BuOrd's reliance on its captive contractors; it had no development and test facilities of its own."[118]

This reliance stemmed from the melee over IP rights and the structure of the US patent system. Without patent protection, contractors had little incentive to innovate, not only because experiments were expensive and risky but also because inventions were likely to be stolen. The commitment of the US patent system to "democratizing invention" made it relatively easy for them to secure patent protection.[119] Paradoxically, however, contractors' demand for patent protection and the ease of acquiring it limited competition and innovation. Patents are monopoly grants: that is, they give their owners a monopoly on the inventions they cover. Thus, even as the Bureau of Ordnance secured a corporate oligopoly containing some competitive pressures in the fire-control industry, avoiding an outright monopoly with no competitive pressures, the monopolistic character of patents limited the potential for competition—including from the government—with negative consequences for technological innovation. Notably, the inverse problem afflicted the Bureau of Ordnance in the area of torpedo development and production, where a noncompetitive government monopoly, rather than a private-sector oligopoly, led to the infamous debacle with the Mark 14 torpedo during World War II.[120] There were simply no easy answers to the question of how to secure naval-technological innovation in a liberal society with strong protections for intellectual property.

The fragile equilibrium that had emerged in the fire-control industry by the late 1930s involved elements of both competition and consolidation. Viewed from the inside out, the competitive pressures appeared dominant, the roiling currents palpable beneath the surface calm. Firms had battled each other and the Navy amid an ever-shifting array of alliances—GE and Ford Instrument now working together to build the synchronous director system and then contesting each other's patent rights thereto; GE now fighting off the government's attempt to extract an indemnity guarantee, then cooperating with the government against Sperry Gyroscope's lawsuit; and so on. Viewed from the outside in, however, the cartelistic pressures, seemingly abetted rather than resisted by the government, appeared dominant; the competition and fragility were invisible. Especially to an outsider lacking corporate resources, the military-industrial complex looked like a well-oiled corporatist conspiracy, as we will see in the next chapter.

[CHAPTER 9]

Outside the Military-Industrial Complex

"[T]his fight with Ford is a private fight, and I'd rather the Navy would
stay out until I lick that gang of freebooters, because I'm going to do
it anyway whether the Navy butts in or not."
JOSEPH DUGAN, 14 NOVEMBER 1938

Knowing their own and the US government's piratical proclivities, the
handful of defense contractors inside the fire-control military-industrial
complex had good reason to secure as much intellectual property protection as they could in the form of patents. But in the absence of British-style
secret patents, US patents had to be published to the world, raising obvious
problems from the Navy's national security perspective. For the military-
industrial complex to function, contractors' interests in IP protection, the
requirements of US patent law, and the Navy's concern for national security
secrecy had somehow to be reconciled with each other.

This chapter explores how a reconciliation was effected, how it exposed
the military-industrial complex to criticism from outsiders, and how it was
vulnerable to legal attack. It does so by focusing on a figure forgotten to history: Joseph Dugan, a patent examiner turned patent lawyer, as well as an
independent inventor in an age of growing corporate dominance of R&D,
who became interested in problems of naval fire control in the 1920s.[1] His
story is not important for technological reasons; his inventions probably
would not have worked, and the Navy did not adopt them. Rather, his story
matters for two other reasons. First, he drew on his insider knowledge of
the patent system to identify the contradictions and tacit complicity of
the Patent Office in the US Navy's attempts to reconcile national security
secrecy with the default liberal norms of the patent system. Second, his
exploitation of the same jurisdictional pluralism that we saw Sperry Gyroscope exploit in the last chapter provided a model for Pollen and Isherwood, with whose American lawsuits Dugan's became connected.

More broadly, Dugan experienced and identified an aspect of modern liberalism that has received little attention from historians. As liberalism transformed from its "classical" (or laissez-faire) nineteenth-century form, characterized (at least in theory) by low levels of government intervention in the economy, to its twentieth-century form, characterized by high levels of government intervention in the economy, many liberals, including some architects of the New Deal, accepted limits on their policy ambitions as the price of reform. Nowhere was this acceptance clearer than in the realm of antitrust policy, where the older nineteenth-century hostility to monopoly per se as a threat to republican liberty gave way to a new distinction between "good" and "bad" monopolies, depending on whether the monopoly's products and prices were "good" for consumers or "bad" for them.[2] As we saw in the last chapter, the US Navy and its major fire-control contractors worked out a similar distinction in the military-industrial complex, between "bad" oligopolists with subpar products (like Sperry Gyroscope) and "good" oligopolists like Ford Instrument. To Dugan, by contrast, any oligopoly was a bad oligopoly. Although his nineteenth-century outlook blinded him to the complexity of the twentieth-century military-industrial complex, that same perspective also enabled him to see how the military-industrial complex made certain compromises with liberal-republican principle in its quest for patent secrecy. These were compromises that many others found it convenient not to see.

THE WORLD IS JUST A GREAT BIG TRUNNION

Very little is known about Joseph Dugan. Born in 1877, he became an examiner at the Patent Office in 1910. He rose through the ranks to become assistant chief of Division 33, which had charge of geometrical instruments, including some fire-control instruments. After fourteen years, he left the Patent Office to become a patent attorney and at some point joined Mason, Fenwick & Lawrence, a well-established law firm specializing in patent and trademark cases.[3] Working also as an expert witness in patent cases, he focused on handling US patent applications by foreign nationals on inventions related to naval gunnery and fire control.[4] No fly-by-night operator with a case of sour grapes, he succeeded in his chosen profession.

Somewhere along the way, Dugan became fascinated by problems connected to naval fire control and aerial navigation, and he began working on his own inventions in those fields.[5] After abandoning two early patent applications, he filed a third in February 1927 for a "Sight Controlled Gunnery System."[6] It was intended to correct errors in fire control caused by "trunnion tilt," the movement of the gun's mountings parallel to the deck as a ship rolled and pitched due to wave action. Trunnion tilt could cause errors for range and/or for line.

Dugan's woes began when he forced an interference with a patent for a trunnion-tilt corrector held by two General Electric engineers.[7] He expected to win because he believed that the language at issue called for a fully mechanized system, like his, whereas the GE patent relied on human beings to implement corrections at multiple moments in the transmission of data from the corrector to the sighting device.[8] But unlike the British Royal Commission on Awards to Inventors, which had agreed with Pollen's argument that mechanical automata and human automata differed fundamentally, the US Patent Office held that the GE engineers were entitled to claim the language at issue—or put differently, that there was no essential difference between human and mechanical automata.[9] Dugan was forced to concede the claims and to substitute new ones.[10]

As if to add insult to injury, the Patent Office then declared a new interference between his application and one by the Ford Instrument Company. Dugan was furious, because he believed that the interference had a nefarious backstory. In his telling, he had approached the Bureau of Ordnance several months after filing his patent application in what he later termed "a fit of patriotic boobery."[11] Two officers took his specifications, promised him a report within a few weeks, and advised him to contact Ford Instrument and GE about his invention. When Dugan met with Henry Moakley, Ford Instrument's patent counsel, Moakley allegedly told Dugan that Ford and GE had a "stranglehold" on fire control for the Navy. Nevertheless, he took a copy of Dugan's specifications and promised a report from Ford's engineers within days. Five weeks later, without having supplied the promised report, he met with Dugan again. This time, Moakley informed him that Ford Instrument had already made his invention, offered him $500 for his application, and warned him that if he did not take the money, Ford Instrument would file its own patent application containing his claims and tie him up in interference proceedings.[12] The firm had done just that. In December 1927—ten months after Dugan filed his application, and two months after he gave Moakley a copy—Ford and one of his engineers, Elliott Ross, filed an application containing seventeen claims taken from Dugan's, leading the Patent Office to declare an interference in October 1928.[13]

The interference created problems for Ford Instrument, not just for Dugan. As discussed in previous chapters, interference proceedings were a nightmare from the perspective of national security secrecy. The Ford application in question covered a secret invention produced under contract with the Bureau of Ordnance and embodied in part of the Mark 19 anti-aircraft director. The Mark 19, which was the precursor to the better-known Mark 33 and Mark 37 directors, represented the state of the art in anti-aircraft fire control for its day. Like all fire-control technology, it was highly secret, and Ford Instrument was contractually bound to preserve its secrecy—yet the interference required that Dugan have access to Ford's application, and thus to the design of US Navy equipment.

In an effort to escape this problem, Ford Instrument sent another of its patent attorneys, Walter Gill, to pay Dugan a visit. Gill pressed Dugan to sign a secrecy pledge at the instigation, Dugan believed, of the Bureau of Ordnance.[14] When Gill returned to Dugan's office the next day, Dugan arranged for a stenographer to take shorthand notes of the meeting, from which she produced a sworn transcript. An edited version of the transcript reads as follows:

GILL: Mr. Dugan, we want you to sign a letter or an agreement that you will not disclose the contents of the Ford application or any information you may obtain from the Ford application to anyone else.
DUGAN: No, why should I? . . . I don't want to tie myself in any way whatever. I'm looking out for me. The Ford Instrument Company doesn't give a damn about me. . . .
GILL: This is an unusual procedure on account of the secret character of the application.
DUGAN: Why should I bother about the Ford Instrument Company or the Navy Department. They are not considering me a damn bit. I will take any medicine coming to me, and I will put any down their throats if I can.
GILL: . . . Will you agree to a further extension of time for filing preliminary statement?
DUGAN: No. . . . I want to get through this so I can go back to California.
GILL: If this is keeping you from going to California, you better make up your mind to camp here two or three years longer.[15]

Enraged, Dugan fired off a letter to the Bureau of Ordnance. "This is to advise you that, in any controversy that may arise between myself and the Ford Instrument Company with regard to the gun control system I disclosed to you over a year ago, I am not concerned with any agreement between the Navy Department and the Bureau of Ordnance with regard to keeping any of their inventions secret," he wrote. "I take neither threats nor insults lightly."[16]

Several days later, in a slightly calmer mood, Dugan tried a different approach with the Bureau by depicting Ford Instrument as the common enemy. In his colorful words (emphasis in the original, as always with Dugan):

> Evidently that Ford gang thought I was going to lie down and thank them for wiping their big brogans on me. Now, they are yelping when they see they are going to get licked unless the Lord Almighty and the U.S. Navy helps them. They have the unmitigated brazen gall to ask me to sign some instrument that will bind <u>me</u> to secrecy on the subject matter of the <u>seventeen</u> broad claims they swiped from <u>my application</u>, giving as their reason that the Navy won't let them disclose to me unless I bind myself to secrecy. The Navy, evidently, has paid them for secrecy, and now they are trying to welch on the Navy.

At the same time, he drew a line that the Navy should not cross: "this fight with Ford is a private fight, and I'd rather the Navy would stay out until I lick that gang of freebooters, because I'm going to do it anyway whether the Navy butts in or not." He wanted to make clear that "<u>I will not bind myself to secrecy at the behest of the Ford Instrument Company</u>, and they have no right to ask it so long as they continue to act like a bunch of cowardly cur dogs." Dugan signed the letter "with kindest personal regards."[17]

·.·

Having warned the Navy off, Dugan next approached the Commissioner of Patents. "Just where the U.S. Navy has any right to be considered in this controversy is a mystery," Dugan complained. Given that Ford had taken seventeen claims from Dugan's own patent, the firm's demand that he keep secret what he learned from the interference amounted to a demand that he keep *his own invention* secret. "The Navy Department is <u>not</u> a party to this interference," Dugan maintained, "and has no right to demand that your petitioner <u>bind himself to keep his own invention in secrecy</u>." Dugan declared his confidence that the Commissioner "will never permit the procedure of the Patent Office to be used as a bludgeon by an arrogant corporation to club an independent inventor out of his invention."[18]

Furthermore, Dugan argued that Ford Instrument's decision to develop its invention in secret precluded patent protection, and thus that it had filed the application in bad faith. "[I]t is quite evident that the Ford invention, if reduced to practice at all, was reduced in <u>secret</u>," Dugan wrote. Accordingly, "the application was evidently <u>not</u> filed for the purpose of obtaining a patent for the invention, because that would disclose the invention to the public in violation of Ford's contract with the Navy Department."

Instead, Ford had filed it "for the sole purpose" of blocking a patent grant to Dugan. In effect, Dugan charged, Ford was trying to combine two incompatible forms of intellectual property protection: trade secrets and patents. "The Ford Instrument Company has elected to obtain its special reward by practice in <u>secret</u> for the Bureau of Ordnance," Dugan argued. "Having elected to seek its reward in this direction of secrecy, it is estopped from attempting to prolong its monoply [sic] by making a pseudo application for patent." Citing a string of legal cases to buttress his contention that secret development barred Ford Instrument from receiving patent protection, Dugan asked the Commissioner to dissolve the interference and allow his patent to issue.[19]

Dugan's argument about the incompatibility of secrecy and patent protection rested on contested legal ground. The thrust of the cases he cited was that inventors who kept their knowledge secret from the public were not entitled to patent protection. US case law generally held that inventors guilty of "unexcused delay" in applying for patents had "abandoned" or "forfeited" their right to patent protection.[20] There was also a well-established tradition of public opprobrium for corporate inventors who delayed their patent applications for commercial gain, though the commercial gain in such cases was unrelated to national security secrecy.[21] Such attitudes were consistent with the United States' status as a "patent republic." By compelling inventors to disclose their knowledge to the public in return for a temporary patent monopoly, the United States cleansed patents of their unsavory association with early modern private privileges and turned them into modern public rights suitable for a liberal-democratic republic.[22] However, there were exceptions (or, from the perspective of skilled users of the patent system, loopholes) to the general requirement for prompt filing. The question was whether Ford Instrument could squeeze through them.

Dugan's argument also raised an issue to which the case law did not speak clearly: namely, the relationship between secrecy and public use in the context of inventions with obvious relevance to national security. In the "patent republic," and in the case law cited by Dugan, secrecy and public use were *antithetical*: if inventive knowledge was kept secret, the public could not use it. But in a national security context, secrecy and public use may be *complementary*. In working an invention, the armed forces may provide maximum use to the public by keeping it secret from foreign powers in order to maintain the nation's technological edge. The national security context complicated the secrecy/public use dichotomy in a further way. Under US patent law, as we saw in chapter 8, inventors were barred from receiving patents for inventions in "public use" for more than two years prior to their application. If Ford Instrument sold fire-control technology to the US Navy, and both parties worked to maintain its secrecy, was the sale analogous to, say, Coca-Cola selling soda while keeping its recipe the most famous trade secret in history—a conventional commercial sale that clearly constituted "public use" within the meaning of the statute—or was it something different? Certainly Ford Instrument reaped commercial advantage from selling to the US Navy, much as Coca-Cola benefited from selling to the public, and in that sense its inventive knowledge was a typical *trade* secret. But unlike the recipe for Coke, Ford Instrument's inventive knowledge was also a *national security* secret. Neither the patent law nor the existing jurisprudence contemplated a secret of this dual character. Such a secret involved a category of public use that was, from the perspective of the liberal-democratic norms on which the US patent system was grounded, an unthinkable contradiction in terms: namely, secret public use.[23]

To meet Dugan's attack, Ford Instrument unsurprisingly opted to avoid the thorny question of secrecy and instead to focus on the question of whether its delay in applying for a patent was "excused." One of the exceptions to the rule of unexcused delay was that inventors were permitted to carry out good-faith experimental efforts to get their inventions into a sufficiently developed state for patent protection. This is exactly how the firm explained its delay.[24] In reality, the Mark 19 director was installed on the USS *Maryland* in August 1926 and manifestly was no longer experimental by this time (indeed, Ford Instrument and the US Navy subsequently used the installation as evidence that the Ford invention predated Dugan's).[25] Yet Ford Instrument waited more than a year before filing its patent application. Of course, from the firm's perspective, it was only doing its good-faith best to honor its contractual obligation to preserve the national security secrecy of its inventions while protecting its intellectual property (not least against the predatory US Navy) within the confines of a patent system not designed for national security secrecy. For this business model to work, Ford Instrument needed the Patent Office to turn a blind eye to its exploitation of the system—and for that matter, if the US Navy wanted the military-industrial complex to work, it too needed the Patent Office to play along.

BORN SECRET, REDUX

Before the Commissioner of Patents could weigh in on Dugan's accusations against Ford Instrument, the Navy Department jumped directly into the fray. Refusing to waive secrecy restrictions on its contractor for the purposes of the Dugan interference, the Navy wrote Dugan a threatening letter. It directed his attention "to the Act of Congress of 15 June 19[1]7, known as the Espionage Act," violations of which could result in a fine up to $10,000 and a two-year prison sentence.[26] The Navy did not specify exactly which part of the Act it had in mind, but most likely it was Section 1(b), which criminalized the following:

> Whoever, for the *purpose* [of obtaining information respecting the national defense], and with . . . *intent or reason to believe* [that the information to be obtained is to be used to the injury of the United States, or to the advantage of any foreign nation], copies, takes, makes, or obtains, or attempts, or induces or aids another to copy, take, make, or obtain, any sketch, photograph, photographic negative, blue print, plan, map, model, instrument, applicant, document, writing, or note of anything connected with the national defense. [emphasis added][27]

The Navy then declared Dugan on notice "not to disclose, and to keep secret

> the subject matter of *your adversaries' application* involved [in the interference] with which you may pursuant to law become familiar with [sic], as well as the subject matter of *your own application* involved therein together with the subject matter of *any other kindred inventions or applications you may have or claim,* because the same involve matters essential to the National Defense embraced by the aforesaid Act. [emphasis added][28]

This language was broad: the Navy was ordering Dugan to keep secret his own inventions (plural)—not just what he learned about Ford's invention, and not just his own invention involved in the interference. Moreover, the Navy was evidently ignoring the statutory requirement that someone have a certain "purpose" and "intent or reason to believe" to come within the Act. Instead, it was implying that the very *nature* of Dugan's inventions, regardless of his purpose or intent, brought them within the meaning of the Act. In characteristically piquant terms, Dugan later referred to the Navy's sweeping language as "a clamp on my mind."[29]

The Navy's approach to secrecy anticipated the practices of atomic secrecy. As we saw in chapter 3, one crucial implication of the "restricted data" provision of the 1946 Atomic Energy Act, which treated nuclear information as "born secret," was that it divorced secrecy from classically liberal ideas about property and ownership. It was one thing to classify information as secret by making a property claim to control it or by inserting a secrecy clause into a defense contract. It was another thing to insist on secrecy when the government, as in Dugan's case, had no property claim

whatsoever in the inventions. He had developed them entirely independent of the Navy. Accordingly, the ground on which it asserted secrecy was
that his inventions "involve matters essential to the National Defense embraced by the [Espionage] Act." That is, they were secret by their nature.
Like nuclear "restricted data," "matters essential to the National Defense"
were being treated as a de facto secret category of information.

The effect of the Navy's secrecy order on Dugan was tantamount to expropriation of a US citizen. By preventing him from selling his inventions,
it was limiting his control of his own property and endangering his financial
interests. "Under your communication to me," he protested to the Navy,
"I am completely tied up, and cannot negotiate for the sale of these inventions, even though they cover matter not involved with the Ford application." The secrecy order potentially covered five of his patent applications,
eight of his inventions, and twelve claims in his application involved in the
Ford interference that were not at issue in the interference. He therefore
asked the Navy to tell him more precisely what it considered "essential to
the National Defense."[30] The Navy replied that it would let him know exactly what was covered "[i]f and when you disclose to the Navy Department the subject matter of these claims, applications and inventions." It
added language to which Dugan subsequently attached great importance:
"[i]f and when it becomes apparent that the Navy Department is enjoining
you to secrecy on an application which is *about to issue into a valid patent* to
be owned by you, the Navy Department will be glad to cooperate with you
in determining a reasonable compensation to you for an assignment of such
application" (emphasis added).[31] Optimistically reading this as an uncon-
ditional promise to compensate him as soon as his applications matured
into patents, without any inquiry into their validity, Dugan authorized the
Patent Office to let the Navy Department to make copies of his pending
applications.[32]

∴

While trying to parry the Navy with one hand, Dugan engaged Ford Instrument with the other. Grumbling to the Commissioner of Patents that Ford
Instrument "have evidently decided on scaring your petitioner out of his
inventive existence by bringing pressure from the U.S. Navy Department
to bear upon your petitioner and the officials of the U.S. Patent Office," he
launched a barrage of motions intended to bring an immediate end to the
interference.[33] Most of them sought, in procedurally irregular ways, to get
evidence on record of the secrecy in which Ford Instrument had developed its invention, on the logic that secret development precluded patent

protection and thus mandated the dissolution of the interference.[34] From Ford Instrument's perspective, Dugan was trying to make end runs around procedure.[35] From Dugan's perspective, Ford Instrument's decision to develop its invention in secret and the Navy's irregular attempt to influence Patent Office proceedings in which it had no standing as inventor, owner, or assignee fatally tainted the interference, and fairness justified procedurally extraordinary means to terminate it rapidly.

Denying all of Dugan's pretrial motions, the Patent Office rejected his argument that secret reduction to practice precluded patent protection.[36] "If it can be satisfactorily established that Ford and Ross are under contract to preserve the invention of the issue in secrecy and not obtain a patent," a Patent Office official wrote, "such contractual obligation may be at any time hereafter lifted or waived by the Navy Department and no one can say such a course will not be followed."[37] The official cited no case law to support these contentions, presumably because none existed. A contractual obligation to maintain the secrecy of an invention, for national security reasons or otherwise, was not a recognized category of "excused delay" in filing for a patent. However overwrought Dugan's allegations of a corporatist conspiracy against him may have been, it is difficult to avoid the conclusion that the Patent Office was making itself complicit in Ford Instrument's and the Navy's attempts to make the patent system do something it was not designed to do.

Dugan soon suffered another defeat. In April 1929, the Patent Office ruled that its prior holding in the interference between Dugan and the GE engineers as to the equivalence of human and mechanical automata debarred Dugan from making most of the claims at issue in the Ford interference.[38] Exasperated, Dugan decided to cut his losses and concede the claims at issue in the interference to Ford so as to speed the path to issue for his own patent.[39] His application was allowed with twenty-nine claims in July 1929.[40]

DUGAN V. UNITED STATES

Dugan lost no time alerting the Navy to the allowance of his patent, believing that the Navy had promised to negotiate compensation with him as soon as this condition was met. He submitted a copy of the file (known as the "file wrapper") for the application just allowed, a copy of the interference with Ford, and his own certified copy of Ford's application involved in the interference. Were it not for the Navy's injunction of secrecy and promise to arrange compensation for him once his patent issued, he wrote, he would immediately sue Ford Instrument for infringing several of his allowed claims. As it was, the Navy's injunction had already caused him to miss his opportunity for filing foreign patent applications under the Paris Convention for the Protection of Industrial Property (discussed in chapter 4). In order to avoid endangering his rights further, he asked the Navy to let him know by 15 September 1929 whether it wanted his invention. He needed the matter settled, and thus far he felt "that the Navy has not been fair with me."[41]

The Navy's response only made the feeling worse. In an interview at the Bureau of Ordnance, Dugan learned that it had consulted with Ford Instrument about the validity of his claims, was seeking an additional report on them, and would at most buy a mere license for the invention, not the outright assignment upon the issue of patents referred to in the Navy's letter of February 1929. Dugan was outraged, so much so that he wrote to the Secretary of the Navy personally about the Bureau's perfidy. "I am beginning to believe that the Bureau of Ordnance is also a branch of the Ford Instrument Company," he protested.[42]

Dugan's remonstration to the Secretary of the Navy led to an interview with William Leahy, the then-Chief of the Bureau of Ordnance and future aide to President Roosevelt, in an attempt to clear the air. According to the transcript of the meeting, Dugan complained to Leahy about the appearance of collusion between Ford Instrument and the Bureau—including the Bureau's consultation with Ford attorneys about Dugan's patent application. Leahy assured Dugan that there was no collusion. The Bureau had required that Dugan be enjoined to secrecy in the Ford interference for its own reasons of national defense, not at the firm's behest. While insisting that he could not spend public money on Dugan's inventions without getting a legal opinion on the validity of the patent, Leahy promised that if the Bureau did decide to use something belonging to Dugan, he would make sure that Dugan was properly reimbursed—"That is a basic principle on which I work."[43] Confronted with Leahy's denials, Dugan apologized.

Days later, however, Dugan sent another aggrieved letter to the Secretary of the Navy. He complained that Leahy had told him that he should not submit his patent applications to foreign governments, and a JAG officer had then confirmed that he was still enjoined to secrecy about his own inventions.[44] Moreover, Dugan was still unquestionably enjoined to secrecy about his knowledge of the Ford application acquired during the interference. "Solve this puzzle for yourself, if you can—I am released from secrecy, and I am still enjoined to secrecy," Dugan sarcastically told the Secretary. "Verily, the ways of the Naval mind are beyond the understanding of a mere civilian."[45] He notified the Secretary that the Navy had four days either to make him an offer or to return all his papers, including his certified copy of Ford's application, so that he could show them to prospective purchasers, who would need to see all the papers in his patent file and interference record to assess the value of his rights. Whether these purchasers existed is impossible to say, and in any case irrelevant to the question of principle Dugan was raising.

Leahy's official denials notwithstanding, access to behind-the-scenes correspondence would have convinced Dugan of the righteousness of his accusations, even as it demonstrates how naval officers rationalized their behavior as noncollusive. In reply to a query from the Bureau of Ordnance about Dugan's charges of collusion with Ford Instrument, Commander Henry Markland, the officer with whom Dugan had originally dealt, wrote that he had not attempted "any matters of negotiation with or through any contractors to affect Mr. Dugan's fortunes." Yet at the same time he acknowledged that representatives of both GE and Ford Instrument "discussed Dugan's ideas with me, and I felt it my duty to find out what their opinions were in regard to the practicability of building apparatus in accordance with Dugan's ideas."[46] That is, Markland had shared Dugan's intellectual property, given to him in confidence, with rival inventors. Similarly, in a letter to the Department of Justice defending the Bureau, Leahy rejected Dugan's charge of collusion. But in the next breath, he acknowledged that Bureau officials spoke with Ford's attorneys about Dugan's claim that Ford's application infringed his.[47] Markland and Leahy were not *trying* to violate Dugan's trust; their inquiries to GE and Ford Instrument were practical necessities in view of the Bureau's own lack of in-house technical expertise. But the technical experts in this case were also Dugan's potential commercial rivals, and that element of commercial rivalry meant that their advice, from Dugan's perspective, could not be disinterested. To the contrary, treating it as disinterested appeared collusive. In effect, the Bureau's denials of Dugan's accusations actually confirmed them.

Seeing Dugan's grievances as unreasonable, the Navy reacted angrily to his call for a quick decision. Although it had lifted the injunction of secrecy under the Espionage Act concerning Dugan's own inventions, it had not lifted the injunction regarding his knowledge of the Ford application, which Dugan had indicated he would share with prospective purchasers if the Navy did not meet his deadline—the Navy had not respected his interest in commercial secrecy vis-à-vis Ford Instrument, so why should he respect the Navy's interest in national security secrecy vis-à-vis potential purchasers? The Navy chose to interpret this as an implied threat to violate the Espionage Act. "In view of your attitude in this matter," the Secretary of the Navy told Dugan, the Navy was not returning his papers, including his certified copy of Ford's application, but instead turning them over to the Department of Justice for investigation.[48] As far as the Navy was concerned, the matter was closed.

Dugan went ballistic. No longer feeling the slightest obligation to preserve the secrecy of his patent application involved in the Ford interference, he paid the final fee and removed the last barrier to its public issuance in October 1929. He also composed a long letter to the Secretary of the Navy explaining his anger. Not only had the Navy reneged on the deal he (dubiously) believed it had made with him to cooperate on compensation once his application issued as a patent, it was now trampling on his rights by refusing to return his copy of the Ford application. "This certified copy of the Ford application is my personal property, for which I, personally, had to pay cold cash to the Commissioner of Patents," Dugan maintained. Withholding part of Dugan's patent file record effectively destroyed his ability to sell his patent rights, because any prospective purchased needed to see the whole file in order to assess risk. "[N]o sane person would ever consider buying a patent," Dugan explained, "unless he had access to the opponents [sic] applications involved in interference." He demanded that the Navy return all his papers and notified the Secretary that he would sue for patent infringement if the Navy did not come to terms with him.[49] The question was in which court he would sue.

.·.

As we saw in chapter 8, the question of where aggrieved third parties should file suit for patent infringement by government contractors was a fraught one, which had provoked confusing rulings by the Supreme Court. Its latest word on the subject was its 1928 decision in *Richmond Screw Anchor Co. v. United States*, which, in a seeming reversal of its decision in *Sperry v. Arma* two years earlier, held that third parties had to sue the US government in the Court of Claims, not contractors in district court, for infringement on government contracts.[50] Accordingly, in March 1930, Dugan filed suit in the Court of Claims. He averred that Ford Instrument had produced over five hundred anti-aircraft fire-control systems infringing five claims in his patent involved in the Ford interference, and he asked the Court to award him $1 million—half for the infringement, and half for the injury to his property rights caused by the Navy's injunction of secrecy.[51]

Unfortunately, only scraps of evidence about *Dugan v. United States* survive, likely because of the extraordinary measures taken by the Navy to preserve secrecy. The court's decisions were not reported—that is, there were no public copies of them. Moreover, at the Navy's request, the court placed a secrecy order on the case file in 1930.[52] It was lifted only in the 1960s, at the instigation of the National Archives.[53] The Court of Claims file, which should contain copies of all the motions and briefs submitted, as well as transcripts of the hearings, contains almost none of them.[54] The file instead consists mainly of fragmentary correspondence between the court and the Department of Justice. Paired with documents from the Navy Department and Department of Justice records, as well as a stray copy of an important document in a Patent Office file, the basic outlines of the case can be established, but not much more. Even the chronology is difficult to determine, though it makes clear that the wheels of justice turned no faster in the 1930s than today: Dugan filed suit in 1930; hearings occurred sometime thereafter; the parties prepared suggested findings of fact for the commissioner (as trial judges on the Court of Claims were then known) in early 1933; the case reopened in 1935; and the ruling came down in early 1937.[55]

Fortunately, one aspect of the case that can be reconstructed relates to the Navy's response to Dugan's attempts at discovery—the issue that had caused Pollen and Isherwood so much difficulty in their RCAI claim and would soon cause them difficulty in their attempts to recover compensation from the US government. At Dugan's request, the Court of Claims issued at least two "calls" for evidence on the Navy Department.[56] Instead of refusing to comply on the grounds that the evidence was privileged and could not be disclosed for reasons of national defense, as it would in the later Pollen and Isherwood case discussed in chapter 10, the Judge Advocate General (future Admiral David Sellers) advised that the Navy submit to the call, albeit with certain precautions. The Navy had the right to refuse on secrecy grounds, Sellers claimed, but

> It is believed that the present case is one in which the Government interests can best be served by not withholding the evidence. This need not endanger the secrecy of the subject matter. In fact its secret nature should be emphasized and safe-guarded in every manner possible as for example by submitting the evidence in the custody of a commissioned officer, and by requiring the trial to be in chambers with all present enjoined to secrecy under the Esp[io]nage Act. In this manner the importance of the subject matter may be emphasized and its secrecy safeguarded without the appearance that the Government is trying to suppress evidence.[57]

Sellers contemplated a sort of ceremony of secrecy, in which the performance of rituals—the officer arriving with evidence in a locked briefcase, the invocation of the Espionage Act—would remind all parties involved (including the judiciary) of the national security stakes. The evidence was duly dispatched in the custody of a commissioned officer.[58] The Navy also arranged for serving officers to testify about the Mark 19 anti-aircraft fire-control system that Dugan accused of infringing his patent, and it permitted Dugan and court officers to inspect the system.[59] The Navy's relative liberality in answering the call of the Court likely impelled it to demand a secrecy order on the Court of Claims file. Had the Navy refused to turn over evidence, the secrecy order would not have seemed necessary.

That said, the Navy's liberality was far from complete. Dugan complained to the Court of Claims that the ongoing secrecy of the Ford application prevented him from disposing of his patent rights; when the Department of Justice advised the Navy that his complaint was hurting the government's case, it agreed to release the Ford application from secrecy.[60] Dugan seems to have had less success in removing other parts of the proceedings from secrecy. For instance, in April 1932, he tried and failed to get the secrecy order lifted for most of the case so that he could submit to the Commissioner of Patents excerpts from the hearing transcripts that proved, in his view, that Ford and Ross had perjured themselves by swearing to have made their invention as early as 1919.[61]

Another aspect of Dugan's case that can be reconstructed from the extant evidence is the cast of characters involved. There was a high degree of personnel overlap with Pollen's and Isherwood's US lawsuits, and with the nuclear-secrecy regime of World War II and the Cold War. Two repeat characters were John F. Mothershead and Paul Stoutenburgh, patent specialists in the Claims Division (renamed the Civil Division in 1933) of the Department of Justice. Another was Victor Borst, the new patent counsel for Ford Instrument, who was appointed special assistant to the attorney general to help fight Dugan's lawsuit in the Court of Claims. A fourth was Robert Lavender, the Navy's own leading expert on patents, whom the Department of Justice asked to be made available whenever needed in Dugan's case.[62]

INTERLUDE: "AN IDENTITY OF INTEREST"

In April 1930, just weeks after Dugan filed suit against the government in the Court of Claims, the Patent Office declared a second interference involving the same patent that had been at issue in the Ford interference.[63] Dugan's opponent this time was not Ford but Mortimer Bates, a Sperry Gyroscope engineer. In October 1923, four years before Dugan, Bates had filed a patent application on an invention for correcting for trunnion tilt, which operated on same principle of construction as Dugan's (but not the same as Ford's).[64]

Dugan's interference against Bates supplied him with what he took to be further evidence of a conspiracy in his battles against Ford Instrument and the Navy. Noting that Sperry Gyroscope and Ford Instrument were both subsidiaries of North American Aviation, as discussed in chapter 8, Dugan alleged to the Commissioner of Patents that Sperry Gyroscope was doing Ford Instrument's dirty work, and that the Bureau of Ordnance was in on the collusion.[65] Sperry Gyroscope's attorney dubbed Dugan's accusations "outrageous and unfair."[66] Nevertheless, Dugan managed to score a rare victory. His decision to concede the single claim at issue in the interference bore fruit when, in a complicated series of decisions that largely turned on the meaning of "automaticity" in Dugan's claims, the Examiner of Interferences sided with Dugan and declined to add new claims to the interference sought by Sperry Gyroscope.[67]

As if to vindicate Dugan's accusations of collusion, the government and Ford Instrument now joined the proceedings. John Mothershead of the Department of Justice was appointed associate attorney for Bates.[68] The government then successfully motioned for leave to file an amicus brief on the grounds that the Patent Office had contradicted itself about the meaning of "automaticity" in Dugan's claims, and that the public interest demanded clarification.[69] Unlike the government, Ford Instrument could not cite the public interest as a reason to intervene. Instead, the firm explained that both it and Sperry Gyroscope were owned by North American Aviation, "so that there is an identity of interest on the part of the assignees of the said application."[70] So much for Dugan's accusations of collusion between the North American subsidiaries being "outrageous and unfair."

Dugan had a field day with these developments. Ford Instrument was acting in concert with its North American Aviation cosubsidiary, he told the Patent Office, while the government was "acting as counsel for the North American Aviation Company."[71] The Department of Justice, he submitted, "is not honestly before this Honorable Board of Appeals as an amicus curiae, but most decidedly amicus North American Aviation, Inc., and rather inimicus Dugan."[72] At last, bureaucratic self-interest favored Dugan: the Patent Office held that it had been perfectly consistent in construing his claims. It upheld the Examiner's decision not to add claims to the interference, which accordingly came to an end.[73] The victory availed Dugan not at all; the significance of the Bates interference was its illustration of how moves—like cartelization among contractors and cooperation with the government—that appeared defensive to those inside the military-industrial complex looked offensive to outsiders.

DUGAN V. FORD INSTRUMENT COMPANY

The Ford application at issue in the interference with Dugan emerged from pending status and issued as a patent in November 1933. In April 1935, Dugan launched an attack on it by suing Ford Instrument in district court, with the goal of advancing his ongoing Court of Claims lawsuit by other means. Because US law, as we have seen, generally channeled patent-infringement suits against government contractors to the Court of Claims, Dugan did not sue Ford Instrument for patent infringement. Instead, he brought suit under a section of the patent laws giving the courts jurisdiction over interference proceedings.[74] He asked the Eastern District of New York to declare that his patent and Ford's were interfering patents, that he was the true and first inventor of the invention covered by the patents, and that Ford's patent was void on the grounds of inoperativeness and insufficient disclosure.[75] Dugan explained his reasons for proceeding with the district court suit in a letter to the Commissioner of Patents. According to Dugan, neither the Commissioner himself nor the examiner in charge of the Ford and Ross patent application had shown any interest in his perjury charge against them. "The only way I could find to expose the fraud" was to file suit in district court, Dugan concluded.[76] This was quixotic, of course, but Dugan was in full tilting-at-windmills mode.

Ford Instrument and the government cooperated to foil him. At a deposition intended to draw out Patent Office officials as to the scope of the Ford and Ross patent, a US attorney blocked most of his questions on the ground that "it is contrary to public policy for such a witness to give testimony in a suit between private litigants in relation to the interpretation or construction of a patent."[77] Per usual, Dugan took this assertion of privilege as evidence of an attempt to cover up fraud and negligence at the Patent Office. "I brought this particular bill of complaint," Dugan declared, to get Ford Instrument's patent counsel, Victor Borst, "right out here in the open instead of sneaking always and eternally behind the question of privilege."[78]

Stymied at the deposition, Dugan continued to make a nuisance of himself by firing off a series of angry letters accusing Ford Instrument and various government agencies of malfeasance—and his complaint to the Attorney General actually touched off an FBI investigation into his charges.[79] In New York, Special Agent W. B. Moran interviewed Borst and his assistant, George Gill. The Ford Instrument attorneys struggled to get their stories straight. Borst insisted that his discussion with Leon Habecker, the examiner of the Ford and Ross patent application, "was in the interest of the Government and not of the Ford Instrument Company." However, Gill stated "that it was his understanding that Borst was discussing matters with Habecker as counsel for the Ford Instrument Company and not as Special Assistant to the Attorney General." (Moran observed parenthetically, "It is to be noted that this is in conflict with the claim of Attorney Borst.") Both Borst and Gill questioned Dugan's mental competence—though it did not require insanity to detect collusion between the government and a corporation when the corporation's lawyers themselves contradicted each other as to which hat Borst was wearing.[80]

At last, hearings in the case took place over four days in March 1936. Borst's skillful cross-examination forced Dugan to admit that he had made a mistake, the significance of which they debated, by reversing the elevation correction for trunnion tilt in his patent specifications.[81] More important, for present purposes, was how the government and Ford Instrument approached the issue of secrecy. After consulting with Borst about whether to hold the hearings *in camera* or take other precautions to preserve secrecy, the Navy Judge Advocate General decided not to, since the patents were public.[82] What was not necessarily public, however, was the information that the Ford patent disclosed the construction of the Navy's secret Mark 19 anti-aircraft director (for which the Navy then used the Roman numerals XIX).

This information came out at Borst's instigation, with an assist from Dugan. In the context of arguing that the disclosure of Ford's patent was insufficient to meet the requirements of US patent law, Dugan remarked, "this [Ford] patent is supposed to disclose the mark XIX that is in actual use and installed on the battleships, and I know what it is, and it is not in this patent, and I dare not disclose it to you because I am under the order of secrecy of the Court [of Claims] and the Secretary of the Navy, and so is Mr. Borst, and they dare not disclose what this patent is supposed to disclose." To keep it secret while obtaining patent protection, Dugan charged that Ford Instrument had used five constants (designated K, K_1, K_2, K_3 and K_4) in the trigonometric equations given in the patent specifications without explaining how to derive them.[83] That is, Dugan was claiming that the Ford patent did *not* disclose the Mark 19 director sufficiently to enabled someone "skilled in the art"—the standard in patent law—to make the invention. When he examined Ford's copatentee Elliott Ross on this point, Dugan asked, "Now, your instrument purports to show a fire control system in actual use, known as the mark XIX?" To this Ross replied, "The mark XIX includes it, yes."[84] In order to sharpen the contrast between Ford engineers and Dugan with respect to their "skill in the art," Borst had the Ford engineer confirm that the US Navy actually used the invention disclosed in the patent.[85] Together with Dugan's identification of the Mark number, Borst and the Ford engineer had matched the disclosure in the public Ford patent with at least part of a secret Navy instrument. The Navy had threatened Dugan with prosecution under the Espionage Act if he disclosed secret information about fire control—but it did not punish Borst or the Ford engineer for having done so.

In a June 1936 ruling, the presiding judge, Clarence Galston, sided with Ford Instrument. He ruled that his court lacked jurisdiction over the case because the patents were not interfering within the meaning of the law. "With this view of the case, it becomes unnecessary to discuss the matter of the sufficiency of the disclosure of the Ford and Ross patent," Galston added. "However, it would seem pertinent to observe that 'Mark XIX,' the instrument manufactured by the defendant for the United States government, according to the testimony of Ross, follows the instruction of the defendant's patent."[86] Here was further confirmation that Ford's public patent disclosed a secret Navy instrument.

DENOUEMENTS

Dugan's defeat in district court sent him back to the Court of Claims, where he also lost. Due to the extraordinary secrecy surrounding the case, Commissioner Hayner Gordon's decision was not publicly reported, and no copy survives. The only summary that exists is a brief entry in Robert Lavender's diary, and it makes clear that the ruling went against Dugan: "Report by Commissioner Gordon on Dugan case. [Dugan's] Patent invalid, was never reduced to practice, anticipated by others and not infringed."[87]

The ever-persistent Dugan of course decided to appeal. Borst, Mothershead, and Lavender worked closely together on the government's reply.[88] The Court of Claims' "judges," who heard appeals from the "commissioners," handed down their decision in February 1939. It remained adverse to Dugan.[89] He next appealed to the Supreme Court.[90] This appeal raised certain evidentiary difficulties because of secrecy. Dugan took advantage of a new rule that required the Supreme Court, once it had agreed to grant certiorari (i.e., to review a case), to receive not only the findings of fact and judgment by the lower court, but also the evidence, namely, the testimony and exhibits.[91]

Borst sensed danger. The clerk of the Court of Claims had given Dugan a copy of the transcript of record, which probably included copies of motions, briefs, court orders, and exhibits, as well as transcripts of hearings and testimony.[92] Borst opined that nothing therein was confidential, but the "general ban of secrecy on the case has not been removed," and he supposed "that the Solicitor General should oppose a motion by Dugan to remove the order of secrecy."[93] The Solicitor General duly did so, despite being told by the Navy that "there is probably nothing of real moment disclosure of which would prejudice the United States" in the transcript of record.[94]

The government also responded to Dugan's Supreme Court appeal by generating some of the legal arguments that it would rely on in meeting

Pollen's and Isherwood's lawsuits. Francis M. Shea, the Assistant Attorney General in charge of the Claims Division (who would go to argue the famous patent case *Marconi Wireless Telegraph Company v. United States* in 1943), asked Paul Stoutenburgh, one of the staff attorneys in the division, to research whether the head of an executive department could refuse a call of the Supreme Court for evidence, with particular reference to the famous Aaron Burr case (in which President Thomas Jefferson had refused a subpoena from the Supreme Court to turn over certain documents). Stoutenburgh traced a line of cases, statutes, and opinions of the Attorney General forward from Burr holding that the head of a department could refuse a call of the court, so long as he provided a reason for withholding the evidence called for. The line of cases included the Supreme Court's 1876 ruling in *Totten v. United States*—often cited today as the first case in the genealogy of the state secrets privilege.[95] Lavender helped to arrange an affidavit to the Supreme Court by Admiral Harold Stark, the Chief of Naval Operations and acting Secretary of the Navy, affirming that the record in the case was secret for reasons of national defense.[96] The Supreme Court duly denied Dugan's petition to release the proceedings in the case from secrecy as well as his petition for certiorari.[97]

Dugan refused to quit. He had two cards left to play, neither of them promising. Within weeks of his rebuff at the Supreme Court, Dugan opened up a new front in his ongoing war by suing Sperry Gyroscope, its president Thomas Morgan, Ford Instrument, its president Hannibal Ford, Lavender, and Borst in the Southern District of New York for violating the Sherman Antitrust Act. Dugan's attorney for this lawsuit was John Lizars, Pollen's and Isherwood's attorney in the lawsuits discussed in the next chapter.[98] Very few traces of this case survive, and it likely went nowhere. Then, in early 1943, Dugan filed a motion with the Court of Claims to disbar Borst and Lavender, who was by then the patent advisor to the Manhattan Project.[99] By this time, Dugan had joined Lizars as counsel in the Pollen and Isherwood lawsuits; apparently, while arguing on the Englishmen's behalf, he had charged Borst with perjury and felt he had to follow it up with a motion to disbar.[100] Unsurprisingly, this attempt failed. Dugan's efforts to achieve justice ended only with his death.[101]

Looking in from the outside, Dugan saw his opponents in the military-industrial complex as operating from a position of strength, and he was not wrong to do so. The US naval fire-control industry appeared to him like a government-supported oligopoly because it walked like one and quacked like one. Looking out from the inside, however, participants in the military-industrial complex felt themselves to be operating from a position of weakness, and they were not wrong to do so. They were frantically trying to plug leaks in a liberal-democratic order that was not really designed for what they wanted to do, which was to combine patent protection in a "patent republic" with national security secrecy. The only way that Ford Instrument could seek some degree of IP protection—if not full-fledged patent protection—while meeting its contractual obligation to preserve the secrecy of its inventions was to apply for patents and keep the applications in pending status for as long as possible. But this tactic rendered the firm vulnerable to charges of trying to combine trade secrecy with patent protection. If one of its applications ended up in interference proceedings, the secrecy problem only got worse. Interferences operated according to liberal norms of due process, with each side entitled to see the other's evidence. In these proceedings, conducted under the jurisdiction of the Patent Office, the Navy could not assert a secrecy privilege as it could in the courts. The only card it had to play against Dugan was the Espionage Act. But that, of course, meant interfering with his IP rights in defiance of liberal norms.

Dugan's lawsuits shaped the landscape that Pollen and Isherwood encountered when they initiated the lawsuits that form the subject of the next chapter. John Mothershead, the Justice Department lawyer handling Dugan's ongoing case, noted that their suit against the US government "pertains to gun firing mechanisms used by the Navy Department and is similar to that involved in the Dugan case."[102] But the Navy and Justice Departments chose a different strategy against Pollen and Isherwood. Having elected not to deploy a secrecy privilege against Dugan when proceedings moved out of the Patent Office and into the courts, but instead to fence him in with the Espionage Act, they had to endure his using his access to evidence to make their lives difficult. Faced with equally stubborn plaintiffs in Pollen and Isherwood, whose inventions—unlike Dugan's—unquestionably worked and the United States had unambiguously stolen, the US government was not about to make the same mistake.

CHAPTER 10

State Secrets and the Pax Americana

"The defendant is in effect saying, You have a right but I shall prevent this Court from hearing your right. And they do that by coming
before this Court and saying, We refuse to answer, it is all secret and
confidential."

JOHN LIZARS, 7 JUNE 1937

In its 1953 ruling in *United States v. Reynolds* formally establishing the state
secrets privilege, the Supreme Court cited five cases as precedents supporting its statement that "the privilege against revealing military secrets . . .
is well established in the law of evidence."[1] One of those cases, which involved what might be called the proto-state secrets privilege, was Arthur
Pollen's and Harold Isherwood's patent-infringement lawsuit against the
Ford Instrument Company. Whereas *Reynolds* pitted the right to hold
the government accountable for tortious wrongdoing against the government's national security claims, the Pollen and Isherwood lawsuit pitted
property rights—specifically, the property right in patents—against those
claims. This chapter tells the story of that lawsuit, their lawsuit against the
US government in the Court of Claims, and the entanglement of both in
Anglo-American relations at the start of World War II. In so doing, it traces
the accumulation of the legal knowledge that came to undergird the power
of the Cold War national security state to classify information as secret, as
well as the process by which global hegemony passed from Britain to the
United States.

Pollen's and Isherwood's efforts to gain compensation for the use of their
inventions by the US government took a different course from their efforts
to do the same from the British government. As we saw in chapter 7, their efforts in Britain benefited from the quasi-judicial forum provided by the Royal
Commission on Awards to Inventors (RCAI), which did not tie them to the
rigid standards of proving patent infringement, and from the hostility of the
RCAI chair, Lord Justice Tomlin, to the crown's assertions of a privilege not

to produce evidence on secrecy grounds. Pollen and Isherwood enjoyed neither of these advantages in the United States. Even so, the jurisdictional map offered certain opportunities. Pollen's and Isherwood's attorney, John Lizars, like Sperry Gyroscope and Joseph Dugan before him, saw that he could exploit the uncertainty as to whether third-party patent owners should sue the US government in the Court of Claims or government contractors in district court for patent infringement to probe for weaknesses in the shield of national security secrecy. A stubborn and fiery ex-naval officer, Lizars, like Dugan—who later joined Pollen's and Isherwood's legal team—was a former insider. And like Dugan, Lizars was outraged by what he regarded as the illiberal, collusive, and downright un-American conduct of the US Navy and Ford Instrument. Lizars decided to exploit the question mark over district court jurisdiction to test whether the proto-state secrets privilege could reach into litigation between private parties.

While Pollen's and Isherwood's US lawsuits were ongoing, World War II began in Europe, France fell, and Britain dispatched a high-level mission to the United States to kickstart scientific and technological cooperation. The reaction of the Navy's Bureau of Ordnance to this mission makes clear that at least one key US naval official knew that Pollen's and Isherwood's lawsuit had merit. The British mission was also significant because it resumed the overwhelmingly one-way flow of scientific and technological knowledge from Britain to the United States that had begun in World War I and eroded British power relative to its erstwhile colony. The US Navy took advantage of round two to cover up what it had done to Pollen and Isherwood during round one.

THE STATE SECRETS PRIVILEGE

On 1 August 1936, Pollen and Isherwood filed suit in the Court of Claims, alleging that the US government had infringed their US patents by procuring the Ford rangekeeper. Due to the loss of records, it is impossible to say why Pollen and Isherwood chose to sue when they did. The driving force behind the lawsuit seems to have been Isherwood, not Pollen; it was Isherwood who worked with Lizars, helped to interview potential witnesses, and testified in court. Pollen was alive for the beginning of the suit but died suddenly in January 1937, leaving Isherwood to press on alone.

The most likely explanation for the timing of Pollen's and Isherwood's lawsuit has to do with the timing of Ford's patents. In 1924, the Patent Office issued to Ford a patent for a "Calculating Instrument" (hereafter the 1924 patent). According to this patent, "Instruments having the general structural details of that shown in [the 1924 patent], have been used in connection with range keepers of the type shown in my co-pending application Serial No. 280,150, filed March 1, 1919, and which are particularly intended for use with guns of large calibre, such apparatus being known in the United States Navy as Mark I, range keeper."[2] Serial no. 280,150, for a "Range and Bearing Keeper," though filed for in 1919, did not issue as patent no. 1,827,812 until 1931.[3] The reason for the delay was not that Ford Instrument had worked the invention in secret before filing for patent protection, as it had in Dugan's case, but rather that, after filing in a timely manner, it exploited two provisions in US patent law—one giving inventors up to a year to respond to any action on their application by the Patent Office, another allowing them to amend their claims and thus restart the process of communicating with the Patent Office—to keep the application in pending status (and thus effectively secret) for a dozen years.[4] Not until the patent application issued in 1931, in other words, did Isherwood possess both pieces of the puzzle—a statement that a certain patent described US Navy equipment, plus the patent describing it—and not until then could he see how closely the Ford clock resembled the instruments described in his and Pollen's US patents.[5] Hence a lawsuit for patent infringement was not viable before 1931 at the earliest.

In their suit, Pollen and Isherwood accused the government of infringing three of their US patents.[6] At the Justice Department's request, the Bureau of Ordnance produced an analysis comparing the Pollen patents with the Ford machines. It pointed to a number of differences. For instance, where the Pollen patents resolved the motions of own and target ship into a single vector by displacing own course and speed onto the target, Ford rangekeepers resolved own and target motion separately, then combined them by means of a differential.[7] The analysis also claimed "radical differences in the mechanical means."[8] In fact, Patent Office examiners had originally rejected Ford's separation of own and target motion as insufficiently different from Pollen's patents to count as patentable, suggesting that the significance of the difference was not as self-evident to experts as the Bureau claimed.[9] Moreover, although Ford may have avoided mechanically infringing Pollen's patents, he had unquestionably plagiarized the text in their machine.

Since US laws provided a remedy only for patent infringement, not for plagiarism, Pollen and Isherwood would likely have faced an uphill battle to prove their case under the best of circumstances. But the hill got even steeper when the Navy Department decided to obstruct their discovery of evidence. In September 1936, the Bureau of Ordnance, led by Harold R. Stark (better known as the author of the famous "Plan Dog" memorandum of 1940), produced a highly misleading memorandum for the Judge Advocate General, who in turn passed it along to the Department of Justice.

Stark maintained that "that no structures have been built for or used by the government which embody the inventive idea of the patents now in suit." He enclosed copies of only two letters between Pollen and then-chief of the Bureau Ralph Earle during the crucial months of October–December 1917, when the Bureau had completed its plagiarism of the Argo clock. These were the letters (covered in chapter 4) in which Earle denied infringing Pollen's patents and Pollen withdrew an accusation of plagiarism made in a letter of 31 October 1917, which Stark excluded on the grounds that it was a *personal* letter not in the Bureau's files. Stark did not make clear on what grounds he omitted various *official* papers in the Bureau's files— such as then-head of the fire-control section Wilbur Van Auken's memorandum to Earle noting that the Bureau would be obliged to pay Pollen for the predicted-bearing feature that it had ordered Ford Instrument to incorporate in the rangekeeper—from the material sent to the Judge Advocate General and thence to the Department of Justice.[10] The omission is especially striking given that Van Auken's memorandum carried the same file number as the two letters that Stark included, and it would have been bundled with them (as it is in the archives today).[11]

Besides suppressing evidence within the government, the Bureau of Ordnance declined, on national security grounds, to disclose any evidence whatsoever to Pollen and Isherwood. In October 1936, the plaintiffs filed a call for evidence on the Navy Department asking the Court of Claims to compel it to turn over information about its rangekeepers.[12] Stark protested that disclosure of such information would be "injurious to the public interest."[13] Nevertheless, the court ordered that the Navy permit Isherwood and Lizars to examine and photograph Ford rangekeepers.[14] In contrast to the strategy that it had pursued in Dugan's case—permitting discovery but enjoining the plaintiff to secrecy under the Espionage Act—the Navy bluntly refused to comply. Not only would it not permit the plaintiffs to view the actual machines, the Secretary of the Navy informed Lizars, but it would withhold blueprints and descriptions, on the grounds that they "relate to the National Defense."[15] The Navy was claiming an evidentiary privilege, akin to Britain's crown privilege, to keep information secret in the name of national security.

·.·

The Navy's refusal to comply with the court order set the stage for a pivotal hearing in the Court of Claims on 7 June 1937, presided over by Commissioner Clyde Norton.[16] Victor Borst attended wearing the same two hats that he had worn in Dugan's case: one as Ford Instrument's patent attorney, the other as a special assistant to the attorney general.[17] Borst objected

Figure 10.1. Robert Lavender, shown here in 1919, at the time of the NC-3 flight. (George Grantham Bain collection, LC-B2-4902-3, LoC.)

when Lizars tried to ask his first two witnesses—the president of Arma Engineering and a former Ford Instrument employee—about the construction of rangekeepers, and the witnesses declined to answer on the grounds that the rangekeepers were confidential. In any case, Commissioner Norton directed Lizars, if he wanted to use secondary evidence about the construction of rangekeepers like testimony from former employees, he needed to prove first that he could not use the best evidence, namely, the rangekeepers themselves.[18]

To supply this proof, Lizars called Commander Robert A. Lavender to the stand. The Navy's leading patent expert, Lavender, shown in figure 10.1, was one of those fascinating and important figures who has been mostly lost to history.[19] He graduated from the Naval Academy in 1912 and quickly developed expertise in radios. In 1919, he served as radio officer of the NC-3, one of three aircraft that the Navy hoped would make the first trans-Atlantic flight, albeit with stops (only NC-4 made it across).[20] He continued to build his technical expertise, picking up a master's degree in electronics from Harvard. In 1924, the Navy ordered him to the Judge

Advocate General's office to head the Patent Division—so many questions about patents in the electronics field were coming up that the Navy needed someone technically qualified. When Lavender matched his electronics degree from Harvard with a law degree from George Washington University in 1927, the results were formidable; a pioneering Navy researcher of underwater acoustics once wrote that he got "quite similar" pleasure reading a patent application prepared by Lavender as he got "from attending a symphony concert."[21] After a stint at sea, Lavender returned for his second tour as head of the Patent Division, this time also serving as the Navy's representative on a commission to consider claims put forward by British inventors who alleged that the United States had used their inventions without compensation during World War I. He did a third tour as head of the Patent Division in the 1930s, earning the Judge Advocate General's praise as "[a]n excellent officer of unique value to the Navy in the patent field where he has peculiar knowledge and experience."[22] Lavender took secrecy seriously—so seriously that the Commissioner of Patents alleged that Lavender had threatened him with prosecution under the Espionage Act if he allowed a certain patent to issue.[23] When Lavender retired from the Navy in 1939, he joined the law firm of Victor Borst, Ford's patent attorney, who had become a personal friend. Indeed, a drink with Court of Claims Commissioner Norton in February 1937 was one of several social engagements involving Borst noted by Lavender in his diary.[24]

But Lavender's most important work still lay before him. In 1941, the Navy recalled him to active duty and assigned him to serve as chief patent advisor to the Office of Scientific Research and Development, the head of which, Vannevar Bush, had specifically requested him.[25] Lavender was read into the Manhattan Project in the spring of 1942 and became the principal legal architect of the atomic secrecy regime. President Roosevelt decided that the best way to secure government control of atomic energy and preserve secrecy was through the patent system, while Bush was determined to incorporate private industry into the nuclear program.[26] The decisions to preserve secrecy through the patent system and through reliance on profit-oriented contractors built on decades of (often unsuccessful) efforts to marry the patent system and the private sector to national security needs. As it had done during World War I, Congress passed legislation in 1940 and 1941 establishing a patent secrecy regime on a temporary wartime basis.[27] Lavender supervised almost a hundred lawyers and engineers working in the "Manhattan District" alone; he was also closely involved with the famous "Rad Lab" (Radiation Laboratory) at MIT. When the war ended, he became the patent advisor to the Atomic Energy Commission. He retired from the Navy in 1947 but continued to work as an advisor to an Air Force contractor studying the nuclear propulsion of aircraft. Thus, he quite literally embodied connections between World War I–era patent secrecy practices and the atomic secrecy regime.

Lizars used his examination of Lavender to probe the nature of the secrecy that the Navy was claiming. Lavender had brought with him a letter from the Secretary of the Navy, dated two days earlier, giving notice that

> all information concerning the details of range keepers in use by the Navy Department, past and present, come within the provisions of the Acts of Congress as defined in 50 U.S. Code [i.e., the Espionage Act]. Such information relates to the National Defense and its disclosure will be injurious to the public interest of the United States.[28]

Brandishing the Secretary's letter, Lavender refused to answer questions that would require him to disclose secret information. When asked about the "mathematical propositions" underlying the Ford rangekeeper, for instance, Lavender replied, "I am unable to make any statement whatever as to any arrangement or mechanism in any rangekeeper that the United States Government or the United States Navy uses."[29] In effect, Lavender was asserting a testimonial privilege complementing the Navy's claimed evidentiary privilege.

Lizars tried to poke holes in the secrecy argument. Handing Lavender copies of two Ford patents for rangekeepers, Lizars asked, "Now would you conclude from the fact that range keepers are actually described in United States patents that it is not quite so pressing a secret as you were led to believe?" "You have failed to see the main point in confidential," Lavender retorted. "[W]hether or not an individual range keeper contains certain things is confidential and I refuse to disclose any of the details of any range keeper that is used in the United States Navy."[30] Nor, Lavender testified, would the government permit the case to proceed *in camera*—as it had in Dugan's case. "If [the defendant] will not consent to conducting in camera what he means of course to do is to object to everything that we propose to say and do," Lizars inferred. "How can we present a case if as a matter of fact he says, 'It is all secret and confidential; we can not produce it'?"[31] Anticipating criticisms of the modern state secrets privilege, Lizars argued that the evidentiary and testimonial privilege claimed by the Navy had constitutional implications:

> I propose to show that the defendant is actually divesting the Supreme Court of its power to declare a statute invalid, and in this way the defendant says in effect that whether you have a case or not is no matter; and

particularly if you do have a case we shall through this fog of secrecy preclude you from presenting it to the Court. There is no statutory right which gives this defendant any such power and giving him the right to offer such an attitude is abrogated by Article I, Section 8 of the United States Constitution in which a patentee is given a definite property right. The defendant is in effect saying, You have a right but I shall prevent this Court from hearing your right. And they do that by coming before this Court and saying, We refuse to answer, it is all secret and confidential.[32]

The invocation of the privilege, in other words, threatened the separation of powers between the executive and judicial branches, as well as property rights.

Stonewalled by Lavender, Lizars called his final two witnesses. The first was Harold Isherwood, who testified about the disclosure of the Argo system to the United States before and during World War I and walked the court through the technical claims made in his and Pollen's US patents.[33] The second was Charles Infante, a former Ford Instrument employee. When Lizars asked him to describe the construction of Ford rangekeepers, Borst objected that the Navy had classified the information as secret, adding "I should like incidentally to ask this witness if he has divulged this information to Mr. Lizars."[34] "The attorney for the defendant is attempting to intimidate the witness," Lizars protested.[35] Commissioner Norton ruled that Lizars could ask the question, but "I wish to instruct the witness and have him thoroughly understand that he does not have to answer that question, if he does not wish to, on the ground that it violates his constitutional rights by possibly tending to incriminate him."[36] This was a reference to the Fifth Amendment right against self-incrimination—in this instance, the right not to incriminate himself for having violated the Espionage Act. When asked again whether he had previously disclosed the information sought to Lizars, Infante answered, "I do not care to answer the question."[37] In addition to claiming privilege to avoid disclosing information itself, the Navy was also using the Espionage Act to dissuade other witnesses from testifying.

Commissioner Norton decided not to decide the questions before him. The legal issues involved—whether to order the case to proceed *in camera* and whether to permit Infante to testify about the construction of Ford rangekeepers—were so weighty, he reasoned, that the full Court of Claims should render judgment. He referred the case to them without prejudice to either side.[38] "Commissioner Norton has not the decision to make," Lavender recorded in his diary.[39]

· ·

Two weeks later, the Chief of Naval Operations and Acting Secretary of the Navy William Leahy wrote to the Justice Department to ask it to investigate Lizars and two former Ford Instrument employees whom he had called as witnesses for possible violation of the Espionage Act.[40] The Justice Department put the Federal Bureau of Investigation on the case.[41] FBI Special Agent Robert Boyle interviewed all three men, as well as other former Ford employees contacted by Lizars. All denied having disclosed confidential information. As for Lizars, Boyle wrote, he "assumed a very arrogant and offensive attitude, stating that he was well aware that an investigation by the Bureau was being made and that in his opinion the investigation was nothing more nor less than an underhanded method devised by the Navy Department to intimidate their witnesses." When the perplexed agent asked him, evidently in all sincerity, what was intimidating about being investigated by the FBI, Lizars explained "that the mere fact that [Boyle] identified himself as an agent of the Bureau in requesting an interview with any of the witnesses would have a frightening effect upon any of the witnesses who were laymen."[42]

While the FBI conducted its investigation, the parties prepared their briefs for the court. Lizars argued that two constitutional issues were at stake: first, whether a government department could abrogate the patent rights protected under Article I, Section 8 of the Constitution by appropriating those rights to itself; and second, whether a government department could violate the Fifth Amendment by destroying the property right in patents without due process. If the Court of Claims refused to permit the plaintiffs to establish proof of infringement, Lizars reasoned, it would nullify the jurisdiction conferred upon it by the Acts of 1910 and 1918 (discussed in previous chapters). If the government could use the Espionage Act to expropriate patents without just compensation, then this act was unconstitutional. In effect, Lizars was invoking liberal norms about private property and due process to attack the ramshackle legal architecture governing the relationship of the military-industrial complex to intellectual property and secrecy.[43]

The government's brief, signed also by Borst, Ford Instrument's attorney, offered a full-throated defense of the Navy's right to assert a secrecy privilege. While the government had waived its sovereign immunity insofar as it empowered the Court of Claims to issue calls for evidence on executive departments, the brief argued—drawing on the knowledge amassed for the Dugan case discussed in chapter 9—that it had reserved the right for a department head to "refuse and omit to comply with any such call for information or papers when, in his opinion, such compliance would be injurious to the public interest."[44] If claimants decided to avail themselves of the privilege to sue the government conferred by the waiver of sovereign immunity, they did so subject to conditions imposed by the government, which had singled out national security information for special protection in the Espionage Act. The government pointed to the 1876 case *Totten v. United States* as precedent.[45]

In its November 1937 ruling, the Court of Claims upheld the government's assertion of privilege. The court had jurisdiction to issue calls for evidence, the ruling held, but department heads had the right not to comply with them. While the judges accepted as uncontroversial Lizars's argument that patent rights were a constitutionally protected form of property, they explained,

> The vital issue is one of proof. May an officer of the Navy [i.e., Lavender] be compelled to disclose what he and his superior officer declare to be military secrets, the disclosure of which they assert would be detrimental to the National defense? The patented devices involved and the devices used by the defendant are obviously of great importance in the field of Naval armament. If a testimonial privilege does not extend to a Naval officer, especially with respect to armament employed in actual service, the Government would in many instances be precluded from availing itself of instrumentalities of defense unknown to all the other Naval powers of the World.

"In time of war the rule prevails," the court went on, "and there is no reason assignable for its non-application in times of peace." Pointing to *Totten*, the court observed that the privilege "is predicated upon the principle of the public good and the right of the Sovereign to maintain an efficient National defense—a public interest of such paramount importance as in and of itself transcends the individual interests of a private citizen." Since the government had the right to assert the privilege, the motion to proceed *in camera* had to be overruled. Moreover, the privilege extended to contractors. While Infante, the Ford employee, was a private citizen, the court reasoned, "the knowledge he possesses is vital to the Government's National defense, and he obtained it in confidential relationship with the Navy Department."[46]

Accordingly, the court rejected Lizars's constitutional arguments. It was not substantively preventing the plaintiffs from proving their case, contra Lizars, merely "passing upon a rule of evidence as it pertains to two certain witnesses." By the same token, "[a]n established rule of evidence does not nullify a jurisdictional act": "[i]t may and often does preclude recovery under the act," but "[t]he remedy is not impaired." As for Lizars's argument that the privilege would enable the government to defeat all patent suits brought against it, the court held, "[t]he presumption obtains that in the exercise of the authority good faith will characterize the conduct of the Government officials," adding, "in this case there is no proof that it has been exercised arbitrarily, capriciously, or with intent to injure plaintiffs."[47] Since the effect of the court's ruling was to prevent the plaintiffs from supplying such proof, this logic had a circular quality. The case was not over, but the court had already decided that Pollen and Isherwood would be denied normal due process.

STAGING AN INTERVENTION

Having failed in his bid to compel the Navy Department to turn over evidence in the Court of Claims, Lizars pivoted at the end of 1937 to sue Ford Instrument for patent infringement in the Eastern District of New York, where the firm was located. On the one hand, this jurisdiction posed obstacles to their case that the Court of Claims had not. Because the Supreme Court had held in *Richmond Screw Anchor*, as we saw in chapter 9, that the government should be sued in the Court of Claims for patent infringement by its contractors, the suit in the Eastern District was limited to rangekeepers sold by Ford Instrument to foreign governments. In another respect, however, the new jurisdiction potentially removed obstacles that Lizars had confronted in the Court of Claims. Because the US government was not a party to the suit and had not established the court through a waiver of sovereign immunity, it had less power to assert secrecy and control the parameters of the case—at least in theory.

Alleging that the Navy had shared information about Pollen's system with Ford Instrument following his communications with the Navy in 1913–14 and 1916–17, the plaintiffs charged Ford Instrument with infringing six of Pollen's and Isherwood's US patents.[48] The first move of Ford Instrument's attorney, Borst, was to enlist the aid of the US government, just as the government had enlisted his in the Court of Claims. Alerting the Navy Department of the new suit, Borst wrote that it was "obviously an attempt to evade the consequences of the decision of the Court of Claims on plaintiff's motions" to compel the production of evidence, and he might need assistance from the Navy "to avoid disclosure of confidential information regarding matters touching the national defense."[49] The Secretary of the Navy asked the Justice Department to prevent such disclosure, and the Justice Department suggested a conference with Borst before he formally responded to the new suit.[50]

There then ensued ten months of jockeying between Lizars and Borst over the form of the Bill of Complaint, which set the parameters of the case that Ford Instrument had to answer. Borst received advice on his drafts from the Justice Department.[51] One of the principal points at issue centered on the statute of limitations for patent infringement. US law limited recovery for patent infringement to the six years preceding the filing of the Bill of Complaint—in this case, to infringement occurring after December 6, 1931.[52] When this time limit was combined with the jurisdictional limit, Pollen and Isherwood could recover only for exports between 1931 and 1937—at best a narrow window. The seventeen-year term of US patents limited them further.[53] To widen the window, Lizars had to find some reason why the statute of limitations would not apply, or, in legal terminology, something that would "toll" or "suspend the running" of it. He therefore argued that Ford Instrument had conspired with the Navy Department to fraudulently conceal its infringing acts from Pollen and Isherwood, and that the statute of limitations did not apply where fraud was involved.[54] In his vigorously capitalized words:

PLAINTIFFS' ALLEGATIONS OF FRAUDULENT CONCEALMENT . . . AVER THAT DEFENDANT REPRESENTS HIS INFRINGING ACTS AS COMING WITHIN MILITARY SECRETS OF THE UNITED STATES GOVERNMENT. THE ALLEGATION ACCORDINGLY SETS UP THE DEFENDANT'S ATTEMPT TO CLOAK HIS WILFULL [sic] INVASIONS OF PLAINTIFFS' PROPERTY RIGHTS UNDER A CRIMINAL STATUTE [the Espionage Act] OF THE UNITED STATES GOVERNMENT. . . . IT IS SUBMITTED THAT NO MORE COGENT REASON FOR SUSPENSION OF THE RUNNING OF THE STATUTE COULD BE ALLEGED.

Lizars filed the final amended version of the Bill of Complaint in early October 1938.[55] Once Borst's formal Answer was in, denying all of Lizars's claims, the case was ready to proceed.[56]

∴

Lizars initiated the next phase of the case with two depositions in Washington in December 1938. Borst attended to represent Ford Instrument; the Justice Department, alerted by Borst, sent John Mothershead, who had been the point man on the Dugan lawsuits; and the Navy Department, alerted by the Justice Department, sent two officers.[57] The first deponent was none other than Joseph Dugan. Lizars's principal line of questioning sought to establish that Ford Instrument and the Navy were cynically using claims of secrecy in order to maintain the firm's monopoly on fire-control instruments and to hide wrongdoing. Having had Dugan explain the background to his interference proceeding at the Patent Office against Ford Instrument, Lizars began to ask him about the patent infringement suit he had filed against the United States in the Court of Claims. Borst, who of course was familiar with the Dugan lawsuits, immediately interjected. Dugan was under a secrecy order concerning his own cases and could not divulge secret information about Navy fire-control material "under the penalties of the Espionage Act," as Borst reminded him "for his own protection."[58] Lizars noted for the record "the efforts of Mr. Borst to intimidate this witness" and then turned to probing the nature of the secrecy claimed by the Navy and Ford Instrument.[59] In the course of Dugan's suit against Ford Instrument in district court, as we saw in the last chapter, Borst had confirmed that Ford's patent at issue described at least part of the Navy's Mark 19 anti-aircraft director.[60] In so doing, he evidently divulged the sort of information about the construction of Navy fire-control instruments that Ford Instrument and the Navy were claiming must be kept secret under the penalty of the Espionage Act. Lizars was suggesting that secrecy did not attach to the knowledge itself, as Ford and the Navy were claiming, but to the person(s) who knew it.

Here, like Sperry Gyroscope and Dugan before him, Lizars was exploiting strains in the marriage between the national security state and the private sector. Had antigovernment ideological forces not compelled the US government, since the early national period, to rely at least partly on private contractors to meet its defense procurement needs, it would have been able to limit patent infringement suits to the Court of Claims. But its employment of contractors, combined with their desire to sell across national boundaries, opened up a second jurisdictional front in district court—where, as the Dugan case showed, secrets could slip out.

Lizars's second witness at the deposition was Vernon Durst, the chief of the Records Division of the General Accounting Office (now the Government Accountability Office, or GAO). Durst's usefulness to Lizars derived from long-running efforts to strengthen Congress's financial oversight of the executive branch and to make government contracting more transparent to the public. In 1862, with the Civil War having vastly increased the federal government's reliance on contractors, Congress passed an act "To prevent and punish fraud on the part of officers intrusted with making of contracts for the government."[61] It established a Returns Office to hold "returns copies" of federal contracts within the Department of the Interior, and it required the Secretaries of War, the Navy, and the Interior to file copies of all contracts there. These returns copies were to be available "to any person desiring to inspect the same."[62] In 1921, after another war-induced boom in federal spending, Congress passed the Budget and Accounting Act.[63] On top of establishing the framework of the modern federal budget, the act also created the General Accounting Office as the legislature's independent, nonpartisan auditing arm. In 1929, Congress moved the Returns Office from the Department of the Interior to the GAO.[64] The history of the Returns Office was thus the history of legislative efforts to control government spending in accordance with liberal-democratic principles of transparency.

In the Returns Office, Lizars had located another tension between the national security state and liberal-democratic norms, and another way of probing the Navy Department's secrecy. His subpoena obliged Durst to bring to the deposition the returns copies of all contracts between the Navy and Ford Instrument, numbering seventy-eight in total. Of these, the Navy Department had marked four as confidential and several others as "restricted."[65] Durst confirmed that the returns copies were open to the public by law, except "those portions of such contracts that are marked Confidential" by the Navy Department.[66] Lizars asked whether the contracts marked confidential contained any drawings or descriptions; Durst answered that they did not.[67] When Lizars offered all seventy-eight contracts into evidence, Borst objected: "So far as they might disclose any military secrets, it is obviously improper that they should be produced for public inspection."[68] Borst asked that the two Navy officers present at the deposition be permitted to inspect the documents. "As the officials from the Navy Department do not represent the defendant in this hearing, I do not consent to their inspection of the documents," Lizars objected.[69] Moreover, he argued, neither the Navy Department nor the GAO had any right to usurp the court's power to decide on the admissibility of evidence by asserting secrecy: "The witness is here under a subpoena from a United States Court and has properly produced documents called for in that subpoena. It is not within the power of the defendant or anyone here to change in any regard the order of the United States Court."[70]

In an effort to establish the arbitrary nature of the secrecy claim, Lizars asked Durst to read an excerpt from one of the unmarked contracts into the record. Borst again objected: "The matter which the witness is asked to read into the record is a statement that contains information of a restricted military character and the witness is asked to refrain from making a record of this statement at least until he is instructed by a court to do so."[71] When Lizars persisted, Borst cautioned, "I wish to warn counsel that that matter is of a confidential military character, and that if he makes this a matter of public record he must be prepared for the consequences." Addressing Durst, he said, "I advise the witness that he may refuse to answer until instructed to do so by a court."[72] After the witness duly refused, Lizars proceeded to read extracts from several contracts into the record over Borst's objections.[73]

∵

What Lizars saw as witness intimidation, Borst and the Navy Department regarded as necessary efforts to safeguard military secrets. Borst described Lizars's decision to read extracts of the returns copies into the record as "shocking" to the two naval officers in attendance.[74] Fire-control technology really was highly secret, and Ford Instrument really was contractually bound to preserve the secrecy of its instruments. Furious at Lizars's actions, the Navy's Judge Advocate General wrote to the chief of the Bureau of Navigation, who was responsible for personnel, ominously noting that Lizars was a lieutenant in the Naval Reserve, yet his efforts "to elicit evidence which he knew to be confidential clearly shows that he has not always had the best interests of the United States in mind."[75] The Bureau of Navigation duly threatened Lizars with dismissal from the Naval Reserve.[76] In addition, the Justice Department ordered the US attorney in Brooklyn to confer with Borst and to file a motion to intervene in the case, as the proceedings might divulge secret information "and be in conflict with the ruling of the Court of Claims in the suit by the same plaintiffs and upon the same subject-matter."[77] By intervening, the US government sought to erase the separation between the Court of Claims and the district court that Lizars was exploiting.

Intervention as a "party defendant" was not a straightforward maneuver. According to the government, its interests in the case met the test of "permissive intervention" in the new *Federal Rules of Civil Procedure*: "[A]nyone may be permitted to intervene in an action . . . when an applicant's claim or defense and the main action have a question of law or fact in common."[78] The government argued that intervention was necessary to "enable it to act directly in the public interests [sic] and in the prevention of the disclosure of matters relating to the National Defense," that its defense against Pollen's and Isherwood's lawsuit in the Court of Claims was "substantially jeopardized by the proceedings" in the district court, and that the district court suit was "an effort to circumvent the effect" of the Court of Claims' ruling on the production of evidence."[79] Lizars countered that the district court suit was entirely separate from the Court of Claims suit: its subject matter concerned sales to others than the US government by a private contractor, not sales to the US government.[80] The court scheduled a hearing on the motion.

FIRE-CONTROL INSTRUMENTS.

The following table shows the more important instruments which have been developed or the manufacture of which was greatly increased during the continuance of hostilities:

	Total ordered or delivered to Apr. 6, 1917.	Total ordered or delivered to Nov. 11, 1918.	Total ordered or delivered during hostilities.
Alidades, illuminated....................................		12,000	12,000
Battle tracers (Sperry), Mk. I-1 and 2..............................	2	20	18
Destroyer direct.rse.pes...........................		205	205
Ford range keepers, Mk. I and II....................................	9	946	937
Multiple turret indicat.rs..................................	12	33	21
Plotting boards, Mk. II-3.............................		200	200
Plotting indicat.rs, Mk. I-0 and 1..........................	37	55	18
Range and deflecti.n receivers (Cory), Mk. VI...................		308	308
Range and deflecti.n transmitters....................		152	152
Range clocks (Vickers), Mk. II........................	404	404	....
Rate of change of range pr.ject.r, Mk. II............	206	206	....
Range receivers, electrical, fr.m R. F., Mk. I-0 and 1...........	12	17	5
Range transmitters, electrical, fr.m R. F. t. plot, Mk. I-0..........	15	17	5
Target bearing transmitters, Mk. I-3, 4, and 5....................		82	82
Target bearing transmitters, Mk. II-0, 3, and 4....................		14	14
Target bearing transmitters, Mk. III-0 and 1.....................		14	14
Target bearing transmitters, Mk. IV..............................		30	30
Target turret indicators, single, Mk. III-1.......................		205	205
Target turret indicators, double, Mk. I-0, 1, and 2.................	29	96	67
Target turret indicat.rs, triple, Mk. I.........................		14	14
Target turret transmitters, Mk. II-1..............................		117	117
Time of flight clocks.............................		278	278
Turret train transmitters, Mk. I-0, 1, and 2......................	48	169	121
Bearing indicators, Mk. III and Mk. XII-1........................		128	128

Figure 10.2. Information about fire-control equipment published by the US government. (Bureau of Ordnance, *Navy Ordnance Activities, World War, 1917–1918*, 152.)

Judge Robert Inch (who had presided over one of the hearings in *Sperry v. Arma*) presided at the hearing, which took place in late December 1938. The argument focused on two main questions. The first was the nature of the secrecy claim. Lizars asserted that Ford Instrument was claiming secrecy in bad faith, and that the information it claimed to be secret was already public.[81] Moreover, he observed, the US government had also published the information in the returns copies that Durst had brought to the deposition and that it now claimed to be secret. One of the excerpts that Lizars had read into the deposition record over Borst's objections came from a contract between Ford and the Navy dated 28 January 1918, reading as follows: "Delivery F O B factory at the rate of 50 per month beginning one May 1918 150 Mark II Ford range keepers at 840.00 each . . . . $126,000."[82] In *Navy Ordnance Activities, World War, 1917–1918*, the Government Printing Office had printed the table shown in figure 10.2. The information in the published table was very similar to information in the ostensibly secret contracts. Finally, Lizars suggested to Judge Inch, the very fact that Ford had exported its fire-control technology abroad weakened its claim to secrecy.

Judge Inch expressed uncertainty as to whether he could even consider the evidence that Lizars presented regarding secrecy.[83] He felt Lizars's concern about the separation of powers, but from the other direction. "If the Secretary of the Navy says that it is a military secret, and that the public interest is so involved that it should not be disclosed, you want to get some kind of procedure and have me review the Secretary of the Navy," he fretted. "How am I going to tell the Secretary of the Navy, who is running the Navy?"[84] In effect, he shared the "presumption . . . [that] good faith will characterize the conduct of Government officials" articulated by the Court of Claims. Lizars asked how the Secretary of the Navy was going to tell him how to run the Eastern District of New York: "Your Honor, the rulings of the Secretary of the Navy are not binding on this Court on a question of law." "It is going to bind me if they say they are going to use it for the National Defense," Inch shot back.[85] Lizars pointed to the exports: "How can the Secretary of the Navy tell your Honor that something manufactured for Ben Smith of Venezuela is a military secret of the United States Government?" "You mean they have disclosed it themselves?" the judge asked, showing some openness to weighing Lizars's evidence.[86] Borst scoffed: if Ford had sold rangekeepers abroad, it had done so "through the United States Navy, and any secrecy was not thereby released."[87] Overall, Borst felt he had the better of this exchange. "On the whole the Judge's attitude was very favorable," he reported to the Justice Department.[88]

The second main question at issue in the hearing was whether the United States had sufficient interest in the case to justify intervention. Lizars maintained that it did not, because the district court lacked jurisdiction to make any judgment binding the US government. "[I]f the Government intervenes," Judge Inch agreed, "it can only be tried out in the Court of Claims."[89] Borst rebutted this argument. "There is no cause of action obvious in this Court against the United States," he acknowledged, "but I see no reason why this Court cannot entertain jurisdiction with the United States as an intervenor" given that the government's interests were being "directly challenged."[90] By way of analogy, he pointed to the Supreme Court's confusing 1926 ruling in *Sperry v. Arma*, Judge Inch's former case, which held (in apparent contradiction to the Act of 1918 and to the 1928 ruling in *Richmond Screw Anchor*) that district courts could inquire whether patentees alleging infringement in work performed for the US government had any basis for recovery, even though only the Court of Claims could issue a judgment binding the government. Here was a precedent suggesting that district courts might permit the government to intervene without impairing the jurisdictional division with the Court of Claims. Borst thought the argument worked: "I drew an analogy from the Sperry v. Arma case and it seemed to register."[91]

He was right. Judge Inch granted the government's motion to intervene. "While no judgment is sought or could be obtained against the Government in this suit and forum," he wrote, "nevertheless it seems plain that there is a community of interest both of law and fact on the part of the Government and the defendant that necessitates the presence of the Government at a trial of the suit."[92] He left the question of whether the case should proceed *in camera* to the trial judge. The government quickly filed its formal Answer to the plaintiffs' Bill of Complaint, averring that the subject matter in the district court was identical to that in the Court of Claims case, and that it was a military secret.[93]

∴

With the issue now joined, Lizars sought a new test of the government's assertion of a secrecy privilege. He moved the court to order Ford Instrument to produce drawings and descriptions of any rangekeepers it had sold to others than the US government.[94] In response, the firm and the government arranged for two affidavits: one from Ford Instrument's treasurer stating that its government contracts enjoined secrecy; and the other from the new chief of the Bureau of Ordnance, William Furlong, attesting to the secret character of fire control and to the Navy's authorization of any exports by Ford.[95] In his capacity as Acting Secretary of the Navy, Leahy wrote a letter for submission to the district court averring that if the court compelled Ford Instrument to produce the evidence sought by Lizars, it would be causing the company to violate the Espionage Act.[96] Both the government and the firm submitted briefs opposing Lizars's motion.[97]

Judge Clarence Galston, the trial judge, who had also presided over Dugan's suit against Ford Instrument, scheduled another hearing.[98] Unfortunately, no transcript of this hearing survives. However, Borst, who appeared on behalf of both Ford Instrument and the government, supplied a brief report to the Justice Department:

> Judge Galston evidenced considerable interest in the issues raised. He indicated some sympathy with the plaintiffs' position. He asked me, for example, how the Government could reconcile its conflicting attitudes in

first granting a patent and then making it impossible for a patent owner to prove infringement.

However, I am sure that that was only an expression of a passing thought. He said very definitely that he would not lightly disregard the statement of the Secretary of the Navy regarding the need for keeping military secrets inviolate.[99]

Once again, Borst's instincts proved sound. "The situation disclosed is exceedingly interesting," Galston philosophized in his opinion:

> On the one hand we have, through the issuance of these various letters patent, a grant by the Government itself of an absolute monopoly. On the other hand we have the assertion of a paramount government right, the inherent right of self-preservation for purposes of national defense.

Citing *Totten*, Galston noted that "during a state of war there is not the slightest doubt that the public interest calls for the maintenance of secrecy upon inventors of military ordnance." Should it be argued that the rule should not extend to peace, "the answer is found in the exercise of a sound discretion by the executive branch of the Government. Certainly when the Secretary of the Navy formally announces to the Department of Justice that the disclosure would be detrimental to the national defense, the suggestion cannot lightly be ignored at any time." This testimonial privilege covered Ford Instrument as well, because the government had clearly enjoined the firm to secrecy: "It is as though the Government were manufacturing the alleged infringing devices itself."[100] Accordingly, the judge denied Lizars's motion. Through the legal procedure of intervention, which enabled it to surmount the jurisdictional fence separating the Court of Claims from the district court, the US government had found a way to reap the benefits of contracting with the private sector without paying the potential costs in secrecy.

The trial, conducted over three days in February 1939, went poorly for the plaintiffs. According to a report by a Justice Department lawyer (which includes details not in the official *Transcript of Record* for the case), Judge Galston opened by stating that Lizars could offer Ford Instrument's patents and other published material into evidence, and he could call the firm's officers "to testify whether those published structures were manufactured for others than the United States," but he could not "go beyond this disclosure and call for details of construction" of actual Ford rangekeepers—that is, he could not do what Borst had done in the Dugan case and link the disclosure of a patent to the construction of US Navy equipment.[101] Accordingly, when

Lizars tried to examine two former Ford Instrument employees about the details of construction, the judge ruled that he could not.[102] So Lizars was left with trying to prove infringement by having Isherwood compare the Pollen and Ford patents.

Isherwood's testimony was crystal clear, but it did nothing to address the statute of limitations. Having no proof that Ford Instrument had exported its rangekeeper within the six years preceding the start of the suit, Lizars fell back on the fraudulent-concealment argument in order to try to toll the statute. Judge Galston would have none of it. The rangekeepers were "properly military secrets," as represented by the United States, and Galston could not say that such secrecy as existed at Ford "was not called for by the circumstances of manufacture."[103] Moreover, the judge could find no precedents for the fraudulent-concealment argument in infringement cases, and he would "not be the person to blaze the way in establishing any such proposition as reading into the patent statutes that which is not there."[104] He made no judgment concerning the validity of the Pollen and Isherwood patents or their infringement, since his decision on the statute of limitations rendered those issues moot.

What the district judge would not do, Lizars hoped in vain the Second Circuit Court of Appeals would do. In June 1939, he filed an appeal, alleging that Galston had erred in ruling that certain testimony and evidence about fraudulent concealment were inadmissible and that there was no proof of fraudulent concealment.[105] The court of appeals rejected these arguments in its January 1940 decision.[106] Isherwood and Lizars had suffered another defeat.

THE TIZARD MISSION

Isherwood and Lizars now shifted back to the lawsuit against the United States in the Court of Claims. Presided over by Commissioner Melville D. Church, hearings resumed there in May 1940. Robert Lavender, now in private practice at Borst's law firm, appeared as counsel for the United States. In mid-June 1940, the court held another set of hearings. This time, Dugan appeared as counsel for the plaintiffs. (Lizars would soon be representing Dugan in the latter's new lawsuit against Sperry Gyroscope.)[107]

The first witness was William Leahy, the former chief of the Bureau of Ordnance and Chief of Naval Operations, whom Lizars called to testify mainly as an authority on the Navy Department's understanding of secrecy. An extended conversation, edited and compressed here for clarity and length, ensued:

LIZARS: Admiral, as an academic matter, will you define what is a military secret?

LEAHY: I venture it entirely safe to say that a military secret, in the understanding of the Department of the Navy, consists of information in regard to military policy that it is not desired should be made known to possible enemies.

LIZARS: . . . Do you know, in advance, who possible enemies may be?

LEAHY: Well, I would assume that any foreign power, or the agents of any foreign power, would come under the classification of possible enemies.

LIZARS: So that, in concept, at least, secrecy has not geographical scope whatever; it is either a secret or it is not a secret? Is that true, Admiral?

LEAHY: I think that is correct, from the point of view of a military secret.

LIZARS: Then would you say, Admiral, that knowledge of a military character, which is enjoyed by, say, ten foreign powers, is not a military secret?

LEAHY: It would be considered by the Navy Department as a military secret, if it is at that time so classified in the Navy Department's instructions to its own agents. . . .

LIZARS: So that a military secret may, in reality, according to your definition, be common knowledge of one or more powers, and yet be classified as a military secret.

LEAHY: I think that is correct. The Navy Department might still classify as a military secret information that presumably was, at that time, in the possession of some foreign power. . . .

LIZARS: Do I understand you to say that a military secret, then, is whatever the Navy Department wishes to call a secret, without regard to whether the substance of the secret is actually made public?

LEAHY: So far as I am concerned, that is correct.[108]

That evening, Leahy recorded in his diary, "My presence at the hearing was of no value to either party to the controversy."[109] Technically he was correct, in that his testimony swayed no one. But Lizars had led the admiral to the point he wanted to make: from the Navy's perspective, secrecy inhered not in the nature of information, nor in the degree to which it was known, but in the department's executive judgment and authority. A secret was what the Navy said it was.

Lizars's examination of Leahy also provided insight into Commissioner Church's understanding of secrecy. When Lizars asked Leahy to read from a publication marked "confidential," Borst objected that a JAG officer needed to review it first. Lizars retorted that decisions on the admissibility of evidence belonged to the judge, not a naval officer. Church disagreed, echoing Judge Inch of the Eastern District of New York: "I would like to state that the determination of the Secretary of the Navy as to what is, or is not, a military secret, pervades, so far as I am concerned, all branches of the Government."[110] Church sustained Borst's objection, again blocking Lizars from introducing evidence.

•.•

These hearings occurred against the backdrop of the Nazi invasion of western Europe, which had, among its lesser-known consequences, implications for Pollen's and Isherwood's legal position. In his diary entry on the June 13 hearing, Leahy went on to note that "[n]ew dispatches report that Paris is today occupied by the German Army and the French Army is on a point of surrendering."[111] The French surrender a week later transformed the strategic situation confronting Britain and the United States. In response, Britain decided to boost scientific and military cooperation with the United States by sending a mission under the leadership of Sir Henry Tizard, a distinguished scientific administrator, across the Atlantic.

The Tizard Mission has rightly been called "one of the most important events of the Second World War."[112] However, it is not widely known (especially to Americanists), perhaps because it contradicts the blanket depictions of a rising United States and declining Britain that dominate so much writing on twentieth-century global power rankings. Those depictions contain much truth; the problem is that they obscure very significant exceptions. One such exception, as noted by the historian Michael Falcone, relates to the distinction between raw manufacturing capacity and cutting-edge technology—in a sense, the distinction between quantity and quality.[113] With regard to the former, the United States had long since overtaken Britain, but with regard to the latter, Britain remained on the cutting edge, especially in nuclear research, jet-engine development, pharmaceuticals, and radar. Indeed, the Tizard Mission brought what one American historian famously dubbed "the most valuable cargo ever brought to our shores," namely, the cavity magnetron—essential for the development of miniaturized radar sets.[114] It gave the Americans the other crown jewels of British technical development, and it created a framework for additional information to follow in its wake.[115] Many of the "prestige technologies" of the Cold War United States actually had British origins.[116] These were obscured by the US government's practice of sharing British research with US industry for further development and large-scale manufacture—while simultaneously using secrecy restrictions to prevent a reverse flow back to

Britain.[117] Thus, the Tizard Mission scaled up and formalized the transfer of science and technology from Britain to the United States that had occurred during World War I, with major long-term consequences for both nations' postwar positions.

Arriving in late August 1940, Tizard found US officials generally cooperative—with the exception of the Navy's Bureau of Ordnance. He recorded in his diary on August 28, "At one p.m. I went to see Admiral Furlong at his request. He is Chief of Naval Ordnance. What he wished to say was that he did not want to exchange any information on gunnery, including anti-aircraft gunnery."[118] Furlong, whom we encountered earlier in his career in chapter 8, had been gunnery officer on the USS *Nevada* when it received one of the first Ford rangekeepers. He had then spent time in the Bureau of Ordnance in the spring of 1918, when Isherwood oversaw the setup of the Argo clock ordered by the Navy Department and when Wilbur Van Auken acknowledged in writing that Ford had plagiarized Pollen, before taking over the fire-control section from Van Auken in 1919.[119] In short, Furlong had played a role in the disclosure of information from Pollen and Isherwood to the Bureau during World War I, as well as in the early development of the Ford rangekeeper.

On September 10, Tizard went to see the Director of Naval Intelligence, Admiral Walter Anderson, in the hopes of learning the reasons for Furlong's uncooperative attitude. He recorded what happened next in his diary:

> Admiral Anderson telephoned to Admiral Furlong in my presence. He had quite a long conversation, at the end of which Admiral Anderson explained to me that the real difficulty was connected with the design of the predictor known as the Ford Predictor and, I believe, made by the Sperry Company. It appears that an English firm (?Paul and Isherwood) [sic] had sued the U.S. Government for infringements of patents. They had been refused access to the latest US predictors for ship work and had been unable to prove their case. They had shifted their attack on Ford and were suing him. *It was felt by Admiral Furlong that if we had full information about the predictor, it might afterwards be said that we handed some of this information to Paul [i.e. Pollen] & Isherwood to enable them to fight their case.* [emphasis added]
>
> Admiral Anderson asked Admiral Furlong to write to Ford and the Sperry Company to ask them if they would have any objection to complete disclosure if the Navy Department had an assurance from us that we should not pass on any information to a British firm.
>
> I said we would be quite willing to give such an assurance and that I thought the somewhat difficult position caused by the legal action might

be better cleared up in another way and I would consult the Embassy about this.[120]

The italicized passage suggests that Furlong feared the evidence sought by Pollen and Isherwood incriminated the Navy Department, or, put differently, that he believed Pollen's and Isherwood's lawsuit had merit. Within the government, he may well have been an exception to the rule, since most other Navy and Justice Department officials had no personal knowledge of the World War I–era disclosures of information from which Pollen and Isherwood alleged that Ford's infringement had flowed. But the fact that the official who knew about the case from firsthand experience was willing to stall Anglo-American cooperation over it speaks both to his sense of its importance and to the equity of the lawsuit.

His position was even more audacious in the broader context of Anglo-American relations. In the overwhelmingly one-way technology transfer from Britain to the United States that had occurred during World War I, Furlong had played his own small part not only through his early involvement with the Ford rangekeeper but also by witnessing James Henderson's eponymous Firing Gear (discussed in chapter 5) as an observer in the British Grand Fleet and then overseeing its incorporation into US fire-control systems.[121] After the war, British inventors and firms whose work their government shared with the United States struggled to gain compensation for its use—Lavender, as we saw, sat on the commission that heard those claims. Pollen and Isherwood were far from the only British inventors whose inventions the United States had acquired without compensation during the war. Now, as the Britain-to-United States technology transfer repeated itself on a larger scale in World War II, Furlong was trying to cover US tracks from the first time around.

∴

As in World War I, more forward-looking British officials worried about the implications of free technology transfer for Britain's postwar position but prioritized the short-term benefits. "The Patent [sic] position was not very clear," Tizard recorded after meetings with US firms that might produce British jet engines. "If we decided to send detailed information to America so as to get manufacture started there, I said that we must get the fact properly recorded so as to reserve commercial rights after the war."[122] The Americans did their best to prevent this. According to a fellow British official, Britain's point man on the patent negotiations (John Galway Foster, the legal advisor at the British Embassy) warned that a "somewhat bad impression has already been created especially in Navy by what was described as 'Haggling' on commercial rights to prejudice of joint defence programme."[123] This was a geopolitical guilt trip: here the Americans were, trying to help the British in their hour of need, and all perfidious Albion wanted to do was safeguard her postwar economic position. Certainly Britain was getting something out of the deal—but so was the United States.

Isherwood had the misfortune to experience this dynamic twice over, in both world wars, at each transformative puncture of the twentieth-century Anglo-American equilibrium. The United States had stolen his invention during World War I. Now it used World War II to hinder his quest for justice. Tizard followed through on his promise to Admiral Anderson to see if "the somewhat difficult position" might be cleared up by applying pressure to Isherwood. The Embassy legal adviser, Foster, spoke directly to Isherwood at Tizard's request. Tizard wrote in his diary, "[Foster] says Isherwood is an ex-Naval officer, now in U.S. Hopes it may be possible to settle case if [the British naval attaché] sees him and explains position."[124] Several days later, Tizard saw the naval attaché and "told him I thought Isherwood probably had a reasonable case against the Ford Instrument Company and it was only for the general good that I wanted the case abandoned."[125] These efforts bore fruit. On September 23, Tizard "saw Mr. Foster, who has had a talk with Isherwood. Isherwood says he will drop the legal action against Ford if we think it desirable but would like out-of-pocket legal expenses paid. Foster will find out what these amount to."[126] Isherwood's wife recalled these dealings in her memoirs:

> [T]he second world war was going on, and my Husband was trying in every way to get back to England and do something, and suddenly the British Naval Attaché in Washington wired him please to come and see him. Of course he went, full of hope that he was to be sent to duty in England, but what he was told was, "The American Navy Department has been very pleasant, but suddenly has grown awfully 'sticky', and I think it's your case about your patents". So that was the end of the Isherwood patents as of course my Husband dropped his case.[127]

Tizard's diary makes no further reference to Isherwood, but from other evidence it seems likely that the Embassy found a way to pay Isherwood off: he appears in the directory of salaried employees of the British Purchasing Commission for the first time in October 1940, as an assistant inspector of miscellaneous technical items.[128] He kept his part of the bargain by not appealing the court of appeals' ruling in the case against Ford Instrument to the Supreme Court.

The case against the United States meandered along for another three years. It finally reached its anticlimactic end in October 1943, when the full Court of Claims ruled that the plaintiffs had not proved what rangekeepers the United States had used in the six years preceding the filing of the suit, and that it could make no findings as to the validity or infringement of the Pollen and Isherwood patents. Accordingly, it dismissed the case.[129] Both lawsuits were over.

∴

The *Pollen and Isherwood* cases brought into conflict two fundamental principles: private property rights and national security. The Court of Claims and the district court both privileged the latter over the former in deferring to the government's assertion of the proto-state secrets privilege. This judicial permission enabled the executive branch to withhold the only evidence by which Pollen and Isherwood might have proved their case. But for all the appearance of a powerful state crushing individual inventors, the Pollen and Isherwood lawsuits reveal as much about the persistent weakness of the American state as about its growing strength. The dam of secrecy constantly sprang leaks, skillfully identified by Lizars, that executive-branch officials scrambled to plug—here a nonsecret patent, there the alternative jurisdiction of a district court. For the Navy's exasperated Judge Advocate General, the lesson of the Pollen and Dugan lawsuits was not that there was too much secrecy but that there was not enough: "it would be a wise policy to forever classify all contracts for range keepers as 'restricted' or 'confidential.'"[130] Leahy's affirmation of Lizars's statement that "a military secret . . . is whatever the Navy Department wishes to call a secret" sprang from the same impulse. Though radical in the extent of the power claimed, the radicalism was double-edged: it reflected not only how emboldened naval officials felt in the face of the judiciary, but also how weak a legal regime for secrecy Congress had provided. The executive power claimed by Leahy went well beyond the "born secret" provision of the Atomic Energy Act of 1946, and without any legislative sanction. It was a bully's arbitrariness and insecurity rolled into one.[131]

The officials in the Navy Department and the Justice Department who conducted the cases against Pollen and Isherwood did not see themselves as bullies any more than the judges who tried the cases saw themselves as stooges of the executive branch. Officials lacking personal knowledge of the development of Ford Instrument's system had every reason to believe that this was a straightforward case of maintaining the secrecy of technology that obviously ought to be kept secret for national security reasons. In effect rather than intent, however, the assertion of the privilege was cynical and permitted the concealment of government wrongdoing, namely, the fact that the US Navy and Ford Instrument had pirated Pollen's and Isherwood's invention. Thus the state secrets privilege was a dual-use legal technology, capable of being used to protect true military secrets or of being used to conceal government wrongdoing—or both at the same time, in Pollen's and Isherwood's cases.

If it was dual-use in the context of the domestic political economy, the privilege acquired a third use in the context of the global political economy: it helped the United States conceal evidence that its growing national power was due not simply to Yankee ingenuity or vast structural forces outside anyone's control, but to deliberate policy choices to pirate foreign technology. The Tizard Mission, and technology transfer from Britain to the United States more broadly, facilitated the United States' climb up the global power rankings. It formed a crucial part of the transition from the Pax Britannica to the Pax Americana. If the technological knowledge acquired from Britain helped constitute the material basis of the Pax Americana, then the legal knowledge of how to preserve secrecy—such as the Espionage Act and the state secrets privilege—helped to conceal the technology's origins. It is a double irony that some of this legal knowledge also had British origins. Britain, it might be said, gave its former colony the tools not only to surpass it but also to hide the history of the transfer.

One result has been to obscure Pollen's and Isherwood's key role in US computer development. Perhaps the most powerful, if unintentional, example of this obscurantism comes from the memoirs of Vannevar Bush, Lavender's boss at OSRD. Prior to the war, Bush was best known as the inventor of the differential analyzer, widely regarded as a landmark in computing history.[132] Constructed from 1928 to 1931 at the Massachusetts Institute of Technology, the analyzer was a combined integrator and integraph—or, in naval terms, clock and plot—that interconnected no fewer than six ball-and-disc drives to solve differential equations and automatically graphed the results on paper. As shown in chapter 2, Bush's student assistants (including his fellow computer pioneer Harold Hazen) knew of Kelvin's nineteenth-century work on ball-and-disc drives but saw that the Englishman had not overcome the critical problem of slippage. They were unaware of the improvements that Pollen and Isherwood had made to Kelvin's design to overcome the problem of slippage without resorting to a servomechanism, or of Pollen's and Isherwood's inter-connection of multiple integrators to increase the Argo clock's processing power.

Thus the extraordinary tribute that Bush paid to the importance of Pollen's and Isherwood's work in his reflections on the invention of the differential analyzer was unwitting. "There is no question that my young assistants and I developed the differential analyzer at M.I.T. during the twenties," Bush wrote in his memoirs. "But who invented it?" He continued:

> I can name an inventor who made a differential analyzer long before I did, or rather who readily could have done so if he had put his mind to it. This was Hannibal Ford. He was about as ingenious an individual as I ever heard of. He made the devices, the computers, if you will, to aim the great guns of battleships, to take into account the flight of the shell, including the effect of the rotation of the earth upon its path, the air density at the time, the speed and direction of the enemy target, and so on. This he did principally by interconnecting integrators. And he made a new form of integrator which could do the job without the help of a servomechanism. The resulting mechanism was a marvel of precision and completeness.[133]

"Did he invent the differential analyzer?" Bush asked.

> One can say merely that he not only could have, but that he could have been the leader in the whole movement toward the modern computer, if he had wanted to. And the only reason he did not is probably that he did not move about in academic circles to see the need and the opportunity. I hail his memory.[134]

Of course, Bush was actually hailing Pollen's and Isherwood's memory.[135]

Everything Old Is New Again

RED IS THE NEW RED, WHITE, AND BLUE

Today, digital is the new analog. The supply chains for digital-computing technology are more global, the manufacturing is more precise, and the technology has more uses, to be sure. But much as digital technology— not least the semiconductor and artificial intelligence (AI)—features in the contemporary Sino-US competition, so naval analog computers featured in the Anglo-American rivalry a century ago. Pollen and Isherwood intended their "system of systems," with an integrated mechanical circuit enabling AI at its heart, to transform naval warfare by aiming naval munitions more precisely and leveraging networked information. In recent decades, AI, precision-guided missiles, and networked information have transformed warfare. Moreover, the analogy extends to the manufacturing process. Pollen and Isherwood emerged from a printing firm, Linotype, that made both scientific instruments and machine tools so precise as to blur the boundary between machine tool and instrument; they soon moved into optics with their purchase of Cooke's, while Linotype eventually moved into photo-typesetting, which used light rather than hot metal to set the print.[1] Semiconductors are "printed" through a process known as photolithography, which uses light to set the print, by machine tools so precise as to blur the boundary between machine tools and scientific instruments; optics firms have long played a key role in the photolithographic process.[2]

Naval analog computers not only supply an analogy for digital computing today: they also influenced it. In the United States, many of the key early players in the development of semiconductors came out of the worlds of bombsight technology and missile guidance, which had close historical connections with naval fire control. Charles Draper, for instance, who gave the chip startup Fairchild Semiconductor its first big order for NASA's Apollo Program, ran the MIT Instrumentation Lab, which worked closely with Sperry Gyroscope and the Navy Bureau of Ordnance on anti-aircraft fire control. The NASA administrator who gave Draper's lab the Apollo contract was the same man who, as Sperry Gyroscope vice president, had handled the anti-aircraft fire control contract with Draper's lab.[3] Pollen and Isherwood, of course, were deeply enmeshed in the "gyro culture" that gave rise to missile guidance systems and had (nonconsensually) given Sperry Gyroscope its start on computing technology. Sperry Gyroscope, as we saw in chapter 8, hired Percy Gray, Isherwood's former assistant, to head its anti-aircraft fire-control work in Britain. Pollen and Isherwood themselves had invented a bombsight containing an analog computer, not unlike the computer in the better-known bombsight invented by the ex-Sperry engineer Carl Norden.[4] Their fingerprints, however partial and faint, were on the subsequent development of digital computing in the United States.

Indeed, British fingerprints were everywhere on US technological and economic development more broadly. In 1917, the British naval officer who pronounced (in chapter 4) the Ford rangekeeper "<u>very</u> similar to Pollen's Clock" misattributed its invention to "Mr Ford (of Motor fame)."[5] The attribution to the wrong Ford was more apt than he knew. A decade before Hannibal Ford learned how to build fire-control computers from Pollen and Isherwood, Henry Ford learned about the vanadium steel alloys used in the Model T from a British metallurgist.[6] The US Navy was already experimenting with vanadium alloys for use in armor plate and shells, having imported the plant and know-how to build armor and heavy ordnance from Britain and other European countries.[7] Financed by British capital, the US steel industry, which grew in concert with the US Navy, had imported the Bessemer process—the nineteenth century's closest analog to twentieth-century Fordist mass production—from Britain.[8] Much as Hannibal Ford struggled to match the quality of British fire-control instruments, so US steel firms like Andrew Carnegie's struggled to match the quality of British steel produced in Sheffield, the home of Henry Bessemer's works.[9] Henry Ford needed vanadium alloys to make up the quality gap with European cars. "With"—only with—"proper steels at our command," he boasted, "the 'Yankee peril' would become a reality."[10] Like China in the late twentieth and early twenty-first centuries, the United States in the late nineteenth and early twentieth centuries depended on multiple rounds of technology transfer and capital infusions from the then-ruling hegemon, and it was known for turning out low-quality goods in high quantities. The "Yankee peril" was the "yellow peril" of its day.[11]

And yet, somehow the United States has largely managed to escape the narrative of "catch-up development" that historians and political scientists impose on everyone else. Perhaps scholars have been so busy "decolonizing" their fields by exposing development models as Trojan horses for imperialism that they have missed equally subversive opportunities to re-colonize the United States by turning developmental theory against it. The turn-of-the-century United States ought to be seen as part of the periphery or semi-periphery to a global order dominated by Great Britain.[12] At the same time as Germany was pursuing world politics (*Weltpolitik*), Russia was undergoing its "great spurt" of industrialization, China was engaged in its self-strengthening movement (*ziqiang yundong*), and Japan was seeking to enrich itself and strengthen its army (*fukoku kyōhei*), the United States—whose slogan under the late nineteenth-century Republican Party might as well have been, with apologies to Meiji Japan, "rich nation, strong navy"—was also engaged in catch-up industrialization and overseas imperialism. All of them were ultimately chasing Great Britain, the world's first industrial nation and still the global hegemon.

Seeing the United States as a catch-up developer means revisiting powerful narratives about American exceptionalism, the Anglo-American relationship, and the sources of national (or rather imperial) power. There is nothing more British than arguing that the United States acquired global hegemony in a fit of absentmindedness. Yet that is effectively the argument that Americans (including many historians critical of American power) make when they describe US hegemony as the inevitable result of its "exceptional" continental scale, economic productivity, Yankee ingenuity, divine favor, or some other vast impersonal force—rather than as the result of deliberate and profoundly unexceptional policy choices to pursue power at others' expense. The wheels of this argument have been greased by the narrative of the Anglo-American "special relationship," which represents the transition from the Pax Britannica to the Pax Americana as consensual—exceptionally, specially consensual—rather than as rivalrous and contested, the way hegemonic transitions usually are, and the way this one was too.[13] Moreover, both the inevitability and the special-relationship narratives draw strength from a model of national power that emphasizes raw manufacturing capacity, which the United States had a great deal of, at the expense of research and development, technological sophistication, and product quality (to say nothing of financial services, telecommunications, shipping, etc.), which the United States had considerably less of. These narratives are how US history, in the face of ample contrary evidence, has managed to escape the catch-up-development storyline.[14]

The escape attempt is itself unexceptional, indeed imitative. Having relied, like the United States, on technology imports to increase its power—and having become widely regarded, alternately with admiration and loathing, as uniquely imitative—Britain developed a similar set of narratives about its own historical exceptionalism.[15] Unlike others across the

English Channel, it was an island, not a continent; a naval power, not a land power; a cosmopolitan commercial society, not a primitive extractive economy; a benevolent civilizer, not an oppressive empire; the home of liberty, not despotism. The United States took these British narratives, as it did British fire-control technology, and adapted them to its own needs.[16] Lumping Britain in with continental Europe, it imagined itself as the new home of liberty—a new empire of liberty. China today follows in these Anglo-American footsteps when it portrays Anglo-American governance as tired and corrupt and its preferred alternative as an exceptional, radical break from historical patterns.[17] In fact, it could scarcely imitate the United States more closely than by placing innovativeness at the center of its sense of self and by fusing its ostensibly unique technological prowess with racism to justify its claims of civilizational superiority.[18] Claiming exceptionalism is about the least exceptional thing a rising power can do.

Of course, like inventions, China and the United States have some exceptional qualities. China has its own long history of technological achievement, imperialism, and racial and ethnic discrimination to draw on and distort in framing its sense of self and its relations with the outside world; it does not "merely" mimic the United States.[19] Moreover, there are profound differences between China's and America's governing ideologies and internal structures, just as there were profound differences between what Pollen and Isherwood did and what others in the field of naval fire control had done. But as this book has shown, narratives of inventive exceptionalism can also be exercises in historical myth-making, and the same is true of narratives of national exceptionalism. They stem from the same "anxiety of influence"—the same desire to believe in one's own unique originality— that afflicted Dreyer, Ford, Sperry, Vickers, and others with enormous debts to Pollen and Isherwood. The anxiety of influence drove attempts at what this book has termed "technology laundering": that is, at laundering "inventions" of their origins in order to make them seem more inventive than they really were. Technology laundering, in turn, facilitated more conventional money laundering, by scrubbing redirected development and purchase funds of their origins in technological theft.

When nations rather than defense contractors launder technology, they are laundering themselves, not money. Their "techno-nationalism" is a scaled-up version of the techno-individualism pursued by inventors. For nations, technology laundering is a technology of nation-building— one might speak of nations as "invented" communities no less than "imagined" ones—and the second in a two-step process.[20] First, nations build their strength by importing or pirating foreign technology, be it semiconductors or rangekeepers. China's theft of foreign IP in digital computing technology today imitates the United States' theft of foreign IP in analog computing technology a century ago (digital theft's analog analog, so to speak). Second, nations build their sense of self by laundering technology imports of their foreign origins, just as the United States did with naval fire-control technology, and just as China does when it angrily denounces accusations of technology theft while boasting of its own innovativeness.[21] Anglo-American and Chinese narratives of exceptionalism are bids at nation-laundering. They seek to scrub themselves of debts and connections to other inventive nations, to detach the text of their national algorithm from the context of other national algorithms. These technologies of nation-building are not digital-age. They are analog-age. And hegemonic nations that use them are analog superpowers.

NATIONAL SECURITY IS THE NEW KING

In the Anglo-American imagination, navies are the handmaidens of liberal capitalism, and armies are the henchmen of despotic command economies. "[P]opulation, riches, true religion, virtue, magnanimity, arts, sciences, and learning, are the necessary effects and productions of liberty," wrote the Englishman John Trenchard in 1722, and "an extensive trade, navigation, and naval power, entirely flow from the same source."[22] It took Americans considerably longer to associate naval power (and the necessary supporting fiscal structure) with the blessings of liberty, but they eventually got there in the twentieth century.[23] Britain exploited the virtuous circle between liberty, trade, and naval power to pioneer the strategy of "offshore balancing" later adopted by the United States: it used the immense financial power derived from commercial wealth and Parliamentary taxation to fund the armies of manpower-rich allies on the European continent and a technology-intensive navy in control of the global common.[24]

There has always been another side to naval power that the Anglo-American imagination prefers to ignore. Abroad, it is captured by the phrase "gunboat diplomacy": the spread of liberal capitalism not through peaceful means but through the threat and reality of violence. This book argues that a parallel phenomenon, previously invisible to historians, occurred at home: namely, repeated attempts by the British and US governments, at the instigation of their navies, to take the intellectual property of defense contractors. Sometimes, these takings occurred within the framework of eminent domain, which was nonconsensual and partly rooted in royal prerogative but did provide compensation.[25] At other times, however, they occurred within the framework of national security, not eminent domain, with the governments using secrecy laws to avoid paying compensation and secrecy privileges to foil the recovery of compensation through the legal system. Takings in the latter category give new meaning to the phrase "naval appropriations," and they anticipate by decades the practices of nuclear secrecy, export controls, and national security elaborated during World War II and the Cold War.

Both the fact that government takings through national security powers occurred and the fact that navies instigated them raise questions. What might account for the timing of these attempted takings, decades before the atomic bomb intensified and expanded—but clearly did not originate—the power of the national security state? And what might explain the antiliberal, anticapitalist hostility of the British and US navies, those handmaidens of liberal capitalism, to contractors' expectations of legal due process and respect for private property?

One way to answer these questions is to emphasize the continuities between modern national security powers and early modern royal prerogatives, and accordingly to see the former as existing essentially outside of modern liberal capitalism. There are reasons to do so. Both the Royal Navy and the US Navy trace their institutional histories back before the founding of the nations they ostensibly serve and the spread of liberal-capitalist norms.[26] Thus it should not surprise us to find officers in both navies displaying a quasi-royalist impatience with defense contractors' private property claims. Nor should we be surprised by their enormous, indeed sometimes hubristic, self-confidence in the superiority of naval officers' knowledge over civilians' knowledge—displayed in the utter inability of some British officers to believe that Pollen and Isherwood could understand naval fire control better than they could, and in American officers' conviction that any old contractor or government factory could produce good fire-control equipment. That self-confidence was a relic of the world before the explosive economic growth of the eighteenth and nineteenth centuries under the aegis of liberal capitalism. Similarly, the persistence of sovereign immunity to tort claims like patent infringement was an instance of continuity over time, not change. So too is the rooting of national security powers in the sovereign's right and obligation to defend the realm.

But there are also important differences between modern national security powers and early modern royal prerogatives. These differences have a great deal to do with the ascent of liberal capitalism, and in that sense, modern national security powers exist inside of liberal capitalism no less than outside it. At the most obvious level, the spread of liberal-capitalist norms and practices within British and American society afforded defense contractors powerful new weapons to resist the deployment of national security powers—weapons that did not exist to resist royal prerogative

centuries years earlier. Contractors could seek protection against their ra-
pacious naval clients by cartelizing, reproducing in the private sector con-
centrations of wealth and power once possible only for states. They could
exploit jurisdictional pluralism to fight back on more than one front. They
could assert rights to private property and legal due process unthinkable in
the early modern period. Indeed, naval personnel themselves were quick
to use these weapons when their own inventions (and pensions) were at
stake.[27] Even when government officials seeking to deploy modern forms
of royal prerogative got their way, the ascendancy of liberal capitalism put
them on the ideological defensive. They could not simply say, "we want
your property, therefore it is ours"; they had to justify their recourse to
national security powers through laws passed by (more or less) democratic
legislatures and to (more or less) independent judiciaries. This legal and
ideological playing field was recognizably that of modern liberal capitalism, even as the national security powers themselves had profound continuities with royal prerogative.

At a deeper level, moreover, the recourse of the British and American
governments to antiliberal, anticapitalist national security powers against
defense contractors stemmed from a crisis *within* liberal capitalism at the
turn of the century.[28] In one respect, the crisis was not new, insofar as it
stemmed from the ideological necessity in liberal-capitalist societies to
procure military technology from defense contractors, not just from state-
owned facilities. But in other respects, the crisis was new. On the one hand,
the world's growing economic interconnectedness, which for better or
worse was a product of liberal capitalism, made it easier for defense contractors to supply their products to foreign governments. Their pursuit of
overseas markets, in turn, set up clashes with their home governments. On
the other hand, the success of liberal capitalism at generating capital sur-
pluses in the "global North" intensified the imperial scramble for overseas
investment and export markets in the "global South."[29] This competition,
in turn, increased demand for defense contractors' wares. Thus, even as liberal capitalism was drawing the world together economically, it was driving
the world apart geopolitically. The convergence of these trends paradoxically increased the pressure on the British and US governments to resort to
antiliberal, anticapitalist behavior against defense contractors.

Navies were at the nexus of this convergence. They, not armies or nascent air forces, were—and remain—the principal arms through which
nations could project power on the maritime common, where the new
international and imperial economic connections were forming.[30] In the
event of colonial resistance or inter-imperial rivalry stemming from the intensified quest for overseas markets, navies were necessary to ferry troops

across bodies of water, armies being unable to cross without boats or safe shipping lanes. Navies were also much more technologically intensive than armies; as the army officer Lord Kitchener once put it, equipping the British army "was not much more difficult than buying a straw hat at Harrods."[31] These reasons explain why the British and US navies, which did (and do) so much to spread and maintain liberal capitalism around the globe, instigated government takings at odds with liberal-capitalist norms of private property and legal due process. And they explain why the naval-secrecy regime, rooted in tensions with defense contractors, anticipated by decades the nuclear-secrecy and export-control regimes of World War II and the Cold War, which in turn underlie the even broader secrecy and export-control regimes of today.

∵

None of this is to suggest that secrecy laws and privileges are inherently illegitimate, or that government officials necessarily used them in bad faith. The issues here are genuinely difficult and do not lend themselves to easy moralizing. They arise only because liberal-capitalist norms have such deep ideological (if not always behavioral) purchase in Britain and the United States. As the saying goes, hypocrisy is the homage that vice pays to virtue.[32] Societies that neither attempt nor even pretend to liberal-capitalist virtue do not pay the price of hypocrisy—but abandoning the pursuit of virtue has its own price. One may deplore abuses of national security powers while believing that governments ought to be able to classify some things as secret for the protection of liberal-capitalist societies. Given the importance of fire-control technology, government officials had good reason to want to keep it secret. Moreover, without cooperation from their naval counterparts, law officers in the British Treasury Solicitor's office and the US Department of Justice had no way of knowing when fire-control technology was pirated. And while some naval personnel did know (and preferred to obstruct justice rather than confess), many others did not, due to personnel turnover.

Nor does the deployment of national security powers against defense contractors lend itself to easy political analysis; on the contrary, it does not neatly fit conventional political narratives. In one powerful account, the secretive national security state, understood to mark the political right, uses its power to crush the civil liberties of marginalized minorities, imagined to occupy the political left. Classic examples in this account—notably all but one during hot wars, and the other one during a warm phase of the Cold War—include the jailing of the socialist Eugene Debs and pacifist Bertrand

Russell during World War I; the internment of Japanese-Americans and enemy aliens in Britain during World War II; the Red Scares and McCarthyism after the world wars; the *New York Times* and the Pentagon Papers during the Vietnam War; and Wikileaks and warrantless wire-tapping in the war on terror. Moreover, the paradigmatic civil liberties endangered by the national security state are imagined as freedom of speech and freedom of the press.

In this book, by contrast, the targets of the secretive national security state were defense contractors, and the civil liberty under threat was property rights. A sense of defense contractors as wealthy elites, along with a long Anglo-American tradition of stigmatizing them as unpatriotic profiteers, which reached its apogee in post–World War I depictions of "merchants of death," has largely insulated them from empathy. They have often made up for the absence of empathy with an abundance of self-pity. (Exhibit A in this book would be Sperry Gyroscope.)

But empathy, which is not the same as sympathy, should stimulate awareness that conflicts between the national security state and defense contractors could be no less asymmetric than conflicts between the national security state and more sympathetic victims like left-wing politicians and heroic newspapers. "The problems of raising money, rolling out a product, and trying to keep ahead of the competition—business problems—do not stack up well against protection of fundamental civil rights, or the reach and limits of the state as against the individual," one scholar has written approvingly of the conventional view. "Making payroll is just not as romantic as battling Leviathan on behalf of the citizenry."[33] But when a firm was on the smaller side, like Argo, one does not have to squint very hard to see the individuals whose livelihoods depended on payroll being made; and when individuals in that firm went up against not one but two governments that had pirated their intellectual property, they were indeed battling Leviathan(s). Unless defense contractors were Leviathans themselves, they had far fewer resources than governments and far less personal economic security than government officials and naval officers with guaranteed pensions for life. Even the Leviathans like Vickers and GE did not have sovereign immunity, could not employ eminent domain, and could not classify information as secret on national security grounds. Those are asymmetries. So, while this book is not about heroes and villains, it is about structural power imbalances and conflicts of interest that invited self-delusion, as well as about individuals who accepted the invitation. And it insists on the need to witness the human damage caused by those who chose self-delusion.

Conceptualizing the history of the secretive national security state along these lines suggests an alternative macro-interpretation of the twentieth century. The concept of the "military-industrial complex" captures a widespread notion that two of the great drivers of modern history—the secretive national security state (or militarism) and property rights untrammeled by government regulation (or neoliberalism)—worked together to advance the objectives of the political right against opposition from the political left. The history related in this book suggests that militarism and neoliberalism not only complemented but also opposed each other. If so, then the twentieth century was as much a civil war within the right as a war between right and left. Alternatively, perhaps our political categories need rethinking.

WHO'S AFRAID OF HISTORY?

The history of naval fire control was a dangerous subject to be interested in. As Hugh Clausen, the Royal Navy's leading expert on fire control in the interwar period, recalled, "The more I studied past history, the murkier and more obscure became the background. It seemed such a dangerous thing to write about that I gave it up." We have seen what frightened him. Frederic Dreyer was an egotistical, insecure officer with delusions of grandeur and powerful supporters within the Royal Navy. He was not incompetent, but he was unable or unwilling to recognize the limits of his competence. For the sins of threatening Dreyer's sense of self, pointing out procedural irregularities, and refusing to toe the party line, Pollen suffered financially and psychologically distressing attacks by the Admiralty on his business and his patriotism. By contrast, while Dreyer suffered the soft punishment of unpopularity in the service, bordering on detestation, he nevertheless continued to be promoted, avoiding more serious professional and financial consequences.

Dreyer could not have done what he did or advanced in the service without enablers. Not only was he permitted to plagiarize Pollen and entrusted with responsibility in fire-control matters despite his conflict of interest, but trials of both systems were designed to damage Pollen's chances and aid Dreyer's. At no point did the Royal Navy subject the two full systems to competitive tests, and deliberately so. Those who actively protected Dreyer or chose to turn a blind eye made the institution as a whole complicit in the selection of his system over Pollen's. The Admiralty showed much less interest in correcting its past mistakes than in suppressing the fact that it had made them. The last thing it wanted was honest, rigorous study of the history of its decision-making on fire control. That is why it twice—during the breakdown of negotiations with Pollen before the war and during the preparation of its case before the RCAI after the war—entrusted the task of producing an official history of British naval fire control to Dreyer, the most self-interested historian possible to imagine. By repeatedly ceding control of the historical narrative and its corporate memory to a private interest, the Admiralty limited debate over the public interest with respect to fire control. The deeper the hole it dug for itself, the higher the costs of getting caught in the act of shoveling grew, and the more determined the institution became to hide from its past rather than to confront it. The Admiralty's disparate treatment of Pollen and Dreyer sent a message about how to behave; Clausen received it.

The Admiralty's decision-making process had profound flaws, and its flawed process produced a flawed outcome: a delay of at least a decade in procuring mission-critical technology that the US Navy and eventually the Royal Navy itself recognized as superior. However much Admiralty officials deluded themselves, they knew, on some level, that their process was flawed, or they would not have engaged in a pattern of behavior that frightened off inquiry by the likes of Hugh Clausen. The Admiralty officials complicit in the procedural irregularities that led to the selection of Dreyer's system treated one of Britain's most important public institutions as a private club. Hence Tomlin's remark, quoted in chapter 7, when Greene described the Admiralty's rejection of Pollen's system after the *Ariadne* trials as "a little bit hard" on *Pollen*: "I thought perhaps you meant *the country*" (emphasis added). Whatever Dreyer's enablers were doing, they were not trying to get the best possible fire-control technology for the Royal Navy or the country, upon which the British empire rested.

Their failure to do so was not evidence of national decline, as comparison with the US case makes clear. It was "declining" Britain, not the "rising" United States, that produced the fire-control system—Pollen's—which the US Navy judged to be the best in the world and thus paid the backhanded compliment of pirating. Rather, the breakdown of Admiralty process beginning in 1907 was evidence of institutional decadence. Conversely, the US Navy's relentless pursuit, by fair means or foul, of what it considered the best technology in the world was not evidence of national power—the whole point is that the Navy had to go abroad—but of institutional hunger. US naval officials trampled on Pollen's property rights, but they did so in the interest of the service and the nation. Admiralty officials did so for less elevated reasons.

These statements about the behavior of US naval officials, and about the United States more broadly, are not made for the didactic purpose of praise nor blame. Nor does the history related in this book about the United States and Anglo-American relations dictate any particular US policy toward China now; for all the similarities between the United States and China, there are also some very important differences. But this book is written in the conviction that scholarly history has moral purpose and policy implications. The moral purpose of scholarly history is not to render verdicts that such-and-such was good and so-and-so was bad, but to aid the development of mature judgment through the rigorous examination of a complex reality. Similarly, scholarly history does not provide straightforward lessons for contemporary policy, but it does facilitate informed consideration of how the past structures, without determining, choices made in the present. It can also provide new ways of understanding important things about oneself and others.

At first glance, naval fire control may not seem to lend itself to the exploration of anything important—it appears so narrow and technical. This book has argued, however, that in fact it was far from narrow and technical: important in its own right, it related closely to matters of even greater importance in Anglo-American political economy, technological development, law, and foreign relations. Studying fire control as primarily or only a naval subject renders these relationships invisible; to see them, it is methodologically necessary to range widely across multiple historical subfields as well as legal scholarship. The Admiralty's determination to avoid studying the history of fire control in any context, narrow or broad, for fear of what it might learn about itself, should serve as a cautionary tale. Putting aside the implications for Pollen and Isherwood, the Admiralty did itself—to say nothing of Britain—no favors. To refuse to face the past is to be its hostage. Institutions and nations that decline to engage in rigorous scrutiny of themselves and the world are preparing for failure.

Acknowledgments

When I first heard the phrase "naval fire control" as a graduate student, I thought it referred to fire-fighting on board ships. It has taken a *lot* of help for me to write this book.

Anyone trying to work at the intersection of multiple subfields without formal training in all of them hopes to find natives who will tolerantly correct visitors' clumsy errors rather than hurl spears. I am very grateful to the scholars who resisted such temptation as I gave them.

One of the most intellectually productive hours in my work on this book was spent having lunch with Myles Jackson, who, after generously reading an early and embarrassing draft of my first chapter, walked me through how I could improve. He put me on a much better path; I particularly appreciate his advice to read the work of Matthew L. Jones and Mario Biagioli, which transformed my understanding of how I could tell my story. Dagmar Schäfer offered further valuable suggestions for reading.

I thank Robert Chesney, whose reference to Pollen's and Isherwood's lawsuits in a foundational article on the history of the state secrets privilege gave me the first inklings of this book, for inviting me to present a draft chapter at the Robert S. Strauss Center for International Security and Law at the University of Texas–Austin. There I had the good fortune to meet Oren Bracha and learn of his work on the history of intellectual-property law. And I thank Mary Dudziak, who served as my welcoming committee to the field of legal history, for suggesting that I attend the seminar on national security law at the University of Virginia where I encountered Chesney's work in the first place.

John Krige has been the most generous and knowledgeable guide to the history of science and technology that a tourist could ask for. Encountering his intellectual openness and curiosity since our meeting in the unlikeliest of ways—he actually attended a panel I was on at the American Historical Association annual meeting—has been one of the serendipitous joys of my career.

I have learned a huge amount from the work of Mario Daniels, Michael Falcone, Kathryn Steen, and Alex Wellerstein and benefited from their enthusiasm for studying many of the same issues that interest me (yet, inexplicably, not everyone else).

I will always owe a special debt to Geoffrey Parker, Jon Sumida, and Nicholas Lambert for their inspiring dedication to high scholarly standards and for doing so much to help me try to meet them. For the same reason, I thank the extraordinary teachers at Maret who ensured that no intellectual task since grade 12 has ever felt too daunting for hard work.

I thank Mario Daniels, Michael Falcone, and Sam Lebovic for each reading a draft chapter, and John Krige and Harold James for reading an abandoned draft of my conclusion. Steven Usselman's comments and criticisms on a related paper were most helpful. I am particularly grateful to Norman Friedman (with his PhD in physics on top of his long historical study of fire control) and William Hollander (with his career in instruments-making) for giving me the benefit of their perspectives on the early chapters. Nicholas Lambert, Captain Steve Deal, and Judge Anthony Epstein deserve hazardous-duty pay for reading the whole manuscript. Peter Carrier patiently helped with images.

I am grateful to Esmond Harmsworth, whose great-uncle makes a cameo in this book, for being one of the half-dozen people who read my first book yet nevertheless becoming my agent. His willingness to invest in me means a great deal, and I hope to repay him (so to speak) in due course.

Mine may have been the first manuscript in recorded history to go two for two when it came to the anonymous readers selected by the press providing the sort of report authors dream of—thorough, informed, and critical in the best sense of the word. Both consented to be revealed once the manuscript was through review, and I am delighted to be able to acknowledge them by name. I thank Jeffrey Engel not only for taking the time to read and review with such care, but also for writing *Cold War at 30,000 Feet,* which has long been one of my mental touchstones in working on technology, diplomacy, and Anglo-American relations. I thank Mary Mitchell for her extraordinary help to situate the manuscript more effectively in the histories of law and science and technology, including several extremely fruitful detailed suggestions. I am more grateful than I can convey to both readers for putting so much work into the manuscript, which is far better as a result of their commentary.

At the University of Chicago Press, I thank my editor, Karen Darling, for justifying every good thing I had heard about her. She provided unerring advice and was an ideal shepherd of the manuscript through the publication process. Associate editor Fabiola Enríquez Flores also helped to guide the manuscript through, and I very much appreciate her promptness and courtesy on email. Charles Dibble contributed his copyediting skills. Production editor Caterina MacLean met every deadline she promised, and promotions manager Anne Strother was delightfully on top of things. I am grateful to all of them as well as the rest of the team at the press.

At Rutgers-Camden, I thank my colleagues in the History Department. I also thank law professors Michael Carrier and Kathryn Kovacs, who graciously fielded occasional queries on IP and administrative law, and the law school's gem of a librarian Charlotte Schneider, who helped me navigate legal databases and tracked down particularly elusive statutes and rulings. Kate Blair generously helped with illustrations. Finally, I thank my students, who have served (however unwittingly) as guinea pigs for some of the ideas in this book.

One of the pleasures of this book, unlike my first, was coming into contact with the descendants of some of the people I was studying. I thank Roberta Anne Vena for permitting me to view the papers of her grandfather, Robert Lavender, on her dining table, and for subsequently transferring them to the Library of Congress to facilitate access for other scholars. I am grateful to Anne Pollen and Louis Jebb for telling me about the Pollen family. And I appreciate Martha Specht Corsi sharing her reminisces and photographs of Harold Isherwood. I thank them all for permission to quote and/or publish photographs.

At the US National Archives and Records Administration, which for the most part is a national embarrassment (would that it imitated its British counterpart as effectively as the US Navy did its!), I thank Robert Beebe of the Kansas City branch, whose enthusiastic knowledge of his collections saved me much work, as well as the rest of the crackerjack staff there (especially Sarah LeRoy). At the Churchill Archives Centre, I thank Andrew Reilly for his help and good cheer. At the Admiralty Library, I thank Jenny Wraight for her assistance.

I am grateful for the generous financial support that funded research trips and enabled me to take time off from teaching. Grants from the American Philosophical Society and the America in the World Consortium covered numerous archival visits. I owe special thanks to the American Council of Learned Societies for awarding me a Frederick Burkhardt Fellowship and to the Institute for Advanced Study for awarding me membership during my fellowship year. The Institute was a blissful place to spend time, and I benefited hugely from the opportunity to interact with scholars outside my usual ambits. I particularly thank librarian Marcia Tucker for her help tracking down an image.

Serendipitously, when I was searching for images for the cover, it emerged that a Mark VII Ford rangekeeper was located an hour's drive from my home. I am very grateful to Michael Pearson, the director of the Pennsylvania Computer and Technology Museum (a.k.a. "The Computer Church"), for permitting my husband and me to come photograph it and to use one of the photographs on the cover.

Finally, I thank the colleagues and institutions, too numerous to list here, who afforded me opportunities to present and get feedback on work in progress.

My first book was dedicated to my parents and sister, my wonderful family of birth. This book is dedicated to my husband and stepdaughters, my wonderful family of choice. They know why. Pooshy.

Abbreviations

Adm	British Admiralty file
ADM	British Admiralty file series, TNA
AsstSecNav	US Assistant Secretary of the Navy
AsstSecState	US Assistant Secretary of State
Atty Gen	US Attorney General
AVIA	British Air Ministry file series, TNA
B	Box
B&S	Barr & Stroud
BT	British Board of Trade file series, TNA
BuC&R	Bureau of Construction and Repair, US Department of the Navy
BuEng	Bureau of Steam Engineering, US Department of the Navy
BuNav	Bureau of Navigation, US Department of the Navy
BuOrd	Bureau of Ordnance, US Department of the Navy
BuS&A	Bureau of Supplies and Accounts, US Department of the Navy
CLSN	Hugh Clausen papers, CAC
CommPat	Commissioner of Patents, US Patent Office
CoO	Chief of the Bureau of Ordnance, US Department of the Navy
CP	Contract and Purchase Department, British Admiralty
Ct.Cl.	US Court of Claims
DeptNav	US Department of the Navy
DNI	Director of Naval Intelligence, US Department of the Navy
DNO	Director of Naval Ordnance, British Admiralty

DoJ	US Department of Justice
D. of C.	Director of Navy Contracts
DRYR	Frederic Dreyer papers, CAC
DUFC	Alfred Duff Cooper (Viscount Norwich) papers, CAC
E	Entry
EAS	Elmer A. Sperry papers, Hagley Museum and Library, Wilmington, DE, USA
EDNY	Eastern District of New York
f(f)	Folio(s)
F	Folder
FIC	Ford Instrument Company
FO	British Foreign Office file series, TNA
G	Gunnery file, British Admiralty
GBP	Great Britain, Patent
HTT	Henry Tizard papers, IWM
IF	Interference File
IQDNO	Important Questions Dealt with by the Director of Naval Ordnance
IP	Intellectual Property
JAG	Judge Advocate General
Nav Att	Naval Attaché
NIO	Naval Inspector of Ordnance
ONI	Office of Naval Intelligence, US Department of the Navy
p(p)	Page(s)
P	Part
Pat Off	US Patent Office
PF	Patent File
PLLN	Arthur Pollen papers, CAC
PP	Uncatalogued Arthur Pollen papers, CAC
PQDNO	Principal Questions Dealt with by the Director of Naval Ordnance
RG	Record Group
ROSK	Stephen Roskill papers, CAC
SecAdm	Secretary of the British Admiralty
SecInterior	US Secretary of the Interior
SecNav	US Secretary of the Navy

SecState	US Secretary of State
SGC	Sperry Gyroscope Company papers, Hagley Museum and Library, Wilmington, DE, USA
T	British Treasury file series, TNA
ToH	Transcript of Hearing
ToR	*Transcript of Record*
Treas	British Treasury file
USP	US Patent
V	Volume

ABBREVIATIONS OF ARCHIVES

AL	Admiralty Library, Portsmouth Naval Base, England
CAC	Churchill Archives Center, University of Cambridge, Cambridge, England
IWM	Imperial War Museum, London, England
LoC	Library of Congress, Washington, DC, USA
NARA-I	National Archives and Records Administration, Washington, DC, USA
NARA-II	National Archives and Records Administration, College Park, MD, USA
NARA-KC	National Archives and Records Administration, Kansas City, MO, USA
NARA-NY	National Archives and Records Administration, New York, NY, USA
TNA	The National Archives, Kew, London, England
UGA	University of Glasgow Archives, Glasgow, Scotland
VA	Vickers Archive, University of Cambridge, Cambridge, England

ABBREVIATIONS OF PUBLISHED WORK

BHAM	*Between Human and Machine*, by David Mindell
FNR	*Sir John Fisher's Naval Revolution*, by Nicholas Lambert
IDNS	*In Defense of Naval Supremacy*, by Jon Sumida
NF	*Naval Firepower*, by Norman Friedman
PP	*The Pollen Papers*, edited by Jon Sumida

Notes

INTRODUCTION

1. Mindell, *BHAM*.

2. See, e.g., Grier, *When Computers Were Human*; Ceruzzi, "When Computers Were Human."

3. Integraphs are mechanical devices for solving integral functions and graphing (or plotting) the results on paper.

4. See Miller, *Chip War*.

5. Belfanti, "Between Mercantilism and Market"; Bracha, "The Commodification of Patents"; Biagioli, "Patent Republic"; Bottomley, *The British Patent System during the Industrial Revolution*, esp. 46–50, 85–103, 112–26.

6. For the early modern period, see, e.g., Jones, *Reckoning with Matter*; for the modern, see, e.g., Diaz, *Software Rights*. A partial exception for the early twentieth century is Sumida, *IDNS*, which is, among other things, a pioneering study of the connections between fire-control computers and the British IP system. Three works—Mindell, *BHAM*; Wright, "Questions"; and Friedman, *NF*—are excellent on the development of US fire-control computers, but none of them focus on IP.

7. See Brock and Lécuyer, "From Nuclear Physics to Semiconductor Manufacturing"; Mody and Lynch, "Test Objects."

8. The most notable exception is the only book-length study of patent secrecy in existence, namely, O'Dell, *Inventions and Official Secrecy*—which is pioneering but leaves a great deal of room for further research. There is brief coverage of patent secrecy on the US side in Farley and Isaacs, *Patents for Power*, 54–58. A few articles deal with patent secrecy in the nuclear context: see Turchetti, "'For Slow Neutrons, Slow Pay'"; Turchetti, "The Invisible Businessman"; and most comprehensively Wellerstein, "Patenting the Bomb."

9. Quoted in Bracha, *Owning Ideas*, 16.

10. Cf. Khan, *The Democratization of Invention*, 13.

11. Biagioli, "Patent Republic"; Bottomley, *The British Patent System during the Industrial Revolution*, esp. 46–50, 85–103, 112–26.

12. The phrase "national security" is anachronistic, but the advantages of its use in this book outweigh its disadvantages. During the World War I era, Britain and the United States spoke of "defense" rather than "security," and Britain used the term "imperial" rather than "national": thus the Committee of Imperial Defence in Britain, and the Council of National Defense in the United States. For the United States,

Andrew Preston has shown how the change from "national defense" to "national security" in the 1930s was not a mere terminological change: the new language denoted a new concept (see Preston, "Monsters Everywhere"). Accordingly, some historical accuracy is lost by speaking of "national security" before the term and the concept it denoted entered wide use in Britain and the United States. But "national security" involved continuities with the older ideas of "national defense" and "imperial defense" as well, and it is the contemporary term closest to them. For present purposes, the meanings that it evokes are more, rather than less, historically accurate.

13. Edgerton, "Liberal Militarism and the British State," and Edgerton, *England and the Aeroplane.*

14. See Fagal, "The Political Economy of War in the Early American Republic"; Fagal, "American Arms Manufacturing and the Onset of the War of 1812." Although there is excellent work on British defense contracting (see esp. McNeill, *The Pursuit of Power*, 223–41, 262–99), and some briefly make the argument about its underlying ideology that Fagal makes for the United States (see, e.g., Bond, *War and Society in Europe*, 44), I do not know of any that develop the point as Fagal does.

15. See here the very insightful remarks in Trebilcock, "A 'Special Relationship,'" esp. 375–77.

16. Galison, "Removing Knowledge," esp. 238, 243.

17. Dudziak, *War Time*, 15–16.

18. The argument that defense contractors' quest for scale—for instance, through cartelization—had a defensive logic is not new (see, e.g., Trebilcock, "Legends of the British Armament Industry," 13–15), though my emphasis on their vulnerability to government national security powers, I believe, is.

19. Wellerstein, *Restricted Data*, esp. 145–58.

20. Hewlett, "'Born Classified' in the AEC."

21. See here Sexton, "From Triumph to Crisis."

22. Epstein, "Scholarship and the Ship of State."

23. Epstein, "The Conundrum of American Power in the Age of World War I"; Berghahn, *American Big Business in Britain and Germany*; James, "The Warburgs and Yesterday's Financial Deterrent."

24. The classic work is Ben-Atar, *Trade Secrets*; see also Sell, "Intellectual Property and Public Policy in Historical Perspective," 285–87; Johns, *Piracy*, 185–95; Bracha, *Owning Ideas*, 199–201; and Moser, "Patents and Innovations in Economic History," 4–5. See also Shankman, "Toward a Social History of Federalism."

25. Bensel, *Yankee Leviathan*, 2–4, 10, 94, 207–8, 225–28, 236, 363–67, 414–15.

26. Angevine, "The Rise and Fall of the Office of Naval Intelligence."

27. On "catch-up development," see Link, *Forging Global Fordism*. Between his book and his article with Maggor, "The United States as a Developing Nation," Link pointed the way to the argument I make here—except that he did not apply to the development of the United States the "catch-up" part of the "catch-up development" model he used for Germany and the Soviet Union. I also want to acknowledge a special debt to the immense scholarly labors of Richard Franklin Bensel, whose book *The Political Economy of American Industrialization, 1877–1900*, first introduced me to the idea of the United States as a developing country.

CHAPTER 1

1. For the application of the concept of "algorithms" to mechanical analog computers, see Mindell, *BHAM*, 323–26. The "schematic diagrams" in Sumida, *IDNS*, 209–14, 246 are essentially algorithmic diagrams without formal notation.

2. Quoted in Miller, *Chip War*, 221. For more on the difficulty of defining software, see, e.g., Díaz, "The Text in the Machine," esp. 761–69; Díaz, "Contested Ontologies of Software"; Slayton, *Arguments That Count*, 9–10; and Samuelson, "The Strange Odyssey of Software Interfaces as Intellectual Property."

3. For the source / object code distinction at the turn of the century, see Díaz, "Encoding Music," 627–65. See also Díaz, "The Text in the Machine," 769.

4. See Owens, "Where Are We Going, Phil Morse?"

5. For "legal technology," see Biagioli and Buning, "Technologies of the Law / Law as a Technology."

6. Pollen to Hughes-Onslow, 1-Nov-1909, PLLN.5/4/7. See also Hayes to Lavender, 20-Jan-1932, "Career and Commendations" pile, Lavender mss.

7. See Diaz, "The Text in the Machine"; and Diaz, *Software Rights*, esp. introduction and chapter 6.

8. This paragraph borrows heavily from and closely paraphrases Jebb, *Leonardo Da Vinci's Miniature Madonna*, 9–10, and Sumida, *IDNS*, 76–77.

9. Pollen to Selborne, 28-Jan-01, PLLN.5/2/1.

10. Kahan, *Ottmar Mergenthaler*, 123.

11. Jebb, *Leonardo Da Vinci's Miniature Madonna*, 10.

12. Sumida, *IDNS*, 76.

13. "Youth and Beauty at the Altar: The Wedding of Miss Maud Beatrice Lawrence, of Kenley," *Croydon Chronicle*, 10-Sep-1898, p. 3. I owe my awareness of this source to Jackie Macaulay, "Mrs A. H. Pollen (or Maud Beatrice Lawrence) (1877–1962)," at https://glasgowmuseumsartdonors.co.uk/2022/08/05/mrs-a-h-pollen-or-maud-beatrice-lawrence-1877-1962.

14. See the diary in PLLN.5/1/38.

15. Pollen, "The *Jupiter* Letters," May-1906, 73, *PP*.

16. Draft letter from Harding to Usborne, 12-Jan-1913, PLLN.5/3/11. For condolences, see, e.g., those from William James of 29-Jan-1937, Somers Somerset of 30-Jan-1937, and Reginald Hall of 31-Jan-1937, PLLN.5/1/50.

17. Quoted in Jebb, *Leonardo Da Vinci's Miniature Madonna*, 10.

18. Clark, *Another Part of the World*, 146–47; my thanks to Bruce Taylor for the reference. For context, see Jebb, *Leonardo Da Vinci's Miniature Madonna*, 20–23.

19. Sumida, *IDNS*, 76–77; see also Spear, *The Business of Armaments*, 26. For instance, firing a spread of torpedoes at a line of battleships was known as a "browning" attack— one fired "into the brown" of the battleline rather than at one particular vessel, just as hunters fired "into the brown" of a group of gamebirds rather than at an individual bird.

20. Sumida, *PP*, 8; Lawrence to Selborne, 9-May-1904, docket "The Pollen Rangefinder," ADM.1/7733, TNA.

21. Minute by Barry, 31-May-1904, ibid.

22. For the Pollen quotation, see Pollen to Wilson, 24-Jan-1908, PLLN.5/2/4 (and also Pollen to Earle, 26-Sept-1917, RG74/E25A-I/B345, NARA-I); inscription by Isherwood, July 1919, PP, CAC.

23. The word "genius" was used by a contemporary well qualified to judge and does not seem too strong; see Boys report, 1-Nov-1912, p. 11, PLLN.1/13-P2.

24. *Institution of Mechanical Engineers. Membership Proposal Forms A–K, 1917*, pp. 325–26, from Ancestry.com, *UK, Mechanical Engineer Records, 1847–1938* [online database] (Provo, UT, USA: Ancestry.com Operations, Inc., 2013).

25. I am very grateful to Martha Specht Corsi for sharing her memories of the Isherwoods with me. Emails to the author, 10-Aug-2016, 11-Aug-2016, and 24-Sept-2016.

26. Sumida, *IDNS*, 77.

27. Depression rangefinders used the angle subtended by the height of the observer above the waterline to the target on the waterline as an input for the trigonometric calculation.

28. Report of the Cleveland Committee on the *Arethusa* trials, 29-Apr-1892, reproduced in Dreyer and Usborne, *Pollen Aim Corrector System. Technical History and Technical Comparison with Commander F. C. Dreyer's Fire Control System*, Feb-1913, p. 14, AL.

29. Isherwood testimony, 20-Feb-1939, *Supplemental Record*, p. 4, EDNY Equity Case File #8432, RG21/B1381, NARA-NY.

30. I stress this point because I found it totally counterintuitive.

31. Pollen, brief for counsel, c. Jul–Nov 1924, P2, pp. 1–5, PLLN 8/2. Sumida (*IDNS*, 101n24 and 272n134) dates this document to 1925 and suggests that the author was Wilfrid Greene; I think the document more likely dates to late 1924 and was authored by Pollen himself to instruct Greene.

32. ToH, 1-Aug-1925, p. 53, T.173/547-P14, TNA.

33. Pollen to Peirse, 24-Nov-1912, PLLN.5/3/6.

34. This has been questioned, because Pollen and Isherwood did not instrumentalize feedback in the way that subsequent inventors did; see Friedman, *NF*, 54–55, 184 (cf. his statement on p. 56 that "the plot would reveal changes in enemy course and speed, so that the clock could be reset").

35. Pollen, "Fire Control and Long-Range Firing" (Dec-1904), p. 41, *PP*.

36. See, e.g., Pollen to SecAdm, "The Pollen System of Telemetry," 25-Feb-1901, paras. 26–28, PLLN.5/2/1; Pollen, "A Proposed System for Finding Ranges at Sea" (Jul-1904), 21–22, *PP*; Pollen, "Fire Control and Long-Range Firing" (Dec-1904), 28–33, *PP*; Pollen to anonymous, January 1906, and Pollen to Chase-Parr, 2-Feb-1906, reprinted in "The *Jupiter* Letters," pp. 77 and 88–92, respectively, *PP*.

37. MacKenzie, *Inventing Accuracy*, 31.

38. MacKenzie, *Inventing Accuracy*, 5–7.

39. Pollen, brief for counsel, c. Jul–Nov 1924, P2, pp. 5–7, PLLN.8/2.

40. Pollen, "The Pollen System of Telemetry," 25-Feb-1901, PLLN.5/2/1.

41. I owe the invocation of "error budget" to Norman Friedman.

42. Pollen, "Reflections on an Error of the Day" (Sep-1908), 189, *PP*. See also Pollen to Bacon, 27-Feb-1908, PLLN.5/2/4, and Pollen, "The Gun in Battle" (Feb-1913), 318–19, *PP*.

43. See Flandreau and Legentilhomme, "Cyberpunk Victoria."

44. Pollen to Kerr, 26-Jan-1901, PLLN.5/2/1; Pollen to Selborne, 4-Feb-1901, ibid; Pollen to SecAdm, "The Pollen System of Telemetry," 25-Feb-1901, ibid.

45. Pollen to Kerr, 26-Jan-1901, PLLN.5/2/1.

46. Pollen to SecAdm, "The Pollen System of Telemetry," 25-Feb-1901, ibid.

47. See Biagioli, "Between Knowledge and Technology," 288–90.

48. Within the rich and sophisticated literature on the history of instruments-making, particularly valuable to me was Jones, *Reckoning with Matter*.

49. For some examples of how these questions have arisen in intellectual property law, see Sherman and Bently, *The Making of Modern Intellectual Property Law*, 44–47; Bracha, *Owning Ideas*, 284–97; and McClaskey, "The Mental Process Doctrine."

50. Pollen to Kerr, 26-Jan-1901, PLLN.5/2/1.

51. Pollen to Fawkes, 12-Feb-1901, ibid.

52. Armstrong's to Pollen, 27-Aug-1902, ibid.

53. Pollen, "A Proposed System for Finding Ranges at Sea" (Jun-1904), esp. 18 and 22, *PP*. Cf. Friedman, *NF*, 44.

54. Pollen, "Fire Control and Long Range Firing: An Essay to Define Certain Principia of Gunnery, and to Suggest Means for their Application" (Dec-1904), 35, *PP*.

55. Pollen, "Fire Control and Long Range Firing, 35, ibid.

56. The scholar Tim Ingold has dubbed this conception "hylomorphic," according to an Aristotelian model of creation in which form (*morphe*) precedes matter (*hyle*). See his *Being Alive*, 210. Pollen's sense of the hierarchy eroded as he came to understand the difficulty of constructing the instruments.

57. See, e.g., Pollen to SecAdm, 22-Aug-1906, para. 11, PLLN.5/2/2; Pollen to Bacon, 27-Feb-1908, PLLN.5/3/5; Pollen to Bayly, 20-Jan-1909, PLLN.5/2/5. Pollen never explicitly defined what he meant by "scientific," but his meaning can be inferred from his use of the term in various contexts.

58. See Beauchamp, *Invented by Law*, 168.

59. Slayton, *Arguments That Count*.

60. In 1876 and 1878, the Thomsons published a series of papers in the *Proceedings of the Royal Society* describing their ideas about mechanical integrators. These were reprinted as an appendix in the 1879 and subsequent editions of the first volume of William Thomson's widely used *Treatise on Natural Philosophy*, co-authored with Peter Tait and first published in 1867, which is where they came to the attention of Vannevar Bush, the American computer pioneer (see Bush, *Pieces of the Action*, 183). See also Owens, "Vannevar Bush and the Differential Analyzer," 87–95.

61. Pollen, "Fire Control and Long Range Firing" (Dec-1904), 29, *PP*.

62. Pollen, "Fire Control and Long Range Firing", 40, ibid.

63. Isherwood's testimony, 21-Feb-1939, *Supplemental Record*, pp. 88–89, EDNY Equity Case File #8432, RG21/B1381, NARA-NY. See also his colloquy with the judge, pp. 91–92, ibid.

64. MacKenzie, *Inventing Accuracy*, 26–94. For the inertial guidance system in torpedoes, see Epstein, *Torpedo*, esp. 5–6, 22–25.

65. ToH, 22-Jun-1925, p. 62, T.173/547-P6, TNA.

66. Pollen, "Fire Control and Long-Range Firing" (Dec-1904), 40–41, *PP*. See also Pollen, brief for counsel, c. Jul–Nov 1924, P2, p. 21, PLLN.8/2.

67. McCrary, "Pollen Fire-Control System," n.d. but c. Apr-1914, File U-1-i, Register 6925, RG38/E98/B1294, NARA-I.

68. Standage, *The Victorian Internet*; Lambert, "Strategic Command and Control for Maneuver Warfare," esp. 379–83; Friedman, *Network-Centric Warfare*.

69. See Goble, "The Obituary of a Machine," 22–106, situating Mergenthaler's invention in the context of long-running attempts to develop labor-saving machinery in the printing trade, and 448, reprinting remarks by Mergenthaler ("now we compose a line, justify and cast it all in one machine and by one operator").

70. Pollen to SecAdm, 21-Dec-1904, PLLN.5/2/1; SecAdm to Pollen, 3-May-1905, Adm.CP.7491/9793, ibid.

71. See Sumida, *IDNS*, 86–87.

72. Barr & Stroud to Heather, 24-Dec-1908, UGD.295/4/1, B&S mss., UGA. ("Find out—without appearing to do so—all about their affairs.")

73. Pollen to SecAdm, 18-Jun-1906, and enclosed memorandum, PLLN.5/2/2.

74. Mokyr, *The Lever of Riches*, 12–14.

75. Pollen to Tweedmouth, 27-Aug-1906, PLLN.5/3/1.

76. See Hughes, *Networks of Power*, 14–15, 79–81, and 95; also MacKenzie, *Inventing Accuracy*, 93, and Boast, *The Machine in the Ghost*, 113.

77. I thank Mary Mitchell for pushing me to consider pioneer patents.

78. The subject of Beauchamp, *Invented by Law*.

79. Ceruzzi, *Computing*, 8–16.

80. MacLeod, *Heroes of Invention*; Beauchamp, *Invented by Law*, 113, 133–34, 156–61.

81. Pollen to Fiske, 17-Feb-1911, PLLN.5/4/4. See also Pollen to Fawkes, 12-Feb-1901, PLLN.5/2/1.

82. Bently and Sherman, *The Making of Modern Intellectual Property Law*, 37–38, 47–50, and 173–82; Pottage and Sherman, *Figures of Invention*, esp. 9–11; Biagioli, "Between Knowledge and Technology," esp. 287–89.

83. Bently and Sherman, *The Making of Modern Intellectual Property Law*, 14–18, 95–100; and Bottomley, *The British Patent System during the Industrial Revolution*, 162–68. See also Bracha, *Owning Ideas*, 64–93, 108–11; Samuelson, "The Story of *Baker v. Selden*," 159–93, esp. 163n30, 177, 187–88; and Swanson, "Authoring an Invention," esp. 45–50 (the term "ghostwriter" is hers).

84. Pollen later made exactly this argument about "master" patent protection; see Pollen, untitled ms., n.d. but likely 1923, para. 27, PLLN.8/2.

85. Pollen to SecAdm, 21-Dec-1904, PLLN.5/2/1.

86. Mindell, *BHAM*, 44, 55.

87. Pollen, brief for counsel, c. Jul–Nov 1924, P2, pp. 11–12, PLLN.8/2.

88. "Pollen's Aim-Correcting Apparatus," minutes of a meeting held on 9-Aug-1906, PLLN.5/2/2.

89. Brewer, *The Sinews of Power*, 70, 130–32, 139, 143–46, 151–52.

90. "Pollen's Aim-Correcting Apparatus," PLLN.5/2/2.

91. Pollen to SecAdm, 24-Aug-1906, PLLN.5/2/2; Pollen to Tweedmouth, 27-Aug-1906, PLLN.5/3/1.

92. "Pollen's Aim-Correcting Apparatus," PLLN.5/2/2; Pollen to Tweedmouth, 27-Aug-1906, PLLN.5/3/1.

93. Black to Pollen, 12-Jun-1906, Adm.CP.8659/15093, PLLN.5/2/2.

94. See Epstein, "Intellectual Property and National Security."

95. Draft letter from Harding to Usborne, 12-Jan-1913, PLLN.5/3/11. For a similar assessment, see Backhouse to Pollen, 1906 [no month or day], PLLN.5/5/4. Backhouse, then a lieutenant, would eventually become First Sea Lord.

96. Draft letter from Harding to Usborne, 12-Jan-1913, PLLN.5/3/11.

97. Parrott, *The Business of War*, esp. 1–24.

98. "Pollen's Aim-Correcting Apparatus," PLLN.5/2/2.

99. Pollen to Tweedmouth, 27-Aug-1906, PLLN.5/3/1.

100. Pollen to SecAdm, 14-May-1906, PLLN.5/2/2.

101. Pollen to Tweedmouth, 27-Aug-1906, PLLN.5/3/1.

102. Pollen to Jellicoe, 20-Mar-1906, PLLN.5/3/4.

103. Pollen to SecAdm, 22-Aug-1906, PLLN.5/2/2.

104. Biagioli, "From Ciphers to Confidentiality," 214–15.

105. See Trebilcock, "A 'Special Relationship,'" 375–77, and Pollen to Crease, 12-Feb-1908, para. 15, PLLN.5/2/4; also Epstein, "Intellectual Property and National Security," 132–33, and Spear, *The Business of Armaments*, 44.

106. Patents for Inventions (Munitions of War), 22 Vict. c. 13, sec. 12; Patents, Designs, and Trade Marks Act of 1883, 46 & 47 Vict. c. 57, sec. 44, para. 12.

107. Pollen to SecAdm, 3-Apr-1906, PLLN.5/2/2.

108. Patents, Designs, and Trade Marks Act of 1883, 46 & 47 Vict. c. 57, sec. 27; *Feather v. Regina* (HPC 8 at 744–62); O'Dell, *Patents and Official Secrecy*, 25–30. See also Pollen to Tweedmouth, 27-Aug-1906, PLLN.5/3/1; Mossoff, "Patents as Constitutional Private Property," 705–10; O'Connor, "Taking, Tort, or Crown Right," 160–66.

109. Pollen to Jellicoe, 20-Mar-1906, PLLN.5/3/4.

110. Biagioli, "Recycling Texts or Stealing Time?"

111. Pollen to Jellicoe, 27-May-1909, PLLN.5/3/4.

112. "Pollen's Aim-Correcting Apparatus," PLLN.5/2/2.

113. Pollen to SecAdm, 10-Aug-1906, ibid.

114. SecAdm to Pollen, 21-Aug-1906, ibid.

115. Pollen, brief for counsel, c. Jul–Nov 1924, P2, pp. 24–26, PLLN.8/2.

116. ToH, 1-Aug-1925, pp. 8–11, 16–17, 45, 47–48, 51, 98–99, T.173/547-P14, TNA; "Statement of the Claimants' Case," n.d. but early Jul-1925, para. 3.ix, T.173/91-P11, TNA; Pollen, brief for counsel, c. Jul–Nov 1924, P2, pp. 26–31, PLLN.8/2.

117. ToH, 1-Aug-1925, pp. 10–11, T 173/547-P14, TNA.

118. Pollen to SecAdm, 10-Aug-1906, PLLN.5/2/2.

119. SecAdm to Pollen, 21-Aug-1906, Adm.CP.13418/20603, PLLN.5/2/2.

120. Pollen, brief for counsel, c. Jul–Nov 1924, P2, pp. 36–38, PLLN.8/2.

121. SecAdm to Pollen, 21-Sep-1906, Adm.CP.14079/24002, PLLN.5/2/2.

122. Pollen, brief for counsel, c. Jul–Nov 1924, P2, p. 39, PLLN.8/2.

123. Harding to Pollen, 4-Sep-1906, PLLN.5/3/11.

124. Harding to Jellicoe, 4-Sep-1906, T.173/91-P7, TNA.

125. Harding, "Memorandum upon the Professional and Financial Value of the A.C. System" [hereafter Harding report], 4-Sep-1906, f.39, T.173/91-P7, TNA.

126. Harding report, f.41.

127. Harding report, ff.43–44.

128. Harding report, f.44.

129. For this language, see testimony of Henry Sokolski, Jun-1998, quoted in Krige, "Regulating the Transnational Flow of Intangible Knowledge of Space Launchers," 181.

130. Harding report, f.46.

131. Harding report, f.46f.

132. Harding report, f.47; see also Pollen to Bacon, 25-Feb-1908, PLLN.5/2/4.

133. Harding report, ff.40–41.

134. Scott to Pollen, 31-Jul-1906, PLLN.5/5/4.

135. Harding to Pollen, 29-Jun-1906, PLLN.5/3/11; Pollen, brief for counsel, c. Jul–Nov 1924, P2, pp. 22–23, PLLN.8/2; ToH, 1-Aug-1925, pp. 14–15, T.173/547-P14, TNA.

136. Fisher to Tweedmouth, 10-Sep-1906, in *Fear God and Dread Nought*, ed. Marder, 87.

137. Sumida, *IDNS*, 37–70, 98–100.

138. Fisher to Tweedmouth, 14-Sep-1906, in *Fear God and Dread Nought*, ed. Marder, 88.

139. See the correspondence between Pollen and the Admiralty from Aug–Nov 1906 in PLLN.5/2/2, as well as Pollen to Tweedmouth, 31-Oct-1906, and Tweedmouth to Pollen, 2-Nov-1906, in PLLN.5/3/1.

140. Beauchamp, *Invented by Law*, 112.

141. Pollen to SecAdm, 15-Mar-1907, PLLN.5/2/3.

142. Black had also missed a crucial meeting to discuss the terms of a monopoly agreement in August 1906, for which see "Pollen's Aim-Correcting Apparatus," PLLN.5/2/2.

143. Pollen to Minter, 18-Apr-1907, PLLN.5/2/3; for the Admiralty letter, see SecAdm to Pollen, c. 1-Apr-1907, Adm.CP.4453, PLLN.5/2/3.

144. Black to Hollams, Sons et al., 19-Jul-1907, Adm.CP.7949/07, PLLN.5/2/3.

CHAPTER 2

1. Certain naval historians may notice that I do not cite or engage with John Brooks's *Dreadnought Gunnery and the Battle of Jutland: The Question of Fire Control* (London: Routledge, 2005). Having consulted the major archival sources that Brooks cited in his book (as well as a great many that he did not but should have), I am unable to understand how he could have interpreted the sources as he did or how his press could have found peer reviewers to approve publication. Quantitatively and qualitatively, the errors therein greatly exceed scholarly tolerances; they are so severe as to render the book unusable.

2. See Trebilcock, "A 'Special Relationship,'" 375–77 (wryly noting on p. 376 that "Trade allegations that the War Office was a den of thieves for inventors were not wholly unfounded").

3. See Lavington, *Moving Targets*, xi–xiii, 14–16, 113–18 (Lavington forthrightly notes that in the absence of extensive archival evidence from Elliotts' early years, he relied in part on corporate memory, in the form of communications with former employees, for his account).

4. For the language of intent-based vs. outcome-based, see Lambert, *The War Lords and the Gallipoli Disaster*, 261. For process-based vs. outcome-based, see Slayton, *Arguments That Count*, 6–8.

5. Bacon to Pollen, 26-Feb-1908, PLLN.5/2/4. See also Bacon to Pollen, 2-Mar-1908, PLLN.5/3/5.

6. See minute by Bacon, 16-Nov-1907, Adm.G.17999/1907, ADM.1/7955, TNA. For insight into Bacon's views on patents, see his minute of 26-Aug-1905, in *The Submarine Service*, ed. Lambert, 120–22.

7. Trebilcock, "A 'Special Relationship,'" 375.

8. Enclosure to minute by Dreyer, 9-May-1918, Adm.G.048282/17, ADM.116/1737, TNA.

9. Dreyer to Jellicoe, 7-Mar-1916, Adm.CP.Patents.3634/16, ADM.1/8464/181, TNA.

10. Davis to Roskill, 29-Apr-1975 and 12-Dec-1975, ROSK.7/210/F3.

11. Davis to Roskill, 5-May-1975, ibid.

12. Graham, *Random Naval Recollections*, 22.

13. Cooper, note assessing admirals, n.d. but c. 1937, DUFC.2/12.

14. See, e.g., Dreyer to Pollen, 22-Mar-1906, PLLN.5/4/3.

15. Dreyer, "Remarks on Channel Fleet Battle Practice 1906," 10-Dec-1906, DRYR.2/1.

16. Dreyer subsequently acknowledged that this visit occurred, though he claimed that he could not remember exactly what he saw. See ToH, 4-Aug-1925, pp. 104–5, T.173/547-P16, TNA; ToH, 5-Aug-1925, pp. 2–3, T.173/547-P17, TNA.

17. Dreyer to Jellicoe, 2-Jul-1907, T.173/91-P3, TNA.

18. See, e.g., Dreyer to Hughes-Onslow, 18-Oct-1908, PLLN.8/2; Dreyer, "Remarks by Commander F. C. Dreyer R.N. on the Question of How to Best Obtain and Maintain the Gun Range in Action," 22-Jul-1910, Adm.G.0450, ADM.1/8147, TNA; minute by Dreyer, 12-Mar-1918, Adm.G.01204/18, DRYR.2/1.

19. Pollen to SecAdm, 2-Nov-1906, PLLN.5/2/2.

20. Although the evidence for the range-rate plot during the preliminary trials comes from two later sources—an account that Pollen wrote for his lawyer in 1924 (see his brief for counsel, c. Jul–Nov 1924, addendum to part II, PLLN.8/2), and Pollen's and Isherwood's testimony in the 1920s—it is corroborated by two other sources: the contemporary patent record, for which see Pollen and Isherwood, "Improvements in Range Finders," GBP 1,367/1908, and "Improvements in Range Finders," GBP 1,368/1908, provisional specifications 20-Jan-1908, complete specifications 20-Jul-1908, acceptance 22-Dec-1908, publication 6-Nov-1913; and Harding (see ToH, 1-Aug-1925, p. 12—also p. 14, which makes clear that "1909" on p. 12 should read "1907"—T.173/547-P14, TNA).

21. Pollen to Dreyer, 18-Dec-1907, PLLN.5/4/3.

22. See Pollen, "An Apology for the A.C. Battle System" (Aug–Dec 1907), 148, *PP*.

23. Pollen to Wilson, 9-Dec-1907, and Wilson to Pollen, 11-Dec-1907, PLLN.5/2/4.

24. For a careful and reliable account of the trials, see Sumida, *IDNS*, 128–30.

25. Pollen to Wilson, 19-Dec-1907, PLLN.5/2/4; Pollen to SecAdm, 17-Jan-1908, ibid.; Pollen, "Re A.C. System," 25-Feb-1909, PLLN.5/2/5.

26. Contract between Pollen and the Admiralty, 18-Feb-1908, Adm.CP.18141/07, ADM.1/7991, TNA; SecAdm to Pollen, 10-Mar-1908, CP.8383/8026, PLLN.5/2/4. For the incorporation of the clauses negotiated in 1906, see preamble and para. 6.

27. "Proof of Evidence of Colonel E. W. Harding, R.M.A.," Jan-1920, para. 19, PLLN.5/3/11. For Wilson's acknowledgment of the difficulty of taking rangefinder readings without a gyro-stabilized mounting, see his report on the *Vengeance* experiments, 17-Mar-1908, reproduced in *Fire Control*, Adm.G.4023/08, p. 27, T.173/91-P1, TNA.

28. See "Application for a Certificate of Incorporation," filed 31-Dec-1907, and accompanying papers, BT.31/18318/96287, TNA.

29. Pollen to Jellicoe, 23-Jan-1908, PLLN.5/3/4.

30. Pollen to Crease, 12-Feb-1908, PLLN.5/2/4.

31. See the correspondence between Pollen and the Admiralty from Apr–Jun 1908, PLLN.5/2/4.

32. Pollen and Isherwood, "Improvements in Range Finders," GBP 1,368/1908, and "Improvements in Means for Indicating and Transmitting Ranges or Changes of Range," GBP 2,497/1908.

33. See Pollen to Jellicoe, 13-Feb-1906, PLLN.5/3/4.

34. Pollen, brief for counsel, c. Jul–Nov 1924, addendum to part II, PLLN.8/2. Note that the brief misidentifies the patent in question as 360/1908 rather than 1,368/1908 (Pollen did eventually hold a patent numbered 360, but it was 360/1911—he likely confused them).

35. Pollen, "Reflections on an Error of the Day," pp. 178–93, *PP*.

36. Dreyer to Hughes-Onslow, 18-Oct-1908, PLLN.8/2. A "deal table" was a table made of relatively soft, cheap wood.

37. Pears, in "The Military View," 104. See also "Hooligan" to Gipps, n.d. but 1908, PLLN.5/4/3.

38. *Fire Control*, Adm.G.4023/08, p. 54, T.173/91-P1, TNA.

39. Hughes-Onslow, "Fire Control," n.d. but c. Feb-1909, PLLN.1/10; Pollen to Bacon, 27-Feb-1908, PLLN.5/2/4. For Dreyer's tendency to multiply personnel, see Dreyer to Eustace, "Remarks on Local Turret Control by Commander Frederic C. Dreyer, Royal Navy, of H.M.S. 'Vanguard,' " 5-Sep-1910, p. 12, Adm.G.0539/10, ADM.1/8147, TNA.

40. Flandreau and Legentilhomme, "Cyberpunk Victoria," 1084.

41. Pollen to McKenna, 18-Mar-1906, PLLN.5/3/2.

42. Pollen to Bacon, 19-Mar-1909, PLLN.5/3/5.

43. Scott to Pollen, n.d. but c. 31-Mar-1909, PLLN.5/4/12.

44. Pollen to SecAdm, 5-Jan-1909, and enclosure, PLLN.5/2/5.

45. November 1909 was the end of the eighteen-month period agreed to in the June 1908 settlement. The correspondence on these negotiations is extensive and may be found mainly in PLLN.5/2/5 and 5/2/6. For a summary, see minute by Black, 25-Feb-1910, Adm.CP.450/10, ADM.1/8123, TNA.

46. The key pieces of evidence are SecAdm to Argo, 19-Aug-1910, para. 7, Adm. CP.G.0419/10/175S, PLLN.5/2/6; Pollen to SecAdm, 26-Oct-1910, ibid.; and Pollen to Henley, 9-Dec-1910, ibid.

47. Hughes, *Networks of Power*, 14–15, 79–81; Brock and Lécuyer, "Digital Foundations," 564.

48. Pollen to Hughes-Onslow, 1-Nov-1909, PLLN.5/4/7.

49. Pollen to Moore, 30-Dec-1909, PLLN.5/3/8; ToH, 6-Jul-1925, p. 61, T.173/547-P8, TNA; "Linotype and Machinery," *Economist* 69, no. 3455 (13 November 1909): 985.

50. SecAdm to Pollen, 11-Apr-1910, with enclosure, PLLN.5/2/6; Pollen to Spender, 12-Apr-1910, PLLN.5/4/14.

51. Pollen to Spender, 22-Apr-1910, PLLN.5/4/14.

52. Pollen to Thomas, 1-Mar-1910, PLLN.5/2/6.

53. Pollen to Spender, 13-Apr-1910, PLLN.5/4/14; Pollen to McKenna, 13-Apr-1910, PLLN.5/3/2; Pollen to Jellicoe, 13-Apr-1910, PLLN.5/3/4; Pollen to McKenna, 19-Apr-1910, PLLN.5/3/2.

54. SecAdm to Pollen, 29-Apr-1910, Adm.CP.14084/93S, and Pollen to SecAdm, 29-Apr-1910, PLLN.5/2/6.

55. Pollen to SecAdm, 17-Jun-1910, PLLN.5/2/6; Pollen to Moore, 17-Jun-1910, PLLN.5/3/8; Moore to Pollen, 17-Jun-1910, ibid.; Pollen to Moore, 18-Jun-1910, ibid.; SecAdm to Pollen, 20-Jun-1910, Adm.G.0381/14167, PLLN.5/2/6; Pollen to SecAdm, 21-Jun-1910, ibid. The Admiralty had also done this in the first round of the *Natal* trials; see Pollen to SecAdm, 16-Nov-1909, PLLN.5/2/5.

56. Plunkett, "Report by Torpedo Lieutenant of H.M.S. 'Natal' (General Impressions of the Pollen A.C. Apparatus)," enclosed in Plunkett to Fisher, 28-Jun-1910, PLLN.5/2/6; Hall, undated note but likely 1922, PLLN.8/2.

57. Dreyer, "Remarks by Commander F. C. Dreyer R.N. on the Question of How to Best Obtain and Maintain the Gun Range in Action," enclosed in Dreyer to Eustace, 22-Jul-1910, Adm.G.0450, ADM.1/8147, TNA.

58. SecAdm to Pollen, 19-Aug-1910, Adm.CP.G.0419/10/175S, PLLN.5/2/6.

59. Pollen to McKenna, 23-Aug-1910, PLLN.5/3/2; Pollen to SecAdm, 25-Aug-1910, PLLN.5/2/6; SecAdm to Pollen, 30-Sep-1910, Adm.CP.18774/199S, PLLN.5/2/6.

60. Pollen, "Fire Control and Long Range Firing," 41, *PP*.

61. Pollen, brief for counsel, c. Jul–Nov 1924, addendum to part II, PLLN.8/2. For corroboration of Pollen's account in the brief, see the contemporary patent record as well as Pollen to Henley, 9-Dec-1910, PLLN.5/2/6.

62. Henley to Dreyer, 13-Aug-1910, DRYR.2/1; Pollen to SecAdm, 25-Aug-1910, PLLN.5/2/6.

63. Minute by Moore, 13-Aug-1910, Adm.CP.Patents.582/1910, ADM.1/8131, TNA.

64. Minute by Black, n.d. but c. 17-Nov-1913, Adm.CP.Patents.1981/1913, enclosed in minute by Black, 12-May-1914, Adm.CP.Patents.2246/1914, ADM.1/8464/181, TNA.

65. Henley to Dreyer, 13-Aug-1910, DRYR.2/1.

66. Dreyer to D. of C., 21-Sep-1910, Adm.CP.Patents.598/10, ADM.1/8131, TNA; D. of C. to Dreyer, 23-Sep-1910, Adm.CP.Patents.598/10/196S, ibid.

67. Minutes by Moore and Black on Adm.CP.Patents.600/10/196S, October 1910, ibid.

68. Dreyer to Eustace, 5-Sep-1910, "Remarks on Local Turret Control by Commander Frederic C. Dreyer, Royal Navy, of H.M.S. 'Vanguard,'" pp. 15–19, Adm.G.0539/10, ADM.1/8147, TNA.

69. Compare Dreyer to Eustace, 5-Sep-1910, "Remarks on Local Turret Control by Commander Frederic C. Dreyer, Royal Navy, of H.M.S. 'Vanguard,'" p. 18, Adm.G.0539/10, ADM.1/8147, TNA with Dreyer and Usborne, *Pollen Aim Correction System. Technical History and Technical Comparison with Commander F. C. Dreyer's Fire Control System*, Feb-1913, p. 12, AL.

70. SecAdm to Pollen, 19-Jan-1911, Adm.CP.10328/5S, PLLN.5/2/6.

71. Henley to Dreyer, 21-Feb-1911, DRYR.2/1; see also Henley to Dreyer, 24-Jul-1911, DRYR.2/1.

72. Pollen to SecAdm, 12-Nov-1910, PLLN.5/2/6.

73. Pollen to Henley, 9-Dec-1910, ibid.

74. Oliver to Argo, 10-Aug-1911, Adm.CP5093.F.331/182S, ibid.

75. Pollen to Peirse, 17-May-1925, PLLN.5/4/9; Sumida, *IDNS*, 208.

76. "Extraordinary Resolution of the Argo Company," 24-Jan-1911, and "Copy of Register of Directors or Managers of the Argo Company," filed 10-Feb-1911, BT.31/18318/96287, TNA.

77. Whereas the Argo I clock broke the vector into components one of which was along the line of own course and neither of which was along the line of sight, the new clock broke the same vector into components one of which was along the line of sight and neither of which was along the line of own course. Removing the dependence on own course meant that own ship could apply helm without affecting the solution of the vector. See their British patent 360/1911 (covering the Argo I clock) and their US patent 1,162,510 (covering the Argo IV clock).

78. Argo to SecAdm, 15-May-1911, and Argo to Isherwood, 15-May-1911, PLLN.5/2/6. The enclosure to the former—Isherwood, "The A.C. Range and Bearing Clock Mark II," 8-May-1911—is in PLLN.1/13-P1.

79. Pollen to Isherwood, 22-May-1911, PLLN.5/2/6. Sumida makes a rare mistake when he attributes the suggestion for the autogeneration-of-bearings feature to Henley (*IDNS*, 213); Argo had already indicated that it would embody that feature in the clock,

and Henley merely asked for drawings. Correcting this mistake, which overcredits the Admiralty and undercredits Argo, actually strengthens the thrust of Sumida's analysis.

80. GBP 19,627/1911 was not released from secrecy, so it does not exist in patent databases, but there is a copy in T.173/91-P10, TNA; see also Argo to SecAdm, 17-Nov-1911, PLLN.5/2/6.

81. Isherwood, "The A.C. Range and Bearing Clock, Mark II," 8-May-1911, para. 37, PLLN.1/13-P1.

82. Hazen, "Working Mathematics by Machinery," 327. See also Clymer, "Mechanical Integrators," 21. I owe my awareness of Hazen's article and the significance of the servo issue to Mindell, *BHAM*, 154–57 and accompanying notes.

83. Bush, *Pieces of the Action*, 182.

84. See Isherwood, "The A.C. Range and Bearing Clock Mark II," 8-May-1911, PLLN.1/13-P1; Pollen and Isherwood, "Improvements in Range Clocks," patent 19,627/1911, pp. 2 and 21, T.173/91-P10, TNA; and Clymer, "Mechanical Integrators," 10–16. Clymer went on to become an engineer at Ford Instrument Company.

85. Isherwood, "The A.C. Range and Bearing Clock Mark II," 8-May-1911, para. 38, PLLN.1/13-P1; report by Boys, 1-Nov-1912, p. 9, PLLN.1/13-P2.

86. See Sumida, *IDNS*, 208–11, overlooked in many later accounts of the development of mechanical integrators and differential analyzers, as shown in chapters 4 and 10.

87. Gooday, "Boys, Sir Charles Vernon."

88. Rayleigh, "Charles Vernon Boys," 779; Bush, *Pieces of the Action*, 183.

89. Report by Boys, 1-Nov-1912, p. 9, PLLN.1/13-P2. "Genius" reference on p. 11.

90. Hazen, "Working Mathematics by Machinery," 327 (342 for the mention of Boys' integraph); report by Boys, 1-Nov-1912, p. 9, PLLN.1/13-P2. See also Mindell, *BHAM*, 156–57.

91. Report by Boys, 1-Nov-1912, p. 9, PLLN.1/13-P2.

92. See the correspondence dating from June through October 1911 in T.173/91-P3, TNA.

93. Dreyer to Elphinstone, 1-Jul-1911 (with enclosure) and 19-Jul-1911, ibid.

94. Elphinstone to Dreyer, 11-Oct-1911, ibid.

95. Jellicoe to Dreyer, 11-Dec-1906, DRYR.3/2.

96. Jellicoe to Pollen, 26-May-1909, PLLN.5/3/4.

97. Jellicoe to Pollen, 14-Nov-1912, PLLN.5/3/4; Jellicoe to Dreyer, 10-Jun-1913, DRYR.3/2.

98. Nor was this the first time that Dreyer's equipment had been tried aboard his own ship. In September 1910, HMS *Vanguard*, on which Dreyer was serving as executive officer, carried out special firings to test arrangements for local turret control (i.e., the backup fire-control system in case the primary system failed). To get a sense of how sharply reports on Dreyer's system by someone in Dreyer's chain of command and by someone outside his chain of command could differ, compare the report of the officer of "A" turret (a junior officer under Dreyer's command), with the report on "A" turret by an officer on the staff of the Inspector of Target Practice (outside Dreyer's chain of command) in Adm.G.0433/10, ADM.1/8147, TNA. There was no independent observer from the ITP's staff for the *Prince of Wales* trials.

99. Hopwood to Jellicoe, 20-Nov-1911, T.173/91-P3, TNA.

100. Jellicoe to SecAdm, 25-Nov-1911, ibid.

101. Minute by Moore, 7-Dec-1911, ibid.

102. Minute by Briggs, 9-Dec-1911, ibid.; note by Hall, n.d. but c. 1922, PLLN.8/2.

103. For the date of the order, see ToH, 4-Aug-1925, p. 58, T.173/547-P16, TNA.

104. The "original" table, as it was usually called, was later moved from *Prince of Wales* to *Hercules*, where it was upgraded and redesignated as a Mark III table. The table subsequently designated "Mark I" actually *post*dated the original, Mark III, and Mark IV tables; it was a stripped-down version of the Mark IV table. The Mark II table was a combination of Dreyer's rate plotter with the Argo clock.

105. Pollen to Craig Waller, 16-Dec-1912, PLLN.5/3/9.

106. Report by Craig Waller, c. Nov-1912, quoted in Sumida, *IDNS*, 231; Pollen to Craig Waller, 13-Aug-1912, PLLN.5/3/9.

107. Pollen to SecAdm, 10-Sep-1913, PLLN.5/2/8.

108. Pollen to Leveson, 3-Jan-1913, PLLN.5/3/3.

109. See Lambert, *FNR*, 44, 54–55, 222–32. I am grateful to Lambert for sharing additional research with me about the Admiralty's dealings with Vickers. For a similar story about the Admiralty's relationship with Vickers and Armstrong-Whitworth in the context of gun mountings, see Lambert, *FNR*, 149.

110. Draft letter from Harding to Usborne, 12-Jan-1913, p. 5, PLLN.5/3/11.

111. Pollen to Moore, 11-Apr-1912, PLLN.5/3/8. See also Pollen to Black, 31-Jul-1912, A.1098/8, PLLN.5/2/7.

112. Dreyer, "Some comparisons made between the Argo Clock and the Fire Control table in 'Monarch,'" n.d. but summer or fall 1912, T.173/91-P7, TNA.

113. Dreyer to DNO, 19-Dec-1912, T.173/91-P3, TNA.

114. No copy of this patent survives, but its timing and evidence from other documents suggests that it covered the improvements to the Mark III table. See enclosure of 9-Feb-1916 in Elphinstone to Black, 14-Feb-1916, Adm.CP. Patents.3568/1916, Docket "Dreyers Fire Control. Patent position of," ADM.1/8464/181, TNA.

115. The one who had served "only" four years and four months in rank, George H. Baird, was widely regarded—i.e., by both the Fisher and Beresford camps—as one of the finest officers in the fleet; see ADM.196/43/271, TNA.

116. Biagioli, "Recycling Texts or Stealing Time?" 455.

117. Bloom, *The Anxiety of Influence*.

118. To borrow terms from the history of science, Dreyer's invention was "mimeomorphic" rather than "polimorphic"; see Collins and Kusch, *The Shape of Actions*.

119. Sonnet 18 by way of *Richard III*.

120. Dreyer to Jellicoe, 2-Jul-1907, T.173/91-P3, TNA.

121. Martin to Bingham, 14-May-1917, BuOrd.30309, RG74/E25A-I/B743, NARA-I. Note also Kimmel letter, 3-Dec-1917, quoted in Sumida, *IDNS*, 310.

122. Sumida, "A Matter of Timing"; Friedman, *NF*, 46–47, 88–91.

123. Gordon, *The Rules of the Game*; Lambert, *FNR*, 212–20, 252, 284–88.

124. Miller, *Chip War*, 35–44, 57–61, 73–78, 141–54.

125. Miller, *Chip War*, 143.

126. Dreyer to Jellicoe, 22-May-1916, Adm.CP.Patents.3877/1916, ADM.1/8464/181, TNA. For similar language, see Dreyer to Jellicoe, 1-Feb-1916, Adm.CP.Patents.3516/1916, ibid.; and Dreyer, "Remarks on the Admiralty Counter Statement to Rear Admiral Dreyer's Claim," n.d. but c. Jul-1924, pp. 13–14, DRYR.2/1.

127. See Elphinstone to Black, 18-Mar-1914, Adm.CP.Patents.2246/1914, and Elphinstone to Black, 14-Feb-1916 (with enclosure of 9-Feb-1916), Adm.CP.Patents.3568/1916, ADM.1/8464/181, TNA.

128. Dreyer to Jellicoe, 7-Mar-1916, Adm.CP.Patents.3634/1916, ibid.

129. Dreyer to Jellicoe, 14-Jun-1913, DRYR.4/3.

130. Pears, in "The Military View," 104.

131. Submission unsigned but by Warrender, 9-Jun-1915, DRYR.2/1.

132. SecAdm to Dreyer, 15-May-1916, Adm.CP.33092/28146, ibid.

133. Minute by Moore, 7-Dec-1911, T 173/91-P3, TNA.

134. See Sumida, *IDNS*, 156–58; Epstein, *Torpedo*, 199–200; and "Complement of Electricians and Torpedo ratings in battleships of 'DREADNOUGHT' and later Classes and Battle Cruisers," Adm.N.2424/12, pp. 33–61, V3, IQDNO, AL.

135. Pollen to Peirse, 31-Oct-1912, PLLN.5/3/6.

136. The roster included not only Edward Harding and Percy Scott, encountered in chapter 1, but also Frederick Ogilvy, Constantine Hughes-Onslow, Richard Peirse, and Arthur Craig Waller.

137. On HMS *Excellent*, see chapter 1; on the Inspectorate, see Sumida, *IDNS*, 154–55, 246.

138. Symington to SecNav for ONI, 15-Aug-1913, File R-2-a, Register 3184, RG38/E98/B1254, NARA-I.

139. Castle to CNO, 29-Aug-1917, BuOrd.35371/348, RG74/E25A-II/B117, NARA-I.

CHAPTER 3

1. Pollen to Moore, 11-Apr-1912, PLLN.5/3/8.

2. Pollen diary entry, 12-Jul-1912, "Letters by AHP (compiled by Maud Pollen)," Jebb Accession, PP, CAC.

3. Pollen diary entry, 2-Jul-1912, ibid.

4. SecAdm to Pollen, 20-Aug-1912, Adm.CP.5218/316S, PLLN.5/2/7 (contains quotation); Oliver to Pollen, 20-Aug-1912, Adm.CP.5218/315S, ibid.

5. SecAdm to Coward et al., 30-Apr-1913, Adm.CP.16787, para. 6, PLLN.5/2/8.

6. Oliver to Pollen, 22-Aug-1912, Adm.CP.Patents.1323/346S, PLLN.5/2/7.

7. Pollen to Black, 10-Sep-1912, ibid.

8. Pollen to Black, 5-Sep-1912, ibid.

9. Black to Pollen, 13-Sep-1912, Adm.CP.21830/18772, ibid.

10. Pollen to Peirse, 16-Sep-1912, PLLN.5/3/8; Pollen to Craig Waller, 24-Dec-1912, PLLN.5/3/9.

11. Pollen to Spender, 10-Sep-1912, PLLN.5/4/14.

12. Pollen to Peirse, 31-Oct-1912, PLLN.5/3/6. See also Pollen to Craig Waller, 8-Nov-1912, PLLN.5/3/9.

13. Pollen to Churchill, 21-Oct-1912, PLLN.5/2/7.

14. Pollen diary entry, 24-Dec-1912, "Letters by AHP (compiled by Maud Pollen)," Jebb Accession, PP, CAC.

15. CP Department, *Pollen Aim Correction System. General Grounds of Admiralty Policy and Historical Record of Business Negotiations* [hereafter *Historical Record of Business Negotiations*], Feb-1913, para. 186, AL; Dreyer, "A Short History of Range Plotting in the Royal Navy," n.d. but summer or fall 1912, T.173/91-P7, TNA.

16. Inferred from Pollen to Black, 25-Nov-1912, PLLN.5/2/7.

17. Pollen to Black, 25-Nov-1912, PLLN.5/2/7.

18. SecAdm to Pollen, 19-Dec-1912, ibid.

19. Greene to Pollen, 21-Feb-1913, PLLN.5/2/8; Official Secrets Act of 1911, 1 & 2 Geo. 5 c. 28, sec. 1.

20. SecAdm to Pollen, 8-Jan-1913, PLLN.5/2/8.

21. Pollen to Black, 18-Jan-1913, ibid.

22. The Treasury Solicitor's opinion no longer survives, but it is dated and described in the typescript addendum to CP Department, *Historical Record of Business Negotiations*, para. 203.

23. SecAdm to Pollen, 21-Feb-1913, PLLN.5/2/8.

24. Black to Pollen, 30-Jan-1913, ibid.

25. Pollen to Black, 31-Jan-1913, and Black to Pollen, 3-Feb-1913, Adm.CP.14571/455, ibid.

26. CP Department, *Historical Record of Business Negotiations*, para. 23.

27. CP Department, *Historical Record of Business Negotiations*, paras. 11 and 28a (contains quotation).

28. Dreyer and Usborne, *Pollen Aim Correction System. Technical History and Technical Comparison with Commander F. C. Dreyer's Fire Control System*, Feb-1913, p. 21, AL.

29. Dreyer and Usborne, *Pollen Aim Correction System*, p. 62.

30. On Swinburne, see Arapostathis and Gooday, *Patently Contestable*, 81–84. For the Admiralty's use of him, see, e.g., Admiralty Awards Council, "Award to Engineer Lieutenant S. U. Hardcastle, R.N. for his system of heating air in Whitehead Torpedoes. Recommendation," 3-Nov-1908, p. 5, ADM.245/1, TNA.

31. F. A. Freeth, "Profile: Sir James Swinburne," *New Scientist* (27-Feb-1958), quoted in Arapostathis and Gooday, *Patently Contestable*, 81. Freeth also wrote Swinburne's *ODNB* entry.

32. CP Department, *The Time and Range System: Report of J. Swinburne, F.R.S.* [hereafter *Report of J. Swinburne*], 5-Mar-1913, p. 7, AL.

33. *Report of J. Swinburne*, p. 3.

34. *Report of J. Swinburne*, p. 7.

35. *Report of J. Swinburne*, p. 6.

36. *Report of J. Swinburne*, p. 6.

37. *Report of J. Swinburne*, p. 4; see also enclosure in Swinburne to Black, 16-Sep-1913, Adm.CP.Patents.1897/1913, ADM.1/8464/181, TNA.

38. The Admiralty did not communicate Swinburne's judgment that the Dreyer table infringed Dumaresq's patent to Dumaresq, to whom the Admiralty had recently awarded £1,500 for his invention—considerably less than it would award to Dreyer in 1916. See Docket "Invention of Range Finding Instrument and improved pattern Electric switch," ADM.1/8330, TNA, and report of the Admiralty Awards Council, 23-Jan-1913, ADM.245/1, TNA.

39. *Report of J. Swinburne*, p. 3.

40. *Report of J. Swinburne*, p. 6.

41. Signed draft opinion by Clarke, 12-Mar-1913, PLLN.8/3.

42. Slinn, *Clifford Chance*, 29–66, 211; Pollen to Hawksley, 28-Apr-1913, PLLN. 5/2/8.

43. Coward et al. to D. of C., 15-Mar-1913, PLLN.5/2/8.

44. SecAdm to Coward et al., 30-Apr-1913, Adm.CP.16787, ibid.

45. Coward et al. to SecAdm, 5-May-1913, ibid. See also Pollen, "Detailed Reply," c. 6-May-1913, enclosed in Coward et al. to SecAdm, 7-May-1913, ibid.

46. SecAdm to Coward et al., 31-May-1913, Adm.CP.18966/180S, and 6-Jun-1913, Adm.CP19231/189S, ibid.

47. CP Department, *Historical Record of Business Negotiations*, typescript addendum, para. 211.

48. Pollen to Robinson, 16-Jun-1913, PLLN.5/3/3; Sumida, *IDNS*, 242–43.

49. Hawksley to Pollen, 10-Jun-1913, PLLN.5/2/8.

50. Pollen to Hawksley (contains quotation), 10-Jun-1913, and Argo memorandum, 30-Jun-1913, ibid.

51. Pollen to Hawksley, 5-Jul-1913, ibid.

52. Cf. Sumida, *IDNS*, 244–45, 247, 281n322.

53. Pollen to SecAdm, 8-Jul-1913, Argo A.1192/18, PLLN.5/2/8.

54. Pollen to SecAdm, 14-Jul-1913, Argo A.1195/18, ibid.

55. Pollen to SecAdm, 8-Jul-1913 (covering note to Argo A.1192/18), ibid.

56. Pollen to Spender, 11-Jul-1913, PLLN.5/4/14.

57. SecAdm to Argo, 12-Jul-1913, Adm.CP.22139, PLLN.5/2/8.

58. Pollen to SecAdm, 14-Jul-1913, ibid.

59. SecAdm to Pollen, 21-Jul-1913, Adm.CP.22454, ibid. (emphasis added).

60. Wellerstein, *Restricted Data*, esp. 145–58; see also McManus, "Science, Interrupted," 114–17.

61. Pollen to SecAdm, 22-Jul-1913, PLLN.5/2/8. He was buttressed by the receipt of Finlay's and Clarke's formal opinion of 23-Jul-1913, in ibid.

62. Minute by Tudor, 2-Feb-1914, V2 (1913), IQDNO, AL.

63. Sumida, *IDNS*, 247.

64. CP Department, *Historical Record of Business Negotiations*, typescript addendum, para. 221. See also SecAdm to CINCs et al., 29-Jul-1913, Adm.G.0721/136972–17015A, pp. 135–36, V2 (1913), IQDNO, AL.

65. Pollen to Spender, 22-Apr-1910, PLLN.5/4/14.

CHAPTER 4

1. Babcock to Craven, 29-Feb-1912, RG74/E26/B1 (red vol.), NARA-I. (There are two Box 1's in this Entry at NARA-I.)

2. For classic statements of this theme, see Hughes, *American Genesis*, and Adas, *Dominance by Design*.

3. For overviews of US naval fire control before 1914, see Wright, "Questions," P1, 60–72, and Friedman, *NF*, 182–84.

4. Hughes, *Elmer Sperry*, 153–58.

5. Hughes, *Elmer Sperry*, 103–51.

6. Wright, "Questions," P1, 62–63; Mindell, *BHAM*, 29–30.

7. See correspondence between Sperry and Overstreet in Sep-1911, Folder "Gyroscope Company, Fire Control Devices—Navy, Bureau of Ordnance, Overstreet, William—Long base range finder," B32, EAS.

8. Mindell, *BHAM*, 30–32; see also transcript of interview with Ford, 21-Feb-1942, pp. 17–18, B18a, SGC.

9. See Colvin to Sperry, 4-Jun-1914, Folder "Gyroscope Company, General Correspondence, 1908-24–30," B23, EAS.

10. US naval attaché to ONI, 20-Jan-1908, File R-2-c, Register 07–756, RG38/E98/B1256, NARA-I.

11. Pollen to Symington, 7-Jan-1913, PLLN.5/3/12. NB this letter refers to earlier correspondence from Dec-1912, which has not been found.

12. Pollen diary, 13-Aug-1913, "Letters by AHP (compiled by Maud Pollen)," Jebb Accession, PP, CAC.

13. Symington to SecNav for ONI, 15-Aug- 1913, File R-2-a, Register 3184, RG38/E98/B1254, NARA-I.

14. Ibid.

15. Symington to Sims, 8-Dec-1913, Folder "Symington, Powers," B87, Sims mss., LoC.

16. Endorsement by Strauss, n.d. but c. 15-Aug-1913, BuOrd.28499/1(L)-9/25, RG74/E25A-I/B346, NARA-I; Symington to Sims, 8-Dec-1913, Folder "Symington Powers," B87, Sims mss., LoC.

17. Gillmor to Sperry, n.d. but c. early Sep-1913, enclosed in Sperry to Overstreet, 19-Sep-1913, BuOrd.28499/3, RG74/E25A-I/B345, NARA-I.

18. Havern, "A Gunnery Manqué."

19. Sims to Symington, 13-Jan-1914, Folder "Symington, Powers," B87, Sims mss., LoC. See also Sims to Symington, 11-Jan-1914, ibid.

20. Symington to Strauss, 6-May-1914, RG74/E26/B3/V4, NARA-I.

21. McCrary to Strauss, n.d. but late March 1914, File U-1-i, Register 6925, RG38/E98/B1294, NARA-I.

22. Strauss to McCrary, 27-Apr-1914, RG74/E26/B2, NARA-I; Strauss to Symington, 15-May-1914, RG74/E26/B3/V4, NARA-I.

23. Pollen diary entry, 18-May-1914, "Letters by AHP (compiled by Maud Pollen)," Jebb Accession, PP, CAC.

24. Pollen to Daniels, 26-May-1914, SecNav.8247/248, RG80/E19A/B319, NARA-I. See also Pollen to Strauss, n.d. but probably 9-Jun-1914, RG74/E26/B3/V3, NARA-I.

25. Endorsement by Strauss to Daniels, 22-Jun-1914, SecNav.8247/248, RG80/E19A/B319, NARA-I.

26. Daniels to Pollen, 10-Jul-1914, SecNav.8247/248, ibid. See also Strauss to Pollen, 29-Jun-1914, RG74/E26/B3/V3, NARA-I.

27. See Mindell, " 'Datum for its Own Annihilation,' " 56 and 57n49. Ford's father published the newspaper in his hometown.

28. Hughes, *Elmer Sperry*, 111–12.

29. Transcript of interview with Ford, 21-Feb-1942, p. 28, B18a, SGC. See also Hughes, *Elmer Sperry*, 129–38.

30. Hughes, *Elmer Sperry*, 137.

31. Hughes, *Elmer Sperry*, 137.

32. Hughes, *Elmer Sperry*, 103.

33. MacKenzie, *Inventing Accuracy*, 35–36. One of the expert witnesses in the Anschütz-Sperry patent litigation was a young Albert Einstein.

34. Mindell, *BHAM*, 42.

35. Strauss to Daniels, 1-Sep-1914, BuOrd.28499/12-(L)-9/15, RG74/E25A-I/B345, NARA-I.

36. See Wright, "Questions," P1, 64–67.

37. BuS&A to Strauss, 17-Sep-1914, BuOrd.28499/12, RG74/E25A-I/B345, NARA-I.

38. On Sperry's clock, see Sperry to BuOrd, 14-May-1915, BuOrd.29758/44, RG74/E25A-I/B587, NARA-I. On Ford's, see Ford Marine Appliance Corporation, "Ford Range and Deflection Predictor," 15-May-1915, BuOrd.30199/1, RG74/E25A-I/B696, NARA-I.

39. Pollen's and Isherwood's US clock patents (1,162,510 and 1,162,511) were not published until November 1915.

40. See pp. 3–4 and 8 of Ford Marine Appliance Corporation, "Ford Range and Deflection Predictor," 15-May-1915, BuOrd.30199/1, RG74/E25A-I/B696, NARA-I.

41. Frucht to CoO, 11-May-1916, BuOrd.30309/3, RG74/E25A-I/B748, NARA-I.

42. Sperry's clock was ready for shipment in July 1916 and duly installed on the battleship *New York*, but for reasons unclear in the surviving documentation, the Navy decisively rejected it within a matter of months in favor of Ford's clock. See Sperry to Gillmor, 20-October-1916, Sperry.2930, Folder "Gyroscope Company, Fire Control Devices, Cpt. McEntree, William, 1917–27," B32, EAS; Mindell, *BHAM*, 34–35.

43. Towers report, "Argo Fire Control System," 5-Jan-1916, File R-2-a, Register 6128, RG38/E98/B1254, NARA-I.

44. Towers to ONI, 26-Jul-1916, File U-1-i, Register 6925, RG38/E98/B1294, NARA-I.

45. Symington to Sims, 26-Jul-1916, Folder "Symington, Powers," B87, Sims mss., LoC.

46. Overstreet to CoO, 29-Sep-1927, BuOrd.A13-4/S71(Sperry/10), RG74/E25B/B1406, NARA-I.

47. Earle to CNO, 18-Apr-1917, BuOrd.32156(A2)-4/25, RG74/E25A-I/B1523, NARA-I; Gillmor to Sperry, 1-May-1917, Folder "Gyroscope Company Administrative Records, London Office," B22, EAS; Sims to Daniels, 11-Jul-1917, Reel 61, Daniels mss., LoC.

48. Gillmor to Sperry, 1-May-1917, Folder "Gyroscope Company Administrative Records, London Office," B22, EAS.

49. See Sims to Earle, 20-Nov-1917, Folder "Earle, Ralph, 1913–1917," B55, Sims mss., LoC; and Gillmor to Sperry, 1-May-1917, Folder "Gyroscope Company Administrative Records, London Office," B22, EAS.

50. Pollen to Gillmor, 17-Apr-1916, PLLN.5/3/12.

51. Sumida, *IDNS*, 305–6.

52. Towers to ONI, 26 July 1916, File U-1-i, Register 6925, RG38/E98/B1294, NARA-I; Lambert, *Planning Armageddon*, 241, 246, 264, and *passim*.

53. Gillmor to Sperry, 13-Jul-1916 [hereafter Gillmor Report], p. 4, enclosed in Towers to ONI, 26-Jul-1916, File U-1-i, Register 6925, RG38/E98/B1294, NARA-I.

54. Gillmor Report, p. 18.

55. Gillmor Report, p. 47.

56. Gillmor Report, p. 53.

57. Gillmor Report, pp. 2–3.

58. Gillmor Report, pp. 45–46; see also p. 13.

59. Gillmor Report, p. 3.

60. Bristol to Twining, 25-Jun-1911, RG74/E26/B1 (loose papers), NARA-I.

61. Craven to Twining, 12-Dec-1911, RG74/E26/B1 (red vol.), NARA-I.

62. See Epstein, "Harnessing Invention."

63. Gillmor Report, p. 50.

64. "Tacit knowledge" is a concept from the history of science and technology. See, e.g., Collins, *Tacit and Explicit Knowledge*.

65. I counted the number of patents in the appendix of Hughes, *Elmer Sperry*.

66. Hughes, *Elmer Sperry*, 17–19, 63–70.

67. Sperry to Gillmor, 16-Aug-1916, Folder "Gyroscope Company, Fire Control, General Correspondence," B32, EAS.

68. Sperry to Gillmor, 25-Aug-1916, Folder "Administrative Records, R.E. Gillmor," B24, EAS.

69. Sperry to Gillmor, 13-Feb-1917, Folder "Gyroscope Company, Fire Control Devices, Naval Bureau of Ordnance, Comm. F. C. Martin," B32, EAS.

70. Sperry to Gillmor, 20-Oct-1916, Folder "Gyroscope Company, Fire Control Devices, Cpt. McEntree, William, 1917–27," B32, EAS.

71. Sperry to Gillmor, 16-Aug-1916, Folder "Gyroscope Company, Fire Control, General Correspondence," ibid.; and Sperry to Martin, 17-Aug-1916, Folder "Gyroscope Company, Fire Control Devices, Naval Bureau of Ordnance, Comm. F. C. Martin," ibid.

72. Ford to Martin, 4-Oct-1916, BuOrd.30309/17, RG74/E25A-I/B748, NARA-I.

73. Sperry to Gillmor, 25-Aug-1916, Folder "Administrative Records, R.E. Gillmor," B24, EAS.

74. Sperry to Gillmor, 23-Sep-[1916], Folder "Gyroscope Company, Fire Control, General Correspondence," B32, EAS.

75. Sperry to Gillmor, 20-Oct-1916, Folder "Gyroscope Company, Fire Control Devices, Cpt. McEntree, William, 1917–27," ibid.

76. *Harvard College, Class of 1886, Secretary's Report No. 6, December 1906* (New York: 1907), 137–38. Pollen also received legal advice from Edmund Hurlburt Parry, a Washington, DC–based lawyer, for which see Pollen diary entries of 22 and 29 June 1917, PLLN.5/1/38. On the critical role played by patent attorneys (and agents), see Swanson, "The Emergence of the Professional Patent Practitioner."

77. On Linotype, see Pollen diary entry, n.d. but c. Dec-1906, "Letters by AHP (compiled by Maud Pollen)," Jebb Accession, PP, CAC; on the friendship, see, e.g., Pollen diary entry, 9-Jul-1917, PLLN.5/1/38. Rogers was married to the daughter of Stilson Hutchins, the American who arranged the sale of the Linotype rights to Britain (better known as the founder of the *Washington Post*) (see "Hutchins, Hon. Stilson," *Granite Monthly* 44, no. 5 (May 1912): 158).

78. Article IV, Paris Convention for the Protection of Industrial Property, signed 20-Mar-1883, *British and Foreign State Papers*, vol. 74, pp. 44–51. This period was originally six months under the 1883 Paris Convention, but it was extended to twelve months under the 1911 Amendment to the Paris Convention (for which see *British and Foreign State Papers*, vol. 104, p. 116–32). Under the 1897 enabling US legislation, the period was two years (see "An Act Revising and Amending the Statutes Relating to Patents," 3-Mar-1897, 29 Stat. 692).

79. See Isasawa, "The Doctrine of Self-Executing Treaties in the United States," 627–92, esp. 644, 658, 668, 685. The enabling legislation was "An Act Revising and Amending the Statutes Relating to Patents," 3-Mar-1897, 29 Stat. 692. Cf. Khan, *The Democratization of Invention*, 16–17.

80. Pollen began preparing to file foreign patent applications in late 1912, making late 1910 the rough cutoff point. Only three of his fourteen secret patent applications were filed after that point, meaning that eleven were totally ineligible and that the three filed for in January 1911 were in a legal gray area.

81. Sperry to Gillmor, 25-Aug-1916, Folder "Administrative Records, R.E. Gillmor," B24, EAS. A 1911 amendment to the Paris Convention had muddied the legal waters by raising the possibility, left to the discretion of the member nations, that an inventor could "avail himself of the priority of an anterior filing" (the official US translation, for which see 38 Stat. 1645). The United States had not passed any enabling legislation regarding this amendment when Pollen began to prepare to file for US patents. His

British lawyers initially advised him that the publication date, rather than the filing date, for his British patents would start the countdown on his filing period for US patents, so he requested that the Admiralty delay its waiver of secrecy and publication of the British patents until he had had time to prepare his US applications (Pollen to SecAdm, 8-Oct-1912, Argo.A.1120/18, PLLN.5/2/7). Further investigation by his lawyers revealed that "[i]t is a matter of doubt whether the English Secret Patents may not bar the possibility of getting any American Patents at all" (Pollen to D. of C., 18-Dec-1912, Argo.A.1144/18, PLLN.5/2/7)—as indeed they did.

82. On the challenges of translation in another context, see Beauchamp, *Invented by Law*, 109–31, 139–45.

83. Blair memorandum, 24-Apr-[1919], BuOrd.34086, RG74/E25A-I/B2346, NARA-I.

84. Compare the copy of GBP 19,627/1911 in T.173/91-P10, TNA with the original specifications of USP 1,162,510, Paper #1, filed 5-Sep-1913, PF.1,162,510, RG241, NARA-KC.

85. Newton to Rogers, Kennedy & Campbell, Paper #2, 29-Sep-1913, PF.1,162,510, RG241, NARA-KC.

86. See Rogers, Kennedy & Campbell, Amendment A, Paper #3, filed 15-Sep-1914, ibid. The eight claims in the original specifications increased to twenty-seven claims in this amendment. As finally issued, the patent contained nineteen claims.

87. Why Pollen did not seek copyright protection or a method (a.k.a. process) patent is an interesting question. As for the former, the Supreme Court's ruling in *Baker v. Selden*, which concerned a book of "mathematical science," cannot have provided grounds for confidence, since it did not confer "an exclusive right to the methods of operation which he propounds" (101 US 99 at 103, 1879; see also Samuelson, "The Story of *Baker v. Selden*," 159–93, esp. 176–77). As for the latter, much like pioneer patents, method patents overcame some of the normal limitations on patent scope (see Bracha, *Owning Ideas*, 284–97). Perhaps, for that reason, they required the same heroic-inventor status, difficult to attain for foreigners, as pioneer patents? Perhaps Rogers did not know this particular corner of the IP system well enough to try?

88. Khan, *The Democratization of Invention*, esp. 55–57.

89. Sperry to Gillmor, 20-Oct-1916, Folder "Gyroscope Company, Fire Control Devices, Cpt. McEntree, William, 1917–27," B32, EAS.

90. Sperry to Gillmor, 20-Oct-1916, ibid.

91. Sperry to Gillmor, 13-Feb-1917, ibid.; Gillmor to Sperry, 28-Nov-1916 and 5-Apr-1917, Folder "Gyroscope Company Administrative Records, London Office," B22, EAS.

92. For details of Tobey's service, see McGowan to SecNav, 29-Jan-1920, BuS&A.146-2, Folder "Ed 64, 2 of 3," RG143/E8/B915, NARA-I.

93. See, e.g., Tobey to Earle, 18-May-1917, BuOrd.28499/74, RG74/E25A-I/B346, NARA-I.

94. Babcock to Craven, 29-Feb-1912, RG74/E26/B1 (red vol.), NARA-I.

95. Sperry to Gillmor, 18-Apr-1916, Folder "Administrative Records, R.E. Gillmor," B24, EAS.

96. Sims to McGowan, 5-Jul-1917, Folder "McGowan, Samuel," B71, Sims mss., LoC. See also Sims to McGowan, 1-Jul-1918, ibid., saying that McGowan's suggestion of reassigning Tobey from Sims' staff "came pretty nearly giving me heart failure."

97. Quotation from Tobey to Higgins, 22-May-1917, PLLN.5/3/12. For the official side, see Tobey to Pollen, 28-Aug-1916, ibid. For further material on the personal side, see Tobey to Mary O'Hea [Pollen's secretary], 21-Sep-1916, ibid.; Pollen to Maud Pollen, 23-Aug-1917, PLLN.5/1/38.

98. Strauss [unsigned] to Tobey, 5-Jan-1917, BuOrd.28499/112, RG74/E25A-I/B346, NARA-I; Pollen to Tobey, 29-Mar-1917, PLLN.5/1/38. See also Strauss to Sperry, 4-Mar-1917, Folder "Gyroscope Company, Fire Control Devices, Cmdr. W. R. Auken," General Correspondence," B32, EAS.

99. Martin to Sperry, 24-Feb-1917, Folder "Gyroscope Company, Fire Control Devices, Naval Bureau of Ordnance, Comm. F. C. Martin," B32, EAS.

100. Martin [unsigned] to Earle, 2-Mar-1917, BuOrd.28499, RG74/E25A-I/B346, NARA-I.

101. Earle to CNO, 18-Apr-1917, BuOrd.32156(A2)-4/25, RG74/E25A-I/B1523, NARA-I.

102. Navy League to Earle, 28-Jun-1917, BuOrd.28499/21, RG74/E25A-I/B345, NARA-I.

103. Buchan to Pollen, 16-May-1917, 21-May-1917, 24-May-1917, and 22-Jan-1918, PLLN.5/1/38; see also Sims to Earle, 31-May-1917, Folder "Earle, Ralph, 1913–1917," B55, Sims mss., LoC.

104. Tobey to Earle, 18-May-1917, BuOrd.28499/74, RG74/E25A-I/B346, NARA-I.

105. He first appears in the April 1916 *Navy List* with 1-Jan-1916 listed as his seniority date.

106. Earle to Sims, 9-Feb-1918, Folder "Earle, Ralph, Ja-Je 1918," B55, Sims mss., LoC.

107. Pollen to Maud Pollen, 12-Oct-1917, PLLN.5/1/38.

108. Pollen to Earle, 8-Oct-1917, BuOrd.28499/35, RG74/E25A-I/B345, NARA-I.

109. Sperry to Gillmor, 25-Jul-1917, Folder "Gyroscope Company, Fire Control Devices, Naval Bureau of Ordnance, Comm. F. C. Martin," B32, EAS. In this document, Pollen is referred to as "Pollak."

110. Down to Browning, 27-Jun-1917, p. 7, Docket "United States Navy. Proposed visit of British Naval Technical Experts. Commander R. T. Down," ADM.137/1621, TNA.

111. Earle to SecNav, 23-Jun-1917, BuOrd.28499(A2)-7/3, RG74/E25A-I/B346, NARA-I.

112. Earle to Sims, 20-Jun-1917, Folder "Earle, Ralph, 1913–1917," B55, Sims mss., LoC.

113. Earle to Sims, 29-Dec-1917, ibid.

114. Gillmor to Sperry, 19-Oct-1917, Folder "Gyroscope Company Administrative Records, London Office," B22, EAS.

115. Commander, Battleship Force to CINC Atlantic, 5-Oct-1916, quoted in Mindell, *BHAM*, 44.

116. Quoted in Earle to Pollen, 19-Nov-1917, BuOrd.28499/53(A2)-0, RG74/E25A-I/B345, NARA-I. The original of Pollen's letter has not been found.

117. Earle to Pollen, 19-Nov-1917, BuOrd.28499/53(A2)-0, RG74/E25A-I/B345, NARA-I.

118. Pollen to Maud Pollen, 30-Nov-1917, PLLN.5/1/38.

119. Pollen to Earle, 27-Nov-1917, BuOrd.28499/58, RG74/E25A-I/B345, NARA-I.

120. Pollen to Earle, 28-Nov-1917, BuOrd.28499, RG74/E25A-I/B346, NARA-I.

121. Martin to Bingham, 14-May-1917, BuOrd.30309, RG74/E25A-I/B743, NARA-I.

122. Mayo to CNO, 4-Feb-1918, para. 11, DeptNav.C-25–29, RG80/UD-E2/B58, NARA-I.

123. Van Auken to BuOrd and BuEng, 8-Apr-1918, para. 19, BuOrd.29068/229, RG74/E25A-I/B429, NARA-I.

124. Tobey report, 10-Aug-1917, File U-2-e, Register 9124, RG38/E98/B1334, NARA-I. Tobey did not specify a particular mark of the Dreyer table.

125. Kimmel to Plunkett, 3-Dec-1917, p. 5, File R-2-d, Register 8750, RG38/E98/B1257, NARA-I.

126. Van Auken to BuOrd and BuEng, 8-Apr-1918, para. 20, BuOrd.29068/229, RG74/E25A-I/B429, NARA-I.

127. Van Auken to Earle, 3-May-1918, BuOrd.28499, RG74/E25A-I/B346, NARA-I. See also Earle to FIC, 27-Dec-1917, BuOrd.30309/129(S1)-0, RG74/E25A-I/B747, NARA-I, and Earle to CINC Atlantic Fleet, 18-May-1918, para. 7, DeptNav.C-26–245, RG80/UD-E2/B71, NARA-I.

128. Van Auken to Earle, 3-May-1918, BuOrd.28499, RG74/E25A-I/B346, NARA-I.

129. Note here Sumida, *IDNS*, 326n127. Although he got some details wrong (for instance about the nature of the Mark II Ford rangekeeper), considering how far beyond the scope of his book the development of the Ford rangekeeper was, Sumida's insight into the gradual incorporation of automatic bearing generation in the Ford rangekeeper was remarkable.

130. Van Auken to Earle, 3-May-1918, BuOrd.28499, RG74/E25A-I/B346, NARA-I.

131. Van Auken to Earle, 3-May-1918, ibid.

132. Van Auken, *Notes on a Half Century of United States Naval Ordnance*, 27–28.

133. I became more familiar than anyone should be with the Navy's usual standards for issuing new Mark and Mod. numbers while working on *Torpedo*. The Mark II Ford rangekeeper was a stripped-down version of the Mark I intended for local turret control on battleships and as the primary fire-control system on smaller ships like destroyers.

134. Terrill, "Notes on the Theory of the Ford Range Keeper," p. 2, n.d. but spring 1918 to July 1919, Folder Conf. 59(93), RG38/E178/B3, NARA-I. Compare to p. 2 of Pollen's and Isherwood's USP 1,162,510.

135. Sadler to Rosenbaum, Stockbridge & Borst, Paper #4, 10-May-1917, PF.1,317,915, RG241, NARA-KC.

136. Compare Ford's USP 1,317,915, "Mechanical Movement," filed 13-Mar-1916, patented 7-Oct-1919, with Pollen's and Isherwood's GBP 17,441/1912, "Improvements in Ball and Disk Variable Speed Mechanism," application filed 4-Apr-1912, accepted 24-Oct-1912. Ford's rollers 18 functioned as Isherwood's rollers 67.

137. USS *Louisiana* report, 31-Mar-1919, BuOrd.28499/711 (also marked 111), p.4, RG74/E25A-I/B345, NARA-I.

138. See Anderson et al. to Mayo, 1-Mar-1918, enclosed in May to SecNav, 21-Mar-1918, BuOrd.28499/79, RG74/E25A-I/B346, NARA-I; Davis to Earle, 12-Apr-1918 and 12-Jun-1918, ibid.; Earle to Mayo, 10-Jul-1918, BuOrd.28499/99(L2)-0, ibid. Of course, the Bureau did not apprise Pollen of his influence, for which see Earle to Pollen, 5-Aug-1918, BuOrd.28499/94, enclosing digest dated 29-Jul-1918, ibid.

139. Ford to Earle, 17-Dec-1917, BuOrd.30309/129(S1)-0, RG74/E25A-I/B747, NARA-I.

140. Mossoff, "Patents as Constitutional Private Property," 702–11; O'Connor, "Taking, Tort, or Crown Right," 153–69.

141. 36 Stat. 851. As O'Connor notes ("Taking, Tort, or Crown Right," 183–85), Congress did not use the term "infringement," since patent infringement was a tort, and settled law at this time held that the government was immune to suits for tortious wrongdoing. For an introduction to sovereign immunity and the debates it has provoked, see Kovacs, "Revealing Redundancy."

142. 224 US 290.

143. O'Connor, "Taking, Tort, or Crown Right," 183–88; see also Epstein, *Torpedo*, 143–45.

144. 246 US 28.

145. O'Connor, "Taking, Tort, or Crown Right," 188 (c.f. Strauss to Solicitor, 23-Aug-1916, and Roosevelt to Strauss, 12-Sep-1916, BuOrd.31734(A1)-8/28, RG74/E25A-I/B1184, NARA-I); Public Law 65-182, "An Act Making appropriations for the naval service," 40 Stat. 704 at 705.

146. Earle to FIC, 27-Dec-1917, BuOrd.30309/129(S1)-0, RG74/E25A-I/B747, NARA-I.

147. Roosevelt to FIC, 30-Apr-1918, DeptNav.26817–88, RG80/E19A/B2023, NARA-I. Ford's second request does not survive, but Roosevelt's letter dates it as 25-Apr-1918. For his dining with Pollen, see Pollen diary entries of 25-Jun-1917 and 1-Nov-1917, PLLN.5/1/38.

The Bureau of Ordnance filed its copy of Roosevelt's letter—the copy that historians have cited (Wright, "Questions," P3, 62 and 96n218; Mindell, *BHAM*, 42 and 346n64)—with a bundle of correspondence (BuOrd.30309) regarding Ford's clock (as BuOrd.30309/274, in RG74/E25A-I/B747, NARA-I), rendering the letter's connection with the *Cramp* decision archivally invisible.

148. USS *Louisiana* report, 31-Mar-1919, BuOrd.28499/711 (also marked 111), RG74/E25A-I/B345, NARA-I.

149. Earle to Pollen, 8-Nov-1918, BuOrd.28499/10, RG74/E25A-I/B345, NARA-I.

150. This document is undated but is clipped to a letter from Pollen to Earle dated 12-Apr-1918 (BuOrd.28499, RG74/E25A-I/B346, NARA-I), so it presumably dates from around that time.

CHAPTER 5

1. Epstein, "The Conundrum of American Power in the Age of World War I."

2. See the draft clause written by the Navy Solicitor in Neagle to Strauss, 22-Sep-1916, BuOrd.31734/2, RG74/E25A-I/B1184, NARA-I, likely included in a letter from Martin to Ford in late September 1916, for the existence of which see Ford to Martin, 4-Oct-1916, BuOrd.30309/17, RG74/E25A-I/B748, NARA-I.

3. Mindell, *BHAM*, 44, 55.

4. On Bingham, apparently a complicated personality, see Sims to Mayo, 29-Jun-1916, Folder "Mayo, H.T., 1914–18," B71, Sims mss., LOC. On tension between Bingham and the Bureau, see Earle to Mayo, 8-Dec-1917, BuOrd.30309/94(L2), RG74/E25A-I/B748, NARA-I, and Van Auken to Earle, 29-Dec-1917, BuOrd.30309/136, RG74/E25A-I/B747, ibid.

5. CNO to Mayo, 12-Jan-1918, enclosed in Mayo to CNO, 4-Feb-1918, DeptNav.C-25–29, RG80/UD-E2/B58, NARA-I; Mayo to CNO, 16-Jan-1818, enclosed in

DeptNav.C-25–29, ibid. For a pioneering deconstruction of the usual knight-dragon narrative, which explores the possibilities for subaltern solidarity between dragons and princesses too intelligent to marry chivalric buffoons, see Patricia C. Wrede, *Dealing with Dragons*.

6. USS *Louisiana* report, 31-Mar-1919, pp. 8–9, BuOrd.28499/111, RG74/E25A-I/B345, NARA-I. See also Earle to Ford NIO, 13-Feb-1918, BuOrd.30309(L2)-1–26–18, RG74/E25A-I/B743, NARA-I; Van Auken to Desk A, 14-Mar-1918, BuOrd.30309/279, RG74/E25A-II/B54, NARA-I; and Wright, "Questions," P1, 56. For an unfavorable comparison of Ford Instrument's workmanship with Elliotts's, see Kimmel to Plunkett, 3-Dec-1917, p. 4, File R-2-d, Register 8750, RG38/E98/B1257, NARA-I.

7. Bingham to Rodman, 2-Apr-1918, Folder "Correspondence, 1917–19," B1, Bingham mss., LOC. See also Martin to Bingham, 14-May-1917, BuOrd.30309, RG74/E25A-I/B743, NARA-I.

8. Padfield, *Aim Straight*, 189–92, 197, 206–12; Sumida, *IDNS*, 90, 146–55, 206–7, 252; Friedman, *NF*, 73–81, 104–5.

9. For the Vickers offer, see Van Auken, "Memorandum on Vickers Follow-the-Pointer System," 21-Jun-1918, BuOrd.33921/80, RG74/E25A-I/B2277, NARA-I.

10. Strauss to BuC&R, 16-Mar-1914, BuOrd.29048, RG74/E25A-I/B414, NARA-I.

11. See, e.g., CINC Atlantic Fleet to Battleship Squadron, 14-May-1915, BuOrd.29048/94, RG74/E25A-I/B422, NARA-I, and Symington to Sims, 26-Jul-1916, Folder "Symington, Powers," B87, Sims mss., LOC; Sperry to Martin, 8-Nov-1916, Folder "Gyroscope Company, Fire Control Devices, Naval Bureau of Ordnance, Comm. F. C. Martin," B32, EAS; Strauss to Sperry, 10-Nov-1916, ibid.; Sperry to BuOrd, 20-Nov-1916, ibid.

12. "Follow-the-pointer" systems were similar to "zero-reading" systems, in which the gunner attempted to keep two pointers (one showing actual gun settings, the other showing predicted gun settings, as in a follow-the-pointer system) hovering over the zero point on a dial. See Gillmor to Sperry, 2-Nov-1924, Folder "Gyroscope Company, Fire Control Devices, Battle Tracer," B32, EAS. Both follow-the-pointer systems and zero-reading systems bore a family resemblance to straight-line plotting, as adopted by the Royal Navy during World War I and discussed in chapter 6. Follow-the-pointer displays, zero-reading displays, and straight-line plotting all sought to minimize the need for mental calculation by operators by displaying two sets of data in a user-friendly way, in order to enable them to "tune" their machines such that actual data matched predicted data, or vice versa.

13. "Follow-the-Pointer Method in Elevation for turrets," 5-Jul-1918, enclosed in Earle to CINC Atlantic, 8-Jul-1918, BuOrd.29048(L2), RG74/E25A-I/B414, NARA-I. In the archival box, the memorandum is separated from the covering letter. See also Naval Proving Ground, Indian Head to BuOrd, 19-Jun-1915, BuOrd.29048/100, RG74/E25A-I/B422, NARA-I.

14. Gillmor to Sperry, 13-Jul-1916 [hereafter Gillmor Report], p. 53, File U-1-i, Register 6925, RG38/E98/B1294, NARA-I.

15. Gillmor to Sperry, 17-Jan-1917, pp. 3–4, Folder "Gyroscope Company, Fire Control Devices, Naval Bureau of Ordnance, Comm. F. C. Martin," B32, EAS.

16. Sperry to Gillmor, 20-Oct-1916, Sperry.2930, Folder "Gyroscope Company, Fire Control Devices, Cpt. McEntree, William, 1917–27," ibid.

17. Sperry to Martin, 21-Feb-1917, BuOrd.29758/150, RG74/E25A-I/B586, NARA-I.

18. Gillmor to Sperry, 17-Jan-1917, Folder "Gyroscope Company, Fire Control Devices, Naval Bureau of Ordnance, Comm. F. C. Martin," B32, EAS.

19. Gillmor Report, p. 55.

20. CoO to JAG, 1-May-1925, BuOrd.37182/34-(L5)-0, RG74/E25A-I/B2924, NARA-I.

21. Earle to SecNav, 26-May-1917, BuOrd.37182, RG74/E25A-I/B2924, NARA-I.

22. Kearney to FIC, 26-Jul-1917, BuOrd.32649(L2)-8/20, RG74/E25A-I/B1686, NARA-I.

23. Kearney to Nav Att London, 15-Aug-1917, BuOrd.37182, RG74/E25A-I/B2924, NARA-I.

24. Down to Browning, 27-Jun-1917, p. 5, Docket "United States Navy. Proposed visit of British Naval Technical Experts. Commander R. T. Down," ADM.137/1621, TNA.

25. Castle to CNO, 29-Aug-1917, BuOrd.35371/348, RG74/E25A-II/B117, NARA-I.

26. Earle to Sims, 4-Oct-1917, Folder "Earle, Ralph, 1913–1917," B55, Sims mss., LoC.

27. Symington to Sims, 30-Mar-1917, Folder "Symington, Powers," B87, ibid.

28. Waterfield to Barstow, 15-Apr-1918, Treas.9237/18, T.1/12325, TNA; the edge of the document has been cut off, requiring surmise as to a missing word, which I think is probably "to." For more on the context of this conference, see Epstein, "Intellectual Property and National Security," 141–42.

29. Jellicoe minute, 3-Dec-1917, Adm.G.40672, ADM.137/1621, TNA.

30. Murray, "Notes for Conference on the rules for supply of secret information to Allied and Neutral Representatives," enclosed in Murray to Hope [Deputy First Sea Lord], 24-Oct-1918, Adm.CSecO4934/19, ADM.1/8541/280, TNA.

31. Rev. Stat. 4894.

32. See *Annual Report of the Commissioner of the Patents for the Year 1913* (Washington, DC: Government Printing Office, 1914), xi.

33. See SecNav to CommPat, 15-Jan-1910, File 1–28, RG241/EA1–1038/B114, NARA-II.

34. Rev. Stat. 490–92.

35. Rev. Stat. 4904.

36. Patents and Designs Act of 1907 (7 Edw. 7. Ch. 29), sec. 7, 9, and 11.

37. Public Law 64-143, "An Act Making appropriations for fortifications and other works of defense, for the armament thereof, for the procurement of heavy ordnance for trial and service, and for other purposes," 39 Stat. 345 at 348 (1916).

38. By contrast, British law required the government to make only "the benefit" of the patent its property, leaving legal title to the patent-owner (Patents and Designs Act of 1907, sec. 30, clause 1).

39. See CoO to JAG, 7-Dec-1923, BuOrd.39853(Sp-1)-0, RG74/E25A-I/B3436, NARA-I; SecNav order of 25-Feb-1924, BuOrd.39853/35, ibid.; JAG to BuOrd, 15-Feb-1927, BuOrd.A13–1(2/14), RG74/E25B/B1406, NARA-I; and "Department of Justice Patent Policy Survey. Navy Department," n.d. but 1940, pp. 54–56, Folder "Navy Department," RG60/E418/B2, NARA-II.

40. Daniels and Krige, *Knowledge Regulation and National Security in Postwar America*, 37–41.

41. CommPat to SecInterior, 14-May-1917, File 2–39, RG241/EA1–1038/B153, NARA-II.

42. Rule 77, *Rules of Practice in the United States Patent Office, Revised-Jan-1, 1916 (Reprint of November 6, 1919)* (Washington, DC: Government Printing Office, 1919), 26. According to the front matter of the 1919 edition, this amendment was made on 19-Jun-1917. But the statute upon which at least one contemporary expert believed it rested (see Shoemaker, "Secrecy of War Invention," 112) was not passed until October 1917, in the form of Public Law 65-80, "An Act to Prevent the publication of inventions by the grant of patents that might be detrimental to the public safety or convey useful information to the enemy, to stimulate invention, and provide adequate protection to owners of patents, and for other purposes," 40 Stat. 394 (1917).

43. Public Law 65-80, "An Act to Prevent the publication of inventions," 40 Stat. 394 (1917); and Public Law 65-91, "Trading with the Enemy Act," 40 Stat. 411 (1917). See also Coates, "The Secret Life of Statutes," 156–60; Steen, *The American Synthetic Organic Chemicals Industry*, 149–71; Daniels and Krige, *Knowledge Regulation and National Security in Postwar America*, 37–41.

44. Woodrow Wilson, Executive Order 2729-A, 12-Oct-1917, "Vesting Power and Authority in Designated Officers and Making Rules and Regulations under Trading with the Enemy Act and Title VII of the Act Approved June 15, 1917," *FRUS* 1917, Supplement 2, *The World War*, Volume II, Document 101, p. 968, https://history.state.gov /historicaldocuments/frus1917Supp02v02/d101.

45. *The Official Gazette of the United States Patent Office* 247, no. 4 (26-Feb-1918): 749.

46. British Embassy to State Dept, 20-Jul-1917, enclosed in Polk to SecInterior, 31-Jul-1917, State.811.542/79, File 1–132, RG241/EA1–1038/B142, NARA-II.

47. Polk to SecInterior, 28-Sep-1917, ibid.

48. Lambert, *Planning Armageddon*, 353–61, 428–29.

49. For the loss of the letter and ensuing finger-pointing, see SecInterior to SecState, 8-Aug-1918, and AsstSecState to SecInterior, 17-Sep-1918, File 1–132, RG241/ EA1–1038/B142, NARA-II.

50. See, e.g., Temple-Franks to Ewing, 19-Jun-1917, and Ewing to Temple-Franks, 7-Aug-1917, ibid.

51. MacDougall for CoO, 14-Sep-1917, BuOrd.37182, RG74/E25A-I/B2924, NARA-I.

52. Earle to Nav Att London, 4-Oct-1917, BuOrd.29048/747(A2)-11/4, RG74/E25A-I/B420, NARA-I.

53. Earle to Sims, 1-Jun-1918, BuOrd.33291(A2)-0, Folder "Patents Royalties etc," RG74/E25A-I/B2277, NARA-I. See also Norton to Earle, 28-May-1918, BuOrd.33291(S1–2)-0, ibid.

54. Sheridan to FIC, 30-Nov-1917, quoted in Ford to Vickers, 4-Dec-1917, enclosed in FIC to BuOrd, 19-Sep-1918, BuOrd.29048/1635, RG74/E25A-I/B416, NARA-I.

55. For Vickers's relationship with Cooke and Argo, see Documents 618 and 771, VA; Isherwood's testimony, 21-Feb-1939, *Supplemental Record*, pp. 83–84, EDNY Equity Case File #8432, RG21/B1381, NARA-NY. The Vickers documents indicate that the purchase of Argo's patent rights occurred in 1929, but that date cannot be correct, since Vickers paid Argo royalties as early as 1926, and Argo was wound up in 1927 (see BT.31/3343/96287, TNA).

56. For the Gray-Isherwood connection, see Isherwood's testimony, 21-Feb-1939, *Supplemental Record*, pp. 84–85, EDNY Equity Case File #8432, RG21/B1381, NARA-NY.

57. Vickers's corporate memory performed this airbrushing by understating the mechanization of fire control before World War I (enabling it to date Gray's postwar

work under Vickers's auspices as a radical break from anything that had come before), by reducing Pollen's output to the plotting table rather than the clock (enabling it to sever Gray's interest in computers from Pollen), and by attributing the Vickers-Ford Instrument connection to Gray's interest in Ford's work on film projectors, which was not what Ford worked on (enabling it to ignore the prior connection between Ford Instrument and Pollen). See "Note of conversations with Mr P.G.H Jeffrey, (Superintendent) and Mr H.C. White (Technical Manager), and of an interview with Mr L. Lane (Section Leader) at Crayford Works on the 14th-Jan-1960," Document 674, VA. See also "Cooke, Troughton & Simms Limited. Recording by Mr. E. Wilfred Taylor lately joint Managing Director," 16-May-1957, Document 618, VA.

58. Arwine to CoO, 17-Oct-1922, BuOrd.35156/1008, RG74/E25A-II/B71, NARA-I.

59. Earle to Ford NIO, 25-Feb-1918, BuOrd.29048(L2)-3/15, RG74/E25A-I/B414, NARA-I. See also Friedman, *NF*, 78 and 185.

60. Earle to Ford NIO, 25-Feb-1918, BuOrd.29048(L2)-3/15, RG74/E25A-I/B414, NARA-I; Norton to CoO, 28-May-1918, BuOrd.33291(S1–2)-0, Folder "Patents Royalties etc," RG74/E25A-I/B2277, NARA-I.

61. Henderson to SecRCAI, 22-Jul-1930, paras. 12–17, and enclosed Schedule A, Group A, pp. 22–30, T.173/273-P2, TNA.

62. The Henderson Firing Gear is described in GBP 3,683/1915, "Improvements in and relating to Fire-Control Apparatus for Naval Guns," applied for 8-Mar-1915, complete specifications left 8-Oct-1915, complete specifications accepted 1-Mar-1916 (but withheld from publication), and published 6-Jan-1927. Two other British patents (6,977/1915 and 16,669/1915) covered elements of the Henderson Firing Gear, but 3,683/1915 was the master patent, for which see ToH, 30-Apr-1923, p. 16, T.173/653-P1, TNA. See also "Director Firing Handbook" (1917), pp. 96–97, ADM.186/227, TNA.

In "Harnessing Invention," I misidentified Henderson as the inventor of Gyro Director Training rather than the Henderson Firing Gear. The actual inventors of GDT were John Dove and Hugh Clausen, as discussed in the next chapter.

63. Gillmor to Sperry, 17-Jan-1917, Folder "Gyroscope Company, Fire Control Devices, Naval Bureau of Ordnance, Comm. F. C. Martin," B32, EAS.

64. Schuyler to Earle, 6-Feb-1918, BuOrd.32977/35, RG74/E25A-I/B1924, NARA-I. See also Frederick Van Auken to BuOrd and BuEng, 8-Apr-1918, para. 19, BuOrd.29068/229, RG74/E25A-I/B429, NARA-I.

65. Earle to DNI, 23-Mar-1918, BuOrd.29048(L2)-0, RG74/E25A-I/B414, NARA-I.

66. Admiralty to Elliotts, 30-Aug-1918, enclosed in Schuyler to SecNav, 25-Sep-1919, BuOrd.37711/23, RG74/E25A-I/B2995, NARA-I.

67. Gillmor endorsement, 10-Jan-1918, BuOrd.29048/837, RG74/E25A-I/B419, NARA-I; Earle to Stratton, 26-Feb-1918, BuOrd.29048/952(L2)-4–15–18, ibid.

68. Mindell, *BHAM*, 44–46.

69. See the correspondence between Sperry and Martin from Nov-1916 to Jan-1917 in Folder "Gyroscope Company, Fire Control Devices, CPT McEntee, William," B32, EAS.

70. Van Auken to Sperry, 10-Nov-1917 and 15-Dec-1917, ibid.

71. Van Auken memorandum, 14-Mar-1918, BuOrd.30309/279, RG74/E25A-II/B54, NARA-I.

72. Gillmor to AsstSecNav, 13-Jun-1918, quoted in Mindell, *BHAM*, 46.

73. Earle to Sheridan, 12-Jun-1918, BuOrd.33291(S1–2)-0, Folder "Patents Royalties etc," RG74/E25A-I/B2277, NARA-I.

74. Ford to BuOrd, 18-Jul-1918, BuOrd.29048/1426, RG74/E25A-I/B417, NARA-I.

75. McCormick to CoO, 26-Jul-1918, BuOrd.35856/1, RG74/E25A-I/B2676, NARA-I.

76. Earle to FIC, 31-Aug-1918, BuOrd.29048(Sp-1), RG74/E25A-I/B414, NARA-I. See also BuS&A to BuOrd, 29-Jun-1918, BuOrd.29048/1339, and Blair to Van Auken, 26-Aug-1918, RG74/E25A-I/B417, NARA-I.

77. Tobey to Earle, 30-Aug-1918, BuOrd.33291/103, Folder "Patents Royalties etc.," RG74/E25A-I/B2277, NARA-I.

78. Specifically, the Bureau would have the right to use the Vickers system for main batteries without payment to Ford Instrument, but Ford Instrument would control the rights for any other use of the Vickers system (for instance, in torpedo-defense batteries).

79. Ford to BuOrd, 19-Sep-1918, BuOrd.29048/1635, and 20-Sep-1918, BuOrd.29048/1634, RG74/E25A-I/B416, NARA-I.

80. Earle to Sheridan, 21-Sep-1918, BuOrd.33921/82(SP-2)-10/1, RG74/E25A-II/B89, NARA-I.

81. Earle to Sims, 25-Oct-1918, BuOrd.33291(Sp-2)-0, Folder "Patents Royalties etc.," RG74/E25A-I/B2277, NARA-I.

82. See Epstein, "Harnessing Invention," and minutes on Adm.CP.Patents.5768/1917, ADM.1/8590/111, TNA.

83. Henderson to Sims, 28-Oct-1918, enclosed in Schuyler to SecNav, 25-Sep-1919, BuOrd.37711/23, RG74/E25A-I/B2995, NARA-I.

84. Sims to Henderson, 19-Dec-1918, enclosed in ibid.

85. A copy of the contract, dated 21-Feb-1919, is enclosed in Jones to CoO, 8-Feb-1932, BuOrd.S71(Ford/80), RG74/E25B/B1740, NARA-I.

86. Minutes of conferences on 21-Oct-1918 and 22-Oct-1918, BuOrd.29048, RG74/E25A-I/B414, NARA-I.

87. Earle to Sims, 25-Oct-1918, BuOrd.33291(Sp-2)-0, Folder "Patents Royalties etc.," RG74/E25A-I/B2277, NARA-I; Tobey to BuOrd, 13-Mar-1919, BuOrd.37182/3, RG74/E25A-I/B2924, NARA-I.

88. Newton to Temple-Franks, 30-Dec-1918, File 1–132, RG241/EA1–1038/B142, NARA-II.

89. Bloch to O'Neil [sic], 1-Apr-1919, BuOrd.37182, RG74/E25A-I/B2924, NARA-I. Charles J. O'Neill was a name partner at Pennie, Goldsborough & O'Neill, located in the McGill Building in Washington, DC.

90. Bloch to Sims, 19-Apr-1919, BuOrd.37182/3(L3)-0, RG74/E25A-I/B2924, NARA-I.

91. Roosevelt to SecState, 30-Jun-1919, enclosed in Polk to SecInterior, 12-Jul-1919, File 1–132, RG241/EA1–1038/B142, NARA-II.

92. See also Polk to SecInterior, 12-Jul-1919, and Newton to Polk, 16-Jul-1919 ibid.; and State Dept files 811.542/164, 811.542/180, and 811.542/181, in Central Decimal File, RG59/EA1–205-A/B7604, NARA-II, which contain a few additional letters.

93. Earle to DNI, 6-Oct-1917, BuOrd.30309/66(L2)-0, RG74/E25A-I/B748, NARA-I; Clausen to Anthony Pollen, 11-Nov-1969, PLLN.1/12.

94. Schuyler [not identified, but he was "X" and the corrections are in his hand], "Ford Range Keeper," 25-Jan-1918, File R-2-d, Register 9822, RG38/E98/B1257, NARA-I.

95. Quoted in Schuyler, "Ford Range Keeper," 25-Jan-1918, ibid.

96. See Terrill, "Notes on the Theory of the Ford Range Keeper," p. 5, n.d. but spring 1918 to July 1919, Folder Conf. 59(93), RG38/E178/B3, NARA-I; Mindell, *BHAM*,

37–38; and Friedman, *NF*, 184 and 304n28. Note that the bearing cross-wire was considered of greater value than the range cross-wire—Pollen having consistently emphasized the importance of bearing as well as range.

97. Quoted in Schuyler, "Ford Range Keeper," 25-Jan-1918, File R-2-d, Register 9822, RG38/E98/B1257, NARA-I.

98. Schuyler, "Ford Range Keeper," 25-Jan-1918, ibid.

99. Van Auken to BuOrd and BuEng, 8-Apr-1918, para. 17, BuOrd.29068/229, RG74/E25A-I/B429, NARA-I.

100. Brownrigg minute, n.d. but c. 17-Mar-1919, Adm.G.0368/19, pp. 1418–23, V3 (Jan-Jun 1919), PQDNO, AL.

101. Brownrigg minute, n.d. but c. 17-Mar-1919, ibid.

102. Furlong to Earle, 7-Feb-1919, BuOrd.30309/546(L3)-0, RG74/E25A-I/B745, NARA-I; Earle to FIC, 26-Feb-1919, BuOrd.33921(Sp-1)-0, RG74/E25A-I/B2277, NARA-I; and Ford to Earle, 27-Feb-1919, BuOrd.37182/2, RG74/E25A-I/B2924, NARA-I.

103. Hannibal Ford, GBP 128,564, "Improvements in or relating to Range Keeping or Predicting Instruments," filed 16-Jun-1919, published 16-Sep-1920; Ford, GBP 128,565, "Improvements in or relating to Calculating Instruments for use in Gunnery," filed 16-Jun-1919, published 16-Sep-1920; and Ford, GBP 128,569, "Improvements in or relating to Range Keepers or like Instruments," filed 17-Jun-1919, published 17-Sep-1920.

104. Earle to Sims, 17-Oct-1919, BuOrd.37182/7-(L3)-0, RG74/E25A-I/B2924, NARA-I.

105. A. T. Dawson et al., USP 1,446,336, "Means for Use in the Laying of Ordnance and Other Apparatus in Training," filed 29-Oct-1919, patented 20-Feb-1923; A. T. Dawson et al., USP 1,479,587, "Means for Use in the Laying of Ordnance," filed 31-Oct-1919, patented 1-Jan-1924; and A. T. Dawson et al., USP 1,529,172, "Means for Use in the Laying of Ordnance," filed 31-Oct-1919, patented 10-Mar-1925.

106. McVay to SecNav, 28-Feb-1921, BuOrd.33921/151, RG74/E25A-I/B2277, NARA-I.

107. FIC to BuOrd, 20-Jun-1919, BuOrd.37711/1, RG74/E25A-I/B2995, NARA-I.

108. McCormick to Craven, 25-Jul-1919, BuOrd.37711/10, ibid.

109. Senn to BuOrd, 29-Jul-1919, BuOrd.37711/14, ibid.

110. Henderson to Controller, 24-Dec-1919, p. 15, Adm.CP.Patents.8573/1920, ADM.1/8590/111, TNA.

111. See Epstein, "The Conundrum of American Power in the Age of World War I."

112. Owens, "Where Are We Going, Phil Morse," 34–41.

113. Schuyler to Earle, 28-Jul-1919, BuOrd.35371/617, RG74/E25A-II/B4114, NARA-I.

CHAPTER 6

1. Ann Gurney (Frederick Ogilvy's daughter) to Anthony Pollen, 29-Jun-1981, PLLN.9/4/6/1.

2. With regard to an article by John Brooks, "The Admiralty Fire Control Tables," in *Warship 2002–2003* (London: Conway Maritime Press, 2003), 69–93, see my comments in chapter 2, note 1 *supra*. Again, the errors in this article are so severe as to render it unusable.

3. Phillpotts committee, "Report of Inspection at York of Pollen Fire Control System," n.d. but Mar-1918, DRYR.2/1.

4. "Pollen Fire Control Apparatus," Dreyer minute of 12-Mar-1918, pp. 309–10, V1 (Jan-Jun 1918), PQDNO, AL.

5. ToH, 2-Apr-1930, p. 26, T.173/612, TNA; and Tobey report, 10-Aug-1917, para. 17, File U-2-e, Register 9124, RG38/E98/B1334, NARA-I.

6. Dove's service record indicates that he had already displayed talent as an inventor and showed an aptitude for working with gunnery equipment; see ADM.196/55/114, TNA.

7. ToH, 2-Apr-1930, pp. 11–12, T.173/612, TNA.

8. This account comes mainly from the ToH, 2-Apr-1930, ibid. See also "Reports of Committee Appointed to Investigate the Question of Continuing Effectively to Engage an Enemy through a Smoke Screen," pp. 1256–1285, V3 (Jan-Jun 1919), PQDNO, AL; Admiralty Technical History Section, *The Technical History and Index: A Serial History of Technical Problems Dealt with by Admiralty Departments*, P23, *Fire Control in H.M. Ships*, Dec-1919, pp. 28–29, AL.

9. In addition to Dove's invention of straight-line plotting for GDT, the same technique was independently invented during the war by two sub-lieutenants, Alfred Langley and Lennox Boswell (see *Reports of the Grand Fleet Dreyer Table Committee, 1918–1919*, p. 11, ADM.186/241, TNA).

10. ToH, 2-Apr-1930, pp. 21–38, T.173/612, TNA.

11. Scott to Beatty, 9-Sep-1918, quoted in *Reports of the Grand Fleet Dreyer Table Committee, 1918–1919*, p. 1, ADM.186/241, TNA.

12. Beatty to GFDT Committee, 18-Oct-1918, quoted in ibid., pp. 5 and 14.

13. The fact that Beatty's trusted flag captain, Alfred E. Chatfield, who also served as the chief gunnery officer of the fleet, was not on the committee suggests that it was he who hand-picked the five members. For Chatfield's double hat, see *Navy List*, Jan-1919, pp. 887–88.

14. Guy Royle, as Flag Commander of HMS *Revenge*, the lead ship of the R-class super-dreadnoughts and the flagship of the 1st Battle Squadron, represented Admiral Sir Charles Madden, the commander of the squadron (ADM.196/126/114, TNA); Royle was also a distinguished gunnery officer, who had served on HMS *Good Hope* during the trials of Percy Scott's director system in 1909. Thomas Binney, as the staff gunnery officer of HMS *Queen Elizabeth*, Beatty's own flagship (i.e., the flagship of the entire Grand Fleet), represented Beatty himself. Charles Prickett, as the staff gunnery officer of HMS *Lion*, the flagship of the Battlecruiser Fleet, represented Vice-Admiral William Pakenham, who succeeded Beatty in command thereof. Julian Patterson, as both the gunnery officer and the staff gunnery officer of HMS *Barham*, the flagship of the 5th Battle Squadron, represented Rear-Admiral Arthur Leveson, the commander of the squadron. Norman Wodehouse (P. G.'s cousin), the most junior member of the committee, from HMS *Revenge* like Royle, was the gunnery officer of Madden's flagship.

15. Royle was on the staff of HMS *Excellent* from Sep-1910 (as soon as he completed the course as a student) to Jul-1911 (ADM.196/50/3, TNA). Binney was on the staff of HMS *Excellent* from Apr-1907 to Dec-1909 (as soon as he completed the course as a student) and again from Aug-1913 to Sep-1914 (ADM.196/143/144). Prickett was on the staff at HMS *Excellent* from Jan-1909 to Mar-1910 (ADM.196/143/9). Patterson was on the staff of HMS *Excellent* from May-1907 (as soon as he completed the course as a student) to Aug-1909 (ADM.196/143/332). Wodehouse was on the staff of HMS *Excellent* from Sep-1911 to May-1913 (ADM.196/144/24).

16. See his service record in ADM.196/126/34, TNA.

17. GFDT Committee, Third Interim Report, n.d. but Feb-1919, in *Reports of the Grand Fleet Dreyer Table Committee, 1918–1919*, p. 6, ADM.186/241, TNA.

18. GFDT Committee, Third Interim Report, p. 7, in ibid.

19. GFDT Committee, Final Report, n.d. but Feb-1919, p. 14, in ibid.

20. GFDT Committee, Third Interim Report, p. 8, in ibid.

21. GFDT Committee, Final Report, p. 18, in ibid.

22. GFDT Committee, First and Second Interim Reports, 19-Nov-1918, p. 5, in ibid. See also GFDT Committee, Third Interim Report, p. 11, ibid.

23. GFDT Committee, Final Report, p. 15, in ibid.

24. GFDT Committee, Final Report, p. 18, in ibid.

25. Beatty to Admiralty, n.d. but c. Feb-1919, pp. 18–19, in ibid.

26. Isherwood testimony, 20-Feb-1939, *Supplemental Record*, pp. 45, 61–62, EDNY Equity Case File #8432, RG21/B1381, NARA-NY.

27. Brownrigg minute, n.d. but c. 17-Mar-1919, Adm.G0368/19, p. 1420, V3 (Jan-Jun 1919), PQDNO, AL.

28. Black minute, 11-Apr-1919, pp. 1425–28, ibid. See also Crooke minute, 19-Mar-1919, p. 1423, ibid.

29. Brownrigg minute, 8-May-1919, p. 1429, ibid. Interestingly, he suggested putting the new section not under the Director of Naval Ordnance but under the Director of Torpedoes and Mining, a suggestion that may or may not say something about the bureaucratic politics of fire control. See also Crooke's minute of 7-Feb-1919, pp. 1123–25 (esp. paras. 3–4), V3 (Jan-Jun 1919), PQDNO, AL: it is open to multiple readings, but his suggestion—which was not taken—of appointing his Assistant Director of Naval Ordnance, who was none other than Dreyer's old friend Joseph Henley, to chair the Admiralty's new Fire Control Table Committee indicates a line of thought different from Brownrigg's.

30. Brownrigg minute, 8-May-1919, Adm.G.0368/19, p. 1429, V3 (Jan-Jun 1919), PQDNO, AL.

31. See Drury-Lowe's service record, ADM.196/43/229, TNA.

32. Its dates can be gleaned from Drury-Lowe's service record, ibid.

33. Drury-Lowe minute, 24-Feb-1920, Adm.CP.Patents.8748/1920, ADM.1/8590/111, TNA.

34. Drury-Lowe minute, 24-Feb-1920, Adm.CP.Patents.8748/1920, ibid.; see also "List of Admiralty Committees and Committees in which the Admiralty is interested," 1-Sep-1919, ADM.1/8568/259, TNA.

35. See Backhouse to Pollen, 1906 [no month or day], and Backhouse to Pollen, 11-Oct-1908, PLLN.5/5/4. See also Backhouse to Pollen, 6-Nov-1925, PLLN.5/5/3.

36. Evelyn Wickham and H. F. Simes, "Branch 5 of the Electrical Engineering Department of the Admiralty: Some Account of Its History," 10-Mar-1954, CLSN.5/3.

37. Jon Sumida, notes of interview with Twiss, 24-May-1979 (document courtesy of Sumida).

38. *Progress in Gunnery Material, 1921*, p. 9, ADM.186/251, TNA. See also *Progress in Gunnery Material, 1922 and 1923*, p. 9 (calling the new design "entirely new"), ADM.186/259, TNA. For confirmation that these pamphlets were prepared by the NOD, see *Progress in Gunnery Materiel, 1920*, p. 8, ADM.186/244, TNA.

39. Backhouse minute, 2-Aug-1922, Adm.G.0908/1922, ADM.1/8654/12, TNA.

40. *Handbook for Admiralty Fire Control Tables, Mk. I (H.M. Ships "Nelson" and "Rodney")*, p. 1, P1, ADM.186/273, TNA. Note also Crooke minute, 7-Feb-1919, p. 1124 (para. 5), V3 (Jan-Jun 1919), PQDNO, AL.

41. Dreyer, *The Sea Heritage*, 59.

42. Henderson to President RNC, "Report of ten years scientific work for the Admiralty," 10-Mar-1915, p. 4, Adm.CP.Patents.2805/1915, ADM.1/8590/111, TNA.

43. *Handbook for Admiralty Fire Control Tables, Mk. I (H.M. Ships "Nelson" and "Rodney")*, p. 31, P2, ADM.186/273, TNA.

44. *Progress in Gunnery Material, 1921*, pp. 20–21, ADM.186/251, TNA.

45. Henley minute, 2-Aug-1923, Adm.G.0485/23, ADM.1/8654/12, TNA.

46. *Handbook for Admiralty Fire Control Tables, Mk. I (H.M. Ships "Nelson" and "Rodney")*, pp. 24–25, P2, ADM.186/273, TNA.

47. Minute by Chatfield, 5-Jan-1926, Adm.G.02137/25, p. 3185, V9, PQDNO, AL.

48. See Pollen to Symington, 29-Apr-1914, PLLN.5/3/12.

49. Minute by DNO, 8-Dec-1925, Adm.G.02137/25, p. 3182, V9, PQDNO, AL.

50. Minute by DNO, 8-Dec-1925, p. 3181, ibid.

51. Minute by DNO, 8-Dec-1925, p. 3181, and minute by Chatfield, 5-Jan-1926, p. 3185, ibid.

52. For more on the legal status of different types of inventors vis-à-vis the crown, see Epstein, "Intellectual Property and National Security," and Epstein, "Harnessing Invention."

53. Pila, " 'Sewing the Fly Buttons on the Statute.' "

54. For confirmation that Isherwood and Landstad signed these agreements in Feb-920, see Drury-Lowe minute, Adm.CP.Patents 8748/1920, ADM.1/8590/111, TNA. For examples of the agreements they signed, see papers "A" and "B" attached to Drury-Lowe minute, 7-May-1920, Adm.G.11058/1919, ibid.

55. Black minute, 11-Apr-1919, Adm.G.0368/19, V3, PQDNO, AL.

56. Exactly how much they were paid is unclear, but some sense may be garnered from paper "A" attached to Drury-Lowe minute, 7-May-1920, Adm.G.11058/1919, ADM.1/8590/111, TNA. It was probably in the region of £3,000/year.

57. For details on this battle, see Epstein, "Harnessing Invention" (just mentally plug in "Henderson Firing Gear" every time "GDT" is mentioned).

58. Annual base pay for a full admiral in 1920 was £2,555. See *Navy List for October 1920, Corrected to the 18 September 1920* (London: HMSO, 1920), 2233.

59. See Epstein, "Intellectual Property and National Security," 146–47.

60. Clausen, "Invention and the Navy," 4.

61. Appendix to Henderson to SecRCAI, 22-Jul-1930, p. 44, T.173/273-P2, TNA.

62. Dove's service record, ADM.196/55/114, TNA.

63. Clausen to Anthony Pollen, 11-Nov-1969, PLLN.1/12.

64. Clausen to Anthony Pollen, 6-Dec-1969, ibid.

65. Clausen to Anthony Pollen, 5-Apr-1970, PLLN.5/4/3.

66. Clausen, "Invention and the Navy," 4.

67. Clausen to Anthony Pollen, 11-Nov-1969, PLLN.1/12.

68. Clausen, "Design and the Conditions Which Influence It," lectures given to the Naval Ordnance Department, May 1947, p. 12, CLSN.3/1. The "previous paper" was Clausen, "A Report on Questions Concerning the Gunnery Efficiency of His Majesty's Navy," 1942 (see para. 59), Pam. 9768, AL.

69. Pollen to Balfour, 1-Feb-1916, PLLN.5/2/9; Reginald Hall's draft letter, n.d., PLLN.8/2.

70. Pollen to Geddes, 9-Apr-1918, PLLN.5/2/9.

71. See correspondence between Pollen and Geddes in Mar–Jun 1918, PLLN.5/2/9; Pollen, "Memorandum to be read in conjunction with a note on the issue between the Admiralty and Mr Pollen, sent to the First Lord on June 6th, 1918," PLLN.8/3; Anderson to Pollen, 18-Dec-1918, Adm.CP.Patents.7118/18/111211, PLLN.5/2/9; Pollen to SecAdm, 20-Dec-1918, T.173/91-P2, TNA.

72. Bousfield was also a practicing scientist and the son of the distinguished lawyer-scientist William Robert Bousfield.

73. See Borchard, "Government Liability in Tort," P1, esp. 1–2; Borchard, "Government Liability in Tort," P4 (mislabeled P6), 17–41; Street, "The Tort Liability of the State," esp. 341–42.

74. Simon and Bousfield opinion, 10-Mar-1920, PLLN.8/3.

75. Baldwin Committee, "Proposed Instructions to Commission," para. 2, in "Report of the Departmental Committee on Awards to Inventors," 1-Nov-1918, Treas.8952/19, T.1/12325, TNA.

76. For the origins of the RCAI and concern over the Treasury's position, see Epstein, "Intellectual Property and National Security," 141–42. For the concern to ensure the appearance of independence, see Tindal Robertson to Chalmers, 6-Feb-1919, Treas.1089/19, T.1/12325, TNA.

77. Simon and Bousfield opinion, 10-Mar-1920, p. 4, PLLN.8/3.

78. Pollen to Milne, 20-Mar-1920, PLLN.5/4/20.

79. Pollen to Beatty, 28-Jun-1920, PLLN.5/5/1.

80. Draft letter from Hall to Beatty, n.d., PLLN.8/2.

81. Brookes to Tindal Robertson, 10-Aug-1920, T.173/88, TNA.

82. Pollen, "Preliminary Statement, comprising a description of the A.C. System of Naval Fire Control, and a Chronological Synopsis outlining its inception and development, including facts relevant to the communication of the System to and its adoption by the Admiralty," Dec-1920, T.173/88, TNA. See also Pollen, "Memorandum Re The Argo Company's Rights," draft copy, n.d. but likely Jun-1918, PLLN.5/2/9.

83. Pollen, "Preliminary Statement," Dec-1920, T.173/88, TNA.

84. Baddeley to Tindal Robertson, 28-Apr-1921, Adm.CP.Patents.9572/26438, ibid.

85. See Sargant minute, c. 10-Oct-1921, and Tindal Robertson minute, 3-Nov-1921, ibid.

86. Royal Warrant of 19-Mar-1919, copy in Treas.1089/19, T.1/12325, TNA.

87. Pollen's claim form, 15-Nov-1921, T.173/88, TNA.

88. Pollen notes enclosed in Pollen to Tindal Robertson, 7-Feb-1923, ibid.

89. Pollen to Peirse, 21-Feb-1911, PLLN.5/4/9.

90. Tindal Robertson to Sargant, 25-Apr-1922, and Pollen to Tindal Robertson, 27-Apr-1922, T.173/88, TNA.

91. See Cobb, Admiralty Counter-Statement, 19-Dec-1922, ibid., and Dreyer's description of his written report, in ToH, 4-Aug-1925, pp. 85–89, T.173/547-P16, TNA. His description matches the undated document titled "Summary" in DRYR.2/1.

92. For the distinction between these two grounds on which to refuse disclosure, see Schwartz, "Estoppel and Crown Privilege in English Administrative Law," 41–42.

93. Pollen to SecAdm, 10-Aug-1906, para. 9, PLLN.5/2/2.

94. Contract of 18-Feb-1908, para. 7, ADM.1/7991, TNA. See also SecAdm to Pollen, 29-Oct-1906, with enclosure, Adm.CP.17731/27926A, PLLN.5/2/2.

95. Cobb, Admiralty Counter-Statement, 19-Dec-1922, T.173/88, TNA.

96. Brookes to Hanscombe, 19-Dec-1922, T.173/91-P9, TNA; Hanscombe to Brookes (contains quotation), 29-Dec-1922, ibid.

97. Pollen to Tindal Robertson, 24-Jan-1923, and Tindal Robertson to Pollen, 27-Jan-1923, T.173/88, TNA. See also enclosure in Brookes to Tindal Robertson, 31-Jan-1923, ibid.

98. Tindal Robertson minutes, 15-Feb-1923, ibid.

99. Brookes to Hanscombe, 3-May-1923, T.173/91-P9, TNA.

100. Porter, "Romer and his Romer."

101. Clark to Pollen, 16-Oct-1925, PLLN.8/2.

102. Brookes to Tindal Robertson, 9-May-1923, and Tindal Robertson minutes, 14-May-1923, T.173/88, TNA.

103. See the correspondence between Brookes and Hanscombe, May–Jul 1923, T.173/91-P9, TNA; Brookes to Tindal Robertson, 17-Jul-1923, T.173/88, TNA; Tindal Robertson minute, 18-Jul-1923, ibid.

104. Arapostathis and Gooday, *Patently Contestable*; Beauchamp, *Invented by Law*, 137–39.

105. For evidence that he understood the challenges from the start, see ToH, 9-Oct-1923, pp. 4–5, T.173/547-P1, TNA.

106. ToH, 9-Oct-1923, p. 7, T.173/547-P1, and 10-Oct-1923, pp. 2, 33–34, T.173/547-P2, TNA.

107. ToH, 9-Oct-1923, p. 39, T.173/547-P1, TNA.

108. See, e.g., ToH, 10-Oct-1923, pp. 11, 34, T.173/547-P2, TNA.

109. ToH, 11-Oct-1923, pp. 54–55, T.173/547-P3, TNA.

110. ToH, 11-Oct-1923, p. 68, ibid.

111. ToH, 11-Oct-1923, p. 82, ibid.

112. Dreyer, "Note," n.d. but c. Oct-1923, DRYR.2/1. See also Dreyer, "The 3 Fire Control System [sic]," ibid.

113. For this account, confirmed by a witness, see ToH, 9-Mar-1925, pp. 22–24, T.173/547-P21, TNA.

114. ToH, 11-Oct-1923, pp. 38–39, T.173/547-P3, TNA.

115. See Cobb, Admiralty Counter-Statement, para. C2, 19-Dec-1922, T.173/88, TNA, for evidence that the Admiralty, like Pollen, understood his claim to include a clock.

116. ToH, 11-Oct-1923, p. 7, T.173/547-P3, TNA.

117. ToH, 11-Oct-1923, p. 11, ibid.

118. ToH, 11-Oct-1923, pp. 11–14 (quotation on p. 13), ibid.

119. ToH, 11-Oct-1923, pp. 14–15, ibid. See also p. 83 for confirmation.

120. ToH, 11-Oct-1923, p. 91, ibid.

121. Pollen to Peirse, 12-Oct-1923, PLLN.5/4/9.

122. RCAI recommendation, 17-Oct-1923, T.173/88, TNA.

CHAPTER 7

1. Note by Maud Pollen, n.d., "Letters by AHP (compiled by Maud Pollen)," Jebb Accession, PP, CAC.

2. Arapostathis and Gooday, *Patently Contestable*, 17.

3. Dreyer to SecAdm, 12-Nov-1923, DRYR.2/1.

4. Pollen's RCAI claim form, 8-Dec-1923, T.173/89, TNA.

5. Dreyer's RCAI claim form, 4-Apr-1924, T.173/204, TNA. For Dreyer's explanation of his thought process, see ToH, 5-Aug-1925, p. 98, T.173/547-P17, TNA. Dreyer offered up this explanation in response to a question by Tomlin, not by Greene, as Anthony Pollen has it (see Pollen, *The Great Gunnery Scandal*, 139).

6. Reginald Dumaresq to RCAI, 13-Jul-1923, and RCAI claim form, 8-Oct-1923, T.173/205, TNA. More than seventy years later, Dumaresq's youngest daughter, Mrs. Lucia Donaldson-Craig, refused to let Dreyer's name be mentioned in her house. My thanks to Nicholas Lambert, whose grandparents lived next door to the Dumaresq family, for sharing with me his memories of conversations with Mrs. Donaldson-Craig.

7. Parry to Tindal Robertson, 29-May-1924, T.173/204, TNA; Tindal Robertson to Tomlin and Tindal Robertson minutes, both 5-Jun-1924, ibid.

8. Cobb, Admiralty Counter-Statement, 25-Jun-1924, ibid.

9. Cobb, Admiralty Counter-Statement, 25-Jun-1924, ibid.

10. Pollen to Peirse, 4-Jul-1924, PLLN.5/4/9.

11. Peirse to Pollen, 6-Jul-1924, ibid.

12. Pollen to Peirse, 4-Jul-1924, ibid; see also Beatty to Pollen, 29-May-1924, and Pollen to Beatty, 2-Jun-1924, PLLN.5/2/10.

13. Hanscombe to Tindal Robertson, 22-Oct-1924, and Tindal Robertson minute, 2-Dec-1924, T.173/89, TNA. See also minute [presumably by Tindal Robertson], 7-Jul-1924, T.173/204, TNA.

14. Tindal Robertson minutes, 2-Dec-1924, T.173/89, TNA.

15. Brookes to Tindal Robertson, 5-Dec-1924, T.173/88, TNA.

16. Pollen, brief for counsel, c. Jul–Nov 1924, P5, para. 10, PLLN.8/2.

17. Tomlin probably consulted with the Treasury because the Royal Warrant implied that the RCAI exercised jurisdiction delegated by the Treasury, which normally exercised it under Section 29 of the 1907 Patents and Designs Act. See the correspondence between the RCAI, the Treasury, and the Admiralty from Dec-1924 to Feb-1925, T.173/89, TNA. For Tomlin's ruling, see ToH, 9-Mar-1925, pp. 99–100, T.173/547-P21, TNA; also ToH, 2-Mar-1925, pp. 1–2, T.173/547-P20, TNA.

18. See also Lord Millett, "Tomlin, Thomas James Chesshyre, Baron Tomlin."

19. Pollen to Peirse, 17-May-1925, PLLN.5/4/9.

20. ToH, 31-Jul-1925, p. 48, T.173/547-P13, TNA.

21. See, e.g., his description of the Argo clock as a sausage grinder, ToH, 22-Jun-1925, p. 30, T.173/547-P6, TNA. Tomlin ate it up (so to speak), for which see ibid, p. 62.

22. See, e.g., Greene to Maud Pollen, 31-Jan-1937, PLLN.5/1/50.

23. ToH, 2-Mar-1925, pp. 3–4, 8–15, 31, T.173/547–20, and 9-Mar-1925, pp. 2–21, 34–45, 56, T.173/547-P21, TNA.

24. ToH, 2-Mar-1925, p. 14, T.173/547-P20, TNA.

25. ToH, 2-Mar-1925, p. 16, ibid.

26. ToH, 9-Mar-1925, p. 24, T.173/547-P21, TNA.

27. ToH, 9-Mar-1925, p. 25, ibid.

28. ToH, 9-Mar-1925, p. 26, ibid.

29. ToH, 9-Mar-1925, p. 27, ibid.

30. ToH, 9-Mar-1925, p. 86, ibid.

31. ToH, 9-Mar-1925, p. 89, ibid.

32. Pollen to Peirse, 17-May-1925, PLLN.5/4/9.

33. Tindal Robertson to SecTreas, 11-Mar-1925, T.173/89, TNA.

34. Brookes to Tindal Robertson, 26-Mar-1925 and 20-Apr-1925, ibid.

35. SecAdm to Tindal Robertson, 14-Apr-1925, ibid.

36. See here Tindal Robertson to Tomlin, 22-Apr-1925, ibid.

37. Tindal Robertson's typed notes on hearing, 9-May-1925, ibid.

38. Tindal Robertson's handwritten notes on hearing, n.d. but c. 9-May-1925, ibid.

39. For Greene's emphasis of this point, see ToH, 2-Mar-1925, pp. 4–7, T.173/547-P20, TNA.

40. See ToH, 27-Jul-1925, pp. 23, 133, 137, T.173/547-P12, TNA; and ToH, 31-Jul-1925, p. 48, T.173/547-P13, TNA.

41. Note also that the crown advocate felt compelled to acknowledge Ballantyne's expertise and credibility; see ToH, 27-Jul-1925, pp. 132–33, T.173/547-P12, TNA.

42. Pollen to Peirse, 17-May-1925, PLLN.5/4/9.

43. ToH, 22-Jun-1925, p. 98, T.173/547-P6, TNA.

44. ToH, 1-Aug-1925, pp. 111–12, T.173/547-P14, TNA.

45. These are in T.173/91, TNA.

46. In British naval-history circles, the assertion that Pollen's documentary bundle duplicated and was otherwise equivalent to his personal papers has been accepted without question (and without examination of the Pollen papers). See Epstein, letter to the editor, 651.

47. Pollen to Isherwood, 22-May-1911, T.173/91-P3, TNA (also PLLN.5/2/6). See also ToH, 13-Jul-1925, pp. 14–24, T.173/547-P9; 1-Aug-1925, pp. 59–60, T.173/547-P14; 6-Aug-1925, pp. 8–12, T.173/547-P18, all TNA.

48. ToH, 27-Jul-1925, p. 18, T.173/547-P12, TNA.

49. ToH, 20-Jul-1925, pp. 14–15, T.173/547-P10, TNA.

50. ToH, 31-Jul-1925, p. 70, T.173/547-P13, TNA.

51. ToH, 4-Aug-1925, p. 39, T.173/547-P16, TNA.

52. [1942] AC 624. See also Spencer, "Bureaucracy, National Security and Access to Justice," esp. 291–98.

53. ToH, 31-Jul-1925, p. 3, T.173/547-P13, TNA.

54. ToH, 4-Aug-1925, p. 22, T.173/547-P16, TNA; see also ToH, 20-Jul-1925, pp. 72–75, T.173/547-P10, and ToH, 1-Aug-1925, p. 66, T.173/547-P14, TNA.

55. ToH, 20-Jul-1925, pp. 122–23, T.173/547-P10, TNA.

56. ToH, 20-Jul-1925, p. 64, ibid.

57. ToH, 20-Jul-1925, p. 5, ibid.

58. ToH, 20-Jul-1925, p. 79, ibid.

59. ToH, 20-Jul-1925, pp. 99–105, ibid.

60. ToH, 1-Aug-1925, p. 43, T.173/547-P14, TNA.

61. ToH, 22-Jun-1925, p. 3, T.173/547-P6, TNA.

62. Elphinstone to Dreyer, 4-Jul-1911, T.173/91-P3, TNA.

63. ToH, 6-Aug-1925, pp. 103–7, T.173/547-P18, TNA. For another example of Greene learning a relevant fact late—specifically, that Pollen had experimented with a device for meaning multiple rangefinder readings—see ToH, 31-Jul-1925, pp. 76–78, T.173/547-P13, TNA.

64. Claim form enclosed in Brookes to Tindal Robertson, 13-May-1925, T.173/88, TNA.

65. ToH, 13-Jul-1925, p. 113, T.173/547-P9, TNA.

66. ToH, 27-Jul-1925, p. 64, T.173/547-P12, TNA. See also "Schedule. Brief Statement of the Essential Features of the Claimants' System," n.d. but c. 6-Jul-1925, para. 1, T.173/91-P11, TNA.

67. ToH, 27-Jul-1925, p. 66, T.173/547-P12, TNA.

68. ToH, 27-Jul-1925, p. 66, ibid.

69. ToH, 27-Jul-1925, p. 67, ibid. For similar discussions about the relationship between system and instrument, mental and material, see, e.g., ToH, 22-Jun-1925, pp. 35–38, T.173/547-P6; 13-Jul-1925, pp. 105–21, T.173/547-P9; 27-Jul- 1925, pp. 110, 133–37, T.173/547-P12; 1-Aug-1925, pp. 17–22, T.173/547-P14; 7-Aug-1925, pp. 6–10, T.173/547-P19, TNA.

70. ToH, 1-Aug-1925, p. 20, T.173/547-P14, TNA. See also ToH, 13-Jul-1925, p. 113, T.173/547-P9, TNA.

71. ToH, 7-Aug-1925, p. 17, T.173/547-P19, TNA.

72. ToH, 7-Aug-1925, p. 18, ibid.

73. "Outline of Admiralty Case," n.d. but mid-July 1925, para. 4, T.173/91-P8, TNA; see also ToH, 20-Jul-1925, p. 83, T.173/547-P10, TNA.

74. ToH, 20-Jul-1925, p. 98, T.173/547-P10, TNA.

75. "Outline of Admiralty Case," n.d. but mid-July 1925, esp. paras. 9a, 9b, T.173/91-P8, TNA.

76. ToH, 4-Aug-1925, p. 90, T.173/547-P16, TNA.

77. ToH, 1-Aug-1925, pp. 5–7, 39–42, T.173/547-P14, TNA.

78. ToH, 31-Jul-1925, pp. 67–74, T.173/547-P13, TNA.

79. ToH, 5-Aug-1925, p. 98, T.173/547-P17, TNA.

80. ToH, 27-Jul-1925, p. 137, T.173/547-P12, TNA. See also ToH, 31-Jul-1925, p. 29, T.173/547-P13, TNA.

81. ToH, 27-Jul-1925, p. 55, T.173/547-P12, TNA; see also p. 127, ibid.

82. ToH, 7-Aug-1925, p. 60, T.173/547-P19, TNA.

83. ToH, 7-Aug-1925, p. 5, ibid.

84. Tomlin understood this point; see ToH, 25-Jul-1925, p. 13, T.173/547-P11, and 7-Aug-1925, p. 28, T.173/547-P19, TNA.

85. For Pollen's and Isherwood's claims regarding rate plotting, see ToH, 6-Jul-1925, pp. 51–64, 73–80, T.173/547-P8; 25-Jul-1925, pp. 35–36, T.173/547-P11; ToH, 1-Aug-1925, pp. 45, 51, 98–99, T.173/547-P14; "Statement of the Claimants' Case," n.d. but early Jul-1925, para 3.xx, T.173/91-P11, TNA.

86. For the discussion of two-rate plotting before the 1906 negotiations, see ToH, 1-Aug-1925, pp. 8–11, T.173/547-P14, TNA. For Harding's 1906 date, see ToH, 1-Aug-1925, p. 64, ibid. For Harding's 1907 date, see ToH, 1-Aug-1925, p. 12 (also p. 14, which makes clear that "1909" on p. 12 should read "1907"), ibid.

87. ToH, 1-Aug-1925, pp. 110–11, T.173/547-P14, TNA.

88. ToH, 3-Aug-1925, pp. 45–49, T.173/547-P15, TNA.

89. ToH, 5-Aug-1925, p. 75, T.173/547-P17, TNA.

90. ToH, 4-Aug-1925, pp. 99–110, T.173/547-P16, TNA.

91. ToH, 7-Aug-1925, p. 14, T.173/547-P19, TNA.

92. For speculation between Greene and the commissioners that Dreyer had gotten the idea of range-rate plotting from Wilson, who had gotten it from Pollen, see ToH, 7-Aug-1925, pp. 14–15, ibid.

93. ToH, 5-Aug-1925, pp. 20–24, 33–36, T.173/547-P17, TNA; see also 6-Aug-1925, pp. 48–51, T.173/547-P18, TNA. The documents were Dreyer's letter to Hughes-Onslow of 18-Oct-1908 and the Admiralty pamphlet G.4023/1908 on fire control. Dreyer and the Admiralty claimed that HMS *Arrogant* had carried out bearing-rate plotting as well as range-rate plotting in 1908 but produced no supporting evidence. The 1910 date is in

Dreyer, "Remarks by Commander F. C. Dreyer R.N. on the Question of How to Best Obtain and Maintain the Gun Range in Action," enclosed in Dreyer to Eustace, 22-Jul-1910, esp. para. 7, T.173/91-P3, TNA.

94. Dreyer, *The Sea Heritage*, 59, 85.

95. See "Statement of the Principles Governing Assessment of Compensation adopted by the Royal Commission on Awards to Inventors," n.d., T.173/21, TNA.

96. ToH, 13-Jul-1925, p. 118, T.173/547-P9, TNA. See also Langdon's comment in ToH, 7-Aug-1925, pp. 21–22, T.173/547-P19, TNA.

97. ToH, 7-Aug-1925, p. 22, T.173/547-P19, TNA.

98. For Pollen's attempts to overcome this point, and the commissioners' skepticism, see ToH, 3-Aug-1925, pp. 3–20, 78–81, T.173/547-P15, TNA; ToH, 7-Aug-1925, pp. 41–50, T.173/547-P19, TNA.

99. ToH, 7-Aug-1925, p. 17, T.173/547-P19, TNA.

100. ToH, 7-Aug-1925, p. 24, ibid.

101. For the RCAI's reasoning on this point, as well as the documents on which it was relying, see ToH, 6-Aug-1925, pp. 84–88, T.173/547-P18, TNA; ToH, 7-Aug-1925, pp. 51–59, T.173/547-P19, TNA; and Pollen to SecAdm, 1-Apr-1908, Thomas to Pollen, 23-Apr-1908, Adm.CP.9389/13894, and Pollen to Thomas, 4-May-1908, T.173/91-P7, TNA.

102. ToH, 4-Aug-1925, pp. 81–83, T.173/547-P16, TNA.

103. ToH, 20-Jul-1925, pp. 89–94, T.173/547-P10; 31-Jul-1925, pp. 20–39, T.173/547-P13; 4-Aug-1925, pp. 22–26, 51–63, T.173/547-P16, TNA.

104. ToH, 29-Jun-1925, pp. 45–49, T.173/547-P7, and 1-Aug-1925, pp. 16–17, T.173/547-P14, TNA.

105. ToH, 5-Aug-1925, pp. 48–54, T.173/547-P17, TNA. See also ToH, 7-Aug-1925, p. 14, T.173/547-P19, TNA.

106. ToH, 5-Aug-1925, p. 46, T.173/547-P17, TNA. See also p. 50, ibid.

107. ToH, 20-Jul-1925, p. 57, T.173/547-P10, and 5-Aug-1925, p. 50, T.173/547-P17, TNA.

108. ToH, 6-Aug-1925, p. 95, T.173/547-P18, TNA.

109. ToH, 22-Jun-1925, pp. 29–32, T.173/547-P6; 29-Jun-1925, pp. 42–49, T.173/547-P7; 6-Jul-1925, pp. 98–116, T.173/547-P8; 20-Jul-1925, pp. 45–58, T.173/547-P10; 27-Jul-1925, pp. 76–104, 119–31, T.173/547-P12; 31-Jul-1924, pp. 19–29, 31–39, T.173/547-P13, TNA.

110. ToH, 20-Jul-1925, p. 89, T.173/547-P10, TNA.

111. ToH, 20-Jul-1925, p. 96, ibid.

112. ToH, 22-Jun-1925, p. 62, T.173/547-P6, TNA.

113. ToH, 29-Jun-1925, p. 45, T.173/547-P7, TNA.

114. ToH, 27-Jul-1925, pp. 79–83, T.173/547-P12, and 31-Jul-1925, pp. 9–11 (quotation on p. 9), T.173/547-P13, TNA.

115. Tomlin understood the point perfectly; see ToH, 27-Jul-1925, pp. 18, 92, T.173/547-P12, TNA.

116. ToH, 6-Aug-1925, p. 102, T.173/547-P18, TNA.

117. ToH, 6-Aug-1925, p. 100, ibid.

118. ToH, 27-Jul-1925, pp. 40–41, T.173/547-P12, and 5-Aug-1925, pp. 2–4, 58–65, T.173/547-P17, TNA.

119. ToH, 6-Jul-1925, pp. 80–94, T.173/547-P8; 13-Jul-1925, pp. 14–27, T.173/547-P9; 1-Aug-1925, pp. 58–61, T.173/547-P14; 6-Aug-1925, pp. 4–12, 75–81, T.173/547-P18, TNA.

120. ToH, 4-Aug-1925, pp. 53–59, T.173/547-P16, TNA.

121. ToH, 6-Aug-1925, p. 57, T.173/547-P18, TNA.

122. ToH, 6-Aug-1925, p. 103, ibid.

123. ToH, 6-Aug-1925, p. 63, ibid.

124. ToH, 6-Aug-1925, p. 104, ibid.

125. ToH, 6-Aug-1925, p. 105, ibid.

126. ToH, 13-Jul-1925, p. 14, T.173/547-P9, TNA. For Dreyer, see ToH, 4-Aug-1925, p. 49, T.173/547-P16, TNA.

127. See ToH, 20-Jul-1925, pp. 58 and 95 (Pollen was cleared out of the hearing on p. 77), T.173/547-P10; ToH, 1-Aug-1925, p. 86, T.173/547-P14; and ToH, 6-Aug-1925, p. 83, T.173/547-P18, TNA.

128. ToH, 6-Aug-1925, p. 54, T.173/547-P18, TNA.

129. ToH, 6-Aug-1925, pp. 97–98, ibid. For the "IV" in brackets, the transcript erroneously reads "B." The ellipsis removes a reference to a particular linkage in the Mark IV Dreyer Table.

130. ToH, 6-Aug-1925, p. 100, T.173/547-P18, TNA.

131. ToH, 7-Aug-1925, p. 62, T.173/547-P19, TNA.

132. ToH, 7-Aug-1925, pp. 62–63, ibid.

133. ToH, 7-Aug-1925, p. 65, also 68–69, ibid.

134. ToH, 6-Jul-1925, pp. 5–9, T.173/547-P8, TNA.

135. ToH, 6-Jul-1925, pp. 26–28, ibid.

136. ToH, 5-Aug-1925, p. 15, T.173/547-P17, TNA.

137. ToH, 5-Aug-1925, p. 79, ibid.

138. ToH, 31-Jul-1925, p. 23–24, 85–102, T.173/547-P14; ToH, 4-Aug-1925, pp. 9–11, 63–76, T.173/547-P16; ToH, 5-Aug-1925, pp. 94–95, T.173/547-P17; ToH, 6-Aug-1925, pp. 44–46, T.173/547-P18, TNA.

139. ToH, 4-Aug-1925, p. 32, T.173/547-P16, TNA.

140. ToH, 4-Aug-1925, p. 59, ibid.

141. ToH, 5-Aug-1925, pp. 10–11, T.173/547-P17, TNA. See also pp. 54–58, ibid.

142. Inglis, "William Ernest Dalby."

143. Dalby, "Argo, Dreyer and Dumaresq Claims," n.d. but c. Oct-1925, p. 23, T.173/205, TNA.

144. Dalby, "Argo, Dreyer and Dumaresq Claims," p. 7, ibid.

145. Dalby, "Argo, Dreyer and Dumaresq Claims," pp. 17 and 21, ibid.

146. Dalby, "Argo, Dreyer and Dumaresq Claims," p. 23, ibid.

147. RCAI recommendation, 30-Oct-1925, T.173/90, TNA.

148. RCAI recommendation, 30-Oct-1925, ibid.

149. See reports of the RCAI, 14-Dec-1920 (Cmd. 1112, 1921), 14-Nov-1922 (Cmd. 1782, 1922), 21-Oct-1924 (Cmd. 2275, 1924–25), 12-Apr-1926 (Cmd. 2656, 1929), 31-Dec-1927 (Cmd. 3044, 1928), 1-Sep-1931 (Cmd. 3957, 1930–31), and 18-Oct-1937 (Cmd. 5594, 1937–38).

150. Tindal Robertson to Tomlin, 20-Oct-1925, T.173/91-P8, TNA.

151. Depending on whether or not the RCAI elected to include the £5,000 for scrapped ships and torpedo-control tables, the award included at least £2,600 (£30,000–£27,400) in damages and perhaps as much as £7,600.

152. Patents and Designs Act of 1907, sec. 33; see also Arnold, *The Law of Damages and Compensation*, 319–25, esp. 320.

153. Killowen [Francis Russell] to Pollen, n.d. but late 1926 or early 1927, PLLN.5/2/10. Russell (the brother of Sir Charles Russell, the first baronet of Killowen,

with whom Pollen also corresponded) was a fellow Catholic, had overlapped with Pollen (and Tomlin) at Oxford, and then entered Lincoln's Inn the same year as Pollen. Tomlin had entered Lincoln's Inn the previous year.

CHAPTER 8

1. Note Merges, *American Patent Law*, 13.

2. McVay to SecNav, 30-Jun-1920, BuOrd.35494-(L3)-0, RG74/E25A-I/B2625, NARA-I.

3. Specifically, the transmission elements supplied by Vickers and Sperry Gyroscope were step-by-step; the transmission elements supplied by Ford Instrument were synchronous, but they were for only one part of the system.

4. This paragraph draws heavily on Mindell, *BHAM*, 46–51. See also Willard affidavit, Paper #16, filed 21-Mar-1927, IF.54,815, RG241, NARA-KC.

5. McVay to SecNav, 11-Aug-1920, BuOrd.35494-(L3)-0, RG74/E25A-I/B2625, NARA-I.

6. This paragraph closely tracks Mindell, *BHAM*, 49.

7. McVay to SecNav, 20-Jun-1930, BuOrd.35494-(L3)-0, RG74/E25A-I/B2625, NARA-I.

8. McVay, "Proprietary Purchase from General Electric Company of Fire Control Equipment for Maryland and California," n.d. but Aug/Sep-1920, BuOrd.35494–8/11/20, ibid.

9. Bloch to GE, 6-Sep-1919, BuOrd.35494-(L3)-0, ibid. See also attached note by Furlong.

10. Niven to CoO, 1-Oct-1919, BuOrd.35494/33, ibid.

11. McVay, "Proprietary Purchase from General Electric Company of Fire Control Equipment for Maryland and California," n.d. but Aug-1920, BuOrd.35494–8/11/20, ibid.

12. This was Contract 2992.

13. A cost-plus contract is one that pays contractors for allowed expenses plus a profit.

14. McVay to SecNav, 30-Jun-1920, BuOrd.35494-(L3)-0, RG74/E25A-I/B2625, NARA-I.

15. McVay to Westinghouse, 6-Aug-1920, BuOrd.39010(L3)-0, and Southgate to CoO, 26-Feb-1921, BuOrd.39010/2, RG74/E25A-I/B3229, NARA-I.

16. Steen, *The American Synthetic Organic Chemicals Industry*, esp. 156–59.

17. See, e.g., Bowyer, "Secretary's Transcript of First Report of Mr. Assistant Attorney General Galloway," 20-Sep-1928, RG60/E209/B1, NARA-II; and McMullen to Atty Gen, 15-Jan-1930, Docket "Survey of Cases—Reports of War and Navy Departments needed to complete cases," ibid.

18. Furlong to Larimer, 8-Jan-1932, Folder "Ordnance—American," B6, Furlong mss, LoC.

19. Public Res. 66-64, "Joint Resolution Declaring that certain Acts of Congress, joint resolutions, and proclamations shall be construed as if the war had ended and the present or existing emergency expired" (1913); Public Law 66-366, "An Act To extend temporarily the time for filing applications for letters patent," etc., 41 Stat. 1313 (1921).

20. Beeler [?] to CoO, 27-May-1921, BuOrd.39117/283(L3)-0, RG74/E25A-I/B3246, NARA-I; McVay to GE NIO, 15-Jun-1921, BuOrd.39117(L3)-0, RG74/E25A-I/B3241, NARA-I.

21. Note Mindell, *BHAM*, 348n87, quoting a handwritten note dated 1922: "GE reports that it has arranged with Sperry, Hammond, Ford to use apparatus. This is covered by clause in contract allowing not over $9000 for patent rights."

22. This point is a staple of histories of GE and of the electrical industry more generally. See, e.g., Hughes, *Networks of Power*, esp. 163–72; Reich, *The Making of American Industrial Research*, esp. 4–6, 81–82; Millard, *Edison and the Business of Innovation*, 43–49, 136–45, 176–78.

23. Minutes of conference, 19-Jul-1921, BuOrd.39117/405, RG74/E25A-I/B3246, NARA-I. On Davis, see "Albert G. Davis Elected a Vice President of the General Electric Company," *General Electric Review* 22, no. 12 (December 1919): 1002–3.

24. The Bureau's surrender can be inferred from later developments. Contract 3270 covered the *Washington*, and Contract 3271 covered the *West Virginia*, for which see McVay to GE NIO, BuOrd.39117(L4)-0, RG74/E25A-I/B3241, NARA-I.

25. See McVay to BuS&A, 21-Jan-1922, BuOrd.39117(L4)-0, ibid.; McVay to GE NIO, 25-Jan-1923, BuOrd.39117/1709(A3)-0, RG74/E25A-I/B3244, NARA-I.

26. See Mindell, *BHAM*, 50–51; *The Engineering Journal: The Journal of the Engineering Institute of Canada* 17, no. 1 (January 1934): 35; Brittain, *Alexanderson*, 84–89.

27. For discussion of the problem, see Evans to Buord, 24-Feb-1922, BuOrd.39117/854, RG74/E25A-I/B3249, NARA-I; McVay memorandum, 18-Nov-1922, BuOrd.39117/1525(A3)-0, RG74/E25A-I/B3244, NARA-I; Clark to BuOrd, 25-May-1923, BuOrd.39117/2141, RG74/E25A-I/B3242, NARA-I; Belknap to BuOrd, 20-Jul-1923, BuOrd.39117/2280, ibid.; Butler to BuOrd, 3-Aug-1923, BuOrd.39117/2316, RG74/E25A-I/B3248, NARA-I; and Adams to BuOrd, 3-Aug-1923, BuOrd.39117/2319, ibid.

28. On Alexanderson's involvement, see Brittain, *Alexanderson*, 203–4.

29. McVay memorandum, 14-Dec-1922, BuOrd.39117/1596(A3)-0, RG74/E25A-I/B3244, NARA-I. See also McVay to CNO, 5-Jun-1922, BuOrd.39117/1108(A3)-0, ibid.

30. Hyatt to CoO, 8-Mar-1924, BuOrd.40974/18(L5–2)-0, RG74/E25A-I/B3633, NARA-I. See also Bailey to Hewlett, 17-Jul-1923, BuOrd.39117/2278, RG74/E25A-I/B3242, NARA-I.

31. Clark to GE NIO, 5-Jan-and 2-Feb-1922, BuOrd.39117/773, RG74/E25A-I/B3249, NARA-I.

32. Evans to BuOrd, 3-Feb-1922, BuOrd.39117/773, ibid.

33. Weiss, *America Inc.?*, 10 and *passim*.

34. Mindell, *BHAM*, 50–51; Brittain, *Alexanderson*, 219–22, 237–42.

35. Mindell, *BHAM*, 54.

36. Hyatt, "Modern Fire Control System," 7-Feb-1925, and Jones, "Modern Fire Control Installation," 23-Feb-1926, File R-4-a, Register 11943, RG38/E98/B1262, NARA-I.

37. Hyatt, 15-Mar-1924, BuOrd.40974/35(L5)-0, RG74/E25A-I/B3633, NARA-I.

38. "Excerpts from Testimony Court of Claims Suit No. L-91—Dugan v. the United States," n.d., p. 3, RG60/EA1-COR27/B41, NARA-II. Underlining removed from the original.

39. Sperry note, 15-Jun-1918, Folder "Gyroscope Company, General Correspondence, 1908–24–30," B23, EAS.

40. See Hughes, *Elmer Sperry*, 103–28, 223–30.

41. McCormick to CoO, 12-Sep-1918, BuOrd.29758/558, RG74/E25A-II/B38, NARA-I; Morgan to Sperry, 30-Dec-1919, Folder "Gyroscope Company, Japan, Business and Patents," B35, EAS; DNI to CoO, 20-Sep-1921, with enclosure,

BuOrd.35156/1057, RG74/E25A-II/B71, NARA-I; Gillmor to CoO, 15-Jun-1936, BuOrd.
A7–2(127), RG74/E25B/B1345, NARA-I.

42. Furlong to CoO, 20-May-1921, BuOrd.37182/21, RG74/E25A-I/B2924, NARA-I.
See also Furlong to Wilson, 4-Apr-1919, Folder "GenCorr, 1919," B1, Furlong mss, LoC.

43. See the bulletins in Folder "Gyroscope Company, Fire Control Devices, Battle
Tracer," B32, EAS.

44. Sperry to London office, 14-Oct-1919, ibid.; Sperry memorandum, 11-Jan-1924, ibid.

45. Gillmor to Sims, 27-Jan-1921, Folder "Gillmor, R.E.," B60, Sims mss., LoC; Hyatt
to CoO, 20-Aug-1923, BuOrd.37224/86-(L5)-0, RG74/E25A-I/B2930, NARA-I. Gillmor
later returned to the firm.

46. Furlong to CoO, 20-May-1921, BuOrd.37182/21, RG74/E25A-I/B2924, NARA-I.

47. This was interference #43,104, between Elemer Meitner's application serial no.118,405, which matured into USP 1,392,959; and Ford's application serial
no. 240,217, which matured into USP 1,472,590.

48. Thompson to Sperry, 27-Feb-1919 and 2-Dec-1919, Folder "Gyroscope Company,
Fire Control Patents, Hamilton [sic] Ford interferences," B32, EAS.

49. Thompson to Sperry, 2-Dec-1919, ibid.; Meitner to CommPat, 31-Oct-1919,
enclosed in Moakley to CommPat, filed 10-Dec-1919, Paper #26, IF.43,104, RG241,
NARA-KC. Cf. Mindell, BHAM, 34 and 344–45n47.

50. See Sperry draft letter to BuOrd, 20-Feb-1920, Folder "Gyroscope Company,
Fire Control Devices, Battle Tracer," B32, EAS.

51. Sperry to BuOrd, 15-Jun-1920, ibid.

52. Thompson to Furlong, 28-Oct-1920, BuOrd.37182/18, RG74/E25A-I/B2924,
NARA-I. The underlining and double underlining were Furlong's.

53. See the correspondence between Sperry and P. R. Jackson (director of the firm's
London office) from August to December 1920, Folder "Gyroscope Company, General
Correspondence," B32, EAS.

54. Note by Sperry, 11-Jan-1924, Folder "Gyroscope Company, Fire Control Devices,
Battle Tracer," B32, EAS; see also Sperry to Irizar, 15-Feb-1924, ibid.

55. See also Davis to Furlong, 6-Apr-1938, BuOrd.S71(Ford/156), Folder "Fire Control Insts & Spare Parts For," RG74/E25B/B1740, NARA-I.

56. Sperry Gyroscope filed suit #34440 against the Navy (for procuring a gyrostabilizer from Carl Norden; see RG123/E1/B2619, NARA-I) in January 1920 and suit 179-A
against the Navy (for procuring gyrocompasses from Carrie Gyroscopic Corp.; see
RG123/E1/B2836, NARA-I) in June 1921. It moved to dismiss both suits in June 1922,
citing the "recent Radio adjustment" as its reason for doing so; see Doran to McVay,
15-Jun-1922, BuOrd.37182/26, RG74/E25A-I/B2924, NARA-I. This was almost certainly a
reference to the report of the Interdepartmental Radio Board of 31-May-1921, on which
see Howeth, *History of Communications-Electronics in the United States Navy*, 375–76.
I am grateful to Jonathan Winkler for explaining the context and sending me the pertinent extract from Howeth. After suing Arma in district court in July 1923 (see *ToR*,
pp. 1–12, *Sperry Gyroscope Co. v. Arma Engineering Co.*, 271 US 232 (1926), available
through the Gale database "The Making of Modern Law: U.S. Supreme Court Records
and Briefs, 1832–1978"), and while awaiting the results of its appeal to the Supreme
Court, Sperry Gyroscope filed suit E-151 in the Court of Claims against the Navy (for
procuring gyrocompasses from Arma; see RG123/E1/3509, NARA-I) in March 1925
before moving to dismiss it just two months later; see also Thompson to Sperry, 3-Mar-
1925, Folder "Gyroscope Company Patent Files," B21, EAS.

57. See the correspondence from May-Oct 1924, BuOrd 37182/28–31, RG74/E25A-I/B2924, NARA-I.

58. Pennie, Davis, Marvin & Edmonds, "Motion to Dissolve," Paper #30, filed 22-May-1926, IF.52,138/F3, RG241, NARA-KC; Lunt, "Motion to Dissolve," Paper #32, filed 24-May-1926, ibid.

59. Thompson, "Brief for Sperry and Meitner in Opposition to Opponents' Motions to Dissolve on the Ground of Non-Patentability of Issue," Paper #44, filed 14-Aug-1926, p. 4, ibid.

60. Pennie, Davis, Marvin & Edmonds, "Brief for Dawson, Watt & Perham," filed 17-Aug-1926, p. 6, ibid.

61. Pennie, Davis, Marvin & Edmonds, "Brief for Dawson, Watt & Perham," filed 17-Aug-1926, p. 12, ibid. See also Lunt, "Brief for Hewlett and Willard in Opposition to Sperry and Meitner's Appeal," Paper #55, filed 17-May-1927, IF.52,138/F2, RG241, NARA-KC.

62. See Disney, Paper #46, 13-Nov-1916, and Board of Appeals, Paper #57, 4-Oct-1927, ibid.

63. Moakley & Gill, "Motion to Dissolve," Paper #24, filed 22-May-1926, IF.52,141, RG241, NARA-KC; Lunt, "Motion to Dissolve," Paper #25, filed 24-May-1926, ibid.; Moakley & Gill, "Brief for Ford," Paper #31, filed 11-Aug-1926, ibid. For the language of the counts, see Colwell to Lunt, Paper #18, 12-Mar-1925, PF.1,894,822, RG241, NARA-KC.

64. Pennie, Davis, Marvin & Edmonds, "Brief for Dawson et al.," Paper #33, filed 11-Aug-1926, p. 1, IF.52,141, RG241, NARA-KC.

65. Thompson, "Brief for Sperry and Meitner Supporting their Motion for Dissolution and Opposing Opponents' Motions for Dissolution," Paper #34, filed 11-Aug-1926, pp. 2–3, ibid.

66. Disney, Paper #35, decision of 13-Nov-1926, pp. 5–6, ibid.

67. Board of Appeals, Paper #39, decision of 31-Jul-1918, esp. p. 2, IF.54,815, RG241, NARA-KC; Tullar letter, Paper #43, filed 10-Sep-1928, ibid.; Moakley & Gill, "Motion for Judgment under Rule 119," Paper #49, filed 5-Feb-1929, ibid.; Houston, Paper #51, decision of 23-Feb-1929, ibid.; Thompson, Paper #53, appeal filed 22-May-1929, ibid.

68. See *Sperry Gyroscope Co. v. Arma Engineering Co.* (271 US 232, 1926).

69. Thompson to Sperry, 10-Jun-1926, Folder "Gyroscope Company Patent Files," B21, EAS. See also Lavenue, "Patent Infringement against the United States and Government Contractors," 421, and O'Connor, "Taking, Tort, or Crown Right?" 188n345.

70. Thompson, Petition, filed 5-Jan-1927, RG123/E1/B3780/F2, NARA-I; see also Doran to Sperry, 17-Feb-1926, Folder "Gyroscope Company, Doran, C. S.," B24, EAS.

71. Doran to CoO, 3-Feb-1927, BuOrd.A13–4/S71(Sperry/2), RG74/E25B/B1406, NARA-I.

72. Doran to Sperry, 11-Feb-1927, Folder "Gyroscope Company, Doran, C. S.," B24, EAS.

73. Doran to Sperry, 11-Feb-1927, ibid.

74. Clark to BuOrd, 8-Jan-1927, enclosing Moakley to GE, 27-Dec-1926, BuOrd.S71–8(37/28)C2992, C3270–1, RG74/E25B/B1814, NARA-I.

75. Seabolt to BuOrd, 29-Jan-1927, BuOrd.S71–8(37/29)C2992,C3270–1, ibid.

76. Moon to BuOrd, 17-Mar-1927, BuOrd.S71–8(37/33)C2992,C3270–1(Sp2), ibid.

77. 35 USC 31, 1925 ed. (Rev. Stat. 4886).

78. See, e.g., "Preliminary Statement of Dawson, Watt & Perham," Paper #13, filed 27-Sep-1925, IF.52,138/F3, RG241, NARA-KC.

79. Moon to BuOrd, 17-Mar-1927, BuOrd.S71-8(37/33)C2992,C3270-1(Sp2), RG74/E25B/B1814, NARA-I.

80. Bloch to JAG, 16-Apr-1927, BuOrd.A13-4/S71(Sperry/9)(Sp2, L6), RG74/E25B/B1406, NARA-I. See also Seabolt to Bloch, 5-Feb-1927, BuOrd.A13-4/S71(Sperry/3), ibid.; Seabolt to Bloch, 23-Feb-1927, BuOrd.A13-4/S71(Sperry/5), ibid.; Markland to CoO, 14-Mar-1927, BuOrd.A13-4/S71(Sperry/2)(L6), ibid.

81. Epstein, *Torpedo*, 141–43; Epstein, "The Other Visible Hand," 46–48.

82. Bloch to JAG, 26-Jun-1928, BuOrd.A13-4/S71(Sperry/12) (Sp5), RG74/E25B/B1406, NARA-I.

83. Fisk, *Working Knowledge*.

84. See, e.g., Norton to JAG, 1-Apr-1922, BuOrd.39853/13(Sp-1)-0, RG74/E25A-I/B3436, NARA-I; Zimermann to CoO, 3-Mar-1928, BuOrd.A13-1(2/39)(Sp5), RG74/E25B/B1406, NARA-I. For the history of the Bureau's patent section (known as Section Sp), see BuOrd, *Navy Ordnance Activities*, 238–39. For more on Norton, who developed his expertise in the context of torpedo procurement, see Epstein, *Torpedo*, 148, 170–71, and "Death of Noted Ordnance Officer," *Army and Navy Register* 71, no. 2188 (24-Jun-1922): 577–600 at 595.

85. *Ordnance Engineering Corporation v. United States* (68 Ct. Cl. 301 at 352–53). Notably, the case involved the procurement of naval ordnance and technology transfer from Britain. The invention at issue related to "star shell," a projectile fired to illuminate an area at night. The Bureau of Ordnance, having failed to design or procure star shells in the United States, turned to the Admiralty for a British design in 1917.

86. Zimermann to Section L, 3-May-1929, BuOrd.A13-4/S71, RG74/E25B/B1406, NARA-I. In all likelihood, a miscommunication occurred between Zimermann and Section L or between the Bureau and the JAG's office. A JAG officer subsequently recalled the Bureau as "the prime mover" in the quest for a settlement (Dodd to Woodson, 12-May-1933, SecNav.L11-15/QM-Sperry Gyroscope Co., RG80/E22/B1062, NARA-I), yet there is no question but that the Bureau opposed the Navy's subsequent settlement with Sperry Gyroscope.

87. Van Auken to BuOrd, 23-Jul-1929, BuOrd.S71(GE Co/5), RG74/E25B/B1740, NARA-I. For the request, see Leahy to Van Auken, 10-Jul-1929, BuOrd.S71(GE Co), ibid.

88. Zimermann to CoO, 10-Jan-1930, BuOrd.A13-4/S71(Sperry/15)(Sp5), RG74/E25B/B1406, NARA-I.

89. Zimermann to CoO, 11-Jan-1930, BuOrd.A13-4/S71(Sperry/14)(Sp5), ibid.

90. Leahy to JAG, 29-Apr-1930, BuOrd.A13-4/S71(Sperry/16/17)(L7), ibid., and Leahy to JAG, 11-Jun-1930, BuOrd.A13-4/S71(Sperry/18)(Sp5, L7), ibid.

91. These were contracts NOd-252 and NOd-253.

92. Smyth to BuS&A, 6-Oct-1930, BuOrd.A13-4/S71(Sperry/21)(L7), RG74/E25B/B1406, NARA-I; Thompson to Comptroller General, 27-Mar-1933, BuOrd.A13-4/S71(Sperry/37), ibid.

93. Bennett memorandum, 26-Jul-1939, BuOrd.A13-4/S71(Sperry/106) (Sp9), RG74/E25D/B33, NARA-I; Bennett memorandum, 13-Sep-1939, BuOrd.A13-4/S71(Sperry/109)(Sp9), ibid.; France to McClaine, 24-Sep-1939, BuOrd.A13-4/S71(Sperry)(L11), ibid.; Woodson to GAO, 26-Sep-1939, BuOrd.A13-4/S71(Sperry/110), ibid.

94. Leahy to JAG, 8-Apr-1929, BuOrd.S71–8(37/53)C2992,C3270–1(Sp5), RG74/
E25B/B1814, NARA-I.

95. "Sperry Plants Join Curtiss in Merger: Gyroscope Company, Acquired by Keys
Holding Concern, a Leader in Instrument Field," *New York Times*, 24-Dec-1928, p. 30.

96. "$3,000,000 Aviation Deal: North American Buys Control of Ford Instrument
Company," *New York Times*, 18-Feb-1930, p. 42.

97. Badger to CoO, 2-Jan-1931, BuOrd.S71(28), Folder "S71(Arma)," RG74/E25B/
B1740, NARA-I; Isherwood's testimony, 21-Feb-1939, *Supplemental Record*, pp. 84–85,
EDNY Equity Case File #8432, RG21/B1381, NARA-NY.

98. Badger to CoO, 2-Jan-1931, BuOrd.S71(28), Folder "S71(Arma)," RG74/E25B/
B1740, NARA-I.

99. Badger to CoO, 2-Jan-1931, ibid.

100. Davis to Furlong, 6-Apr-1938, BuOrd.S71(Ford/156), Folder "Fire Control Insts &
Spare Parts For," RG74/E25B/B1740, NARA I.

101. Dawson, Watt, and Perham, "Means for Use in the Laying of Ordnance," USP
1,695,483, filed 13-Aug-1920 (serial no. 403,432), patented 18-Dec-1928.

102. Jones to CoO, 8-Feb-1932, BuOrd.S71(Ford/80), RG74/E25B/B1740, NARA-I.

103. Jones to CoO, 7-Apr-1932, BuOrd.L4–2/6–32/245, RG74/E25B/B1618, NARA-I.

104. Jones to CoO, 7-Apr-1932, ibid.

105. The evidence is fragmentary; I am inferring this agreement from Willard to
BuS&A, 15-May-1933, para. 4, BuOrd.S71/Nos29791/23, RG74/E25B/B1758, NARA-I.

106. Borst to SecNav for JAG, 31-Jul-1933, enclosed in Dean memorandum, 12-Aug-
1933, BuOrd.S71(Ford/98), RG74/E25B/B1740, NARA-I.

107. Borst to SecNav for JAG, 31-Jul-1933, ibid.

108. Murfin endorsement to BuOrd, 5-Aug-1933, DeptNav.A13–1(330731), RG80/
E22/B522, NARA-I.

109. Larimer endorsement to JAG, 10-Aug-1933, BuOrd.S71(Ford/98)(Sp6, L9),
RG74/E25B/B1740, NARA-I.

110. Dean memorandum, 12-Aug-1933, BuOrd.S71(Ford/98)(L9), RG74/E25B/
B1740, NARA-I.

111. Proprietary purchases (i.e., purchases without advertisement) were governed
by 34 USC 569, which says nothing about a patent requirement. I could not find any
opinion by the Attorney General passing on this question. The Comptroller General
issued several opinions relating to the meaning of "proprietary," but they do not speak
specifically to the question of whether a proprietary purchase required that an item
be patented. Indeed, his language was ambiguous, sometimes using "proprietary" and
"patented" as synonyms (e.g., "considering the question of purchases of patented or
copyrighted articles without advertising," Opinion A-19811 of 24-Oct-1927, 7 Comp.
Gen. 283), other times implying that they were separate categories (e.g., "patented or
proprietary product," Opinion A-32080, 13-Oct-1930, 10 Comp. Gen. 160). It may be
that the Navy Judge Advocate General had issued an opinion holding that "proprietary"
meant patented (or copyrighted).

112. Dean memorandum, 12-Aug-1933, BuOrd.S71(Ford/98)(L9), RG74/E25B/
B1740, NARA-I.

113. See, e.g., Furlong to CoO, 2-Jun-1921, BuOrd.39853/2(L2)-0, RG74/E25A-I/
B3436, NARA-I.

114. Rousseau to SecNav, 22-Apr-1929, DeptNav.QN/A18(280810), RG80/E22/
B3946, NARA-I.

115. See Woodson to BuOrd, 6-Dec-1933, DeptNav.QN/A18(280810)(IV), ibid.

116. This was Contract NOd-551. See Bloch diary, 21-Nov-1934, Folder "Journal, 1934-July 3, 1935," B4, Bloch mss., LoC; Ford to SecNav, 26-Nov-1934, enclosed in Ford to Dean, 26-Nov-1934, BuOrd.S71(Ford/118), RG74/E25B/B1740, NARA-I; Ford to SecNav, 21-Jan-1935, DeptNav A13–1(330721–6), RG80/E22/B522, NARA-I. For the clause making the license renewable on an annual basis, see Swanson to Comptroller General, 16-Feb-1935, DeptNav A13–1(330721–6)IV(AJ:lg), RG80/E22/B522, NARA-I.

117. Comptroller General to SecNav, 9-Nov-1934, enclosed in Bloch to BuOrd, 16-Nov-1934, BuOrd.S71(Ford/117), RG74/E25B/B1740, NARA-I; Swanson to Comptroller General, 16-Feb-1935, DeptNav A13–1(330721–6)IV(AJ:lg), RG80/E22/B522, NARA-I.

118. Mindell, *BHAM*, 217.

119. Khan, *The Democratization of Invention.*

120. Milford, "US Navy Torpedoes, Part Two." I am quite sure that the government established its monopoly because it tired of headaches and lawsuits over intellectual property rights with private-sector torpedo manufacturers. In *Torpedo*, I did not go past 1914, but the IP disputes I covered in chapter 5 continued through World War I; the government and its lead torpedo contractor landed at the Supreme Court in 1920 (*E. W. Bliss Co. v. United States*, 253 US 187).

CHAPTER 9

1. The most recent major study is Hintz, *American Independent Inventors in an Era of Corporate R&D*, which cites much of the previous literature.

2. See esp. Brinkley, *The End of Reform*, 106–36.

3. See Beauchamp, *Invented by Law*, 31.

4. Dugan's testimony, 19-Mar-1936, "Stenographer's Minutes," pp. 13–15, EDNY Equity Case File #7550, RG21/B1241, NARA-NY.

5. In addition to his foreign patents, I have found five US patents in his name, though there may be others: #1,733,531, "Sight-controlled gunnery system," filed 7-Feb-1927, issued 29-Oct-1929; #1,800,931, "Synchronous bomb sight," filed 11-Oct-1928, issued 14-Apr-1931; #1,880,174, "Continuous aim gunfire control system," filed 25-May-1932, issued 27-Sep-1932; #1,959,264, "Radio direction and position indicating system," filed 15-Mar-1930, issued 15-May-1934; and #2,363,948, "Gunfire control system," filed 19-Jan-1942, issued 28-Nov-1944.

6. The abandoned applications were serial nos. 746,238, filed 27-Oct-1924, and 29,843, filed 12-May-1925.

7. Edward Hewlett and Waldo Willard, "System and Apparatus for Gun-fire Control," filed 9-Apr-1924, issued 3-May-1927; Dugan, Amendment D, Paper #9, filed 10-Oct-1927, PF.1,733,531, RG241, NARA-KC.

8. See Dugan's Amendment B, Paper #5, filed 7-Jun-1927; Amendment C, Paper #7, filed 3-Oct-1927; Dugan, Paper #10, filed 17-Oct-1927; Dugan, Paper #17, filed 20-Feb-1928, ibid.

9. Board of Appeals, Paper #19, 5-Jul-1928, f. 84, ibid.

10. Dugan, Amendment E, Paper #20, filed 10-Jul-1928, f. 86, ibid.

11. Dugan to SecNav, 9-Sep-1929, copy of Dugan's Petition to the Court of Claims, IF.59,824, RG241, NARA-KC.

12. Dugan told this story on several occasions. The most detailed version is in Dugan to CommPat, "Petition under Rule 295," Paper #7, filed 15-Nov-1928, IF.57,411, RG241,

NARA-KC. See also Dugan to SecNav, 9-Sep-1929, copy of Dugan's Petition to the Court of Claims, IF.59,824, ibid. See also his secretary's sworn statement corroborating his account (Lida Gregg Patterson, statement of 16-Nov-1928, ff. 36–37, enclosed in Dugan, "Supplementary Petition under Rule 199," filed 19-Nov-1928, IF.57,411, ibid.).

13. The claims were numbered 57–73 in the Ford application, corresponding to claims 1–15, 18, and 22 in Dugan's.

14. Dugan to Gill, 1-Nov-1928, f. 26, IF.57,411, RG241, NARA-KC; Dugan to CommPat, "Petition under Rule 295 [sic—actually Rule 199]," Paper #7, filed 15-Nov-1928, ff. 16–17, ibid.

15. Transcript of meeting on 10-Nov-1928 by Hilda Millan, sworn to 19-Nov-1928, enclosed in Dugan, "Supplementary Petition under Rule 199," filed 19-Nov-1928, ibid.

16. Dugan to Markland, 10-Nov-1928, BuOrd.S71(Ford/27), RG74/E25B/B1740, NARA-I.

17. Dugan to Markland, 14-Nov-1928, BuOrd.S71(Ford/28), ibid.

18. Dugan to CommPat, "Petition under Rule 29," Paper #7, filed 15-Nov-1928, ff. 12–25, IF.57,411, RG241, NARA-KC.

19. Dugan to CommPat, "Petition under Rule 29," ibid. The cases he cited were "the old Patent Office standby" *Mason v. Hepburn* (13 App.D.C. 86, 1898), *In re Appeal of Mower* (15 App.D.C. 144, 1899), *Brown v. Campbell* (41 App.D.C. 499, 1914), and *Macbeth-Evans Glass Co. v. General Electric Co.* (231 F. 183, 1916). I have converted Dugan's law-report citations to their modern form.

20. See "Forfeiture of the Right to the Issuance of a Patent through Unexcused Delay," *Harvard Law Review*.

21. Beauchamp, *Invented by Law*, 103.

22. Biagioli, "Patent Republic." See also Bottomley, *The British Patent System during the Industrial Revolution*, 46–50.

23. Nor has this problem disappeared; see Galison, "Removing Knowledge," 238–40.

24. Ford and Ross, "Affidavit under Rule 75," Paper #8, filed 8-Jan-1930, f.88, PF.1,937,336, RG241, NARA-KC.

25. Sweeney to DeptNav, 19-Feb-1935, BuOrd.S71(Ford/128), RG74/E25B/B1740, NARA-I.

26. SecNav to Dugan, 17-Nov-1928, BuOrd.S71(Ford/26)(L6), ibid.

27. 40 Stat. 217–19, chapter 30. The penalty mentioned by the Navy applied only to offenses listed in sec. 1 of the Act.

28. SecNav to Dugan, 17-Nov-1928, BuOrd.S71(Ford/26)(L6), RG74/E25B/B1740, NARA-I.

29. ToH, 21-Dec-1938, p. 37, EDNY Equity Case File #8432, RG21/B1381, NARA NY.

30. Dugan to SecNav, 26-Jan-1929, in copy of Dugan's Petition to the Court of Claims, IF.59,824, RG241, NARA-KC. Dugan apparently sent the Navy two other letters, dated 27-Dec-1928 and 22-Jan-1929, seeking clarification, but these do not seem to survive.

31. SecNav to Dugan, 8-Feb-1929, in copy of Dugan's Petition to the Court of Claims, IF.59,824, RG241, NARA-KC.

32. Dugan to CommPat, "Power to Inspect and Make Copies," Paper #74, 12-Feb-1929 [no filing date], IF.57,411, RG241, NARA-KC.

33. Dugan to CommPat, "Supplementary Petition under Rule 199," filed 19-Nov-1928, ff. 31–32, ibid.; see also Dugan, "Petition to Make Special," Paper #36, filed 8-Jan-1929, f. 147, ibid.

34. Dugan, "Second Supplementary Petition under Rule 199," Paper #9, filed 20-Nov-1928, ibid.; "Motion for Judgment on the Record," Paper #10, filed 20-Nov-1928, ibid.; "Motion for Judgment on the Record," Paper #18, filed 26-Nov-1928, ibid.; "Motion to Dissolve under Rule 122," filed 30-Nov-1928, ibid.; "Motion for Permission to Take Special Testimony," Paper #21, filed 30-Nov-1928, ibid.; "Motion for Dissolution under Rule 122," Paper #23, filed 3-Dec-1928, ibid.; "Request for Judicial Notice," Paper #27, filed 10-Dec-1928, ibid.; "Request for Judicial Notice," Paper #28, filed 10-Dec-1928, ibid.; and "Petition to Make Special," Paper #36, filed 8-Jan-1929, ibid.

35. See, e.g., Moakley & Gill, "Memorandum Opposing Dugan's Motion for Permission to Take Special Testimony," Paper #25, filed 6-Dec-1928, ibid.

36. Kinnan, Paper #29, 17-Dec-1928, ibid.; Waite, Paper #30, c. 21-Dec-1928, ibid.; Robertson (CommPat), Paper #37, 10-Jan-1929, ibid.

37. Kinnan, "Appeal on Motion," Paper #33, 5-Jan-1929, ibid.

38. Disney (Law Examiner), Paper #53, 12-Apr-1929, ibid.

39. Dugan, "Disclaimer under Rule 125," Paper #71, filed 11-Jun-1929, ibid.

40. CommPat to Dugan, 15-Jul-1929, f. 109, PF.1,733,531, RG241, NARA-KC.

41. Dugan to SecNav, 8-Aug-1929, copy in Dugan's Petition to Court of Claims, IF.59,824, RG241, NARA-KC.

42. Dugan to SecNav, 9-Sep-1929, ibid.

43. "Report of Conference between the Chief of the Bureau of Ordnance, Navy Department, Rear Admiral W. D. Leahy, U. S. Navy, Captain D. E. Theleen, U.S.N., and Mr. Joseph Dugan, held in the Bureau of Ordnance on September 12, 1929," 12-Sep-1929, BuOrd.S71(Ford/49), p. 16, RG74/E25B/B1740, NARA-I.

44. This is not borne out by the transcript of the meeting, but the transcript indicates that Dugan and Leahy continued talking informally after the end of the formal interview covered by the transcript, so Leahy could possibly have made the remark during the informal chat.

45. Dugan to SecNav, 16-Sep-1929, f. 52, in Dugan's Petition to the Court of Claims, copy in IF.59,824, RG241, NARA-KC.

46. Markland to Badger, 20-Sep-1929, BuOrd.S71(Ford/79), RG74/E25B/B1740, NARA-I.

47. Leahy to Atty Gen, 24-Sep-1929, BuOrd.S71(Ford/47)(A5), ibid.

48. SecNav to Dugan, 30-Sep-1929, BuOrd.S71(Ford/51), ibid.

49. Dugan to SecNav, 19-Nov-1929, copy in Dugan's Petition to the Court of Claims, IF.59,824, RG241, NARA-KC.

50. *Richmond Screw Anchor Co. v. United States*, 271 US 331 (1928), esp. at 346–47.

51. Dugan, "Petition," 30-Mar-1930, copy in IF.59,824, RG241, NARA-KC.

52. Mentioned in Rugg to DeptNav, 9-Dec-1932, RG80/E22/B1071, NARA-I.

53. See Campbell to Peartree, 24-Apr-1967, and subsequent correspondence, Ct.Cl.L-91, RG123/E1/B4212, NARA-I.

54. This is a sad loss, since the testimony apparently ran to more than 2,300 pages, which would have been a gold mine about the development of US naval fire control. See Dugan, "Motion for Extension of Time to File Petition for Writ of Certiorari," 3-Aug-1939, Case 488, RG267/E21/B1860, NARA-I.

55. Bauer to Mothershead, 4-Feb-1933, DoJ.27–580, RG60/EA1-COR27/B41, NARA-II; Lavender diary, 19-Nov-1935, "Datebook, 1930s I," Lavender mss.

56. Dugan, "Motion for Call," 31-Mar-1930, DeptNav.L11-15/QQ-Dugan,Jos. (300415), RG80/E22/B1071, NARA-I, and Dugan, "Motion for Call, 23-Apr-1930, enclosed in Sellers to BuOrd, 9-Jun-1930, ibid.

57. Sellers to BuOrd, 9-Jun-1930, ibid.

58. SecNav to Clerk of the Court of Claims, 14-Jun-1930, and correspondence thereon, ibid.

59. See, e.g., Smyth to JAG, 24-Dec-1931, ibid.; Gatch to Atty Gen, 20-Jul-1935, ibid.; and Stott to CNO, 21-Mar-1935, BuOrd.S71(Ford)(L9), RG74/E25B/B1740, NARA-I.

60. Rugg to DeptNav, 21-Jan-1931, BuOrd.S71(Ford/68), RG74/E25B/B1740, NARA-I.

61. Dugan, "Memorandum in Support of Motion to Amend," 5-Apr-1932, DoJ.27-580, RG60/EA1-COR27/B41, NARA-II.

62. Rugg to DeptNav, 23-Dec-1931, DeptNav.L11-15/QQ-Dugan,Jos.(300415), RG80/E22/B1071, NARA-I.

63. Colwell, Paper #1, 7-Apr-1930, IF.59,824, RG241, NARA-KC.

64. By the time of the interference with Dugan's patent, Bates had already fought and lost an interference with the same GE patent that Dugan had fought and lost, for which see IF.56,158, RG241, NARA-KC. Bates's concession of priority to GE was part of a negotiated settlement between GE and Sperry Gyroscope.

65. Dugan, "Petition to Make Special," Paper #8, filed 7-Jul-1930, ff. 17-22, IF.59,824, RG241, NARA-KC.

66. Thompson, "Reply Memorandum and Request to Make Special," Paper #10, filed 10-Jul-1930, f. 57, ibid.

67. For Dugan's concession, see Dugan, "Disclaimer," Paper #18, filed 9-Sep-1930, and "Concession of Priority," Paper #19, filed 23-Sep-1930, ibid. For the examiner's three decisions, see Jacobs, Paper #24, 30-Sep-1930, ibid.; Jacobs, Paper #26, 14-Oct-1930, ibid.; and Jacobs, Paper #31, 24-Oct-1930, ibid. For the arguments by both parties, see Dugan, "Petition for Rehearing," filed 3-Oct-1930, Paper #25, ibid.; Thompson, "Supplementary Motion for Rehearing," Paper #29, filed 21-Oct-1930, ibid; Dugan, "Brief Opposing Bates' Supplementary Motion for Rehearing," Paper #30, filed 22-Oct-1930, ibid.

68. Brearley to Dugan, Paper #32, 27-Oct-1930, ibid.

69. Rugg, "Motion by Government for Leave to File Brief Amicus Curiae," Paper #35, filed 15-Nov-1930, ibid.; Kinnan (Acting CommPat), Paper #36, 25-Nov-1930, ibid. See also Rugg, "Government's Brief Amicus Curiae," Paper #42, filed 12-Dec-1930, ibid.

70. Moakley & Gill, "Memorandum in Support of Motion to Intervene," Paper #38, filed 2-Dec-1920, ibid. The Patent Office rejected its motion; see Kinnan, Paper #39, 5-Dec-1930, ibid.

71. Dugan, "Dugan's Brief on Appeal," Paper #41, filed 12-Dec-1930, f. 191, ibid.

72. Dugan, "Dugan's Brief on Appeal," ff. 191-92, ibid.

73. Board of Appeals, Paper #47, 22-Dec-1930, IF.59,824, RG241, NARA-KC.

74. Sec. 4918, Rev. Stat. Dugan also sued on his second patent (USP 1,880,147), rather than on his first (USP 1,733,531), which was the basis of his suit in the Court of Claims.

75. Dugan, "Bill of Complaint," 1-Apr-1935, DoJ.27-740, RG60/EA1-COR27/B51, NARA-II. The requirements for disclosure and operativeness were governed by Sec. 4888, Rev. Stat.

76. Dugan to CommPat, 10-Jun-1935, DoJ.27-740, RG60/EA1-COR27/B51, NARA-II.

77. Deposition transcript, 17-Jun-1935, p. 4, EDNY Equity Case File #7550, RG21/B1242, NARA-NY.

78. Deposition transcript, 17-Jun-1935, p. 12, ibid.

79. See Dugan to Atty Gen, 29-Jun-1935 and 2-Jul-1935, DoJ.27–740, RG60/EA1-COR27/B51, NARA-II; Dugan to McFarlane, 25-Jun-1935, ibid.; and Dugan to Roper, 28-Jun-1935, ibid.

80. Moran report, 24-Sep-1935, ibid.

81. "Stenographer's Minutes," hearings of 20- and 23-Mar-1936, pp. 160–99, EDNY Equity Case File #7550, RG21/B1242, NARA-NY; Borst, "Brief on Behalf of Defendant," filed 24-Apr-1936, pp. 45–48, ibid.

82. Bloch diary, 18-Mar-1936, Folder "Journal, 6 Jul 1935–1936," B4, Bloch mss., LoC; and Spellman to CoO, 25-Mar-1936, BuOrd.S71(Ford/144), RG74/E25B/B1740, NARA-I.

83. "Stenographer's Minutes," hearing of 20-Mar-1936, p. 128, EDNY Equity Case File #7550, RG21/B1241, NARA-NY. Dugan had made the argument about insufficient disclosure of the "K-constants" consistently from the interference proceedings through the court proceedings.

84. "Stenographer's Minutes," hearing of 20-Mar-1936, p. 221, ibid.

85. "Stenographer's Minutes," hearing of 20-Mar-1936, pp. 296–97, ibid.

86. *Dugan v. Ford Instrument Co.*, 15 F. Supp. 442 at 447.

87. Lavender diary, 15-Jan-1937, "Datebook, 1930s I," Lavender mss.

88. See their correspondence from Sep-1937 in Ct.Cl.L-91, RG123/E1/B4212, NARA-I.

89. No copy of the ruling survives, but see Mothershead to Whitaker, 14-Feb-1939, ibid.

90. Whitaker to Borst, 15-Apr-1939, and Mothershead to Borst, 12-Sep-1939, ibid.

91. Public Law 76-81, "An Act to provide that records certified by the Court of Claims to the Supreme Court, in response to writs of certiorari, may include material portions of the evidence, and for other purposes," 53 Stat. 752, ch. 140. See also S. Rep. 339, 1-May-1939, 76th Congress, 1st session; Mothershead to Borst, 12-Sep-1939, Ct.Cl.L-91, RG123/E1/B4212, NARA-I.

92. Transcripts of record typically included such matter, and on balance, documents in the Supreme Court's case file support this interpretation, though they are not definitive. See Dugan, "Motion for Extension of Time to File Petition for Writ of Certiorari," 3-Aug-1939, Case 488, RG267/E21/B1860, NARA-I; Hart to Dugan, 20-Oct-1939, ibid.; Hart to Cropley, 20-Oct-1939, ibid.; Jackson to Cropley, 7-Nov-1939, ibid.

93. Borst to Atty Gen, 2-Nov-1939, DoJ.27–580, RG60/EA1-COR27/B41, NARA-II.

94. Jackson to Cropley, 7-Nov-1939, Case 488, RG267/E21/B1860, NARA-I. Jackson's brief no longer survives, but for evidence that he opposed Dugan's motion to release the proceedings from secrecy, see Dugan to Jackson, 20-Nov-1939, ibid.

95. Stoutenburgh to Shea, 8-Nov-1939, Ct.Cl.L-91, RG123/E1/B4212, NARA-I.

96. Stark affidavit, 9-Nov-1939, DeptNav.L11–15/QQ-Dugan,Jos.(300415–2), RG80/E22/B1071, NARA-I; Lavender to Robinson, 13-Nov-1939, ibid.

97. *Dugan v. United States*, 308 US 614 (1939).

98. Borst to Mothershead, 29-Dec-1939, Ct.Cl.L-91, RG123/E1/B4212, NARA-I.

99. Shea to Navy JAG, 24-Mar-1943, DoJ.27–740, RG60/EA1-COR27/B51, NARA-II.

100. Campbell memorandum, 10-Feb-1943, ibid.

101. Newell to Sumida, 6-Jun-1994 (document courtesy of Jon Sumida).

102. Mothershead to Asst Atty Gen, 28-Oct-1936, DoJ.95–51–54, RG60/EA1-COR95/B60, NARA-II.

CHAPTER 10

1. *United States v. Reynolds*, 345 US 1 at 6–7 (1953). On *Reynolds*, see Siegel, *Claim of Privilege*. On the privilege, see Chesney, "State Secrets and the Limits of National Security Litigation," and Donohue, "The Shadow of State Secrets." On the use of the privilege in the context of patent litigation, see Farley and Isaacs, "Privilege-Wise and Patent (and Trade Secret) Foolish?", and Farley and Isaacs, *Patents for Power*, 63–65.

2. Ford, "Calculating Instrument," p. 1, USP 1,484,823, filed 24-Feb-1921, issued 26-Feb-1924.

3. Ford, "Range and Bearing Keeper," USP 1,827,812, filed 1-Mar-1919, issued 20-Oct-1931.

4. 29 Stat. 693, sec. 4 (revising Rev. Stat. sec. 4894, 1878 edn., to change the time limit from two years to one year), repeated in 39 Stat. 348. The one-year limit was later reduced to six months, for which see 44 Stat. 1335, sec. 1 and 1337, sec. 15. For correspondence between Ford's attorneys and the Patent Office showing how they exploited these provisions, see PF.1,827,812, RG241, NARA-KC.

5. ToH, 16-May-1940, p. 183, RG123/E1/B4937, NARA-I.

6. "Petition," filed 1-Aug-1936, ibid.

7. Enclosure (N), "Remarks under Patent No. 1,232,968," enclosed in Stark to Rowcliff, 21-Sep-1936, BuOrd.A13–4(360610–1), Folder "A13–4," RG74/E25C/B1396, NARA-I.

8. Enclosure (O), "Patent No. 1,162,511," enclosed in ibid.

9. Groesbeck to Moakley, 7-Feb-1919, PF.1,450,585, RG241, NARA-KC. See also Groesbeck to Moakley, 2-May-1919 and 24-Jul-1920, ibid.

10. Stark to JAG, 21-Sep-1936, BuOrd.A13–4(34)(L10–3, Sp8), Folder "A13–4," RG74/E25C/B1396, NARA-I; Rowcliff to Atty Gen, 26-Sep-1936, DeptNav.A13–4(D4), RG80/UD-E8/B48, NARA-I.

11. This was file number 28499, the Bureau's main file on Pollen during the World War I years.

12. This motion has not been found, but its date is given and its contents can be inferred from Mothershead, "Opposition to Plaintiffs' Motion for Call on the Navy Department," filed 6-Nov-1936, RG123/E1/B4937, NARA-I.

13. Stark to JAG, 3-Nov-1936, BuOrd.A13–4(34)(A7), Folder "A13–4," RG74/E25C/B1396, NARA-I; Mothershead, "Opposition to Plaintiffs' Motion for Call on the Navy Department," filed 6-Nov-1936, RG123/E1/B4937, NARA-I.

14. See ToH, 7-Jun-1937, p. 31, RG123/E1/B4937, NARA-I.

15. Swanson to Lizars, 9-Dec-1936, DeptNav A13–4(360610)(D4), RG80/E22/B532, NARA-I.

16. At this stage in its evolution, the court consisted of "commissioners," who functioned as trial judges, and "judges," who functioned as appellate judges. See Bennett, "Section Three," 85–94.

17. ToH, 7-Jun-1937, pp. 1–4, RG123/E1/B4937, NARA-I.

18. ToH, 7-Jun-1937, pp. 7–24, ibid.

19. Unless otherwise noted, the following biographical information comes from a statement by Lavender in the "Patents" pile, Lavender mss.

20. The British fliers John Alcock and Arthur Brown made the first *nonstop* trans-Atlantic flight two weeks later.

21. Harvey C. Hayes to Lavender, 20-Jan-1932, "Career and Commendations" pile, Lavender mss.

22. Entry for 1-Oct-1936, Lavender's service record, ibid.

23. Bloch diary, 21-Aug-1935, Folder "Journal, 6 Jul 1935–1936," B4, Bloch mss., LoC.

24. Lavender diary, 2-Feb-1937, "Datebook, 1930s I," Lavender mss.; see also entries for 23-Jan-1936, 27-Oct-1936, and 19-Feb-1937.

25. Bush to SecNav, 7-Oct-1941, "Career and Commendations" pile, Lavender mss.

26. Wellerstein, "Patenting the Bomb."

27. PL 76-700, "To amend the Act relating to preventing the publication of inventions in the national interest, and for other purposes," 54 Stat. 710 (1940); Public Law 77-239, "To amend the Act relating to preventing the publication of inventions in the national interest, and for other purposes," 55 Stat. 657 (1941).

28. Swanson, 5-Jun-1937, RG123/E1/B4937, NARA-I.

29. ToH, 7-Jun-1931, p. 29, ibid.

30. ToH, 7-Jun-1931, p. 56, ibid.

31. ToH, 7-Jun-1931, p. 61, ibid.

32. ToH, 7-Jun-1931, p. 58, ibid.

33. ToH, 7-Jun-1931, pp. 62–84, ibid.

34. ToH, 7-Jun-1931, p. 89, ibid.

35. ToH, 7-Jun-1931, p. 91, ibid.

36. ToH, 7-Jun-1931, p. 90, ibid.

37. ToH, 7-Jun-1931, p. 92, ibid.

38. ToH, 7-Jun-1931, p. 92, ibid.

39. Lavender diary, 7-Jun-1937, "Datebook, 1930s I," Lavender mss.

40. Leahy to Attorney General, 19-Jun-1937, DoJ.95–51–54, RG60/EA1-COR95/B60, NARA-II; see also Stark endorsement, 11-Jun-1937, Folder "A13–4," RG74/E25C/B1396, NARA-I.

41. McMahon to Hoover, 29-Jun-1937, DoJ.95–51–54, RG60/EA1-COR95/B60, NARA-II.

42. Boyle report, 25-Aug-1937, enclosed in Hoover to McMahon, 1-Sep-1937, ibid.

43. Lizars, "Motion and Citation of Authorities in Support Thereof and Offer of Proof," 2-Jul-1937, RG123/E1/B4937, NARA-I.

44. 28 USC 272, 1934 ed.

45. Whitaker, "Brief in Opposition to Plaintiff's Motion to Direct the Commissioner to Receive Evidence," 23-Sep-1937, RG123/E1/B4937, NARA-I.

46. *Pollen and Isherwood v. United States*, 85 Ct.Cl. 673 (1937).

47. *Pollen and Isherwood v. United States*.

48. Bill of Complaint, 6-Dec-1937, EDNY Equity Case File #8432, RG21/B1381, NARA NY.

49. Borst to JAG, 11-Jan-1938, DoJ.27–938, RG60/EA1-COR27/B59, NARA-II.

50. Swanson to Atty Gen, 26-Jan-1938, and Whitaker to Borst, 28-Jan-1938, ibid.

51. See Mothershead to Borst, 7-Mar-1938 and 11-May-1938, ibid.

52. 35 USC 70, 1934 ed.

53. These were USP 1,077,965 (issued 1913, expired 1930); 1,123,795 (issued 1915, expired 1932); 1,162,510 (issued 1915, expired 1932); 1,162,511 (issued 1915, expired 1932); 1,232,968 (issued 1917, expired 1934); and 1,314,208 (issued 1919, expired 1936).

54. Lizars, "Plaintiffs' Brief in Opposition to the Defendant's Motion," 2-Mar-1938, EDNY Equity Case File #8432, RG21/B1381, NARA-NY.

55. See Lizars, "Amended Bill of Complaint," 20-Apr-1938; Borst, "Motion for an order striking the amended bill of complaint," 9-May-1938; Borst, "Memorandum in Support of Defendant's Motion to Strike," 25-May-1938; Lizars, "Plaintiffs' Brief in Opposition to Defendant's Motion to Strike the Amended Bill of Complaint," 25-May-1938; Judge Byers, ruling on motion, 14-Jun-1938; Judge Byers, Order on motion, 28-Sep-1938; and Lizars, "Amended Bill of Complaint," 6-Oct-1938, all in ibid.

56. Borst, "Answer to amended bill of complaint," 25-Oct-1938, ibid.

57. Borst to Attorney General, 9-Dec-1938, DoJ.27–938, RG60/EA1-COR27/B59, NARA-II; Whitaker to JAG, 13-Dec-1938, ibid. The transcript of the depositions lists the two naval officers but not Mothershead as present; however, his letter to Whitaker of 14-Dec-1938 (ibid.), shows that he was present.

58. *ToR*, pp. 87–88, EDNY Equity Case File #8432, RG21/B1381, NARA-NY.

59. *ToR*, pp. 88, ibid.

60. *ToR*, pp. 89–92, 99–100, ibid.

61. 12 Stat. 411.

62. 12 Stat. 411, sec. 4.

63. 40 Stat. 29.

64. 45 Stat. 1147.

65. *ToR*, p. 113, EDNY Equity Case File #8432, RG21/B1381, NARA-NY; ToH, 21-Dec-1938, p. 12, ibid.

66. *ToR*, p. 108, ibid.

67. *ToR*, pp. 109, 113–14, ibid.

68. *ToR*, pp. 109–10, ibid.

69. *ToR*, p. 110, ibid.

70. *ToR*, p. 112, ibid.

71. *ToR*, pp. 116–17, ibid.

72. *ToR*, p. 117, ibid.

73. *ToR*, p. 118–20, ibid.

74. ToH, 21-Dec-1938, p. 14, EDNY Equity Case File #8432, RG21/B1381, NARA-NY.

75. Woodson to BuNav, 29-Dec-1938, DeptNav.A13–4(D4), RG80/UD-E8/B48, NARA-I.

76. See Woodson to CoO, 1-Mar-1939, para. 7, ibid.

77. Whitaker to Walsh, telegram and letter, 15-Dec-1938, DoJ.27–938, RG60/EA1-COR27/B59, NARA-II; see also Mothershead to Cooper, 14-Dec-1938, ibid.

78. Walsh, "Memorandum (1) On Behalf of Petition to Intervene (2) On Behalf of Defendant in Opposition to Plaintiff's Motion," n.d. but c. 23-Dec-1938, EDNY Equity Case File #8432, RG21/B1381, NARA-NY. This test was, and remains, Rule 24b of the *Federal Rules of Civil Procedure*, which had become effective only three months earlier, replacing the old *Federal Equity Rules*.

79. "Petition to Intervene as Defendant," filed 19-Dec-1938, EDNY Equity Case File #8432, RG21/B1381, NARA-NY. For further development of these arguments, see Walsh

and Borst, "Memorandum (1) On Behalf of Petition to Intervene (2) On Behalf of Defendant in Opposition to Plaintiff's Motion," n.d. but c. 23-Dec-1938, ibid.

80. Lizars, "Memorandum in Opposition to Petition to Intervene," filed 21-Dec-1938, ibid. For further development of these arguments, see Lizars, "Reply Memorandum to Memorandum (1) On Behalf of Petition to Intervene (2) On Behalf of Defendant in Opposition to Plaintiff's Motion," filed 27-Dec-1938, ibid.

81. ToH, 21-Dec-1938, pp. 44–72, ibid.

82. *ToR*, p. 119, ibid.

83. For context on the considerations affecting judges, see Trenga, "What Judges Say and Do in Deciding National Security Cases."

84. ToH, 21-Dec-1938, pp. 47–48, EDNY Equity Case File #8432, RG21/B1381, NARA-NY.

85. ToH, 21-Dec-1938, p. 48, ibid.

86. ToH, 21-Dec-1938, pp. 50–51, ibid.

87. ToH, 21-Dec-1938, p. 107, ibid.

88. Borst to Mothershead, 21-Dec-1938, DoJ.27–938, RG60/EA1-COR27/B59, NARA-II.

89. ToH, 21-Dec-1938, pp. 100–1, EDNY Equity Case File #8432, RG21/B1381, NARA-NY.

90. ToH, 21-Dec-1938, p. 105, ibid.

91. Borst to Mothershead, 21-Dec-1938, DoJ.27–938, RG60/EA1-COR27/B59, NARA-II.

92. Inch memorandum, 28-Dec-1938, p. 44, *ToR*, EDNY Equity Case File #8432, RG21/B1381, NARA-NY.

93. Walsh, "Answer of Intervener," 6-Jan-1939, p. 46, *ToR*, ibid.

94. Lizars, "Motion for Production of Documents, Etc.," filed 12-Jan-1939, pp. 49–50, *ToR*, ibid.

95. Affidavits by Holden, 16-Jan-1939, and by Furlong, 20-Jan-1939, DoJ.27–938, RG60/EA1-COR27/B59, NARA-II.

96. Leahy to Attorney General, 20-Jan-1939, DoJ.27–938, ibid.

97. Borst, "Memorandum on Behalf of Defendant, Ford Instrument Company, Inc., in Opposition to Plaintiffs' Motion," filed 25-Jan-1939, EDNY Equity Case File #8432, RG21/B1381, NARA-NY; Smith, "Memorandum of the United States of America as Intervener, In Opposition to Plaintiff's Motion for the Production of Documents," n.d. but c. 25-Jan-1939, pp. 51–61, *ToR*, ibid.

98. Galston's role is of additional interest because ten years later, he wrote the opinion in *Cresmer v. United States* (9 FRD 203, 1949), cited by the Supreme Court in *Reynolds* alongside *Pollen and Isherwood*.

99. Borst to Attorney General, 25-Jan-1939, DoJ.27–938, RG60/EA1-COR27/B59, NARA-II.

100. *Pollen et. al v. Ford Instrument Co., Inc. (United States, Intervener)*, 26 F.Supp. 583 (1939). The Supreme Court's citation of this case in *Reynolds* dropped the "(United States, Intervener)" from the title; see *United States v. Reynolds*, 345 US 1, note 11 (1953).

101. Stoutenburgh to Whitaker, 25-Feb-1939, DoJ.27–938, RG60/EA1-COR27/B59, NARA-II.

102. Stoutenburgh to Whitaker, 25-Feb-1939, ibid. Presumably these rulings, described by Stoutenburgh, occurred at those times during Peter Bruce's and Charles Infante's testimony when the *ToR* reads "balance of argument deleted" (*ToR*, pp. 123–24, EDNY Equity Case File #8432, RG21/B1381, NARA-NY).

103. "Decision by the Court," received 4-Apr-1939, DoJ.27–938, RG60/EA1-COR27/B59, NARA-II.

104. *ToR*, pp. 157–58, EDNY Equity Case File #8432, RG21/B1381, NARA-NY.

105. Lizars, "Assignment of Errors," filed 14-Jun-1939, *ToR*, pp. 170–71, ibid. See also his "Brief for Plaintiffs-Appellants," filed 2-Dec-1939, 2nd CCA #16805, RG276/B4908, NARA-KC.

106. *Pollen et al. v. Ford Instrument Co., Inc.*, 108 F.2d 762 (1940).

107. See "Bill of Complaint," filed 19-Jul-1940, EDNY Civil Case File #1406, RG21/B154, NARA-NY; and *Dugan v. Sperry Gyroscope Co.*, 35 F.Supp. 902 (EDNY 1940). This case concerned a radio direction finder, not a fire-control invention.

108. ToH, 13-Jun-1940, pp. 221–27, RG123/E1/B4937, NARA-I.

109. Leahy diary, 13-Jun-1940, Reel 2, p. 66, Leahy mss., LOC.

110. ToH, 13-Jun-1940, p. 234, RG123/E1/B4937, NARA-I. In a biographical twist, the Commissioner's father, Melville W. Church, had been the Firth Sterling Steel Company's lawyer in its litigation with the Bethlehem Steel Company, one of the cases cited in *Reynolds* (*Firth Sterling Steel Co. v. Bethlehem Steel Co.*, 199 F. 353, (1912)). In that capacity, Church *pere* had argued against the Navy Department's assertion the proto-state secrets privilege to drawings of steam turbines that Firth Sterling wanted in order to prove patent infringement. Church *fils* took a different line in the *Pollen* case.

111. Leahy diary, 13-Jun-1940, Reel 2, p. 66, Leahy mss., LoC.

112. Zimmerman, *Top Secret Exchange*, 3.

113. See Falcone, "The Rocket's Red Glare." Falcone also emphasizes how much the Americans learned from the British about the organizational infrastructure necessary to guide public-private cooperation in the development of strategically significant technologies.

114. Baxter III, *Scientists Against Time*, 142.

115. Zimmerman, *Top Secret Exchange*.

116. This phrase comes from Falcone, "The Rocket's Red Glare," 173 and *passim*.

117. Falcone, "The Rocket's Red Glare," 50–176; Falcone, "Culture Diplomacy." For those wanting a deeper dive, Falcone provides citations to the work of previous scholars on several of these technologies in "The Rocket's Red Glare," 142–57.

118. Tizard diary, 28-Aug-1940, HTT.16/42, IWM.

119. Furlong to Bingham, 26-Dec-1917, Folder "GenCorr, 1911–1917," and Furlong to Bingham, 14-Feb-1918, Folder "GenCorr, 1918," B1, Furlong mss., LoC; Earle to Sims, 27-Mar-1918, Folder "Earle, Ralph, Ja-Je 1918," B55, Sims mss., LoC; Earle to Thomson, 29-Mar-1918, BuOrd.32977/41(A2)-0, RG74/E25A-I/B1924, NARA-I. For the dates of Furlong's 1918 stint in the Bureau, see Furlong to CoO, 20-May-1921, BuOrd.37182/21, RG74/E25A-I/B2924, NARA-I.

120. Tizard diary, 10-Sep-1940, HTT.16/116, IWM. This passage was brought to my attention by Zimmerman, *Top Secret Exchange*, 114.

121. Furlong to SecNav for BuOrd, 13-Jul-1918, BuOrd.35371/169, RG74/E25A-II/B116, NARA-I.

122. Tizard diary, 25-Nov-1940, HTT.16/173, IWM.

123. Self to Ministry of Aircraft Production, 11-Nov-1940, Briny.1406.11/11, Docket "Miscellaneous papers from Director of Contracts (D) on Patent Interchange agreement dated Nov. 1940-Aug 1944," AVIA.15/2437, TNA.

124. Tizard diary, 13-Sep-1940, HTT.16/119, IWM.

125. Tizard diary, 18-Sep-1940, HTT.16/127, IWM.

126. Tizard diary, 23-Sep-1940, HTT.16/134, IWM.

127. Isherwood, *Round the World in 80 Years*, 182.

128. October 1940 directory, Docket "British Purchasing Commission (Organisation)," FO.115/3768, TNA. See also Isherwood, *Round the World in 80 Years*, 182.

129. *Pollen et al. v. United States*, 58 F.Supp. 653 (1943).

130. Woodson to CoO, 1-Mar-1939, DeptNav.A13–4(D4), RG80/UD-E8/B48, NARA-I.

131. I am grateful to Michael Falcone for pushing me to think along these lines.

132. See, e.g., Boast, *The Machine in the Ghost*, 83–87.

133. Bush, *Pieces of the Action*, 183–84. I thank Jon Sumida for calling my attention to this passage in Bush's memoirs.

134. Bush, *Pieces of the Action*, 184–85.

135. Bush's error has been widely reproduced in one form or another. See, e.g., Clymer, "Mechanical Integrators," 20–27; Bowles, "US Technological Enthusiasm and British Technological Skepticism in the Age of the Analog Brain," 6–7; Bromley, "Analog Computing Devices," 172–91; Clymer, "The Mechanical Analog Computers of Hannibal Ford and William Newell," esp. 18–24; Zachary, *Endless Frontier*, 49; Mindell, *BHAM*, 38 (a rare error, due to relying on two authors, Clymer and Bromley (see *BHAM*, 345n56), unaware of Isherwood's improvements to the Kelvin drive); and Boast, *The Machine in the Ghost*, 84–85 (which elides Pollen and Isherwood by stating that Kelvin had built his integrator for naval gunnery).

CONCLUSION

1. Seybold, *The World of Digital Typesetting*, 80–82, 114–23.

2. Miller, *Chip War*, 23–28, 91–92, 183–89, 225–34; Brock and Lécuyer, "From Nuclear Physics to Semiconductor Manufacturing"; Mody and Lynch, "Test Objects."

3. Mindell, *BHAM*, ch. 8; Miller, *Chip War*, 20.

4. Bradley, "The History and Development of Aircraft Instruments," 10, 181–87, 194–202.

5. Down to Browning, 27-Jun-1917, p. 7, Docket "United States Navy. Proposed visit of British Naval Technical Experts. Commander R. T. Down," ADM.137/1621, TNA.

6. Nevins with Hill, *Ford*, 349–50; Watts, *The People's Tycoon*, 112–5.

7. Cooling, *Gray Steel and Blue Water Navy*, 40–50, 66–82.

8. Misa, *A Nation of Steel*, 5.

9. Tweedale, *Steel City*, 99–154; Misa, *A Nation of Steel*, 15–28.

10. Ford, "Special Automobile Steels," 386G.

11. And warnings about the foreign "Yankee peril" were no less useful at home than warnings about the "yellow peril"; see Marin, "Did the United States Scare the Europeans?"

12. In the language of postcolonial theory, the United States needs to be "provincialized."

13. For a good example of the (flawed) conventional view, see the entry for "Early 20th century—United Kingdom vs. United States—NO WAR," in Harvard's "Thucydides Trap Project," at https://www.belfercenter.org/thucydides-trap/case-file.

14. For fuller development of the ideas in this paragraph, see Epstein, "The Conundrum of American Power in the Age of World War I," and Epstein, "A Useful Category of Analysis?"

15. MacLeod, *Inventing the Industrial Revolution*, 10–12; MacLeod, "The European Origins of British Technological Predominance," 111–26; and Reinert, *Translating Empire*, 13–15.

16. Historians of technology might call this "indigenization," "hybridization," or "creolization." See, e.g., Edgerton, "Creole Technologies and Global Histories," 75–112, esp. 100–101.

17. Doshi, *The Long Game*, 261–91; Gries, *China's New Nationalism*, esp. 30–42, 128–34, 141–44.

18. See Hughes, *American Genesis*; Adas, *Machines as the Measures of Men*; Adas, *Dominance by Design*; Mitter, *Bitter Revolution*, 233–38; Westad, *Restless Empire*, 456.

19. See, e.g., Freymann, *One Belt One Road*, 44–91; Dikötter, *The Discourse of Race in Modern China*; Wyatt, "A Certain Whiteness of Being."

20. Anderson, *Imagined Communities*.

21. For historical perspective, see Krige, "Regulating the Transnational Flow of Intangible Knowledge," 185–90; Westad, *Restless Empire*, 372–73. For contemporary examples, read the news.

22. Trenchard, Letter 64, p. 267, in *Cato's Letters* (I have modernized the capitalization). See also Semmel, *Liberalism and Naval Strategy*, 1–8.

23. See Epstein, "Conundrum."

24. Rodger, "From the 'Military Revolution' to the 'Fiscal-Naval State,'" 119–28.

25. Meidinger, "The 'Public Uses' of Eminent Domain"; Benson, "The Evolution of Eminent Domain."

26. The Royal Navy (there is a clue in the name) originated as the English king's personal navy in medieval times, not as the Parliamentary Navy after the Glorious Revolution or as the British Navy after the Acts of Union. The US Navy considers its founding to have been the establishment of the Continental Navy in 1775, prior to the Declaration of Independence, the Articles of Confederation, and the Constitution.

27. In addition to the evidence provided in this book, see Epstein, "Intellectual Property and National Security," and Epstein, "Harnessing Invention."

28. I thank Mary Mitchell for suggesting this framing to me, though I have developed it in a somewhat different way than contemplated.

29. This is both a Marxist argument and an anti-Marxist argument. See Parrini, "Theories of Imperialism"; and Cain and Hopkins, *British Imperialism*, 453.

30. Here I owe a deep intellectual debt to Nicholas Lambert and his work, especially *Planning Armageddon* and *The Neptune Factor*.

31. Quoted in Sumida, "Forging the Trident," 217.

32. The saying is attributed to François de La Rochefoucauld; see *Réflexions ou Sentences et maximes morales de La Rochefoucauld*, ed. Louis Lacour (Paris: Académie des Bibliophiles, 1869), 70. See also Orwell, "Reflections on Gandhi."

33. Merges, *American Patent Law*, 22 (cf. p. 13).

Sources Cited

I wish to record my appreciation for the work of four historians—Jon Sumida, Christopher Wright, David Mindell, and Norman Friedman—who have written about naval fire control. In the course of researching this book, I went back over a number of archival records that they had used (in addition to a number of previously untapped records). Though I disagree with them on the occasional minor point, the thoroughness of their research and the skill with which they interpreted very difficult material continually impressed me and made my job easier than it would have been.

A note on two of the archival collections that I used for the book is in order. First, I saw the Arthur Pollen papers at the Churchill Archives Centre (CAC) over the course of multiple research trips, initially while they were still in the course of being catalogued. For ease of reference, I have done my best to translate the original box numbers into the new catalog numbers, prefixed by PLLN. However, there was a small accession for which I cannot hazard a guess as to its new catalog number; files in that accession are cited in my notes as "Jebb Accession, PP [Pollen Papers], CAC." I also could not determine the new catalog number for the inscription by Harold Isherwood cited in chapter 1, and thus I have cited the source as as PP, CAC. Finally, while I was able to determine the new catalog numbers of two files (PLLN.5/1/38 and 8/2) consisting of multiple folders, I was uncertain to which folder any particular document from the files belonged, so I have omitted folder designations.

Second, I saw the Robert Lavender papers arranged in piles on a dining table when they were privately held by his granddaughter, Roberta Anne Vena. She subsequently transferred them to the Library of Congress, where they are currently being catalogued. I have cited the papers as I saw them, with a "pile" or other designation, hoping that this information will help anyone who wishes to check my notes once the papers are available to researchers.

A list of the sources used in the book follows.

PRIMARY SOURCES

Unpublished

United States

Hagley Museum and Library, Wilmington, DE
  Elmer A. Sperry papers (Accession 1893)
  Sperry Gyroscope Company Division papers (Accession 1915)

Robert A. Lavender papers

Library of Congress, Washington, DC
  Donald Bingham papers
  Claude Bloch papers
  Josephus Daniels papers
  William Furlong papers
  William Leahy papers
  William Sims papers

National Archives and Records Administration, Washington, DC
  Record Group 38, Records of the Chief of Naval Operations
      Entry 98, Naval Attaché reports, 1886–1939
      Entry 178, Fleet Training Division: Confidential General Correspon-
        dence, 1914–1926
  Record Group 74, Records of the Navy Bureau of Ordnance
      Entry 25A-I, General Correspondence, 1912–1926
      Entry 25A-II, Formerly Confidential General Correspondence, 1912–1926
      Entry 25B, General Correspondence, 1926–1939
      Entry 25C, Formerly Confidential General Correspondence, 1926–1939
      Entry 25D, Formerly Secret General Correspondence, 1926–1939
      Entry 26, Semi-Official Correspondence of the Chief of the Bureau,
        1904–1920
  Record Group 80, Records of the Office of the Secretary of the Navy
      Entry 19A, General File 1897–1915
      Entry 22, General File, 1926–1940
      UD-Entry 2, Formerly Confidential Correspondence, 1917–1919
      UD-Entry 8, Formerly Confidential Correspondence, 1927–1939
  Record Group 123, Records of the Court of Claims
      Entry 1, General Jurisdiction Case Files, 1855–1939
  Record Group 143, Records of the Navy Bureau of Supplies and Accounts
      Entry 8, General Correspondence File, 1913–1925
  Record Group 267, Records of the Supreme Court
      Entry 21, Case Files

National Archives and Records Administration, College Park, MD
  Record Group 59, Records of the State Department
      Entry A1-205-A, Central Decimal File
  Record Group 60, Records of the Department of Justice
      Entry A1-COR27, Central Files, Classified Subject Files, Correspondence

Entry A1-COR95, Central Files, Classified Subject Files, Correspondence

Entry 209, Records of the Claims Division, 1902–1947: Records Relating to the Defense of Patent Claims before the War Claims Arbiter, 1928–1931: Minutes, Memoranda, Orders, and Decisions

Entry 211, Records of the Claims Division, 1902–1947: Records Relating to the Defense of Patent Claims before the War Claims Arbiter, 1928–1931: Correspondence with the War and Navy Departments concerning Patents

Entry 418, Attorney General's Patent Policy Survey, 1939–1947

Record Group 241, Records of the Patent Office

Entry A1–1038, Commissioner of Patents' Circulars, Orders, etc., 1909–1946

National Archives and Records Administration, Kansas City, MO

Record Group 241, Records of the Patent Office

Patent files

Interference files

Record Group 267, Records of the Courts of Appeals

Second Circuit Court of Appeals files

National Archives and Records Administration, New York, NY

Record Group 21, Records of the District Courts

Eastern District of New York Equity Case Files

Eastern District of New York Civil Case Files

Great Britain

Admiralty Library, Portsmouth, England

Churchill Archives Center, University of Cambridge, Cambridge, England

Hugh Clausen papers (CLSN)

Alfred Duff Cooper papers (DUFC)

Frederic Dreyer papers (DRYR)

Arthur Pollen papers (PLLN and PP)

Stephen Roskill papers (ROSK)

Imperial War Museum, London, England

Henry Tizard papers (HTT)

The National Archives, Kew, England

Admiralty (ADM)

ADM.1, Secretariat Files

ADM.116, Case Files

ADM.137, Historical Section, Records Used for Official History, First World War

ADM.186, Publications

ADM.196, Officers' Service Records

ADM.245, Awards Council Papers

Air Ministry (AVIA)

AVIA.15, Registered Files

Board of Trade (BT)
   BT.31, Companies Registration Office: Files of Dissolved Companies
Foreign Office (FO)
   FO.115, Embassies and Consulates, USA: General Correspondence
Treasury (T)
   T.1, Secretariat Files
   T.173, Royal Commission on Awards to Inventors Files

University of Glasgow Archives, Glasgow, Scotland
   Barr & Stroud papers (UGD.295)

Vickers Archive, University of Cambridge Library, Cambridge, England

Published

Bureau of Ordnance. *Navy Ordnance Activities, World War, 1917–1918*. Washington, DC: Government Printing Office, 1920.

Clark, Kenneth. *Another Part of the World*. Vol. 1. New York: Harper and Row, 1974.

Clausen, Hugh. "Invention and the Navy—The Progress from Ideas to Ironmongery." *The Inventor* 10, no. 1 (March 1970): 2–8.

Dreyer, Frederic. *The Sea Heritage: A Study of Maritime Warfare*. London: Museum Press, 1955.

Ford, Henry. "Special Automobile Steels: Vanadium, the New Element, Imparts Qualities to Steel Which Are Little Less than Magical." *Harper's Weekly* 51, no. 2621 (16 March 1907): 386G.

Graham, Angus Cunninghame. *Random Naval Recollections, 1905–1951*. Privately published, 1979.

Isherwood, Charlotte E. *Round the World in 80 Years*. Self-published, printed by Chiltern Books, 1961.

Lambert, Nicholas, ed. *The Submarine Service, 1900–1918*. Aldershot, UK: Ashgate for the Navy Records Society, 2001.

Marder, Arthur, ed. *Fear God and Dread Nought: The Correspondence of Admiral of the Fleet Lord Fisher of Kilverstone*. Vol. 2, *Years of Power: 1904–1914*. London: Jonathan Cape, 1956.

Pears, Stewart. In "The Military View: Comments by Members of the Royal Navy," in *Command and Commanders in Modern Military History*, ed. William Geffen, 101–8. Office of Air Force History and U.S. Air Force Academy, 1971.

Sumida, Jon, ed. *The Pollen Papers: The Privately Circulated Printed Works of Arthur Hungerford Pollen, 1901–1916*. London: Allen and Unwin for the Navy Records Society, 1984.

Trenchard, John. Letter 64. In *Cato's Letters: Or, Essays on Liberty, Civil and Religious, and Other Important Subjects*. Vol. 2. 6th ed. London: printed for J. Walthoe et al., 1755.

Van Auken, Wilbur. *Notes on a Half Century of United States Naval Ordnance, 1880–1930*. Washington, DC: George Banta, 1939.

SECONDARY SOURCES

Unpublished

Fagal, Andrew. "The Political Economy of War in the Early American Republic, 1774–1821." PhD dissertation, Binghampton University, 2013.

Bradley, John K. "The History and Development of Aircraft Instruments—1909 to 1919." PhD dissertation, Imperial College (University of London), 1994.

Clymer, A. Ben. "Mechanical Integrators." Master's thesis, Ohio State University, 1946.

Falcone, Michael. "The Rocket's Red Glare: Global Power and the Rise of American State Technology, 1940–1960." PhD dissertation, Northwestern University, 2019.

Goble, George. "The Obituary of a Machine: The Rise and Fall of Ottmar Mergenthaler's Linotype at US Newspapers." PhD dissertation, Indiana University, 1984.

Havern, Christopher, Sr.. "A Gunnery Manqué: William S. Sims and the Adoption of Continuous-Aim in the United States Navy, 1898–1910." Master's thesis, University of Maryland, 1995.

Mindell, David. "'Datum for its Own Annihilation': Feedback, Control, and Computing, 1916–1945." PhD dissertation, Massachusetts Institute of Technology, 1996.

Published

Adas, Michael. *Dominance by Design: Technological Imperatives and America's Civilizing Mission.* Cambridge, MA: Belknap Press of Harvard University Press, 2006.

———. *Machines as the Measure of Men: Science, Technology, and Ideologies of Western Dominance.* Ithaca, NY: Cornell University Press, 2014; first ed. 1989.

Anderson, Benedict. *Imagined Communities: Reflections on the Origin and Spread of Nationalism.* Revised ed. London: Verso, 2006.

Angevine, Robert. "The Rise and Fall of the Office of Naval Intelligence, 1882–1892: A Technological Perspective." *Journal of Military History* 62, no. 2 (April 1998): 291–312.

Arapostathis, Stathis, and Graeme Gooday. *Patently Contestable: Electrical Technologies and Inventor Identities on Trial in Britain.* Cambridge, MA: MIT Press, 2013.

Arnold, F. O. *The Law of Damages and Compensation.* 2nd ed. London: Butterworth & Co., 1919.

Baxter III, James Phinney. *Scientists against Time.* Boston: Little Brown, 1946.

Beauchamp, Christopher. *Invented by Law: Alexander Graham Bell and the Patent That Changed America.* Cambridge, MA: Harvard University Press, 2015.

Belfanti, Carlo Marco. "Between Mercantilism and Market: Privileges for Invention in Early Modern Europe." *Journal of Institutional Economics* 2, no. 3 (2006): 319–38.

Ben-Atar, Doron. *Trade Secrets: Intellectual Piracy and the Origins of American Industrial Power.* New Haven, CT: Yale University Press, 2004.

Bennett, Marion. "Section Three." In *The United States Court of Claims: A History.* Part 2, *Origin—Development—Jurisdiction, 1855–1878.* Washington, DC: Committee on the Bicentennial of Independence and the Constitution of the Judicial Conference of the United States, 1978.

Bensel, Richard Franklin. *Yankee Leviathan: The Origins of Central State Authority in America, 1859–1877.* Cambridge: Cambridge University Press, 1990.

———. *The Political Economy of American Industrialization, 1877–1900.* Cambridge: Cambridge University Press, 2000.

Benson, Bruce L. "The Evolution of Eminent Domain: A Remedy for Market Failure or an Effort to Limit Government Power and Government Failure?" *Independent Review* 12, no. 3 (Winter 2008): 423–32.

Berghahn, Volker. *American Big Business in Britain and Germany: A Comparative History of Two "Special Relationships" in the Twentieth Century.* Princeton: Princeton University Press, 2014.

Biagioli, Mario. "Patent Republic: Representing Inventions, Constructing Rights and Authors." *Social Research* 73, no. 4 (Winter 2006): 1129–72.

———. "From Ciphers to Confidentiality: Secrecy, Openness and Priority in Science." *British Journal for the History of Science* 45, no. 2 (June 2012): 213–33.

———. "Recycling Texts or Stealing Time? Plagiarism, Authorship, and Credit in Science," *International Journal of Cultural Property* 19, no. 3 (August 2012): 453–76.

———. "Between Knowledge and Technology: Patenting Methods, Rethinking Materiality." *Anthropological Forum* 22, no. 3 (November 2012): 285–300.

Biagioli, Mario, and Marcus Buning. "Technologies of the Law / Law as a Technology." *History of Science* 57, no. 1 (2019): 3–17.

Bloom, Harold. *The Anxiety of Influence: A Theory of Poetry.* Oxford: Oxford University Press, 1973.

Boast, Robin. *The Machine in the Ghost: Digitality and Its Consequences.* London: Reaktion Books, 2017.

Bond, Brian. *War and Society in Europe, 1870–1970.* New York: St. Martin's Press, 1983.

Borchard, Edwin. "Government Liability in Tort." Part 1. *Yale Law Journal* 34, no. 1 (November 1924): 1–45.

———. "Government Liability in Tort." Part 4. *Yale Law Journal* 36, no. 1 (November 1926): 1–41.

Bottomley, Sean. *The British Patent System during the Industrial Revolution, 1700–1852.* Cambridge: Cambridge University Press, 2014.

Bowles, Mark. "US Technological Enthusiasm and British Technological Skepticism in the Age of the Analog Brain." *IEEE Annals in the History of Computing* 18, no. 4 (1996): 5–15.

Bracha, Oren. "The Commodification of Patents, 1600–1836: How Patents Became Rights and Why We Should Care." *Loyola of Los Angeles Law Review* 38, no. 1 (Fall 2004): 177–244.

———. *Owning Ideas: The Intellectual Origins of American Intellectual Property, 1790–1909.* Cambridge: Cambridge University Press, 2016.

Brewer, John. *The Sinews of Power: War, Money and the English States, 1688–1783.* Cambridge, MA: Harvard University Press, 1988.

Brinkley, Alan. *The End of Reform: New Deal Liberalism in Recession and War.* New York: Vintage Books, 1996.

Brittain, James. *Alexanderson: Pioneer in American Electrical Engineering.* Baltimore, MD: Johns Hopkins University Press, 1992.

Brock, David, and Christophe Lécuyer. "From Nuclear Physics to Semiconductor Manufacturing: The Making of Ion Implantation." *History and Technology* 25, no. 3 (September 2009): 193–217.

———. "Digital Foundations: The Making of Silicon-Gate Manufacturing Technology." *Technology and Culture* 53, no. 3 (July 2012): 561–97.

Bromley, Allan. "Analog Computing Devices." In *Computing before Computers*, ed. William Aspray, 156–99. Ames, IA: Iowa State University Press, 1990.

Cain, Peter, and Antony Hopkins. *British Imperialism: Innovation and Expansion, 1688–1914.* London: Longman, 1993.

Ceruzzi, Paul. "When Computers Were Human." *Annals of the History of Computing* 13, no. 3 (1991): 237–44.

———. *Computing: A Concise History.* Cambridge, MA: MIT Press, 2012.

Chesney, Robert. "State Secrets and the Limits of National Security Litigation." *George Washington Law Review* 75, no. 5/6 (August 2007): 1249–1332.

Coates, Benjamin. "The Secret Life of Statutes: A Century of the Trading with the Enemy Act." *Modern American History* 1, no. 2 (July 1918): 151–72.

Collins, Harry. *Tacit and Explicit Knowledge*. Chicago: University of Chicago Press, 2010.

Collins, Harry, and Martin Kusch. *The Shape of Actions: What Humans and Machines Can Do*. Cambridge, MA: MIT Press, 1999.

Cooling, Benjamin Franklin. *Gray Steel and Blue Water Navy: The Formative Years of America's Military-Industrial Complex, 1881–1917*. Hamden, CT: Archon Books, 1979.

Daniels, Mario, and John Krige. *Knowledge Regulation and National Security in Postwar America*. Chicago: University of Chicago Press, 2022.

Díaz, Gerardo Con. "Contested Ontologies of Software: The Story of *Gottschalk v. Benson*, 1963–1972." *IEEE Annals of the History of Computing* 38, no 1 (2016): 23–33.

———. "The Text in the Machine: American Copyright Law and the Many Natures of Software, 1974–1978." *Technology and Culture* 57, no. 4 (October 2016): 753–79.

———. *Software Rights: How Patent Law Transformed Software Development in America*. New Haven, CT: Yale University Press, 2019.

———. "Encoding Music: Perforated Paper, Copyright Law, and the Legibility of Code, 1880–1908." *Case Western Reserve Law Review* 71, no. 2 (2020): 627–65.

Dikötter, Frank. *The Discourse of Race in Modern China*. Stanford, CA: Stanford University Press, 1992.

Donohue, Laura. "The Shadow of State Secrets." *University of Pennsylvania Law Review* 159, no. 1 (December 2010): 77–216.

Doshi, Rush. *The Long Game: China's Grand Strategy to Displace American Order*. New York: Oxford University Press, 2021.

Dudziak, Mary. *War Time: An Idea, Its History, Its Consequences*. New York: Oxford University Press, 2012.

Edgerton, David. "Liberal Militarism and the British State." *New Left Review* 185 (January–February 1991): 138–69.

———. "Creole Technologies and Global Histories: Rethinking How Things Travel in Space and Time." *History of Science and Technology* 1, no. 1 (2007): 75–112.

———. *England and the Aeroplane: Militarism, Modernity, and Machines*. London: Penguin, 2013.

Epstein, Katherine. *Torpedo: Inventing the Military-Industrial Complex in the United States and Great Britain*. Cambridge, MA: Harvard University Press, 2014.

———. "Scholarship and the Ship of State: Rethinking the Anglo-American Strategic Decline Analogy." *International Affairs* 91, no. 2 (March 2015): 319–31.

———. "The Other Visible Hand: National Security and Intellectual Property in the United States before World War I." *Enterprises et Histoire* no. 85 (December 2016): 40–53.

———. "Intellectual Property and National Security: The Case of the Hardcastle Superheater, 1905–1927." *History and Technology* 34, no. 2 (2018): 126–56.

———. Letter to the editor. *Journal of Military History* 83, no. 2 (April 2019): 651–55.

———. "The Conundrum of American Power in the Age of World War I." *Modern American History* 2, no. 3 (November 2019): 345–65.

———. "A Useful Category of Analysis? Grand Strategy and US Foreign Relations from 1865 to 1918." In *Rethinking American Grand Strategy*, ed. Christopher Nichols,

Elizabeth Borgwardt, and Andrew Preston, 123–42. New York: Oxford University Press, 2021.

———. "Harnessing Invention: The British Admiralty and the Political Economy of Knowledge in the World War I Era." In *Knowledge Flows in a Global Age: A Transnational Approach*, ed. John Krige, 77–102. Chicago: University of Chicago Press, 2022.

Fagal, Andrew. "American Arms Manufacturing and the Onset of the War of 1812." *New England Quarterly* 87, no. 3 (September 2014): 526–37.

Falcone, Michael. "Culture Diplomacy: Penicillin and the Problem of Anglo-American Knowledge Sharing in World War II." In *Knowledge Flows in a Global Age: A Transnational Approach*, ed. John Krige, 103–47. Chicago: University of Chicago Press, 2022

Farley, Robert, and Davida Isaacs, "Privilege-Wise and Patent (and Trade Secret) Foolish? How the Courts' Misapplication of the Military and State Secrets Privilege Violates the Constitution and Endangers National Security." *Berkeley Technology Law Journal* 24, no. 2 (Spring 2009): 785–818.

———. *Patents for Power: Intellectual Property and the Diffusion of Military Technology*. Chicago: University of Chicago Press, 2020.

Fisk, Catherine. *Working Knowledge: Employee Innovation and the Rise of Corporate Intellectual Property, 1800–1930*. Chapel Hill: University of North Carolina Press, 2009.

Flandreau, Marc, and Geoffroy Legentilhomme. "Cyberpunk Victoria: The Credibility of Computers and the First Digital Revolution, 1848–83." *Economic History Review* 75, no. 4 (November 2022): 1083–119.

Freymann, Eyck. *One Belt One Road: Chinese Power Meets the World*. Cambridge, MA: Harvard University Asia Center, 2021.

Friedman, Norman. *Naval Firepower: Battleship Guns and Gunnery in the Dreadnought Era*. Barnsley, UK: Seaforth, 2008.

———. *Network-Centric Warfare: How Navies Learned to Fight Smarter through Three World Wars*. Annapolis, MD: Naval Institute Press, 2009.

Galison, Peter. "Removing Knowledge." *Critical Inquiry* 31, no. 1 (Autumn 2004): 229–43.

Gooday, Graeme. "Boys, Sir Charles Vernon (1855–1944), Physicist and Inventor." 23 September 2004. *Oxford Dictionary of National Biography*. https://doi.org/10.1093/ref:odnb/32016.

Gordon, Andrew. *The Rules of the Game: Jutland and British Naval Command*. London: John Murray, 1996.

Grier, David. *When Computers Were Human*. Princeton, NJ: Princeton University Press, 2005.

Gries, Peter. *China's New Nationalism: Pride, Politics, and Diplomacy*. Berkeley: University of California Press, 2004.

Harvard Law Review. "Forfeiture of the Right to the Issuance of a Patent through Unexcused Delay." *Harvard Law Review* 37, no. 4 (February 1924): 482–86.

Hewlett, Richard. "'Born Classified' in the AEC: A Historian's View." *Bulletin of Atomic Scientists* 37, no. 10 (December 1981): 20–27.

Hintz, Eric. *American Independent Inventors in an Era of Corporate R&D*. Cambridge, MA: MIT Press, 2021.

Howeth, Linwood. *History of Communications-Electronics in the United States Navy*. Washington, DC: Government Printing Office, 1963.

Hughes, Thomas P. *Elmer Sperry: Inventor and Engineer*. Baltimore, MD: Johns Hopkins Press, 1971.

———. *Networks of Power: Electrification in Western Society.* Baltimore, MD: Johns Hopkins University Press, 1983.

———. *American Genesis: A Century of Invention and Technological Enthusiasm, 1870–1970.* New York: Viking, 1989.

Inglis, C. E. "William Ernest Dalby, 1862–1936." *Obituary Notices of the Fellows of the Royal Society* 2, no. 5 (December 1936): 144–49.

Ingold, Tim. *Being Alive: Essays on Movement, Knowledge and Description.* Abingdon: Routledge, 2011.

Isasawa, Yuji. "The Doctrine of Self-Executing Treaties in the United States: A Critical Analysis." *Virginia Journal of International Law* 26, no. 3 (1986): 627–92.

James, Harold. "The Warburgs and Yesterday's Financial Deterrent." In *Peoples, Nations and Traditions in a Comparative Frame: Thinking about the Past with Jonathan Steinberg,* ed. D'Maris Coffman, Harold James, and Nicholas Di Liberto, 59–70. London: Anthem Press, 2021.

Jebb, Louis. *Leonardo Da Vinci's Miniature Madonna: Arthur Hungerford Pollen and the Virgin and Child with a Cat.* Privately published, 2013.

Johns, Adrian. *Piracy: The Intellectual Property Wars from Gutenberg to Gates.* Chicago: University of Chicago Press, 2009.

Jones, Matthew L. *Reckoning with Matter: Calculating Machines, Innovation, and Thinking about Thinking from Pascal to Babbage.* Chicago: University of Chicago Press, 2016.

Kahan, Basil. *Ottmar Mergenthaler: The Man and His Machine.* New Castle, DE: Oak Knoll Press, 2000.

Khan, B. Zorina. *The Democratization of Invention: Patents and Copyrights in American Economic Development, 1790–1920.* Cambridge: Cambridge University Press, 2005.

Kovacs, Kathryn. "Revealing Redundancy: The Tension between Federal Sovereign Immunity and Nonstatutory Review." *Drake Law Review* 54, no. 1 (2005): 77–124.

Krige, John. "Regulating the Transnational Flow of Intangible Knowledge of Space Launchers between the United States and China." In *Knowledge Flows in a Global Age: A Transnational Approach,* ed. John Krige, 173–98. Chicago: University of Chicago Press, 2022.

Lambert, Nicholas. *Sir John Fisher's Naval Revolution.* Columbia: University of South Carolina Press, 1999.

———. "Strategic Command and Control for Maneuver Warfare: Creation of the Royal Navy's 'War Room' System, 1905–1915." *Journal of Military History* 69, no. 2 (April 2005): 361–410.

———. *Planning Armageddon: British Economic Warfare and the First World War.* Cambridge, MA: Harvard University Press, 2012.

———. *The War Lords and the Gallipoli Disaster: How Globalized Trade Led Britain to Its Worst Defeat of the First World War.* New York: Oxford University Press, 2021.

———. *The Neptune Factor: Alfred Thayer Mahan and the Concept of Sea Power.* Annapolis, MD: Naval Institute Press, 2023.

Lavenue, Lionel. "Patent Infringement against the United States and Government Contractors under 28 U.S.C. §1498 in the United States Court of Federal Claims." *Journal of Intellectual Property Law* 2, no. 2 (Spring 1995): 389–507.

Lavington, Simon. *Moving Targets: Elliott-Automation and the Dawn of the Computer Age in Britain, 1947–1967.* London: Springer, 2011.

Link, Stefan, *Forging Global Fordism: Nazi Germany, Soviet Russia, and the Contest Over the Industrial Order.* Princeton, NJ: Princeton University Press, 2020.

Link, Stefan, and Noam Maggor. "The United States as a Developing Nation: Revisiting the Peculiarities of American History." *Past and Present* 246, no. 1 (February 2020): 269–303.

MacKenzie, Donald. *Inventing Accuracy: A Historical Sociology of Nuclear Missile Guidance*. Cambridge, MA: MIT Press, 1990.

MacLeod, Christine. "The European Origins of British Technological Predominance." In *Exceptionalism and Industrialisation: Britain and Its European Rivals, 1688–1815*, ed. Leandro Prados de la Escosura, 111–26. Cambridge: Cambridge University Press, 2004.

———. *Heroes of Invention: Technology, Liberalism, and British Identity, 1750–1914*. Cambridge: Cambridge University Press, 2007.

Marin, Séverine Antigone. "Did the United States Scare the Europeans? The Propaganda about the 'American Danger' in Europe around 1900." *Journal of the Gilded Age and Progressive Era* 15, no. 1 (2016): 23–44.

McClaskey, Norman D. "The Mental Process Doctrine: Its Origin, Legal Basis, and Scope," *Iowa Law Review* 55, no. 5 (June 1970): 1148–95.

McManus, Alison. "Science, Interrupted: Censorship and the Problem of Credit Allocation in the American Advisory Committee on Scientific Publications, 1940–46." *Historical Studies in the Natural Sciences* 52, no. 1 (February 2022): 80–117.

McNeill, William. *The Pursuit of Power: Technology, Armed Force, and Society since AD 1000*. Chicago: University of Chicago Press, 1982.

Meidinger, Errol. "The 'Public Uses' of Eminent Domain: History and Policy." *Environmental Law* 11, no. 1 (1980): 1–66.

Merges, Robert. *American Patent Law: A Business and Economic History*. Cambridge: Cambridge University Press, 2022.

Milford, Frederick. "US Navy Torpedoes, Part Two: The Great Torpedo Scandal." *Submarine Review* (October 1996): 81–93.

Millard, Andre. *Edison and the Business of Innovation*. Baltimore, MD: Johns Hopkins University Press, 1993.

Miller, Chris. *Chip War: The Fight for the World's Most Critical Technology*. New York: Scribner, 2022.

Lord Millett. "Tomlin, Thomas James Chesshyre, Baron Tomlin (1867–1935)." 10 December 2020. *Oxford Dictionary of National Biography*. https://doi.org/10.1093/ref:odnb/36531.

Mindell, David A. *Between Human and Machine: Feedback, Control, and Computing before Cybernetics*. Baltimore, MD: Johns Hopkins University Press, 2002.

Misa, Thomas. *A Nation of Steel: The Making of Modern America, 1865–1925*. Baltimore, MD: Johns Hopkins University Press, 1995.

Mody, Cyrus, and Michael Lynch. "Test Objects and Other Epistemic Things: A History of a Nanoscale Object." *British Journal for the History of Science* 43, no. 3 (September 2010): 423–58.

Mokyr, Joel. *The Lever of Riches: Technological Creativity and Economic Progress*. New York: Oxford University Press, 1990.

Moser, Petra. "Patents and Innovations in Economic History." National Bureau of Economic Research Working Paper 21964 (February 2016).

Mossoff, Adam. "Patents as Constitutional Private Property: The Historical Protection of Patents under the Takings Clause." *Boston University Law Review* 87, no. 3 (June 2007): 689–724.

Nevins, Allan, with Frank Ernest Hill. *Ford: The Times, the Man, the Company*. New York: Columbia University Press, 1954.

O'Connor, Sean. "Taking, Tort, or Crown Right? The Confused Early History of Government Patent Policy." *John Marshall Review of Intellectual Property Law* 12 (2012): 145–204.

O'Dell, T. H. *Inventions and Official Secrecy: A History of Secret Patents in the UK*. Oxford: Clarendon Press, 1994.

Orwell, George. "Reflections on Gandhi." In *The Orwell Reader: Fiction, Essays, and Reportage*, 328–35. San Diego, CA: Harcourt Brace, 1984.

Owens, Larry. "Where Are We Going, Phil Morse? Changing Agendas and the Rhetoric of Obviousness in the Transformation of Computing at MIT, 1939–1957." *IEEE Annals of the History of Computing* 18, no. 4 (1996): 34–41.

Padfield, Peter. *Aim Straight: A Biography of Admiral Sir Percy Scott*. London: Hodder and Stoughton, 1966.

Parrini, Carl. "Theories of Imperialism." In *Redefining the Past: Essays in Diplomatic History in Honor of William Appleman Williams*, ed. Lloyd Gardner, 65–83. Corvallis: Oregon State University Press, 1986.

Parrott, David. *The Business of War: Military Enterprise and Military Revolution in Early Modern Europe*. Cambridge: Cambridge University Press, 2012.

Pila, Justine. "'Sewing the Fly Buttons on the Statute': Employee Inventions and the Employment Context." *Oxford Journal of Legal Studies* 32, no. 2 (2012): 265–95.

Pollen, Anthony. *The Great Gunnery Scandal: The Mystery of Jutland*. London: Collins, 1980.

Porter, R. T. "Romer and His Romer." *Sheetlines* no. 63 (April 2002): 39–43.

Pottage, Alain, and Brad Sherman. *Figures of Invention: A History of Modern Patent Law*. Oxford: Oxford University Press, 2010.

Preston, Andrew. "Monsters Everywhere: A Genealogy of National Security." *Diplomatic History* 38, no. 4 (2014): 477–500.

Reich, Leonard S. *The Making of American Industrial Research: Science and Business at GE and Bell, 1876–1926*. Cambridge: Cambridge University Press, 1985.

Reinert, Sophus. *Translating Empire: Emulation and the Origins of Political Economy*. Cambridge, MA: Harvard University Press, 2011.

Rodger, N. A. M. "From the 'Military Revolution' to the 'Fiscal-Naval State.'" *Journal for Maritime Research* 13, no. 2 (November 2011): 119–28.

Samuelson, Pamela. "The Story of *Baker v. Selden*: Sharpening the Distinction Between Authorship and Invention." In *Intellectual Property Stories*, ed. Jane Ginsburg and Rochelle Dreyfuss, 159–93. New York: Foundation Press, 2006.

———. "The Strange Odyssey of Software Interfaces as Intellectual Property." In *Making and Unmaking Intellectual Property: Creative Production in Legal and Cultural Perspective*, ed. Mario Biagioli, Peter Jaszi, and Martha Woodmansee, 321–38. Chicago: University of Chicago Press, 2011.

Schwartz, Bernard. "Estoppel and Crown Privilege in English Administrative Law." *Michigan Law Review* 55, no. 1 (1956/57): 27–66.

Sell, Susan. "Intellectual Property and Public Policy in Historical Perspective: Contestation and Settlement." *Loyola of Los Angeles Law Review* 38, no. 1 (Fall 2004): 267–322.

Semmel, Bernard. *Liberalism and Naval Strategy: Ideology, Interest, and Sea Power during the Pax Britannica*. Boston: Allen & Unwin, 1986.

Sexton, Jay. "From Triumph to Crisis: An American Tradition." *Diplomatic History* 43, no. 2 (2019): 405–17.

Seybold, John. *The World of Digital Typesetting*. Media, PA: Seybold, 1984.

Shankman, Andrew. "Toward a Social History of Federalism: The State and Capitalism to and from the American Revolution." *Journal of the Early Republic* 37, no. 4 (Winter 2017): 615–53.

Sherman, Brad and Lionel Bently. *The Making of Modern Intellectual Property Law: The British Experience, 1760–1911*. Cambridge: Cambridge University Press, 1999.

Shoemaker, William D. "Secrecy of War Invention." *Journal of the Patent Office Society* (1918): 112–25.

Siegel, Barry. *Claim of Privilege: A Mysterious Plane Crash, A Landmark Supreme Court Case, and the Rise of State Secrets*. New York: Harper Collins, 2008.

Slayton, Rebecca. *Arguments That Count: Physics, Computing, and Missile Defense, 1949–2012*. Cambridge, MA: MIT Press, 2013.

Slinn, Judy. *Clifford Chance: Its Origins and Development*. Cambridge: Granta Editions, 1993.

Spear, Joanna. *The Business of Armaments: Armstrongs, Vickers and the International Arms Trade, 1855–1955*. Cambridge: Cambridge University Press, 2023.

Spencer, Maureen. "Bureaucracy, National Security and Access to Justice: New Light on *Duncan v. Cammell Laird*." *Northern Ireland Legal Quarterly* 55, no. 3 (Autumn 2004): 277–301.

Standage, Tom. *The Victorian Internet: The Remarkable Story of the Telegraph and the Nineteenth Century's On-line Pioneers*. New York: Bloomsbury, 2007.

Steen, Kathryn. *The American Synthetic Organic Chemicals Industry: War and Politics, 1910–1930*. Chapel Hill: University of North Carolina Press, 2014.

Street, Harry. "The Tort Liability of the State: The Federal Tort Claims Act and the Crown Proceedings Act." *Michigan Law Review* 47, no. 3 (January 1949): 341–68.

Sumida, Jon. *In Defence of Naval Supremacy: Finance, Technology, and British Naval Policy, 1889–1914*. Boston: Unwin Hyman, 1989.

———. "Forging the Trident: British Naval Industrial Logistics, 1914–1918." In *Feeding Mars: Logistics in Western Warfare from the Middle Ages to the Present*, ed. John Lynn, 217–49. Boulder, CO: Westview Press, 1993.

———. "A Matter of Timing: The Royal Navy and the Tactics of Decisive Battle, 1912–1916." *Journal of Military History* 67, no. 1 (January 2003): 85–136.

Swanson, Kara. "The Emergence of the Professional Patent Practitioner." *Technology and Culture* 50, no. 3 (July 2009): 519–48.

———. "Authoring an Invention: Patent Production in the Nineteenth-Century United States." In *Making and Unmaking Intellectual Property: Creative Production in Legal and Cultural Perspective*, ed. Mario Biagioli, Peter Jaszi, and Martha Woodmansee, 41–54. Chicago: University of Chicago Press, 2011.

Trebilcock, Clive. "A 'Special Relationship': Government, Rearmament, and the Cordite Firms." *Economic History Review* 19, no. 2 (1966): 364–79.

———. "Legends of the British Armament Industry, 1890–1914: A Revision." *Journal of Contemporary History* 5, no. 4 (1970): 3–19.

Trenga, Anthony. "What Judges Say and Do in Deciding National Security Cases: The Example of the State Secrets Privilege." *Harvard National Security Journal* 9, no. 1 (2018): 1–71.

Turchetti, Simone. "'For Slow Neutrons, Slow Pay': Enrico Fermi's Patent and the US Atomic Energy Program, 1938–1953." *Isis* 97, no. 1 (March 2006): 1–27.

———. "The Invisible Businessman: Nuclear Physics, Patenting Practices, and Trading Activities in the 1930s." *Historical Studies in the Physical and Biological Sciences* 37, no. 1 (September 2006): 153–72.

Tweedale, Geoffrey. *Steel City: Entrepreneurship, Strategy, and Technology in Sheffield, 1743–1993*. Oxford: Oxford University Press, 1995.

Watts, Steven. *The People's Tycoon: Henry Ford and the American Century*. New York: Vintage Books, 2006.

Weiss, Linda. *America Inc.? Innovation and Enterprise in the National Security State*. Ithaca, NY: Cornell University Press, 2014.

Wellerstein, Alex. "Patenting the Bomb: Nuclear Weapons, Intellectual Property, and Technological Control," *Isis* 99, no. 1 (March 2008): 57–87.

———. *Restricted Data: The History of Nuclear Secrecy in the United States*. Chicago: University of Chicago Press, 2021.

Westad, Odd Arne. *Restless Empire: China and the World Since 1750*. New York: Basic Books, 2012.

Wyatt, Don. "A Certain Whiteness of Being: Chinese Perceptions of Self by the Beginning of European Contact." In *Race and Racism in Modern East Asia: Western and Eastern Constructions*, ed. Rotem Kowner and Walter Demel, 309–26. Leiden: Brill, 2013.

Zachary, G. Pascal. *Endless Frontier: Vannevar Bush, Inventor of the American Century*. New York: Free Press, 1997.

Zimmerman, David. *Top Secret Exchange: The Tizard Mission and the Scientific War*. Montreal: McGill-Queen's University Press, 1996.

Index